The Ideal Bishop

THOMISTIC RESSOURCEMENT SERIES

Volume 8

SERIES EDITORS

Matthew Levering, *Mundelein Seminary*

Thomas Joseph White, OP, *Dominican House of Studies*

EDITORIAL BOARD

Serge-Thomas Bonino, OP, *Pontifical University of St. Thomas Aquinas*

Gilles Emery, OP, *University of Fribourg*

Reinhard Hütter, *Duke University*

Bruce Marshall, *Southern Methodist University*

Emmanuel Perrier, OP, *Dominican Studium, Toulouse*

Richard Schenk, OP, *Katholische Universität Eichstätt-Ingolstadt*

Kevin White, *The Catholic University of America*

The Ideal Bishop

Aquinas's Commentaries on the Pastoral Epistles

MICHAEL G. SIRILLA

Foreword by
Archbishop J. Augustine Di Noia, OP

The Catholic University of America Press
Washington, D.C.

Copyright © 2017
The Catholic University of America Press
All Rights Reserved

The paper used in this publication meets the minimum
requirements of American National Standards for Information
Science—Permanence of Paper Printed for Library Materials,
ANSI Z39.48-1984
∞

Cataloging-in-Publication Data available from the
Library of Congress
ISBN 978-0-8132-2910-2

Michael Sirilla exemplifies the careful, sustained study of St. Thomas Aquinas as an interpreter of Sacred Scripture. Sirilla has not only enriched our understanding of St. Thomas on Scripture, he has also substantially enriched our understanding of St. Thomas on the office of bishop. Sirilla's analysis of St. Thomas's commentaries on Timothy and Titus and their intellectual and historical circumstances illuminates in new ways the thought of the Angelic Doctor.

—JOHN F. BOYLE, UNIVERSITY OF ST. THOMAS

The life of St. Thomas Aquinas was one of ecclesial service. Michael G. Sirilla has performed a true work of service to the Church and has contributed a valuable text to the corpus of Thomistic literature. This book helps show how Aquinas's religious consecration as a Dominican priest placed him and his work—then and now—at the center of the Church.

—ROMANUS CESSARIO, OP, SAINT JOHN'S SEMINARY, BRIGHTON, MASSACHUSETTS

Michael Sirilla's superbly researched and astutely argued work fills an important lacuna in Aquinas studies—regarding his biblical commentaries as well as his theology of the ecclesial hierarchy. At the same time it is a timely contribution to contemporary ecclesiology and especially to the theology of the bishop. The Second Vatican Council advanced the theology of the bishop in crucial ways. But *The Ideal Bishop* amply demonstrates how fresh and relevant Aquinas's view is precisely now in the wake of the last ecumenical council's teaching on the episcopacy. No serious Aquinas scholar and no contemporary ecclesiologist can afford to ignore this important book. *Tolle lege*, take and read!

—REINHARD HÜTTER, DUKE UNIVERSITY

The theme of this important book could be summed up as 'hierarchy and holiness.' As Michael Sirilla shows in his erudite investigation of Aquinas's commentaries on the Pastoral Epistles, Aquinas recognized the supreme need for bishops to love the truth of the gospel and to be willing to lay down their lives rather than to compromise the ability of the flock to pursue holiness. Against an overly juridical ecclesiology, which sees only the administrative tasks of maintaining order and filling the pews (often by cultural accommodation), Aquinas's vision of the episcopacy lives up to Vatican II's universal call to holiness—a holiness that is inevitably costly and counter-cultural for bishop and layperson alike.

—MATTHEW LEVERING, JAMES N. AND MARY D. PERRY JR.
CHAIR OF THEOLOGY, MUNDELEIN SEMINARY

Michael Sirilla's *The Ideal Bishop* is important for anyone wanting to see what resources of doctrine and tradition St. Thomas brings to his reading of Scripture, and how St. Thomas's systematic theology is in turn embedded in his close reading of the word of God. It is more important, however, for helping us understand the nature and structure of the Church Christ instituted. We really are all called to help one another grow in charity. Nowhere is that more true than with those who occupy the difficult but grace-filled and grace-giving office of bishop.

—FR. GUY MANSINI, SAINT MEINRAD SEMINARY

For my dear father, George Michael Sirilla
May he rest in Christ's peace

I do not know of any system of constitutional guarantees that will both provide for strong pastoral authority in the Church and preclude the abuse of such authority. The best guarantee is the personal quality of the office-holders.

Avery Dulles, *A Church to Believe In*

Contents

Foreword by Archbishop J. Augustine Di Noia, OP	xi
Acknowledgments	xv
List of Abbreviations	xvii
1. Introduction	1
2. The Theology of the Episcopacy in the Writings of St. Thomas and His Contemporaries	19
3. St. Thomas's Lectures on the Pastoral Epistles	70
4. Lectures on 1 Timothy: *Ut gubernet populum*	104
5. Lectures on 2 Timothy: *Ut pro populo subdito patiatur*	172
6. Lectures on Titus: *Ut malos coerceat*	206
7. Conclusion	231
Bibliography	241
Index	253

Foreword

Archbishop J. Augustine Di Noia, OP

Congregation for the Doctrine of the Faith

In the post-synodal apostolic exhortation *Pastores Gregis* (2003), Pope St. John Paul II wrote (par. 11):

Objective sanctification, which by Christ's work is present in the sacrament through the communication of the Holy Spirit, needs to coincide with subjective sanctification, in which the Bishop, by the help of grace, must continuously progress through the exercise of his ministry. The ontological transformation brought about by episcopal consecration, as a configuration to Christ, demands a lifestyle that manifests a "being with him." Consequently, during the Synod sessions, emphasis was laid on pastoral charity as being the fruit of the character bestowed by the sacrament and of its particular grace. Charity, it was said, is in a sense the heart of the ministry of the Bishop, who is drawn into a dynamic pastoral *pro-existence* whereby he is impelled to live, like Christ the Good Shepherd, for the Father and for others, in the daily gift of self.

To attain the perfection of charity through configuration to Christ: this description of the essence of the spiritual life of the bishop in *Pastores Gregis* accords well with the theology of the episcopacy of St. Thomas Aquinas, both in his *Summa theologiae* and even more amply in his commentaries on St. Paul's letters to Timothy and Titus. Michael Sirilla's timely book makes Aquinas's teaching in his scriptural commentaries accessible to a wide readership in a lucid and comprehensive form. The book is especially welcome as the Church continues to appropriate—as she does in the tenth Ordinary General Synod of which *Pastores Gregis* is the fruit—the immense body of magisterial teaching on the episcopacy that is the legacy of the Second Vatican Council.

Careful study of St. Thomas's substantive theology and spirituality of the episcopal office and life is indispensable to this work of appropriation. The central thesis of his theology of the episcopacy is that the bishop is constituted in a state of perfection in which he, as a mediator under Christ, is charged with the duty of actively perfecting others. Spiritual perfection is thus to be brought about both in faith by the bishop's exercise of his magisterial office of teaching and in charity by the bishop's governing activities and personal example of life. In these ways, Christ works in the bishop to establish and build up the Church as the communion of the faithful in divine love. Drawing upon Paul's directives in the Pastoral Epistles, Aquinas's spiritual theology of the episcopal office studies the role of the particular moral virtues and supernatural gifts necessary to undertake this office fruitfully; the centrality of the mastery of Scripture to which the bishop must attain and which is demanded for the effectiveness of episcopal teaching; and of the charity, courage, and readiness to suffer martyrdom that the episcopal life requires.

Professor Sirilla's close and careful reading of St. Thomas's commentaries on the Pastoral Epistles avoids unnecessary technical terminology and obscure interpretive methodology. He undertook this study of the commentaries precisely because of its importance to the life of the Church and to fill what he identifies as a lacuna in Thomistic scholarship on the episcopacy. Most recent studies of Aquinas on the bishop's office in any language have focused on matters such as its sacramentality. When they have explored the nature, purpose, and moral demands of the episcopacy as outlined by St. Thomas, they have all but ignored his lectures on the Pastoral Epistles. Viewed in this perspective, this book is unique in the literature on Aquinas as much as in that on the theology of the episcopacy.

The book makes a substantial contribution to the study of Aquinas in at least two ways. First, as the author notes, previous studies of Aquinas on the episcopacy have examined Thomas's systematic works but have rarely drawn upon the theological treasures of his Scripture commentaries. This is noteworthy since St. Thomas himself repeatedly identifies Paul's intention in these epistles as instructing all bishops, not just Timothy and Titus, on the grace, duties, and moral demands of the episcopacy. Thus, Professor Sirilla's book serves both as a helpful remedy and as a supplement to the Thomistic and ecclesiological scholarship on this topic. Second, the book contributes to the burgeoning Thomistic *ressourcement*, specifically with respect to St. Thomas as an interpreter of Scripture. By examining Aquinas's commentaries on these epistles, along with the nature and method of thirteenth-century biblical hermeneutics, this book showcases Thomas's work as a *magister in Sacra Pagina*, an interpreter and teacher of Sacred Scripture—an area much in need of exploration.

Beyond the field of Thomistic studies, this book will be welcomed by bishops and their collaborators who seek a more profound examination of the theology of the interior life of the episcopacy in a cultural milieu obsessed with its administrative and managerial roles. What is more, theologians and those interested in the renewed theology of hierarchy and orders that is at the heart of Catholic ecclesiology will find much to ponder in this splendid book. For, as we can conclude after reading it, nothing is more critical for this renewed theology and for its actualization in ecclesial life than the conviction that "each Bishop is configured to Christ in order to love the Church with the love of Christ the Bridegroom, and in order to be in the Church a minister of her unity" (*Pastores Gregis*, par. 13).

Acknowledgments

I am grateful to the many people that helped to make this work possible. First of all, I thank Fr. Joseph Komonchak for suggesting this avenue of study as my doctoral dissertation, for providing me with direction throughout the early stages of research and writing, and for his constant generosity and encouragement. I am also grateful to Msgr. Paul McPartlan and Dr. Kenneth Pennington for devoting time and attention to my work and for their generosity in reading the manuscript in its form as a doctoral dissertation and for providing helpful corrections and suggestions. I owe a special debt of gratitude to Fr. Gilles de Grandpré, OP, of the Leonine Commission, who provided me with precise information regarding the manuscript tradition of Aquinas's Pauline commentaries and the reliability of various published editions of these works. During the process of developing this study into a book, Dr. Matthew Levering afforded me invaluable assistance, as did Drs. Kevin Schmiesing, Stephen Hildebrand, and Christopher Malloy, all of whom so generously devoted their time to read numerous drafts of this work, providing thoughtful advice and identifying early mistakes. Drs. Scott Hahn, Peter Casarella, Barbara Sain, Gregory Vall, and Jonathan Sanford offered counsel, encouragement, and moral support. Fr. Daniel Pattee, TOR, has served as one of my principal motivators, impelling me to complete this project. Additionally, I express gratitude to Ms. Kelly Schaffer, Mr. Michael Kujan, and Mr. John Serafini for their help as my research assistants.

My gratitude also extends to the Franciscan University of Steubenville for support while undertaking this study and to the Hubbard Fellowship committee at the Catholic University of America for awarding me a yearlong grant that helped expedite the process enormously. Tremendous thanks also are due to my parents, who so generously gave me material, emotional, and spiritual support over the years. My father, George Sirilla, passed away before seeing this book in print. It is to him that I dedicate this work. He formed me in the Catholic faith and in the spiritual life in Christ. I hope and pray that I may honor his memory both by reverence and emulation. I am more grateful than words can tell to my dear wife, Laura, and to our children who so patiently endured while praying for the completion of my work. My earnest desire is that this study will be of benefit to the Church and her members. Anything of value in it is to be attributed to the generosity of our Lord. Any errors are solely my own responsibility.

Abbreviations

WORKS OF AQUINAS

Cont imp	Contra impugnantes Dei cultum et religionem
De perf	De perfectione spiritualis vitae
De verit	Quaestiones Disputatae de Veritate
In 1 Cor	Lectura super 1 Corinthios
In Eph	Lectura super Ephesios
In Heb	Lectura super Hebraeos
In Matt	Lectura super Matthaeum
In Philem	Lectura super Philemonem
In Philip	Lectura super Philippenses
In Rom	Lectura super Romanos
In Sent	Scriptum Super libros Sententiarum
In 1 Tim	Lectura super 1 Timotheum
In 2 Tim	Lectura super 2 Timotheum
In Tit	Lectura super Titum
Ioannis	Super evangelium S. Ioannis lectura
Quodl	Quaestiones de quodlibet
SCG	Summa Contra Gentiles
STh	Summa Theologiae

OTHER WORKS

- DTC   *Dictionnaire de théologie catholique* (ed. Mangenot et al.)
- PE   *Pastoral epistles* (St. Paul)
- PG   *Patrologia Graeca* (ed. Migne)
- PL   *Patrologia Latina* (ed. Migne)
- RF   *Decretum magistri Gratiani* (ed. Richter)

TEXTUAL INDICATORS

- a.   articulus
- ad 1   ad primum
- cap.   caput
- co.   corpus
- d.   distinctio
- lect.   lectio
- q.   quaestio
- qua.   quaestiuncula
- s.c.   sed contra
- sol.   solutio

The Ideal Bishop

1

Introduction

In his commentaries on the Pastoral Epistles, St. Thomas Aquinas (1224/25–74) discusses the nature of the episcopacy, its foundation, its role in the Church, its principal aims, and those requisite characteristics that render one a suitable candidate for this office. This book is intended as a particular contribution to the recent Thomistic *ressourcement* by returning to an invaluable yet overlooked source for the renewal of a proper theological understanding of the episcopal office.[1] Recovering what Thomas says about the episcopacy will serve both to renew discourse on this mystery of faith and to assist those who find themselves in this office so that with this understanding they may better fulfill the duties thereof for the good of Christ and the Church.

Aquinas teaches that the episcopacy is an active state of perfection in his *Summa Theologiae* (hereafter "*STh*") II-II, qq. 183–85, and in *De perfectione spiritualis vitae* (hereafter "*De perf*"). The works of Pseudo-Dionysius, in particular his *Ecclesiastical Hierarchy*, exert a primary formative influence on Aquinas's thought and provide a fundamental theological matrix for Aquinas's commentatorial lectures on the PE. The episcopacy is an active state of perfection in which the bishop works to perfect his flock in charity, Christian holiness. Aquinas's

---

1. For an introduction to this current scholarly endeavor, see *Ressourcement Thomism: Sacred Doctrine, the Sacraments, and the Moral Life*, ed. Reinhard Hütter and Matthew Levering (Washington, D.C.: The Catholic University of America Press, 2010).

commentaries on the PE specify the virtues a bishop needs to fulfill the duties of his state. My hope is that this recovery of St. Thomas's thought will supplement Thomistic scholarship on the episcopacy, stimulate theological debate on the episcopal state, and assist bishops as they reflect on and undertake the duties of their office, the fulfillment of which demands a special grace of state.

THE CURRENT QUESTION

Thomas O'Meara, surveying the theological discussion of the episcopacy since the Second Vatican Council, laments: "Very few [theologians] develop (or even mention) a theology of the graces given to a bishop to guide faith and life."[2] To be sure, the Council elicited debates on the role and status of episcopal colleagueiality, episcopal conferences, and the relationship of the local church to the universal Church. While these discussions have played an important role in the reception of the Council, insufficient attention has been devoted to a significant development brought about by the Council itself with respect to the episcopacy. This Council complements the teaching of the First Vatican Council on the Church's hierarchy by reaffirming the perennial teaching that the individual bishop, in his own right, is the true representative of Christ and the source of unity for his particular church.[3] In its *Decree on the Pastoral Office of Bishops in the Church*, the Council confirms: "Individual bishops, to whom the pastoral care of a particular church has been committed, are the proper, official and immediate shepherds of these churches."[4] This affirmation should foster a theological examination of the bishop's office and its exercise in and for the particular church over which a bishop presides. Nonetheless, O'Meara notes, "Studies on ecclesial magisterium, however, lack any adequate

---

2. Thomas F. O'Meara, "Divine Grace and Human Nature as Sources for the Universal Magisterium of Bishops," *Theological Studies* 64 (2003): 685.
3. Vatican Council II, *Lumen Gentium*, November 21, 1964, nos. 20 and 27, in *Decrees of the Ecumenical Councils*, ed. Norman P. Tanner, trans. Robert Murray (London: Sheed and Ward, 1990), 2:863–64.
4. "Singuli episcopi, quibus ecclesiae particularis cura commissa est ... tamquam proprii, ordinarii et immediati earum pastores." Vatican Council II, *Christus Dominus*, October 28, 1965, no. 11, in *Decrees*, ed. Tanner, 2:924. Unless otherwise noted, all translations of foreign language quotations are my own.

discussion of a psychology of the graced teacher."[5] The prospect of the perceived decline of episcopal teaching and the ever-present danger of the episcopacy being perceived as an "isolated oligarchy," as O'Meara puts it, make the development of an adequate episcopal theology all the more urgent.

O'Meara dubiously faults the later scholasticism of the baroque period for developing an overly mechanistic and extrinsic theology of grace. Such an account, he alleges, falsifies the personal and concrete way that grace works in and through the human nature and personality of the bishop. Interestingly, O'Meara finds the basis for a more faithful account of episcopal grace within scholasticism itself, albeit in an earlier form. He examines St. Thomas's theology of the episcopacy in order to retrieve from it and develop an account of grace working through nature in the individual bishop's magisterium. For all that, O'Meara's article fails to address, more narrowly, the operation of the Holy Spirit and grace in the person of the bishop as he exercises his magisterial duties. Yet his initial foray serves at the very least to raise the question of how grace operates in the bishop's office (not limited to the bishop's teaching office), the requisite virtues of this office, the vices that endanger it, the duties that flow from it, and related matters. Unfortunately, he fails to examine Thomas's insights on these matters in his lectures on the PE, which constitute source material that greatly assists this task. While there is no question that his thought cannot simply be transferred into the present context without qualification, in his PE lectures Aquinas identifies essential aspects of the bishop's office and responsibilities that have been eclipsed in recent theological discourse for a variety of reasons.

Since the thirteenth century, the nature and duties of the episcopacy have been discussed by theologians and canonists increasingly within the categories of the power of order (*potestas ordinis*) and the power of jurisdiction (*potestas iurisdictionis*).[6] Within this framework, episcopal acts are generally classified as having to do either with over-

---

5. O'Meara, "Divine Grace," 694.

6. This tendency continued through to the Council of Trent (1545–63) and beyond. See the recent study by Laurent Villemin, *Pouvoir d'ordre et pouvoir de juridiction: Histoire théologique de leur distinction* (Paris: Éditions du Cerf, 2003). See also E. Valton, "Évêques. Questions théologiques et canoniques," in *Dictionnaire de Théologie Catholique* (Paris: Letouzey et Ane, 1930–50), 5.2:1701–25 (hereafter *DTC*).

seeing the sacraments as an expression of the power of order or with teaching and governing as an expression of the power of jurisdiction. Around the time these notions were being developed, Thomas was reflecting on and developing the thought of St. Paul and of Pseudo-Dionysius the Areopagite, conceiving the episcopacy fundamentally as a state of perfection (*status perfectionis*) in which all of the pastoral actions of the individual bishop—whether teaching, governing, or overseeing sacramental activity—are ordered to the spiritual perfection of the faithful in Christ, where such perfection consists above all in the theological and supernatural virtue of charity.[7] These theological conceptions of St. Thomas provide a necessary and proper framework for a fuller understanding of the episcopal exercise of the powers of order and jurisdiction. The spiritual perfection of charity, as manifested particularly in a bishop moved by fraternal charity, ought to form the basis of *all* episcopal actions on behalf of the faithful. Charity should serve as the "soul" that animates all the actions of the episcopal powers. Without it, a bishop's official acts either would be seriously impeded or would simply not *be*, strictly speaking. Moreover, animated by charity, these official acts are empowered to bring about the spiritual perfection of the faithful in divine love, precisely in the way that something or *someone* already "in act" (in this case, the bishop animated by charity) can move something or *someone* else from potency to act (namely, actual charity in the faithful). This foundational understanding of the episcopacy suffuses the episcopal theology Aquinas developed in his commentaries on the PE. It is in these commentaries, more than in any other work of Aquinas, where he examines in detail the movements of God's grace in the ministry of the individual bishop.

Yet theological discourse on the episcopacy in the centuries after the Council of Trent has gradually moved away from these insights, leaving us with the (otherwise laudable) theology of the *potestas ordinis* and *potestas iurisdictionis* in danger of losing its foundation in the supernatural grace of the episcopal state. This book seeks to redress this problem by filling a lacuna in the scholarly work on St. Thomas's

---

7. See Pseudo-Dionysius the Areopagite, "The Ecclesiastical Hierarchy," in *Pseudo-Dionysius: The Complete Works* (New York: Paulist Press, 1987), 193–259, and Aquinas's commentaries on the PE, *STh* II-II, q. 184, aa. 1 and 7, and *De perf.*

Introduction 5

theology of the episcopacy with a study of his commentaries on the PE. These works are singular resources for a theology of the bishop's office that examine the grace and virtues of the episcopal *status perfectionis*. While recent studies have investigated the theology of the episcopacy in Aquinas's systematic and polemical works, no studies have yet emerged on the episcopal theology developed in his scriptural commentaries, and there is little indication that scholars are aware of the scope and value of the substantive theological contribution Aquinas makes therein.[8] This is a significant weakness, since many of St. Thomas's theological reflections on the grace of the bishop's office are found exclusively in his commentaries on the PE.

SCHOLARSHIP ON AQUINAS'S THEOLOGY OF THE EPISCOPACY

Although St. Thomas did not produce a free-standing treatise on the bishop's office, his theology of the episcopacy can be culled from his treatment of the subject in various works (see chapter 2, below). Contemporary studies selectively examine a few of these works and describe many of the principal points of Thomas's episcopal theology. While many of them reference portions of his scriptural commentaries, there are no studies that substantively examine the theology of the episcopacy found in his *lecturae* on the PE.[9] These studies may be organized according to their principal theological concerns: one set examines Aquinas's position on the sacramentality of the episcopal office while the other investigates his treatment of the episcopacy as a *status perfectionis*.[10] What follows constitutes a brief survey of this

---

8. See, e.g., Fr. John Saward's essay "The Grace of Christ in his Principal Members: St. Thomas Aquinas on the Pastoral Epistles," in *Aquinas on Scripture*, ed. Thomas Weinandy et al. (London: T & T Clark, 2005), 197–221. The title sounds promising but Saward limits his study to an examination of Aquinas's comments in the PE lectures on God, the moral life of man, and the Incarnation. Saward theorizes that the commentaries anticipate Aquinas's treatments of the same topics in *STh* I, I-II, and III. Curiously, the essay does not discuss Aquinas's theological reflections on the episcopacy.

9. Thomas delivered his commentaries on the PE to pupils in the form of lectures that were recorded by a professional reporter—in Thomas's case, Reginald of Piperno. The master personally edited the recorded lecture, or *reportatio*, before publication. Chapter 3 of this book discusses the medieval *reportatio*.

10. On the question of sacramentality, see Humbert Bouëssé, "Épiscopat et sacer-

scholarship identifying the *status quaestionis* regarding Aquinas's theology of the episcopacy.

On the question of whether the episcopacy is a sacramental order—that is, whether it is conferred as a sacrament that imparts to the recipient sanctifying grace and an indelible character—the work of Robert Stenger and that of Joseph Lécuyer, CSSp, represent two main divergent positions.[11] In a section entitled "The Episcopacy in

---

doce, pt 2: l'opinion de Saint Thomas," *Revue des Sciences Religieuses* 28 (1954): 368–91; Achilles Darquennes, *De Juridische Structuur van de Kerk volgens Sint Thomas van Aquino*, Recueil de Travaux d'Histoire et de Philologie (Leuven: Bibliothèque de l'Université, 1949); Joseph Lécuyer, CSSp, "Aux origines de la théologie thomiste de l'Épiscopat," *Gregorianum* 35 (1954): 56–89, and "Les étapes de l'enseignement thomiste sur l'Épiscopat," *Revue Thomiste* 57 (1957): 29–52; and Robert Stenger, "The Development of a Theology of the Episcopacy from the Decretum of Gratian to the Writings of Saint Thomas Aquinas" (PhD diss., The Catholic University of America, 1963). On the episcopacy as a *status perfectionis*, see Louis Bertrand Gillon, "L'Épiscopat, état de perfection," in *L'Evêque dans l'église du Christ*, ed. Humbert Bouëssé and Antré Mandouze (Paris: Desclée de Brouwer, 1963), 221–36; Ulrich Horst, OP, *Bischöfe und Ordensleute: cura principalis animarum und via perfectionis in der Ekklesiologie des hl. Thomas von Aquin* (Berlin: Akademie Verlag, 1999); A. H. Maltha, "Heiligheid en macht van de bisschop volgens Thomas van Aquino," in *Episcopale Munus: recueil d'études sur le ministère épiscopal offertes en hommage à Son Excellence Mgr J. Gijsen*, ed. Joannes Matthijs Gijsen et al. (Assen: Van Gorcum, 1982), 287–310; Noel Molloy, OP, "Hierarchy and Holiness: Aquinas on the Holiness of the Episcopal State," *The Thomist* 39 (1975): 198–252; and L. M. Orrieux, "L'Evêque 'perfector' selon le Pseudo-Denys et saint Thomas," in *L'Evêque dans l'église du Christ*, ed. Bouëssé, 237–42. For historical studies of the polemical works of Aquinas that bear upon the theology of the episcopacy at least in part, see Yves Congar, "Aspects ecclésiologiques de la querelle entre mendiants et séculiers dans la seconde moitié du XIIIe siècle et le début du XIVe," *Archives d'histoire doctrinale et littéraire du Moyen Age* 28 (1961): 35–151, and *L'Église de saint Augustin à l'époque moderne* (Paris: Éditions du Cerf, 1970); and O. Rousseau, "La doctrine du ministère épiscopal et ses vicissitudes dans l'église d'Occident" in *L'Épiscopat et l'église universelle*, ed. Y. Congar and D. Dupuy, *Unam Sanctam* (Paris: Éditions du Cerf, 1962), 39:279–308.

11. See also Santiago María Ramírez's treatment of this question in his study, *De Episcopatu ut Sacramento deque Episcoporum Collegio* (Salamanca: Instituto Histórico Dominicano de San Esteban, 1966). Though he recognizes that Thomas denies that episcopal consecration is a sacrament, Ramírez attempts to develop a theological rationale for its sacramentality based on some of what Aquinas says with respect to the permanent character of the episcopacy. Though it is not easily to be supposed that Aquinas denies the sacramentality of the episcopacy simply because he denies its sacramentality relative to the Eucharist, Ramírez admits that Thomas himself did not understand the episcopacy to be a sacramental order, simply speaking. Nevertheless, Ramírez attempts to develop such an understanding based on Aquinas's work. With that said, when developing this line of argumentation, Ramírez repeatedly qualifies his own work with comments such as the one noting Thomas's explicit denial that the episcopacy confers a

the Writings of Thomas Aquinas" within Stenger's doctoral dissertation, he studies Aquinas's reflections on the episcopal office in his commentary (composed around 1256) on Peter Lombard's *Sentences* as well as in certain portions of the *Summa Contra Gentiles* (hereafter *SCG*, composed 1260–65), *De perf* (1269–70), and *STh* (1268–73).[12] He does not mention Aquinas's scriptural commentaries at all.

Stenger argues that Thomas, throughout his career, retained the opinion he expressed in his *Sentences* commentary, namely, that the episcopacy is a genuine ecclesiastical office but not a sacramental order. According to Stenger, Aquinas held that the sacrament of the Eucharist (the *Corpus Christi verum*) is the final cause—the end—of all the other sacraments, including the sacrament of orders. The reason being that all things are ordered to their final end in Christ, whose true body, the *Corpus Christi verum* (as distinct from his mystical body, the *Corpus Christi mysticum*) is present in the Eucharist. Thus the distinction between the sacraments and, in particular, between the sacramental orders arises from the unique way each one is ordered to the Eucharist.[13] For an order to be a distinct *sacramental* order, it must have a distinctive orientation to the Eucharist. But precisely because episcopal consecration does not bestow on its recipient any new power

---

sacramental character (206). Thomas's direct denial of the sacramental character of the episcopacy is found, as cited by Ramírez, in the *Sentences* commentary (IV, d. 25, q. 1, a. 2, ad 2). Ramírez recognizes Thomas's position on this question many times. His work is an attempt to develop further theological thoughts on the episcopacy as a sacramental order—thoughts that Thomas himself never expresses and that he, in fact, repeatedly denies. Ramírez attempts to draw his conclusions in accord with some, but not all, of what Thomas directly says about the episcopacy and the exercise of the episcopal powers of consecration and the conferral of the sacraments of confirmation and holy orders. In the twentieth century, the Church has developed in her understanding of this doctrine, teaching that episcopal ordination is, indeed, an instance of the sacrament of holy orders. See, e.g., Pope Pius XII, *Sacramentum Ordinis*, Apostolic Constitution, November 30, 1947, and Vatican Council II, *Lumen Gentium*, no. 21, both of which teach that episcopal consecration is not only a sacrament, but the *fullness* of the sacrament of holy orders. The implications of this doctrinal development are far-reaching with respect to the grace intrinsic to the episcopal state. *Pace* Ramírez, Aquinas was not in a position to work them out, given his theological commitments.

12. Stenger, "Development," 148. *Summa Contra Gentiles* (Rome: Apud sedem Commissionis Leoninae, 1934).

13. Stenger, "Development," 161. See Aquinas, *Commentum in Quatuor Libros Sententiarum* in *Sancti Thomae Aquinatis Doctoris Angelici Ordinis Praedicatorum Opera Omnia* (New York: Musurgia Publishers, 1948), d. 24, q. 2, a. 2 (7.2:897; hereafter *In IV Sent*).

over the *Corpus Christi verum* than that received by a priest in his ordination, in Thomas's estimation the episcopacy cannot be a sacramental order.[14] Stenger makes a convincing case for his interpretation of Aquinas—extensively citing not only his *Sentences* commentary, but also *SCG* IV, cap. 76, as well as some of Thomas's more mature works, such as *De perf* and *STh*.[15] Had Stenger examined Aquinas's scriptural commentaries, he would not have found anything contrary to this conclusion.

Stenger notes that even though episcopal consecration bestows no new power over the *Corpus Christi verum*, Thomas teaches that it does impart a new power over the *Corpus Christi mysticum* and, thus, it is somehow a distinct order, though not in a sacramental sense. With respect to orders directly concerned with the mystical body of Christ, the episcopacy is evidently a higher order than the priesthood.[16] Yet the episcopacy cannot be reduced merely to the power of jurisdiction that can be given or revoked since the episcopacy is a permanent state. Therefore, Stenger argues that in Aquinas's thought the episcopacy is neither a sacramental order nor merely identical with the power of jurisdiction: "Between the two [Aquinas] saw that there was an *ordo* with a *potestas ordinis* over the Mystical Body."[17]

Though he unconditionally denies any notion of sacramentality in Aquinas's theology of the episcopacy, Stenger nevertheless recognizes that St. Thomas, especially in his mature works such as *STh*, affirms the communication of episcopal power by means of a consecration that communicates grace. The seasoned reflections of St. Thomas

14. To establish this, Stenger cites Aquinas, *De perf*, cap. 24, [Marietti, no. 715] (*Opuscula Theologica*, ed. Raymundo Spiazzi [Turin, Marietti: 1954], 2:150): "Sed quantum ad corpus Christi verum, quod in Sacramento continetur, [episcopus] non habet ordinem supra presbyterum" (But with respect to the true body of Christ which is contained in the Sacrament, a bishop does not have an order higher than the priesthood). Hereafter, numbers in brackets refer to article numbers in the Marietti editions of Aquinas's works.

15. Stenger also briefly reviews Thomas's teaching on episcopal jurisdiction and the episcopal state of perfection found in his three polemical works in defense of the mendicants: *Contra impugnantes* (hereafter "*Cont imp*"), *De perf*, and *Contra retrahentes*.

16. "Saint Thomas ... affirms that the episcopacy is an order with respect to the Mystical Body, for in this area the bishop does have power which the priest lacks." Stenger, "Development," 166–67. See Aquinas, *In IV Sent*, d. 7, q. 3, a. 1, qua. 2, ad 3 (7.1:577), and d. 23, q. 1, a. 3, qua. 3, ad 1 (7.2:878); and *De perf*, cap. 23 [691] (2:146).

17. Stenger, "Development," 198.

in his *STh* on the grace of episcopal consecration led Joseph Lécuyer to a different conclusion, namely, that Aquinas's mature thought affirms that episcopal consecration is, in fact, the sacrament of holy orders. In 1954, in the first of two articles he wrote on the sacramentality of episcopal *ordo* in Aquinas, "Aux origines de la théologie thomiste de l'Épiscopat," Lécuyer argues that Aquinas's thought "was oriented toward the affirmation of the sacramentality of the distinct episcopal character."[18] Uncovering the sources of this teaching, Lécuyer surveys those strands of patristic thought that informed Aquinas on the question of whether the episcopacy is a sacramental order. Acknowledging that he initially denied the sacramentality of the episcopacy, Lécuyer argues that Aquinas's thought developed near the end of his career when he began to describe the episcopacy as a grace-conferring order that cannot be received repeatedly. This explanation, he notes, is descriptive of a sacramental order with an indelible character. Attempting to support this claim, Lécuyer examines Thomas's teaching on episcopal grace found in *De perf*, cap. 24, and in *STh* II-II, q. 184, a. 5; however, he barely mentions Aquinas's comments on the grace of episcopal consecration in the lectures on 1 Timothy 4:14 and 2 Timothy 1:6.[19]

In a second article published three years later, "Les étapes de l'enseignement thomiste sur l'Épiscopat," Lécuyer backpedals a bit and modifies his previous opinion, recognizing that, at most, Thomas inchoately adumbrates the idea of the sacramentality of the episcopacy.[20] Lécuyer frankly admits that, from his *Sentences* commentary onward, St. Thomas calls the episcopacy a type of order while denying its sacramentality. In this article, he cites a few more comments on the grace of episcopal consecration in Thomas's lectures on 1 Timo-

---

18. "Se soit orienté vers l'affirmation de la sacramentalité du caractère épiscopal distinct." Lécuyer, "Aux origines," 56. For similar positions, see Bouëssé, "Épiscopat et sacerdoce," and Darquennes, *De Juridische Structuur*.

19. See Aquinas, lectures on the first epistle to Timothy (hereafter "*In 1 Tim*") in Aquinas, *Super Epistolas S. Pauli Lectura*, ed. Raphael Cai (Turin: Marietti, 1953), cap. 4, lect. 3, [172], 2:245; and *In 2 Tim*, cap. 1, lect. 3 [12] (2:269).

20. "Il semble bien que saint Thomas a, sinon évolué, du moins nuancé et précisé sa pensée, depuis ses premiers ouvrages jusqu'aux derniers chapitres de la *Somme théologique*" (It seems that St. Thomas has, if not evolved, at least nuanced and clarified his thought, from his early works up to the latter chapters of the *Summa Theologica*). Lécuyer, "Les étapes," 29.

thy 3:2 and Titus 1:5.[21] However, as with his prior article, he does not examine them at any length.

The conclusions Lécuyer draws in this second article reveal a development of his understanding of Aquinas's episcopal theology. He lists the following essential points of Thomas's teaching on the episcopacy. First, Thomas clearly posits a distinction not only of jurisdiction, but also of order between bishops and simple priests. Nevertheless, he is constrained to recognize a single sacerdotal order including both bishops and priests because they have equal power to consecrate the Eucharist. Second, episcopal consecration, conferred by imposition of hands, imparts a special episcopal grace and produces a stable and indelible effect similar but not identical to the character conferred in the sacrament of holy orders. Third, by this episcopal grace the bishop is enabled to rule the people *in persona Christi*, his principal duty being to teach the faith.[22]

Lécuyer's work offers valuable insights into one aspect of Thomas's theology of bishops. However, along with Stenger, he neglects virtually the entire body of teaching in Thomas's lectures on the PE. This is all the more striking since, according to Aquinas, the grace of the episcopal state—whether sacramental or not—is the *very subject* of the PE themselves.[23] This grace enables the bishop to direct the spiritual growth and perfection of his flock. To be fair, Stenger and Lécuyer duly limit their studies to the question of episcopal sacramentality. They did not intend to evaluate the ecclesial purpose of the episcopacy.

A second set of studies examines in some detail Aquinas's notion of the episcopacy as a *status perfectionis* or "state of perfection." Decisively influenced by Pseudo-Dionysius's *Ecclesiastical Hierarchy* and, in fact, by his reading of the PE, Aquinas develops the notion of the episcopacy as a state of perfection in which the bishop is established

21. Lécuyer, "Les étapes," 35–37. Lécuyer cites Aquinas, *In 1 Tim*, cap. 3, lect. 1, [91], 2:232, and the lectures on the epistle to Titus in *Super Epistolas* (hereafter *"In Tit"*), cap. 1, lect. 2, [10], 2:305.

22. Lécuyer, "Aux origines," 52.

23. Aquinas states this in the prologue to his commentaries on the Pauline corpus, "Est enim haec doctrina tota de gratia Christi.... Alio modo secundum quod est in membris principalibus corporis mystici, et sic commendatur in epistolis quae sunt ad praelatos" (And indeed this entire teaching is on the grace of Christ.... In another way grace is treated insofar as it is found in the principal members of the mystical body, and it is commended thus in the epistles to the prelates). *Super Epistolas*, prol., [11], 1:3.

as the spiritual perfector of his flock. The Pseudo-Dionysian hierarchical schema of the Church, prevalent in the thought of several medieval theologians (see chapter 2, below), conceived the deacon as the purifier of the beginners in the spiritual life, the priest as the illuminator of the proficient, and the bishop as the *perfector* (the "finisher" or "perfector") of the spiritually advanced. These three orders thus have an inner relation to the stages of the growth of the spiritual life and are directed ultimately to bring about *theosis* or divinization in the faithful. The two outstanding investigations of Aquinas's teaching on this matter have been produced by Dominican theologians: Ulrich Horst, *Bischöfe und Ordensleute: cura principalis animarum und via perfectionis in der Ekklesiologie des hl. Thomas von Aquin*, and Noel Molloy, "Hierarchy and Holiness: Aquinas on the Holiness of the Episcopal State."[24]

In the second part of his book, "Episcopacy and *status perfectionis*," Horst briefly investigates Aquinas's theology of the episcopal state of perfection.[25] He examines the notion of *status* that Thomas applies to the episcopacy and religious life, each of which Aquinas calls a *status perfectionis*. Aquinas uses the word *status* to signify a relatively stable and permanent condition. Classically, the term *status* indicated whether a person was in a state of servitude or of freedom. In the Christian tradition, the notion was extended to identify different positions or ranks in the Church.[26] According to St. Thomas, the religious life is a passive *status perfectionis* since it is a stable condition of life defined by the evangelical counsels of perfection (poverty, chastity, and obedience). Adhering to these counsels

24. See the detailed bibliographical information in footnote 10 above. For other, less comprehensive studies, see Gillon, "L'Épiscopat, état de perfection"; Maltha, "Heiligheid en macht van de bisschop volgens Thomas van Aquino"; and Orrieux, "L'Evêque 'perfector.'"

25. Horst, *Bischöfe und Ordensleute*, 79. In the first part of the book, "Thomas von Aquin und die Anfänge seiner Theologie des Episkopats," Horst examines Aquinas's theology of the episcopacy from its beginnings in his *Sentences* commentary and the *SCG*, and traces its development through his polemical works against Gerard of Abbeville, relevant sections of his *Quaestiones de quodlibet* (hereafter "*Quodl*")—in particular, Quodl III, q. 6, a. 3 (*Quaestiones quodlibetales*, ed. R. Spiazzi [Turin: Marietti, 1956], 55–58), *Cont imp*, and *De perf*. Horst adds to previous scholarship an examination of Thomas's thoughts on some of the prerogatives and pastoral duties of the bishop.

26. See *STh* II-II, q. 183, a. 1 (*Summa Theologiae* [Torino: Edizioni San Paolo, 1999], 1797).

produces spiritual perfection in the religious. For its part, the episcopal office is an active *status perfectionis* because it is a stable condition defined by activity that is essentially ordered to the spiritual perfection of one's neighbor in supernatural charity. The religious state exists for the spiritual perfection of the individual Christian who receives this perfection, whereas the episcopal state is for the action of spiritually perfecting the community of Christians.[27]

Though he does not intend to provide a comprehensive account of Aquinas's theology of the episcopacy, Horst masterfully traces its historical beginnings and Aquinas's subsequent development of a theology of the active state of perfection in the episcopacy. As such, the book is a fine synthesis of some of the principal themes in Aquinas's episcopal theology. However, like other contemporary scholars, Horst does not substantively examine Thomas's PE lectures. Interestingly, in a section entitled "The Duties of the Bishop," where it would be fitting to discuss Aquinas's extensive treatment of episcopal obligations in the lectures on the PE, Horst focuses almost exclusively on *STh* II-II, q. 185, aa. 4–8 (discussed below, in chapter 2).[28] Apart from a few passing references to Aquinas's comments on 1 Timothy 3:1 regarding whether it is licit to seek the episcopacy for oneself, Horst does not mention the PE lectures again.[29]

In a 1975 article in *The Thomist*, "Hierarchy and Holiness," Noel Molloy examines various works of St. Thomas in which he discusses the holiness required of a candidate for the episcopate. Identifying the historical tradition in which the bishop is viewed as the instantiation of the holiness to which his flock is called, Molloy aims "to show how this tradition was taken over and developed by St. Thomas."[30] Thomas's theology of the episcopacy "confronts us with an episcopal ideal that has been largely lost sight of, with a contemplative and charismatic episcopate whose primacy is a real primacy in Christ."[31] Molloy's is one of the more comprehensive and accurate studies of Aquinas's the-

---

27. Horst, *Bischöfe und Ordensleute*, 88–92. In the third and final part of the book, "Das Wesen des Religiosenstandes" (The Essence of the Religious State), 111, Horst examines the state of perfection in the various religious orders and the differences between them.
28. Horst, *Bischöfe und Ordensleute*, 93.
29. Horst cites *In 1 Tim*, cap. 3, lect. 1, [88], 2:231 (Horst, *Bischöfe und Ordensleute*, 106).
30. Molloy, "Hierarchy and Holiness," 199.
31. Molloy, "Hierarchy and Holiness," 199.

ology of the episcopacy. He examines Thomas's teaching on the episcopal state of perfection, on the spiritual and moral prerequisites to fulfill the duties of this office, and on the principal responsibility of this office: to perfect others spiritually through teaching.

Closely following Aquinas's treatise on the states of life in *STh* II-II, qq. 183–85, Molloy shows how Thomas's notion of *status* as a stable and quasi-permanent condition contributes to his understanding of the episcopacy as an active *status perfectionis*. The episcopal office is characterized by the duty to work for the spiritual perfection of the flock. Because the bishop is bound by his office to perfect others in charity (the essence of spiritual perfection), he himself ought to have extraordinary fraternal charity. Enjoying genuine spiritual perfection enables him to guide others in the life of charity. In other words, the excelling love he has (or ought to have) for God and his neighbors impels the bishop to work tirelessly so that his subordinates may acquire the supernatural love of God above all else. While the fit candidate for the episcopacy must be possessed of an exceptionally high moral character, Thomas acknowledges that hierarchical office is received through an act of episcopal consecration, regardless of the recipient's personal holiness. Nevertheless, holiness is demanded of the candidate so that, being conformed to God himself, he may thereby be empowered to bring about the same conformity in others.[32]

Molloy then provides a partial study of Aquinas's teaching on some of the moral and spiritual qualities entailed by episcopal holiness.[33] Like Stenger and Lécuyer, Molloy documents Thomas's teaching on the special grace of the episcopacy. He also follows Lécuyer in briefly citing *Lectura super 1 Timotheum*, cap. 4, lect. 3 (173) and *Lectura super 2 Timotheum* (hereafter "*In 2 Tim*"), cap. 1, lect. 3 (13–14), where Thomas discusses the episcopal grace given to Timothy through the imposition of hands.[34] However, as with the other studies, Molloy's discussion of episcopal grace in the PE lectures is minimal, extending no further than that of Lécuyer.[35]

32. Molloy, "Hierarchy and Holiness," 206–9.
33. Molloy, "Hierarchy and Holiness," 202–3. See *STh* II-II, q. 185, a. 3; *De perf*, cap. 16 [655], 2:135 and cap. 18 [664], 2:137; and *Quodl* VIII, q. 4, a. 1 (*Quaestiones*, 166).
34. Molloy, "Hierarchy and Holiness," 213–14. See the Marietti text of Aquinas, *Super Epistolas*, 2:245 and 2:269.
35. For the most part, Molloy overlooks the lectures. On page 206, Molloy does cite

Molloy discusses the primacy of the bishop's magisterial duty in Thomas's writings, especially *STh* III, q. 67, a. 2. The bishop serves as the image of Christ for his flock, but, according to Thomas, "above all, he is the image of *Christ the Prophet,* for the office of teaching has absolute precedence (*principalissimum*) over the other functions of the bishop."[36] As an act of charity, teaching is the principal means by which the bishop spiritually perfects his flock.[37] As such, the bishop simultaneously possesses a "magisterium of perfection" and a "spiritual magisterium."[38] To exercise this office prelates especially need the gift of wisdom, thus they must devote themselves to the contemplation and diligent study of Scripture.[39] The following chapters of this book clarify why Aquinas views teaching, in particular, as the apex of the perfecting action of the bishop upon the faithful inasmuch as that activity demands superlative erudition and wisdom.

Molloy's study is unique in its emphasis on Thomas's claim that fraternal charity constitutes the essence of the episcopacy, drawing especially, as he does, from Aquinas's remarks to this effect in his *De perf.* The episcopal office places the bishop in a state of life that binds him in charity to procure for his neighbors the greatest of all goods, eternal life. The exercise of the episcopal office is thus construed as a mature and even heroic exercise of charity.[40]

All of these valuable studies identify some of the principal topics in Aquinas's episcopal theology. In particular, Stenger argues that, even though Aquinas denies the sacramentality of the episcopal or-

---

In 1 Tim, cap. 3, lect. 1 [88–90], 2:231–32, where Aquinas argues that it is illicit and presumptuous to desire the episcopate for oneself. However, he does not proceed to consider Thomas's comments on 1 Tm 3:2 (*In 1 Tim,* cap. 3, lect. 1 [91], 2:232) that elaborate upon on the virtues necessary for bishops.

36. Molloy, "Hierarchy and Holiness," 202. See *STh* III, q. 67, a. 2, ad 1.

37. Molloy, "Hierarchy and Holiness," 236–37. See *Cont imp* II, cap. 1 (*Opuscula theologica,* ed. Spiazzi, [45], 2:15–16); *STh* II-II, q. 187, a. 4, ad 2; and *STh* III, q. 39, a. 3, ad 2.

38. Molloy, "Hierarchy and Holiness," 232 and 234. See *STh* II-II, q. 185, a. 8 and *De perf,* cap. 19, [674], 2:139.

39. Molloy, "Hierarchy and Holiness," 239–42. See *Cont imp* II, cap. 4 [196] (*Opuscula theologica,* ed. Spiazzi, 2:44); *STh* II-II, q. 45, a. 5; and *STh* III, q. 40, a. 1, ad 2.

40. Molloy, "Hierarchy and Holiness," 227. See *STh* II-II, q. 184, a. 5. Lending further support to this claim, Molloy cites Thomas's argument in *Quodl* IV, q. 12, a. 1, ad 7 (*Quaestiones,* 90) to the effect that the episcopal state ought to be held by a man possessed of a perfect charity that impels him to work tirelessly for the salvation of his neighbor (Molloy, "Hierarchy and Holiness," 231).

Introduction 15

der, he attempts to show that it is, nevertheless, an *ordo* with a *potestas ordinis* over the mystical body of Christ. Both Stenger and Lécuyer highlight Thomas's teaching that grace is conferred by episcopal consecration. Horst and Molloy examine Thomas's treatment of the episcopacy as a *status perfectionis* essentially ordered to the spiritual perfection of one's neighbor in charity. The episcopal state demands an excelling fraternal charity and it enjoins upon the bishop the special duty of preaching which, for Thomas, is the principal means to perfect others spiritually. In the following chapters, these studies will be supplemented with an examination of St. Thomas's detailed teaching on the grace of the episcopacy in his lectures on the PE. In these commentaries, Aquinas provides unique theological reflections on the foundation of the episcopal office in a divine calling and in grace; the virtues required of suitable candidates for the episcopacy; the proper and virtuous execution of this office on behalf of the faithful, heretics, and unbelievers; the particular vices to which bishops are especially vulnerable; the spiritual, psychological, and social pitfalls they commonly face; and the fruit of everlasting glory promised to the faithful bishop and his flock.

THE VALUE OF AQUINAS'S COMMENTARIES ON THE PASTORAL EPISTLES

Aquinas's commentaries on the PE considerably supplement his treatment of the episcopacy in his other works and any comprehensive account of his writings on the episcopal office ought to consider them as uniquely valuable theological sources in their own right.[41] In his recent biography of Aquinas, Jean-Pierre Torrell writes: "If we wish, therefore, to get a slightly less one-sided idea of the whole theologian and his method, it is imperative to read and use in a much deeper fashion these biblical commentaries in parallel with the great systematic works."[42] In the course of his lectures on the PE, Thomas elaborates a

---

41. The dating of Aquinas's commentaries on the Pauline corpus is a difficult question. In chapter 3, I survey the scholarship on this question and argue for a later dating. Thus, the commentaries would represent the more mature thought of St. Thomas.

42. Jean-Pierre Torrell, *Saint Thomas Aquinas: Volume 1, The Person and His Work*, trans. Robert Royal, 2nd rev. ed. (Washington, D.C.: The Catholic University of America Press, 2005), 55.

unique theology of the episcopacy by means of a probing examination of these epistles.

While none of St. Thomas's polemical works or theological syntheses is dedicated exclusively to the episcopacy, in them he offers substantial reconsiderations of various questions regarding the episcopacy such as the nature of the bishop's office, the extent of the authority over the mystical body of Christ conferred by episcopal consecration, the functional relation of the episcopacy to both the priesthood and the diaconate, the way in which this office constitutes an active *status perfectionis*, and many other matters.[43] Throughout these works he expresses his theology of the episcopacy primarily in speculative and general terms. However, he usually does not examine the practical needs of the bishop in the exercise of his office.

But in his commentaries on the PE, meticulously following the text of these epistles, Thomas approaches the episcopacy as a concrete expression of divine grace. In the prologue to his commentaries on all fourteen Pauline epistles, he writes that Paul's "entire teaching is on the grace of Christ"—particularly as it is found in the Church.[44] Theologian Thomas Prügl remarks that Thomas's Pauline commentaries "amount to an astoundingly original biblically-founded ecclesiology which he deduces consistently from contemplation of the mystical body."[45] The object of this accolade includes the theology of the episcopacy found in his lectures on the PE—a principal element of the ecclesiology in Aquinas's Pauline commentaries.

Although several of the same concerns addressed in his systematic and polemical works are treated in his lectures on the PE, these lectures are the *only* complete works in Aquinas's entire corpus dedicated

---

43. For instance, in his early polemical work defending the rights of mendicant friars to teach and perform pastoral duties, *Cont imp* (1256), Thomas treats the nature and scope of the bishop's power to delegate pastoral responsibilities to the friars. In *De perf*, caps. 15–19 (*Opuscula Theologica*, ed. Spiazzi, 2:134–40), as well as in *STh* II-II, qq. 183–85, Thomas offers extended treatments of the episcopal *status perfectionis* that constitute short treatises on the episcopacy in their own right.

44. "Est enim haec doctrina tota de gratia Christi" (In fact, his entire teaching is on the grace of Christ). Aquinas, *Super Epistolas*, prol., [11], 1:3.

45. Thomas Prügl, "Thomas Aquinas as Interpreter of Scripture," in *The Theology of Thomas Aquinas*, ed. Joseph Wawrykow and Rik van Nieuwenhove (Notre Dame, Ind.: University of Notre Dame Press, 2005), 405.

principally to a discussion of the episcopacy. In the lectures, Aquinas engages the episcopal office both speculatively and practically, with a particular focus on moral and spiritual issues. With profound sensitivity, Aquinas examines what a bishop ought to be and do. He closely traces the contours of the PE themselves as St. Paul considers the graces and virtues demanded by the episcopal office-holder and the particular vices that must be carefully avoided. St. Thomas provides elaborations and practical applications of the general principles of episcopal theology—principles he establishes both in the lectures themselves and in his other works. Among all his writings on the episcopacy, Aquinas's PE lectures are conspicuous for their sensitivity to the concrete exigencies of the bishop's office.

METHOD

This book is, principally, a study of the theological insights of St. Thomas's lectures on 1 and 2 Timothy and Titus. As such, I will contextualize these lectures both within the corpus of Thomas's *opera omnia* and within the writings of several of his principal contemporaries who also examined the episcopacy theologically. Aquinas's PE commentaries are distinctively *theological* in that they both consider the literal sense of the scriptural text (the direct meaning of the words) and seek a more penetrating understanding of the text—either heuristically/dialectically by uncovering the reasons behind the scriptural assertions, or deductively by arguing for conclusions that necessarily follow from the text's claims. Thomas positions himself as an excellent interpreter of Paul, as will be borne out below, especially in chapters 4 through 6.

The core of this study is a careful examination of those portions of Aquinas's PE lectures that bear upon the nature and duties of the office of bishop, the grace of the Holy Spirit communicated in episcopal ordination, the requisite virtues of this office, the vices to be avoided, and the particular instructions for bishops on teaching and church governance. The theological reflections found in the lectures are vital components of Aquinas's theology of the episcopacy and, more broadly speaking, of his ecclesiology as a whole. Chapter 2 offers a conspectus of the theology of the episcopacy in the writings of Aquinas's principal contemporaries and in the entire body of his own works.[46] This will provide the historical, theological, and textual context in light of which Aquinas's PE commentaries ought to be read. Chapter 3 introduces St. Thomas's lectures on the PE, identifying their place in the exegetical tradition of commentaries on the PE, their dating, and the method by which theological insights are developed in the course of a medieval biblical commentary. Chapters 4 through 6 examine the theology of the episcopacy found in Aquinas's lectures on 1 Timothy, 2 Timothy, and Titus respectively. This is followed by a concluding chapter, summarizing the findings and suggesting further avenues of research indicated by this study.

46. Given his understanding of Scripture as providing the first principles of *sacra doctrina* (see *STh* I, q. 1), one might suspect that much of what Aquinas has to say about the episcopacy in his PE commentaries would form the basis for the episcopal theology in his systematic works. Along these lines, a fruitful investigation could compare, e.g., what he says on the NT use of *presbyter* and *episcopus* in *In 1 Tim*, cap. 3, lect. 1, [87], 2:231, with *STh* II-II, q. 184, a. 6, ad 1; also compare his comments on whether desiring the episcopacy is licit in *In 1 Tim*, cap. 3, lect. 1, [89], 2:232, with *STh* II-II, q. 185, a. 1; and, finally, compare his remarks on the solemn obligation imposed by the rite of episcopal ordination in *In 1 Tim*, cap. 6, lect. 2, [259], 2:260, and *In 2 Tim*, cap. 1, lect. 3, [13], 2:269, with *STh* II-II, q. 184, a. 5.

2

The Theology of the Episcopacy in the Writings of St. Thomas and His Contemporaries

Aquinas commented on the PE a few centuries after the writings of Pseudo-Dionysius had been translated into Latin. His immediate predecessors and principal contemporaries had begun to incorporate Dionysius's teachings on the celestial and ecclesiastical hierarchies into their theology. Regarding the episcopacy in particular, this signaled a development or, more accurately, a *recovery* of the notion of the bishop as a hierarchical mediator who brings his subordinates to spiritual perfection. In his writings, Aquinas describes this perfective activity as consisting in the bishop producing supernatural charity in his subjects by means of his hierarchical actions, above all by preaching.

During Aquinas's career, the newly founded mendicant orders were besieged by the secular masters at the University of Paris. This multivalent dispute, known as the "mendicant controversy," was constituted by a constellation of issues which can, for our purposes, be reduced to two principal questions. First, what kind of life constitutes the *status perfectionis* (the state of perfection): that of the secular clergy (as per William of St. Amour) or that of bishops and those in religious orders whose lives were defined by profession of vows of poverty, chastity, and obedience (as per St. Thomas Aquinas)? Second, are the mendicants inspired by the spirit of the antichrist when they exercise preaching and sacramental ministry without permission from the local bishop? William of St. Amour answered this latter question in the affirmative. St. Bonaventure and St. Thomas answer in the negative. For her part, the Church decided the question in favor of the mendicants. For all that, this chapter will focus on Aquinas's theology of the episcopal office and that of his principal contemporaries. His polemical works on the mendicant controversy will be treated in their proper historical setting.

In examining the recovery of Pseudo-Dionysius by St. Thomas and his contemporaries, this chapter provides the historical context for Aquinas's work on the episcopacy so that, seen in its concrete milieu, it may be assessed and valued with greater accuracy. To this end, this chapter surveys the theology of the episcopacy as found in the writings of Thomas's principal predecessors and peers, namely, Peter Lombard (1096–1164), St. Albert the Great (1193–1280), and St. Bonaventure of Bagnoregio (1221–74). By and large, this will frame the proximate historical backdrop for our study of Aquinas's work. Following this is a summary of the salient points of Aquinas's theology of the episcopacy in his *opera omnia,* establishing the immediate textual setting for his lectures on the PE. The theology that Aquinas develops in his PE lectures is unique both with respect to that of his peers and with respect to what he says about the episcopacy in his other writings. For instance, while his contemporaries occasionally recognize that the episcopacy is, in Dionysian terms, the office of "perfector," Aquinas bears this out more fully by developing the notion of the episcopacy as an active "state of perfection" (*status perfectionis*) and an office in which the bishop is charged to bring his subjects to the fulfillment of supernatural charity. Aquinas's theology of the episcopacy in his PE lectures affords insights found neither in his other writings nor in those of his contemporaries regarding the spiritual, intellectual, and moral prerequisites for one to hold and execute the duties of this office.

This chapter concludes with a brief examination of the mendicant controversy, attending to Aquinas's treatment of the state of perfection as manifested in the episcopal office. In the course of his works defending the mendicants, Aquinas identifies essential features of the bishop's office. To produce exhaustive treatments of the theological writings on the episcopacy in Aquinas's corpus and in those of his principal contemporaries would demand an independent tome for each. The brief review found in this chapter identifies Aquinas's foundational insights that serve as a basis for discovering how his treatment of the episcopacy fits into the thirteenth-century discussion of the same.

THE THEOLOGY OF THE EPISCOPACY IN THE WRITINGS OF AQUINAS'S CONTEMPORARIES

Peter Lombard

Peter Lombard's teaching on the episcopacy in his *Sententiae* serves as the primary background text, a point of entry for studying the theology of the episcopacy developed by the thirteenth-century masters.[1] Lombard identifies seven ecclesiastical grades of sacramental order: porter, lector, exorcist, acolyte, subdeacon, deacon, and priest.[2] He also recognizes several ecclesiastical "dignities and offices" which are not sacramental orders, the first among these being the office of bishop. In his usage, an *ordo* signifies a particular grade of cleric in which one is constituted by the sacrament of holy orders. He thus categorizes the episcopacy not as a sacramental clerical *ordo* but as a dignified office (*officium*). In this chapter, he says very directly: "There are certain other names, not of orders, but of dignities and offices. 'Bishop' is both the name of a dignity and of an office."[3] To this end, he cites St. Isidore and Gratian.[4] Following Lombard, the "Master," thirteenth-century theologians likewise held that the episcopacy is not a sacramental order.

Citing Gratian, Lombard says: "The bishop [*pontifex*] is the chief of priests and [serves], as it were, [as] the way [*via*] of those who follow. He is also named the highest priest, for he makes priests and dea-

---

1. Peter Lombard, *Sententiae in IV Libris Distinctae*, 3rd ed. (Rome: Grottaferrata, Editiones Collegii S. Bonaventurae Ad Claras Aquas, 1981), 2:405. He treats the episcopacy directly in IV, d. 24, caps. 14–17.

2. Lombard, *Sententiae* IV, d. 24, cap. 3, 394.

3. "Sunt et alia quaedam, non ordinum, sed dignitatum et officiorum nomina. Dignitatis simul et officii nomen est episcopus." Lombard, *Sententiae*, cap. 14, 405–6.

4. Isidore, *Etymology* 7, cap. 12, n. 11, in *Patrologiae Cursus Completus, Series Latina*, ed. Jacques-Paul Migne (Paris: Garnier and J.-P. Migne, 1844–64; hereafter *PL*), 82:291; Gratian, *Decret.*, C. Cleros, a. 7, Friedberg, 1.68.

cons, and ordains all ecclesiastical orders."[5] The bishop is the "chief of priests" and, as *pontifex*, he is the *via*, the "path" for those to follow on their way to Christ. He is the high priest and the one who consecrates men to be priests and deacons, and the one who distributes all ecclesiastical orders. Finally, Lombard discusses the fourfold distinction of the order of bishops into patriarchs, archbishops, metropolitans, and simple bishops.

In his work *On the Sacraments of the Christian Faith*, Hugh of St. Victor (d. 1141) identifies the same seven grades of clerical order listed by Lombard, adding that the grade of priesthood contains within itself different degrees of dignity. Specifically and in ascending order he mentions bishops, archbishops, primates, and patriarchs, culminating in the highest pontifex, the pope.[6] In the chapter entitled "On bishops," Hugh says that "no one is to be elected as bishop except one who has first lived religiously in the sacred orders," reflecting the ancient tradition that candidates for the episcopacy are to be chosen from among the monastic orders.[7] Regarding the question of the sacramentality of the episcopacy, Hugh's position is essentially the same as Lombard's. In this same chapter Hugh writes: "Only the diaconate and the presbyterate are to be called sacred orders, because the primitive Church is described as having had only these, and only of these have we the precepts of the apostle."[8]

There is no trace in Lombard's *Sententiae* of the Dionysian notion of the episcopal office of perfector. He does use the term *status perfectionis*, but not in connection to the episcopacy. For him, the term principally signifies either the state of humankind in supernatural grace prior to the Fall or the state of humans in beatitude. It is evident from a thorough search of the *opera omnia* of Alexander of Hales (1185–1245), St. Albert the Great, and St. Bonaventure that these authors also use this term almost exclusively in this way. The one exception is found in the corpus of St. Bonaventure as noted below.

---

5. "Pontifex princeps sacerdotum est, quasi via sequentium; ipse et summus sacerdos nuncupatur: ipse enim sacerdotes et levitas efficit, ipse omnes ordines ecclesiasticos disponit." Lombard, *Sententiae*, cap. 16, 406.

6. Hugh of St. Victor, *On the Sacraments of the Christian Faith*, trans. Roy J. Deferrari (Cambridge, Mass.: The Mediaeval Academy of America, 1951), book 2, part 3, cap. 4, 261.

7. Hugh of St. Victor, *On the Sacraments*, cap. 12, 269.

8. Hugh of St. Victor, *On the Sacraments*, cap. 12, 269.

St. Albert the Great

While the writings of Pseudo-Dionysius do not play a role in Lombard's brief treatments of the episcopacy, by the thirteenth century the Dionysian corpus serves as a primary source for Albert, Bonaventure, and Aquinas. How did the Dionysian works come to preponderate in the Latin West?

In 827, imperial ambassadors delivered a copy of the works of Dionysius to the abbey in Saint-Denis, France. Hilduin (775–840), the abbot of St. Denis, translated this corpus into Latin. This first Latin version was, by many accounts, largely incomprehensible and was thus revised by John Scotus Eriugena (815–77) in 862. Along with this revision there emerged the traditional account of St. Dionysius: the convert of St. Paul, author, bishop of Athens, apostle to the French, and the bishop and martyr of Paris.[9]

The historian Maria Theresa d'Alverny notes that later, in the twelfth century, a renewed interest in this supposed apostolic father was initiated when "a new manuscript had been brought from Constantinople to St. Denis by William Le Mire, who knew Greek and himself produced versions of the *Vita Secundi philosophi* and of Greek prologues to the Pauline Epistles, this last at the request of Herbert of Bosham," who was a student of Peter Lombard.[10] A series of new Latin translations was then produced, the most important being John Sarrazin's revision of Eriugena's translation in the middle of the twelfth century. According to d'Alverny, Sarrazin's text was both more accurate and readable. Whether or not Lombard availed himself of this source, this translation of the Dionysian writings was certainly used by Hugh of St. Victor and Albert the Great.

While Albert made broad use of the newly-available Dionysian corpus in his writings on ecclesiology and the theology of hierarchy,

---

9. See Andrew Louth, *The Church in History*, vol. 3: *Greek East and Latin West: The Church AD 681–1071* (Crestwood, N.Y.: St. Vladimir's Seminary Press, 2007), 131–32. I am grateful to Fr. Kevin Augustyn for directing me to the latest scholarship on the reception of the Dionysian corpus in the West.

10. Marie-Thérèse d'Alverny, "Translations and Translators," in *Renaissance and Renewal in the Twelfth Century*, ed. Robert Louis and Giles Constable with Carol Lanham, reprint (Toronto: University of Toronto Press in association with the Medieval Academy of America, 1999), 433.

the Dionysian notion of the bishop as spiritual perfector does not play as significant of a role for him (nor for St. Bonaventure) as it did for St. Thomas. In fact, the notion of the bishop as spiritual perfector appears in a uniquely architectonic manner in Aquinas's writings, functioning for him as the determinative feature of the episcopacy, as we shall see below. Nonetheless, as noted by Edward Mahoney, an expert in medieval philosophy:

Albert the Great was one of the first philosopher-theologians of the thirteenth century to adopt a conceptual scheme of metaphysical hierarchy that had its roots in the writings of Proclus, pseudo-Dionysius and the *Liber de causis*, as well as in some relevant texts in works by Avicenna. The young Thomas Aquinas, one might add, evidently learned about this scheme during the time that he spent at Cologne following Albert's lectures on Dionysius's *De divinis nominibus* [composed around 1250].[11]

In his writings on hierarchy, Albert discerns and employs the dominant Dionysian principle throughout, namely, "the lowest in a higher rank touches the highest in a lower rank."[12] Following Hugh of St. Victor, Albert identifies the essence of the hierarchical state as a participation in the grace of divine illumination in which the hierarch pours forth that same illumination on his subordinates.[13] For one to enter the fullness of the hierarchical state, it is required that he first undergo a conversion by way of purging; second, that he be illuminated in divine knowledge assimilating him to the divine life; and third, that he enter perfection properly speaking, consisting in the activity of illuminating his subordinates.[14]

Albert postulates a broad view of hierarchy as such by identifying the divine hierarchy of the Trinity as the ground and source for the

---

11. Edward P. Mahoney, "Albert the Great on Christ and Hierarchy," in *Christ Among the Medieval Dominicans: Representations of Christ in the Texts and Images of the Order of Preachers*, ed. Kent Emery Jr. and Joseph Wawrykow (Notre Dame, Ind.: University of Notre Dame Press, 1999), 365.

12. Mahoney, "Albert the Great," 365.

13. See Hugh of St. Victor, *Commentaria in Hierarchiam Coelestem S. Dionysii Areopagitae* I, cap. 5, *PL* 175:934. In this work, Hugh comments on Pseudo-Dionysius's writings on the angelic, not the ecclesiastical, hierarchy.

14. Albertus Magnus, *Summa theologiae* II, tr. 10, q. 37, m. 2, ed. Augustus Borgnet, 34 (Paris: Vivès, 1890): 533; also Albertus Magnus, *Super Dionysium de ecclesiastica hierarchica*, in *Opera Omnia*, vol. 36.2, ed. Maria Burger (Cologne: Monasterii Westfalorum in Aedibus Aschendorff, 1999).

angelic and ecclesial hierarchies, though Dionysius himself did not explicitly make this connection.[15] Albert places Christ at the center of both the angelic and ecclesial hierarchies as the one from whom all illumination proceeds to creatures. The ecclesial hierarchy, for its part, is illumined by the third and lowest angelic hierarchy.[16] Closely following Dionysius, he identifies the three orders of the ecclesiastical hierarchy: deacons who purge, priests who both purge and illuminate, and bishops who purge, illuminate, and purify.[17]

Following Lombard, Albert did not consider the episcopacy to be a sacramental order distinct from that of the priesthood. He deploys a theological argument for this position that Aquinas, in turn, adopts and develops: since distinctions between sacramental orders are based on their different relations to the true body of Christ (the *Corpus Christi verum*) in the Eucharist, and because there is no distinction between the episcopacy and the presbyterate on this account, the episcopacy cannot be a sacramental order different from the presbyterate. Nevertheless—and Aquinas follows Albert on this as well (both of whom are evidently heirs of Lombard's thought)—the episcopacy is a higher grade of order than the priesthood since it confers a unique dignity of jurisdiction over the mystical body of Christ (the *Corpus Christi mysticum*).[18] Bishops are the successors of the apostles and they wield the *juridical* power of the keys with a greater scope than simple priests. For Albert, however, in a certain respect this power is subordinate to the *sacramental* power of orders to consecrate the Eucharist in that the bishop's juridical power is principally ordered to prepare the faithful through the forgiveness of their sins to receive the Eucharist worthily.[19]

St. Albert strongly affirms that Christ is the head of the Church,

---

15. Albertus Magnus, *In II Sententiarum*, d. 9, a. 1 (ed. Borgnet, 27:190). This is Albert's commentary on Lombard's *Sentences*, hereafter referenced as "*In [no.] Sent*" where "[no.]" refers to the book number.

16. Mahoney, "Albert the Great," 368. See Albert, *Summa theologiae* II, tr. 10, q. 39, m. 2, ad 3 (ed. Borgnet, 32:469–70).

17. Albertus Magnus, *Super Dion. De eccl. hier.*, cap. 5 (ed. Borgnet, 14:736n29, referenced by Mahoney, "Albert the Great," 373).

18. Albertus Magnus, *In IV Sent*, d. 24, aa. 39–40 (ed. Borgnet, 30:81).

19. See, e.g., Albertus Magnus, *De sacramentis*, tr. 8, q. 3 (ed. Colon., 26:139–41); *De incarnatione*, tr. 5, q. 2, a. 4 (ed. Colon., 26:216).

the chief member of the ecclesial hierarchy. Thus, not only do clerics hold and exercise their juridical and sacramental power in subordination to Christ, but Christ is the preeminent model to which all clerics, but especially bishops, must conform their lives and ministries.[20] It is on this point, in particular, that we may discern a formative influence on Aquinas's writings on the episcopacy. Mahoney summarizes Albert's insights on the qualities of a good bishop and, without a doubt, these points are echoed by Aquinas in his comments on the PE:

Only someone who humbles himself for the benefit of his subjects makes good use of the power that he has received within the Church.... Indeed, nothing is easier than to rule subjects if one does so in humility and meekness. In the early Church (*primitiva ecclesia*), there was not great concern for power and all paid heed to examples of humility and love (*caritas*). Only with the increase of wicked people in the Church has severe rule become necessary and serving as a prelate become intolerable.[21]

In his commentary on Luke 9 (especially verses 49 and following), Albert argues that one who is not conformed to the profound humility of Christ should be barred from ministry.[22] Such persons, preferring their own wealth, power, and luxury, simulate self-effacing virtue in order to mask their invidious malice and self-adulation. Mahoney explains why Albert denounces such persons so scathingly:

Albert excoriates contemporary prelates for being tyrants and oppressors of the souls entrusted to their care rather than being their physicians. Such prelates act most evilly, since they bring about the evil reign within the Church and cause the name of Christ to be blasphemed. Albert considers some prelates of his day to tolerate and even to favor the wicked, since they are more committed to the self-indulgent Sardanapalus [a legendary evil king of Assyria] than they are to Jesus Christ. Popes [sic!], Cardinals, archbishops and bishops, who should be sources of light (*illuminatores*) for others, are in fact darkened because of their ignorance and evil life (*nigra vita*). Given Albert's harsh judgment of highly placed prelates by reason of their failure to live up to the model of Christ, one may conclude that it is not only his theoretical

---

20. Albertus Magnus, *Super Lucam* (ed. Borgnet, 22:601).

21. Mahoney, "Albert the Great," 376–77. See Albertus Magnus, *Super Lucam* on Lk 9:46 (ed. Borgnet, 22:677). Albert cross-references his comments by citing Mt 18:4 and 11:29–30.

22. Albert, *Super Lucam* on Lk 9:49 (ed. Borgnet, 22:686).

conception of the ecclesiastical hierarchy that is Christocentric. So too is his conception of the practical life of the hierarchical Church, in regard both to the celebration of the Eucharist and to what should be expected of its ministers, that is, its priests, prelates, bishops, Cardinals and Popes.[23]

Clearly, Albert's concerns are of great value for those who serve the Church at any time throughout her history.

In sum, St. Albert develops the speculative principles and theological conclusions of a Christ-centered hierarchical office of the episcopacy. Drawing from the Dionysian corpus and Scripture, he begins to identify the moral and spiritual qualities that ought to be found in one suitably disposed for this office. He thus establishes a solid theological platform on which his pupil, St. Thomas Aquinas, builds his highly refined insights demonstrating that the episcopal office is an active state of perfection. Notably, the results of my search of Albert's *opera omnia* both in print and, as available, in electronic format for the phrase *"status perfectionis"* (and variations thereof) show that Albert does not ordinarily use this phrase to describe the episcopal office or its duties.[24] The same is true regarding my search of the works of Alexander of Hales and St. Bonaventure of Bagnoregio. When the phrase (and its variations) appear in Albert's and Alexander's writings, it refers either to the state of mankind prior to the Fall, to the perfection of the spiritual life which is the defining note of religious vows, or to the final state of the blessed in heaven.

St. Bonaventure

St. Bonaventure's brief but fruitful scholarly career (just under five years) was brought to a close when he accepted the office of minister general of the Franciscan order in 1257. In his commentary on Lom-

---

23. Mahoney, "Albert the Great," 377–78. Albertus Magnus, *Super Lucam* on Lk 9:16, 21:25–27, and 22:26 (ed. Borgnet, 22:633, 644, 682).

24. With that said, see Albertus Magnus, *Super Dion. De eccl. hier.*, cap. 5 (ed. Colon, 127 and 144) where he clearly indicates that the bishop's hierarchical role is to perfect: "Deinde concludit quod, sicut ostensum est, ordo episoporum est perfectivus, sacerdotum illuminativus, diaconorum purgativus" (Then he concludes that, as he has shown, the order of bishops is perfective, that of priests is illuminative, and deacons purgative), 127; "Similiter perfectores quidam sunt purgantes, ut diaconi, quidam illuminantes, ut sacerdotes, quidam perficientes, ut episcopi" (Similarly, certain office holders purge, as deacons; others illuminate, as priests; and others perfect, as bishops), 144.

bard's *Sentences* he reaffirms the primary Dionysian principle of hierarchy, namely, that the lower be brought or assimilated to the highest (the first principle, God) by those intermediaries established hierarchically as their superiors.[25] With Albert he affirms that this hierarchical power is found in its fullness in Christ and it is shared (by way of participation) in different degrees by the intermediary members of the Church's hierarchy. According to Bonaventure, the first among these is the pope and from him is derived all other powers in the Church in an orderly fashion: "From whom [namely, from the pope] as from the highest is derived the power of order for the infirm members of the Church, which demands a surpassing dignity in the ecclesiastical hierarchy."[26]

In his seminal work on the ecclesiology of Bonaventure, Fr. Peter Fehlner, FI, explains Bonaventure's contention that the *validity* of the exercise of the episcopal power depends on the power of a legitimate papacy:

> The orderliness of this [ecclesiastical] hierarchy, that which gives it its formal, hierarchical visage, is formally actuated by the power of jurisdiction. And to the extent the exercise of orders depends directly on the actualization of this ordered visage, these cannot be exercised validly except in relation to and in conjunction with the power of jurisdiction. In virtue of this power the papacy differs from the episcopacy and the episcopacy from the priesthood, the first enjoying a certain excellence and dignity in relation to the second, and the second this same in relation to the third, and so on.[27]

Finally, along with Lombard, Albert the Great, Alexander of Hales, and Thomas Aquinas, Bonaventure argues in his *Sentences* commentary that the episcopacy is not a sacramental order.[28] With Albert, Bonaventure recognizes that the bishop, as the spouse of his church, serves to bring the faithful to spiritual perfection. He does not directly call the episcopal office as such a *status perfectionis*, though he comes rather

---

25. Bonaventure, *In II Sent*, d. 11, a. 1, q. 1 (3), ed. Luigi da Parma Canali, 2 (Quaracchi: Collegii S. Bonaventurae, 1882): 277a, and *In IV Sent*, d. 19, a. 3, q. 1: 4.508b.

26. From 278b: "A quo [Papa] tamquam a summo derivantur ordinata potestas usque ad infima Ecclesiae membra, secundum quod exigit praecellens dignitas in ecclesiastica hierarchia." Bonaventure, *Breviloquium*, pars 6, cap. 12:5.

27. Peter D. Fehlner, *The Role of Charity in the Ecclesiology of St. Bonaventure* (Rome: Editrice Miscellanea Francescana, 1965): 148–49.

28. Bonaventure, *In IV Sent*, d. 24, a. 2, q. 3: 4.634.

close when he identifies the sacrament of holy orders with the state of perfection in his comments on book 4 of Lombard's *Sententiae*.²⁹

THE THEOLOGY OF THE EPISCOPACY IN ST. THOMAS'S WORKS

I have excluded from the following conspectus an examination of Aquinas's theology of the episcopacy in his commentaries on the PE. St. Thomas provides us with a remarkable amount of reflections on the episcopacy. His writings on the topic represent a significant advance compared to those of his predecessors. It is likely that the mendicant controversy was a principal historical factor that prompted his detailed reflections on the episcopal office as an active state of perfection, properly speaking. Aquinas's writings constitute a monumental development in the history of the theology of the episcopacy. The following overview is ordered more or less chronologically so that the reader may gain a sense of the development of Aquinas's thought on this topic.³⁰ As a result, certain topics will emerge more than once. With that said, there are few if any points on the episcopacy regarding which Aquinas changed his mind in later writings. What we find, instead, is a development that entails both an elaboration (at times, profoundly significant) of prior insights and the addition of new ones.

---

29. See Bonaventure *In IV Sent*, d. 25, a. 1, q. 1: 4. "Item, eius est in Ecclesia ordines conferre, ad quem spectat ex Ecclesia filios generare perfectos, pro eo quod ordo collocat in statu perfectionis; sed hoc est illius solius, qui est sponsus, hic autem est episcopus" (Likewise, it is for him to confer the sacrament of orders in the Church, which entails generating perfect sons out of the Church, for that order establishes persons in the state of perfection; but this is unique to him who is the spouse, this is the bishop), 641; and "Posset etiam alia ratio assignari sive ex hoc, quod episcopus sponsus est, sive ex hoc, quod Sacramentum ordinis statum perfectionis dicit ... episcopus tanquam sponsus filios, id est perfectos, et filias, id est imperfectos, debuit generare" (And another reason may be assigned either from the fact that the bishop is the spouse of the Church, or from the fact that he calls the sacrament of order the state of perfection ... the bishop as the spouse ought to generate sons, that is the perfect, and daughters, that is the imperfect), 642. Note that Bonaventure is saying that the sacrament of holy orders (*sacramentum ordinis*) is called a state of perfection (*status perfectionis*), not the episcopacy. As mentioned above, he denies that the episcopacy is a sacramental order. Thomas says something similar when he claims that by means of the sacrament a man is made "a perfector of others" in *STh* III, q. 65, a. 2, ad 2.

30. Issues surrounding the dating of Thomas's *opera*, especially with regard to his commentaries on Paul, are treated at some length in the following chapter.

Commentary on Lombard's *Sentences* (1252–56)

In his commentary on Lombard's *Sentences*, St. Thomas articulates the fundamental insights on the episcopacy that he develops in his later works. The seminal source for him, along with Scripture, is the corpus of Pseudo-Dionysius. Robert Grosseteste (1175–1253), bishop of Lincoln, mastered the Greek language and produced a new translation of the Dionysian corpus along with the definitive thirteenth-century edition of Aristotle's *Ethics*. St. Thomas most likely utilized Grosseteste's translations of Dionysius's works as his principal texts; if not, he certainly had access to them.[31]

The Dionysian hierarchical order

In the very beginning of his academic career, we find St. Thomas already closely adhering to the Dionysian scheme of the ecclesiastical offices and duties: deacons purge by exorcism, priests illuminate by baptism, and bishops perfect by confirmation. Thomas makes these arguments in book 4, d. 7, of his *Sentences* commentary, explicitly identifying the work of perfecting others spiritually as proper to the episcopal office.[32] Only bishops serve *ex officio* to perfect the faithful spiritually, and to do so they themselves must be perfect in both the active and the contemplative life.[33] Because they work principally to perfect the faithful, bishops have a greater power than simple priests.[34] In making this point, Aquinas stands out from his predecessors, especially Albert, who saw the episcopal office functioning largely to prepare the faithful for worthy reception of the Eucharist. Aquinas's argument here constitutes a remarkable development in the thirteenth-century theology of the episcopacy, especially as he mounts these claims at the very beginning of his scholarly career and in contradistinction from the position of his master, Albert. The bishop's principal task is to bring the faithful to the perfection of sanctity

---

31. See Colin Morris, *The Papal Monarchy: The Western Church from 1050 to 1250* (Oxford: Oxford University Press, 1989), 510.

32. "In ordine ecclesiasticae hierarchiae, secundum Dionysium, soli episcopi sunt perfectores" (In the order of the ecclesiastical hierarchy, according to Dionysius, the bishops alone are perfectors). Aquinas, *In IV Sent*, d. 7, q. 3, a. 1, qc. 2, s.c. 1–2.

33. Aquinas, *In IV Sent*, d. 7, q. 3, a. 1b, s.c. 1–2.

34. Aquinas, *In IV Sent*, d. 24, q. 3, a. 2a, s.c. 1–2.

not only through the Eucharist but also, and principally, by teaching the mysteries of faith and perfecting the flock in charity and virtue through his governing acts.

The episcopacy is not a sacramental order

Continuing in d. 7, Aquinas argues that the episcopacy is not a sacramental *ordo* but an office with respect to "certain sacred actions" insofar as bishops have a real power over the mystical body, particularly the ability to ordain priests.[35] In d. 24, following St. Albert, Aquinas argues that a sacramental order is determined by its relation to the *corpus domini verum* and bishops have no relation to the Eucharist different from that of simple priests.[36] Thus the episcopacy is distinct from the presbyterate as an office, but not as a sacramental order.

Jurisdiction in the public forum

In d. 18, Thomas notes that bishops, unlike simple priests, have jurisdiction in the external forum which concerns public matters between the members of the faithful as distinct from the internal forum of conscience which concerns private matters. For this reason bishops, but not simple priests, are able to excommunicate as this entails separating someone publically from the communion of the faithful—this being a matter exclusively reserved for the external forum.[37]

The episcopal source of the power of ministry

A little later, in d. 23, Thomas maintains that because bishops are perfectors in the Dionysian sense, they are the ones who constitute the faithful in a higher state by means of the sacraments of confirmation and orders.[38] On this basis, in d. 24 (regarding the sacramental ordination of priests) Thomas demonstrates that the power of ministry finds its proximate source in the episcopacy because only bishops (not priests) can confer orders.[39]

---

35. Aquinas, *In IV Sent*, d. 7, q. 3, a. 1b, ad 3.
36. Aquinas, *In IV Sent*, d. 24, q. 2, a. 1b, co. and q. 3, a. 2b. Thomas explains this most clearly in d. 24, q. 3, a. 2b, co.
37. Aquinas, *In IV Sent*, d. 18, q. 2, a. 2a, co.
38. Aquinas, *In IV Sent*, d. 23, q. 2, a. 1c, co.
39. Aquinas, *In IV Sent*, d. 24, q. 3, a. 3, ad 3.

Moral and intellectual prerequisites for bishops

Continuing in d. 24, Thomas asks what moral and intellectual characteristics are demanded of those in the episcopal state. In general, sanctity of life is required of all those in ecclesial orders, including those holding the episcopal office.[40] Bishops must have a more perfect knowledge of the law—especially when it comes to difficult cases—than simple priests who are required to know only the basics of the law, not its application to difficult questions.[41] Aquinas grounds this requirement of bishops on the difference between the acts proper to simple priests and those that bishops are called to perform. The act distinctive of simple priests is to consecrate and offer the Eucharistic sacrifice, whereas the distinguishing act of bishops is to oversee the mystical body of Christ by teaching and governing in the public forum. Thus, bishops must have a more perfect knowledge of Scripture and its application to particular cases than simple priests.

More specifically, the episcopacy requires a greater Christian perfection than is demanded of simple priests because bishops not only fulfill the priestly ministry but also establish ministers and constitute and preserve the particular church itself. As the one called to inaugurate divine worship for his particular church in conformity to Christ, a bishop is especially called the "spouse" of his church, as Christ is the Spouse of the universal Church, a critical point to which Aquinas returns in his polemical works on the mendicant controversy (see the

---

40. Aquinas, *In IV Sent*, d. 24, q. 1, a. 3a, s.c. 2.

41. "Alii autem promoventur ad alium actum qui est supra corpus christi mysticum; et a talium ore populus legem requirit; unde scientia legis in eis esse debet, non quidem ut sciant omnes difficiles quaestiones legis, quia in his debet ad superiores haberi recursus; sed sciant quae populus debet credere et observare de lege. Sed ad superiores sacerdotes, scilicet episcopos, pertinet ut etiam ea quae difficultatem in lege facere possunt, sciant; et tanto magis, quanto in majori gradu collocantur" (But others [priests] are promoted to another act over the mystical body of Christ; and the people need to hear the law from the mouth of those persons; wherefore those persons ought to have an understanding of the law, not that they would know all the difficult questions of the law, because in those matters he ought to have recourse to his superiors; but he ought to know what the people should believe and observe about the law. But it pertains to the high priests, namely the bishops, that they are able to resolve the difficult matters of the law; and all the more insofar as they are established in a higher grade). Aquinas, *In IV Sent*, d. 24, q. 1, a. 3b, ad 1.

comments in this chapter, below).⁴² Thus, the care of the particular church is chiefly entrusted to the bishop.

To fulfill this duty, in conformity to Christ, the bishop as a *mediator* ought to be perfect in both the active and the contemplative life.⁴³ In chapter 4 of this book, on Aquinas's commentary on 1 Timothy, I cite a lengthy passage from Aquinas's commentary on book 3 of Lombard's *Sentences*, where he shows that the mediatorial role of the bishop demands that he be perfect in his reception of truth and goodness by his contemplation and that he be perfect in his active role of communicating this divine truth and goodness to the faithful by preaching and commanding.⁴⁴ For Aquinas, the bishop's duty to preach the Gospel is most essential to his role as spiritual perfector.

The bishop represents Christ

Finally, in the same distinction (d. 24), Aquinas encapsulates the nature and duties of the episcopal office insofar as the bishop represents the Person of Christ to his flock. To be sure, every priest represents Christ, acting *in persona Christi*. But the bishop does so more fully and perfectly not only by fulfilling priestly duties but also by instituting other ministers and by founding, or at least preserving and fostering his particular church.⁴⁵

Quaestiones Disputatae de Veritate (1256–59)

Bishops perfect by preaching

The main principle that Aquinas deploys when discussing the episcopal office in *Quaestiones Disputatae de Veritate* (hereafter "*De verit*") is the Dionysian insight that inferiors are led back to God by their superior.⁴⁶ In q. 9, a. 3, Aquinas notes that bishops perfect others

42. Aquinas, *In IV Sent*, d. 24, q. 3, a. 2a, ad 3.
43. Aquinas, *In IV Sent*, d. 24, q. 1, a. 3, qua. 5.
44. Aquinas, *In III Sent*, d. 35, q. 1, a. 3, qua. 3, sol. 3.
45. "Every Christian priest, it is true, acts 'in persona Christi,' but the bishop represents Christ in a more perfect way: 'The priest, indeed, represents Christ insofar as he himself fulfilled a certain ministry; but the bishop represents him in this that he instituted other ministers and founded the Church.'" Molloy, "Hierarchy and Holiness," 200, citing Aquinas, *In IV Sent*, d. 24, q. 3, a. 2, sol. 1, ad 3.
46. "Est quod dicit dionysius, hanc legem esse divinitas immobiliter firmatam, ut

above all by preaching. He describes the perfecting duty of bishops as uncovering the spiritual riches concealed in the mystical symbols of Scripture and the sacraments. In the body of this article, Aquinas notes that deacons purify the faithful from those things contrary to illumination. Priests illuminate by giving the people the sacraments as these are the means by which the faithful are led to divine things. But it falls to the office of bishop to uncover and explain spiritual things to the faithful, things which have been veiled in the signification of the sacraments.[47] Though he does not use the term, his description of this distinctive activity of the bishop is commonly called "mystagogy."[48] Compare this with what Aquinas says near the end of his academic career in the corpus of *STh* III, q. 61, a. 2, to the effect that the soul is perfected in knowledge and grace by corporeal means in the sacraments. While his argument in *De verit* would seem also to sustain the idea that bishops should discern and preach on the spiritual senses of Scripture, especially the anagogical, the direct textual reference here, and those found later in his *STh*, show that Aquinas con-

---

inferiora reducantur in deum mediantibus superioribus" (Dionysius says that this divine law is immutably established, that inferiors are led to God by the mediation of their superiors). Aquinas, *De veritate*, q. 9, a. 2, s.c. 1.

47. "Ut hoc modo intelligitur differre illuminatio et perfectio, sicut formatio visus per speciem visibilis, et cognitio ipsius visibilis; et secundum hoc dionysius in eccles. Hierarch., cap. V, dicit, quod ordo diaconorum est ad purgandum institutus, sacerdotum ad illuminandum, episcoporum ad perficiendum; quia scilicet diaconi habebant officium super catechumenos et energumenos, in quibus sunt dispositiones contrariae illuminationi, quae eorum ministerio removentur; sacerdotum autem officium est populo sacramenta communicare et ostendere, quae sunt quasi quaedam media quibus deducimur in divina; episcoporum autem officium erat populo aperire spiritualia, quae erant in sacramentorum significatione velata" (In this way it is understood that illumination differs from perfection, as the form of what is seen by the species of the visible differs from the knowledge of the visible thing itself. According to this distinction Dionysius, in *Ecclesiastical Hierarchy*, cap. 5, says that the order of deacons is to purify the beginners, that of priests is to illuminate, and that of bishops, to perfect. Because deacons have the office over catechumens and those possessed by demons, in whom are dispositions contrary to illumination, and this is removed by the deacons' ministry. The office of priests, however, is to communicate and show the sacraments to the people; for the sacraments are specific means by which we are led to God. However, the office of bishops is to uncover the spiritual mysteries which are veiled in the signification of the sacraments). Aquinas, *De verit*, q. 9, a. 3, co.

48. This episcopal activity is exemplified by St. Ambrose in his work, *De Mysteriis*, a seminal work of mystagogy.

ceives episcopal preaching as an act of making manifest the transcendent mysteries veiled corporeally in the Church's sacraments.

Summa Contra Gentiles IV (1265)
The episcopal power exceeds the priestly power

In *SCG* IV, cap. 76, Aquinas once again argues that the episcopal power exceeds the power of the simple priest in things pertaining to the direction of the faithful, but not in regard to the Eucharist. He reaffirms that the priestly powers and acts are derived from the episcopal power and that difficult matters for the faithful are reserved to the bishops, but he elaborates slightly more on this issue in *SCG* than he does in his *Sentences* commentary:

Now, the bestowal of all of these orders [namely, porters, lectors, exorcists, acolytes, subdeacons, deacons, and priests, identified by Aquinas in IV, cap. 75] accompanies some sacrament, as was said, and the sacraments of the Church require some ministers for their dispensing; there must, therefore, be a superior power in the Church with a higher ministry which dispenses the sacrament of orders. And this is the episcopal power, which, although it does not exceed the power of the priest in the consecration of the body of Christ, does exceed the priestly power in what touches the faithful. For the priestly power itself flows from the episcopal power, and anything particularly difficult to be performed for the faithful is reserved to the bishops; by their authority, even priests are empowered to do that which is committed to them to be done. Hence, even in the tasks which priests perform they employ things consecrated by bishops; thus, in the Eucharistic consecration they use a chalice, an altar, and a pall consecrated by the bishop. Clearly, then, the chief direction of the faithful belongs to the dignity of the bishops.[49]

---

49. "Quia vero omnium horum ordinum collatio cum quodam sacramento perficitur, ut dictum est; sacramenta vero ecclesiae sunt per aliquos ministros ecclesiae dispensanda: necesse est aliquam superiorem potestatem esse in ecclesia alicuius altioris ministerii, quae ordinis sacramentum dispenset. Et haec est episcopalis potestas, quae, etsi quidem quantum ad consecrationem corporis christi non excedat sacerdotis potestatem; excedit tamen eam in his quae pertinent ad fideles. Nam et ipsa sacerdotalis potestas ab episcopali derivatur; et quicquid arduum circa populum fidelem est agendum episcopis reservatur; quorum auctoritate etiam sacerdotes possunt hoc quod eis agendum committitur. Unde et in his quae sacerdotes agunt, utuntur rebus per episcopum consecratis: ut in eucharistiae consecratione utuntur consecratis per episcopum calice, altari et pallis. Sic igitur manifestum est quod summa regiminis fidelis populi ad episcopalem pertinet dignitatem." Aquinas, *SCG* IV, cap. 76, n. 1.

Summa Theologiae, Prima Pars (1265–68)

In his mature work, *STh*, St. Thomas provides us with a great number of insights regarding the episcopal office that both encapsulate and build upon his earlier work. While he adumbrated as much in his earlier works, in his *STh* Aquinas unequivocally identifies the bishop's office as a *state of perfection*. As perfectors, bishops must teach the deeper meaning of the Gospel, and such teaching pertains to their principal and proper office and duty. Not so with priests. They receive the right and duty to preach to their flock from the bishop, who is at liberty to bestow this duty to other clerics as well (for instance, to mendicants) even if this be contrary to the will of the local priest. Regarding this latter point, St. Thomas recognizes that this prerogative extends also to popes who can give preaching faculties to priests even against the will of local bishops. To conduct successfully their particular kind of perfecting preaching, bishops ought to excel both in the contemplative and active lives insofar as they contemplate divine truths in order actively to instruct others in them. In his *STh*, Aquinas also provides a masterful treatment of the grace of the episcopal state.

The bishop is the master and teacher of sacred doctrine

In the first question of the first part of *STh*, Aquinas treats the nature of *sacra doctrina*. To show that sacred doctrine is indeed a matter of argument, that is, something over which legitimate disputes may be conducted, in the *sed contra* of *STh* I, q. 1, a. 8, St. Thomas cites Titus 1:9, where the bishop is exhorted to "embrace that faithful word which is according to doctrine, that he may be able to exhort in sound doctrine and to convince the gainsayers." For such argumentation to be legitimate, the bishop must be able both to convince disputants and to exhort the faithful regarding sacred doctrine. At the very beginning of his magnum opus, Aquinas connects episcopal teaching duties with *sacra doctrina* and with the task of theological understanding and argumentation. Yet he does not return to a discussion of the episcopacy until the *secunda pars*.

Summa Theologiae, Secunda Pars (1268–72)

If the episcopacy is not a sacramental order, how is it that a bishop's sacramental power to ordain cannot be lost? This is an important issue as it pertains to the question of whether Aquinas considered the episcopacy to be a sacramental order. He did not. And yet in treating the vice of schism (opposed to the virtue of charity) he unequivocally states in II-II, q. 39, a. 3, co., that those who have a spiritual power (for example, bishops) possess both a sacramental power and a power of jurisdiction. For Aquinas, the sacramental power is permanent in virtue of the consecration of a bishop; but note that this is not the result of a sacramental ordination according to Aquinas. All consecrations of things and persons in the Church are immovable as long as the consecrated thing or person remains. Thus, the bishop's power to confer sacraments, a power he receives at his consecration, cannot be lost.

However, because the lawful use of this power is given by a mere human appointment (that is, by the pope) by which the bishop is granted jurisdiction, such use can be and indeed is lost by formal schismatics. The clear implication here is that the act of consecration is not merely a human act. This act confers a real spiritual power upon the recipient that, nevertheless, cannot be licitly exercised apart from the human, juridical appointment he receives from his superior. Because a lower power should only act when moved by the higher power, a bishop may lose the lawful use of this power, but not the power itself. At this point, it is important to keep in mind that, in the centuries after St. Thomas's death, there has been a development both in theology and in magisterial teaching on the sacramental nature of episcopal ordination. Yet a careful and fair study of this article in his *STh* shows how Thomas is able to recognize a permanent episcopal consecration that affords grace to the recipient without the act of consecration constituting in any way the sacrament of holy orders. Exegetically speaking, this resolves the textual conundrum addressed by Stenger and Lécuyer (see chapter 1), namely, how Thomas is able to affirm the permanence of episcopal consecration while denying its sacramentality.

The gift of wisdom must be found in prelates to a higher degree

Later in the *secunda secundae*, in treating of the Holy Spirit's gift of wisdom which perfects the virtue of charity, specifically in q. 45, a. 5, Aquinas notes that the gift of wisdom is found in two degrees: the first is present in everyone who is in the state of grace; the other is appropriate to prelates. Bishops need the gift of wisdom to a higher degree and God gives this to them because they have a solemn duty to "manifest to others certain deeper mysteries."[50] This builds upon his remarks in *De verit* to the effect that the bishop must uncover for the faithful the spiritual riches veiled in the sacraments. Here in his *STh*, Aquinas establishes the foundation in grace for the bishop's duty to perfect the faithful by explaining the depths of the faith in his preaching ministry.

To excel in his teaching, the bishop must excel in contemplation

Yet the bishop's gift of wisdom must be accompanied by a life of profound contemplation and vigorous action. In *STh* II-II, q. 182, a. 1, ad 1, when comparing the active and contemplative states of life, Aquinas notes that the episcopal state is both contemplative and active—also called the "apostolic life." The active life of the bishop which consists in teaching must be derived from a plenitude of contemplation. Aquinas writes: "Not only the active life concerns prelates, they should also excel in the contemplative life; hence Gregory says (*Pastor.* II.1), 'A prelate should be foremost in action, more uplifted than others in contemplation.'"[51]

States of life and states of perfection

In an excursus in chapter 4, below, I will examine in greater detail certain distinctive notes of St. Thomas's treatment of the episcopacy as a state of perfection. Here, I provide a brief conspectus of his treatment of the topic in this part of *STh*. Beginning in q. 183, Aquinas examines various states of life, the states of perfection in general,

---

50. Aquinas, *STh* II-II, q. 45, a. 5; see, especially, ad 2 and compare this with the passage from *De verit* cited in footnote 47 above.

51. Aquinas, *STh* II-II, q. 182, a. 1, ad 1. Cf. *De perf*, cap. 18, par. 664 and *In III Sent*, d. 35, q. 1, a. 3, sol. 3.

and the species of these states of perfection: the episcopal and the religious life. But what is a state (*status*)? In this question, St. Thomas notes that a grade (*gradus*) has to do with beauty, a state (*status*) has to do with perfection, and an office/duty (*officium*) with action (a. 1, co. and ad 3). One who is made a bishop is raised to a higher office, a higher grade, and a state of perfection (a. 3, ad 3). For Aquinas, a grade signifies the order of superiors to inferiors, an office regards actions, and a state denotes a stable (*immobilitas*) condition of freedom or servitude. Regarding states in the Church, the freedom or servitude in question is the freedom from sin or from justice and servitude to the same, that is, to sin or to justice (see a. 4). Thus, most generally, the ideal episcopal "state" ought to be one in which the office holder is free *from* sin and *for* righteousness (or justice). And yet that holds true for those in the religious state as well.

The state of perfection consists in charity

Then, in q. 184, Aquinas treats the *state of perfection* in general, identifying that it consists principally in charity (a. 1).[52] To be perfect spiritually requires one to remove from his affections everything contrary to charity and to remove from the mind's inclinations everything that hinders it from tending wholly to God (a. 2, co.). Charity consists primarily in the observance of God's commandments and secondarily in observance of Christ's evangelical counsels of poverty, chastity, and obedience which are directed toward charity (a. 3). Aquinas notes that some who are spiritually perfect are not in the state of perfection and some who are in the state of perfection are wicked and imperfect (a. 4).

The state of perfection in bishops

Although both religious and prelates are in the state of perfection, bishops are *active* perfectors while religious are those who are being perfected in a *passive* sense. Bishops solemnly bind themselves to the pastoral duty of perfecting others to the point of laying down their

---

52. See Thomas's remarks in *Quaestiones Disputatae de Virtutibus* (1272) where, in q. 2, a. 11, obj. 6 and ad 6, he notes that bishops are in the state of perfection which consists chiefly in charity.

lives for their flock and they make this commitment by a profession with a "certain solemnity of consecration" (in this regard, Thomas cites 2 Tm 1:6 in q. 184, a. 5):

> There is required for the state of perfection a perpetual obligation to things pertaining to perfection, together with a certain solemnity. Now both these conditions are competent to religious and bishops.... Bishops bind themselves to things pertaining to perfection when they take up the pastoral duty, to which it belongs that a shepherd "lay down his life for his sheep," according to Jn 10:15. Wherefore the Apostle says (1 Tim 6:1): "Thou ... hast confessed a good confession before many witnesses," that is to say, "when he was ordained," as a gloss says on this passage. Again a certain solemnity of consecration is employed together with the aforesaid profession, according to 2 Tim 1:6: "Stir up the grace of God which is in thee by the imposition of my hands," which the gloss ascribes to the grace of the episcopate. And Dionysius says (*Ecclesiastical Hierarchy*, V) that "when the high priest," that is, the bishop, "is ordained, he receives on his head the most holy imposition of the sacred oracles, whereby it is signified that he is a participator in the whole and entire hierarchical power, and that not only is he the enlightener in all things pertaining to his holy discourses and actions, but that he also confers this on others."[53]

With that said, Aquinas argues that one who is not spiritually perfect may enter the episcopacy as long as he has the intention of reaching perfection (a. 5, ad 2). And in accord with the great patristic tradition, he holds out martyrdom as the most perfect act of charity (ad 3). In

---

53. "Ad statum perfectionis requiritur obligatio perpetua ad ea quae sunt perfectionis, cum aliqua solemnitate. Utrumque autem horum competit et religiosis et episcopis.... episcopi obligant se ad ea quae sunt perfectionis, pastorale assumentes officium, ad quod pertinet ut animam suam ponat pastor pro ovibus suis, sicut dicitur Ioan. X. Unde apostolus dicit, I ad Tim. ult., confessus es bonam confessionem coram multis testibus, idest in tua ordinatione, ut Glossa ibidem dicit. Adhibetur etiam quaedam solemnitas consecrationis simul cum professione praedicta, secundum illud II ad Tim. I, resuscites gratiam Dei quae est in te per impositionem manuum mearum, quod Glossa exponit de gratia episcopali. Et Dionysius dicit, V cap. Eccles. Hier., quod summus sacerdos, idest episcopus, in sua ordinatione habet eloquiorum super caput sanctissimam superpositionem, ut significetur quod ipse est participativus integre totius hierarchiae virtutis, et quod ipse non solum sit illuminativus omnium quae pertinent ad sanctas locutiones et actiones, sed quod etiam haec aliis tradat." Aquinas, *STh* II-II, q. 184, a. 5, co. Citing this article of *STh*, Lécuyer argues that "Il [Thomas] accepte de voir dans l'imposition des mains de II Tim. 1, 6, un rite d'ordination conférant la «grâce épiscopale»" (Thomas sees the imposition of hands in 2 Tim 1:6 as a rite of ordination conferring "episcopal grace"). Lécuyer, "Les étapes," 45.

any event, for Aquinas the episcopal state is more perfect than the religious state insofar as it is the active, not the passive, state of perfection (a. 7). As Aquinas soon makes explicit in q. 188, a. 1, ad 3, this entails the distinctively Dionysian notion that bishops are the active perfectors of religious who are passively perfected by bishops. Ultimately, bishops are to live and act for love of neighbor prompted by their love for God above all else (a. 7, ad 2). To fulfill these solemn duties, prelates must be foremost both in contemplation and in action (ad 3). Underscoring this point, in a. 7 Aquinas says that bishops must lead a *mixed life*, one that is both active and contemplative. He describes this as a life in which the bishop must contemplate divine truths not only for his own benefit but also that he may instruct others in them.[54]

May one desire the episcopacy?

In q. 185, Aquinas treats those things that pertain properly to the episcopal state itself, and in a. 1 he asks whether one may licitly desire the episcopal office for oneself. To resolve this question, he identifies three things involved in the episcopal office: the work of the office, its grade which entails a higher degree in which one is placed over others as their superior, and its honor which involves the possession and use of temporal goods. To desire the office for temporal goods would be covetous or ambitious. To desire it either for its higher degree or even in order to perfect others would be presumptuous—considering oneself suitable to rule over the faithful. Though it would seem, then, that no one may licitly desire this office for himself, Aquinas maintains that if one's desire for the office is predicated on his already being in the episcopal office or if one's desire is based on his trust in his own *potential* to be made worthy by God to fulfill the duties of his office (without judging oneself *actually* able to do so), then such a desire would have as its object the "good work" of the episcopacy rather than a precedence in dignity (here, Aquinas is thinking of Paul's teaching in 1 Tm 3:1, "If a man desire the office of a bishop, he desires a *good work*"). As such, only this last kind of desire would be licit.

54. Aquinas, *STh* II-II, q. 184, a. 7, ad 3.

What kind of man should be chosen?

In a. 3 of this same question Aquinas notes that it is not always necessary to choose the best man for this office, as long as the candidate presented is one who will serve the flock by faithfully dispensing the divine mysteries for the good of the church.[55] Such a man would not seek or accept this office for his private good. The criterion for suitable candidates for the episcopacy, then, is not simply that the candidate be perfected in charity, but that he be "one who is best for governing the Church, one namely who is able to instruct, defend, and govern the Church peacefully."[56] The person appointed should not think himself better than others. To this effect Aquinas adduces the example of Peter who refused to say that he loved Christ more than the others, as recorded in John 21:15, and he ought not perceive anything in himself which would make it unlawful for him to be a bishop. Finally, in a. 3, ad 3, he notes that sometimes a man who does not excel in the grace of holiness can nevertheless be more fit for governing due to his natural prudence.

Being dispensed from the episcopacy to return to the religious life

In q. 185, a. 4, Thomas remarks: "The perfection of the episcopal state consists in this that for love of God a man binds himself [by a vow] to work for the salvation of his neighbor."[57] If for some reason he is no longer able to procure the spiritual welfare of his subjects, he may request to be released from his episcopal vow. Though his vow is otherwise perpetual, he can be dispensed from it by the pope. Being hindered from procuring the spiritual welfare of subjects can arise from: (1) a defect of conscience, for example, the sins of murder or simony, (2) a defect of body, being old and infirm, (3) an irregularity, such as bigamy, or (4) a defect in his subjects because of their wickedness or when they take scandal from the person in authority,

---

55. See also Aquinas, *Quodl* 8, q. 4, a. 1, where Thomas makes the same point.

56. "Et ideo ille qui debet aliquem eligere in episcopum, vel de eo providere, non tenetur assumere meliorem simpliciter, quod est secundum caritatem, sed meliorem quoad regimen Ecclesiae, qui scilicet possit Ecclesiam et instruere et defendere et pacifice gubernare." Aquinas, *STh* II-II, q. 185, a. 3, co.

57. "Perfectio episcopalis status in hoc consistit quod aliquis ex divina dilectione se obligat ad hoc quod saluti proximorum insistat." Aquinas, *STh* II-II, q. 185, a. 4.

as long as the scandal is not caused by the wickedness of his subjects desiring to subvert the faith or the righteousness of the Church. In the first three cases, one may licitly resign from the episcopacy, but in the latter case, Aquinas insists that, for the true spiritual benefit of the bishop's subjects, the episcopacy should not be resigned.

May a bishop ever abandon his flock?

In q. 185, a. 5, Aquinas argues that a bishop may abandon his flock when he is personally endangered if and *only if* doing so would not harm his flock spiritually. This would require the bishop to ascertain that someone else is able to take his place and sufficiently provide for the salvation of his subjects. But when all the faithful are equally threatened (and not just the bishop!), then he must not abandon the flock. Elaborating on this point, in a. 5, ad 1, Thomas adds that the bishop must not prefer his temporal advantage or bodily welfare to the spiritual welfare of his neighbor. After all, the bishop is to be animated by such a love of his neighbors that he would be willing to suffer even death, were that necessary to procure their eternal salvation. Even in circumstances that legitimize his abandoning the flock, the bishop should always retain the intention of devoting himself to his neighbor's salvation and of returning to do so when the opportunity arises.

A magisterium of perfection

In q. 185, a. 8, considering whether religious who are raised to the episcopacy are still bound to observe their vows of poverty, chastity, and obedience, Thomas draws an analogy between the bishop's magisterium and that of professors of theology: "The episcopal state pertains to perfection as a certain teaching office [*magisterium*] of perfection."[58] Just as students are brought to a certain intellectual perfection by professors who actually possess that intellectual perfection, so too religious are brought to the perfection of charity by the magisterial activity of the bishop who personally possesses the spiritual perfection of charity. Upon becoming a bishop, a religious is to retain all the practices arising from his religious vows save those incompatible with

---

58. "Status autem episcopalis ad perfectionem pertinet tanquam quoddam perfectionis magisterium." Aquinas, *STh* II-II, q. 185, a. 8.

episcopal duties (such as silence, solitude, and the like). To this end, in the next question (q. 186, a. 3, ad 5), Thomas notes that, unlike religious, bishops must own and make use of wealth as an instrument to fulfill their duty to administer both spiritual and temporal needs.[59]

Then, in a. 5, ad 3, Thomas notes that the religious vow of obedience principally refers them to their bishop: "The subjection of religious is chiefly in reference to bishops, who are compared to them as perfectors to perfected, as Dionysius states (*Ecclesiastical Hierarchy*, VI), where he also says that the 'monastic order is subjected to the perfecting virtues of the bishops, and is taught by their divine illumination.'"[60] Yet even when religious who are raised to the episcopal office are exempted from obedience to the bishop, they are always bound to obey the pope. This point touches upon an issue at the heart of the mendicant controversy issue, treated below.

A little later, in q. 187, a. 1, Thomas raises the question whether it is lawful for religious to teach, preach, hear confessions, and the like. This issue relates to the mendicant controversy in which certain secular clerics argued that religious ought not do these things because they have no ordinary jurisdiction for these acts. In a. 1, co., Thomas argues:

> Matters of jurisdiction can be deputed to those who have not ordinary jurisdiction: thus the delivery of a judgment is deputed by the bishop to a simple priest. In this sense it is said to be unlawful for monks and other religious to preach, teach, and so forth, because the religious state does not give them the power to do these things. They can, however, do them if they receive orders, or ordinary jurisdiction, or if matters of jurisdiction be delegated to them.[61]

---

59. "The episcopal state is not directed to the attainment of perfection, but rather to the effect that, in virtue of the perfection which he already has, a man may govern others, by administering not only spiritual but also temporal things. This belongs to the active life." Aquinas, *STh* II-II, q. 186, a. 3, ad 5.

60. "Subiectio religiosorum principaliter attenditur ad episcopos, qui comparantur ad eos sicut perfectores ad perfectos, ut patet per Dionysium, VI cap. Eccles. Hier., ubi etiam dicit quod monachorum ordo pontificum consummativis virtutibus mancipatur, et divinis eorum illuminationibus edocetur." Aquinas, *STh* II-II, q. 186, a. 5, ad 3.

61. "Ea vero quae sunt iurisdictionis, committi possunt eis qui non habent ordinariam iurisdictionem, sicut prolatio sententiae committitur ab episcopo simplici sacerdoti. Et hoc modo dicitur non licere monachis et aliis religiosis praedicare, docere, et alia huiusmodi facere, quia status religionis non dat eis potestatem haec faciendi. Possunt tamen ista facere si ordinem accipiant vel ordinariam iurisdictionem, aut etiam si eis committantur ea quae sunt iurisdictionis." Aquinas, *STh* II-II, q. 187, a. 1, co.

Perfecting by teaching

In q. 188, a. 5, co., Aquinas reaffirms that preaching and teaching are acts belonging to the office of bishop. The study of letters (or an extraordinary gift of the Holy Spirit, as was the case with certain apostles who did not study letters) is necessary both for bishops and for those who share in this office by being delegated by the bishop.[62] Aquinas underscores the primacy of preaching in the episcopal office in q. 188, a. 6, in which he prioritizes the active, apostolic life over a life of mere contemplation which, in its turn, is higher than the active religious life centered principally on external activities (such as almsgiving). In this article, he says:

> The work of the active life is twofold. One proceeds from the fullness of contemplation, such as teaching and preaching.... And this work is more excellent than simple contemplation. For even as it is better to enlighten than merely to shine, so it is better to give to others the fruits of one's contemplation than merely to contemplate.... Accordingly the highest place in religious orders is held by those which are directed to teaching and preaching, which, moreover, are nearest to the episcopal perfection.[63]

Commenting on this article, L. M. Orrieux notes that the perfection proper to a bishop lies essentially in teaching: "For St. Thomas, at least such as we understand it, the state of perfection proper to the bishop, as for Dionysius, consists essentially in teaching, 'as it were a certain perfection of the teaching office' (II-II, q. 185, a. 8): this explains the well-known insight on the orders devoted to preaching 'which are most proximate to the perfection of the episcopacy' (II-II, q. 188, a. 6)."[64]

---

62. See Aquinas, *STh* II-II, q. 187, a. 1, co., above. Also, see Thomas's teaching in *Quaestiones Disputatae de Malo* (1270), q. 3, a. 7, co., where he notes that a bishop is bound to know those things which pertain to his office and in q. 5, a. 2, co., where he says that one lacking knowledge of letters is unworthy of promotion to the dignity of episcopal office. Incidentally, in q. 7, a. 3, obj. 7, of the same work, Thomas shows that he is aware of the decretals on the duty of bishops to bring persons in discord into agreement.

63. "Sic ergo dicendum est quod opus vitae activae est duplex. Unum quidem quod ex plenitudine contemplationis derivatur, sicut doctrina et praedicatio.... Et hoc praefertur simplici contemplationi. Sicut enim maius est illuminare quam lucere solum, ita maius est contemplata aliis tradere quam solum contemplari.... Sic ergo summum gradum in religionibus tenent quae ordinantur ad docendum et praedicandum. Quae et propinquissimae sunt perfectioni episcoporum." Aquinas, *STh* II-II, q. 188, a. 6, co.

64. "Pour saint Thomas, du moins tel que nous le comprenons, l'état de perfection

Finally, in q. 189, a. 7, co., it is worth noting that Thomas remarks that bishops and religious are both bound to divine service by a perpetual and solemn vow.

Summa Theologiae, Tertia Pars (1272–73)

In *STh* III, q. 8, a. 6, Thomas provides a helpful analysis of the scope and duration of ecclesial power. The bishop is the head of the Church in a specific place and time; the pope in all places but for a limited time; and Christ in all places for all time. Thus the bishop, who teaches and governs the faithful in his particular church, does so concomitantly with and subordinated to Christ, participating, in a very real sense, in these actions of Christ.

The bishop acts in the person of Christ by teaching and governing

Noel Molloy beautifully summarizes this point in Aquinas:

Christ, in fact, is "the first and principal teacher of spiritual doctrine and of faith," [III, q. 7, a. 7].... Now "every action of Christ serves as instruction for us" [III, q. 40, a. 1, ad 3]. This dictum is verified in a special way when it is a question of preaching, that distinctive activity of Christ, for those who undertake the office of preaching, teaching, and the care of souls are the imitators of Christ *par excellence*.[65]

Bishops, as successors to the apostles, are God's vicars in governing the Church, as Aquinas notes in *STh* III, q. 64, a. 2, ad 3. A little later, Thomas makes it clear that the bishop "takes the place of Christ in the Church."[66]

In his question on baptism (q. 67, a. 1, ad 1), Thomas explains that the principal way by which the bishop perfects the flock is by teaching and explaining the meaning of the Gospel: "To teach, that is, to expound the Gospel, is the proper office of the bishop, whose task it is to perfect, according to Dionysius (*Ecclesiastical Hierarchy*, V);

---

propre à l'évêque est, comme pour Denys, lié essentiellement à l'enseignement, tamquam quoddam perfectionis magisterium (IIa-IIae, 185, 8): ceci explique l'incise bien connue sur les ordres voués à la prédication (religiones) quae et propinquissimae sunt perfectioni episcoporum (IIa-IIae, 188, 6)." Orrieux, "L'Evêque 'perfector,'" 242.

65. Molloy, "Hierarchy and Holiness," 239, citing Aquinas, *STh* III, q. 7, a. 7; III, q. 40, a. 1, ad 3; and Aquinas, *Lectura super Matthaeum* (hereafter "*In Matt*"), cap. 19, par. 1598.

66. Aquinas, *STh* III, q. 72, a. 3, ad 3; see Molloy, "Hierarchy and Holiness," 200.

now to perfect is the same as to teach."[67] And in the next article (a. 2, ad 1), Thomas argues that the principal office of the episcopacy is the preaching office:

> Our Lord enjoined on the apostles, whose place is taken by the bishops, both duties, namely, of teaching and of baptizing, but in different ways. Because Christ committed them to the duty of teaching, that they might exercise it themselves as being the most important duty of all: wherefore the apostles themselves said (Acts 6:2): "It is not fitting that we should leave the word of God and serve tables." On the other hand, He entrusted the apostles with the office of baptizing, to be exercised vicariously; wherefore the Apostle says (1 Cor 1:17): "Christ sent me not to baptize, but to preach the Gospel." And the reason for this was that the merit and wisdom of the minister have no bearing on the baptismal effect, as they have in teaching, as may be seen from what we have stated above (q. 64, a. 1, ad 2, 5, 9). A proof of this is found also in the fact that our Lord Himself did not baptize, but His disciples, as John relates (4:2).[68]

The most important duty, then, for bishops is that of teaching. It is more difficult than simply baptizing since to teach well, merit and wisdom are required.

Later, in q. 71, a. 4, ad 3, Aquinas recognizes that persons in different states of life teach the faith. In comparing the differences between the teaching given by deacons, priests, godparents, and bishops, he notes that the kind of teaching that distinguishes the episcopal office from the others is the bishop's instruction on the profound mysteries of faith and the perfection of the Christian life:

---

67. "Sed docere, id est exponere Evangelium, pertinet proprie ad episcopum, cuius actus est perficere, secundum Dionysium, V cap. Eccl. Hier.; perficere autem idem est quod docere." Aquinas, *STh* III, q. 67, a. 1, ad 1. This text is cited by Molloy, "Hierarchy and Holiness," 238. Compare this to Aquinas's *lecturae* on the PE, esp. his comments on 1 Tm.

68. "Utrumque officium, scilicet docendi et baptizandi, dominus apostolis iniunxit, quorum vicem gerunt episcopi, aliter tamen et aliter. Nam officium docendi commisit eis Christus ut ipsi per se illud exercerent, tanquam principalissimum, unde et ipsi apostoli dixerunt, Act. VI, non est aequum nos relinquere verbum Dei et ministrare mensis. Officium autem baptizandi commisit apostolis ut per alios exercendum, unde et apostolus dicit, I Cor. I, non misit me Christus baptizare, sed evangelizare. Et hoc ideo quia in baptizando nihil operatur meritum et sapientia ministri, sicut in docendo, ut patet ex supra dictis. In cuius etiam signum, nec ipse dominus baptizavit, sed discipuli eius, ut dicitur Ioan. IV." Aquinas, *STh* III, q. 67, a. 2, ad 1. Also Molloy: "The bishop, then, being the only prelate in the strict sense, is the one on whom the preaching office primarily devolves. Among the offices of the bishop this one, and not the administration of the sacraments, is the one that is absolutely primary [*principalissimum*]." Molloy, "Hierarchy and Holiness," 237–38.

Instruction may be of many sorts. One is that which converts to the faith, which Dionysius attributes to the bishop (*Ecclesiastical Hierarchy*, II) and which can pertain to any preacher, and even to any lay person. Another is that instruction by which one is informed about the rudiments of the faith and about how one should prepare oneself to receive the sacraments. This pertains in a secondary way to ministers [that is, deacons], but primarily to priests. The third instruction is that which concerns Christian behavior, and this pertains to godparents. The fourth instruction is that which treats of the profound mysteries of faith and the perfection of the Christian life, and pertains *ex officio* to bishops.[69]

In his treatments of the sacraments of confirmation (q. 72) and the Eucharist (qq. 73–83), Thomas makes several brief but targeted remarks about the episcopacy that ought to be mentioned. In q. 72, a. 3, ad 3, he reaffirms that the bishop acts in the Person of Christ. In a. 10, ad 2, he notes that the *confirmandi* are to be enrolled as Christian "soldiers" and that the bishop is the commander of the army of the faithful. In a. 11, he argues that because bishops wield supreme power, only they properly confirm. In q. 82, a. 3, ad 3, he remarks that the Eucharist perfects the recipients but that simple priests, in distributing the Eucharist, thus share in the bishop's "perfective dispensing" (Dionysius, *Ecclesiastical Hierarchy*, V). Finally, Thomas teaches that the bishop acts on Christ's behalf on his mystical body (in q. 82, a. 5, ad 4), that the bishop gives the power of order instrumentally (in a. 8, ad 2), and that the bishop chiefly represents Christ to his flock (in q. 83, a. 5, ad 6).

Quaestiones Quodlibetales and *Quodlibetum* XII (*Quodlibet* I–VI and XII, 1268–72; *Quodlibet* VII–XI, 1256–59)

In his *Quodlibetal Questions* Aquinas treats the episcopacy in various ways. The topics appear random, yet this should be unsurprising given the nature of an academic session in which the participating au-

---

69. "Multiplex est instructio. Una conversiva ad fidem. Quam Dionysius attribuit episcopo, in II cap. Eccl. Hier., et potest competere cuilibet praedicatori, vel etiam cuilibet fideli. Secunda est instructio qua quis eruditur de fidei rudimentis, et qualiter se debeat habere in susceptione sacramentorum. Et haec pertinet secundario quidem ad ministros, principaliter autem ad sacerdotes. Tertia est instructio de conversatione Christianae vitae. Et haec pertinet ad patrinos. Quarta est instructio de profundis mysteriis fidei, et perfectione Christianae vitae. Et haec ex officio pertinet ad episcopos." Aquinas, *STh* III, q. 71, a. 4, ad 3. See also Molloy, "Hierarchy and Holiness," 238.

dience can ask questions "quodlibetally"—that is, on anything and everything about which they care to inquire. In one of the earlier sessions (*Quodl* XI, q. 7) Thomas notes that only bishops properly confirm and in his argumentation he explains that the episcopacy is a state and an office of perfecting persons spiritually. A few years later, he calls the episcopacy a "state of perfection" in *Quodl* I, q. 7, a. 2.

St. Thomas treats the similarities and differences between the ecclesial magisterium of bishops (the *cathedra pontificalis* or the pontifical chair or office) and the magisterium of academic professors (the *cathedra magistralis* or the professor's chair or office) in several quodlibetals. This is a topic sharply debated in recent decades. Is the magisterium of theologians on par with that of bishops? St. Thomas did not think so. While he argues in *Quodl* I, q. 7, a. 2, that it is a higher act both for bishops and for theologians to teach sacred doctrine, in *Quodl* III, q. 4, a. 1, he notes that there are three principal differences between the two magisteria. First, those elevated to the professorial chair by that very fact do *not* receive any degree of eminence that they did not previously enjoy but only the authority to teach—a distinction from which they did not previously benefit—consisting in the duty to communicate knowledge (*scientia*), whereas those elevated to the episcopacy receive an eminence of power (an *eminentia potestatis*). Second, professors have an eminence of science that pertains to their own personal intellectual perfection, whereas the eminence of bishops pertains to their perfection of power over the faithful of Christ—something that professors lack. Third, the episcopal chair is for those who have attained a high degree of the perfection of charity, whereas those who attain a professorial chair merely attain the recognition of a sufficient perfection in the knowledge of their peculiar intellectual discipline. The upshot of all this is that there is no fundamental parity, as many recently have argued, between the episcopal and professorial magisteria. Those who hold the former office are deputed, consecrated, and thus empowered by Christ to authoritatively and juridically perfect the faithful in holiness; those holding a professorial chair are recognized and empowered merely by other men to communicate the knowledge of their peculiar science to others.[70]

70. "Dicendum, quod ad evidentiam huius quaestionis oportet triplicem differentiam considerare cathedrae magistralis ad cathedram pontificalem. Quarum prima est,

In *Quodl* III, q. 6, a. 3, Aquinas reaffirms that bishops are in the active state of perfection. In q. 11, a. 2, he treats the question whether one should accept the episcopal office or recuse oneself and he resolves the issue precisely as he does in his *STh*, noted above. And in *Quodl* XII (composed between 1268 and 1272), q. 11, a. 3, he argues that it is sometimes licit to desire the episcopacy. His argument there reflects the one he gives in *STh* II-II, q. 185, a. 1 (treated above). He returns once again to this question in his commentary on 1 Timothy 3:1. Finally, in his prologue to *Quodl* XII, q. 19, he asserts that bishops have immediate jurisdiction over everyone in their diocese.

SCRIPTURAL COMMENTARIES

Though St. Thomas adduces numerous citations from the Church Fathers and other early Christian writers in his *Catena Aurea*, I will not treat them at any length here as they represent his own thought some-

---

quod ille qui accipit cathedram magistralem, non accipit aliquam eminentiam quam prius non habuerit, sed solum opportunitatem communicandi scientiam, quam prius non habebat: non enim ille qui licentiat aliquem, dat ei scientiam, sed auctoritatem docendi. Ille vero qui accipit cathedram episcopalem, accipit eminentiam potestatis, quam prius non habebat.... Secunda differentia est, quod eminentia scientiae, quae requiritur ad cathedram magistralem, est perfectio hominis secundum seipsum; eminentia vero potestatis, quae pertinet ad cathedram pontificalem, est hominis per comparationem ad alium. Tertia differentia est, quod ad cathedram pontificalem fit homo idoneus per caritatem excellentem; unde dominus antequam Petro suarum ovium curam committeret, quaesivit ab eo: Simon Ioannis diligis me plus his? Ut dicitur Ioan. XXI, 15; ad cathedram autem magistralem redditur homo idoneus ex sufficientia scientiae" (It must be said that to answer this question it is necessary to consider a threefold difference between the teaching and pontifical chairs. The first is that those who receive the teaching chair do not receive any eminence that they did not previously have, but merely the opportunity to communicate their understanding, which privilege they did not previously enjoy; not that he who bestows the teaching license gives the recipient knowledge, but only the authority to teach. But those who receive the episcopal office receive an eminence of power that they did not previously have.... The second difference is that the eminence of understanding, which is required for the teaching chair, is a perfection of man in himself, whereas the eminence of power, which pertains to the pontifical chair, is a perfection of a man in relation to others. The third difference is that a man becomes fit for the pontifical chair through an excelling charity, wherefore the Lord before committing to Peter the care of his sheep asked him, "Simon, son of John, do you love me more than these?" as is said in Jn 21:15; but the teaching chair is given to a suitable man of sufficient understanding). Aquinas, *Quodl* III, q. 4, a. 1, co.

what indirectly.⁷¹ Also, I will not examine St. Thomas's commentaries on the PE, as noted above, since that constitutes the substance of this study in the following chapters.⁷²

Lectura super Philippenses (1259–68)

Commenting on Paul's opening address in Philippians 1:1, "Paul and Timothy ... to all the saints ... with the bishops and deacons," Aquinas explains that priests are not mentioned in this verse as distinct from bishops because in the early Church there were not distinct names for the orders of the presbyterate and episcopacy even though the orders themselves were indeed distinct.⁷³ This is a matter which he treats at greater length in his PE commentaries.

---

71. With that said, there are at least two significant references in this work relevant to the current study. The first is from *Catena Aurea in Lucam* (1265–68), cap. 10, lect. 1, in which Aquinas quotes St. Augustine (*De quaest. Evang.*, l, ii, q. 14) to the effect that the twelve apostles foreshadowed the order of bishops and the seventy-two disciples represent the presbytery "that is, the second order of priests." The second is from *Catena Aurea in Ioannem* (1265–68), cap. 20, lect. 3, where he quotes St. Gregory the Great to the effect that bishops hold the place of the apostles and that they thus have an urgent need for self-control.

72. Among the remaining works of Aquinas that are not examined at any length in this chapter, I must mention in passing his *De articulis fidei* (1261–65), part 2, in which St. Thomas remarks that the episcopacy is more a dignity than a sacramental order: "Sunt autem septem ordines: scilicet presbyteratus, diaconatus, subdiaconatus, acolytatus, exorcistae, lectoris et ostiarii.... Episcopatus autem magis est dignitas quam ordo" (There are seven orders: namely priests, deacons, subdeacons, acolytes, exorcists, lectors, and porters.... The episcopacy is more of a dignity than an order).

73. "Item cur intermittit presbyteros? Respondeo. Dicendum est quod comprehenduntur cum episcopis, quia in una civitate non sunt plures episcopi. Unde dicens in plurali, dat intelligere etiam presbyteros. Et tamen est alius ordo, quia ex ipso Evangelio hoc legitur quod post designationem duodecim apostolorum (quorum personas gerunt episcopi), designavit septuaginta duos discipulos, quorum locum sacerdotes tenent. Dionysius etiam distinguit episcopos et sacerdotes. Sed in principio, licet ordines fuerint distincti, non tamen nomina ordinum; unde hic comprehendit presbyteros cum episcopis" (Why does he omit priests? It must be said that they are included with bishops, because in one city there were not many bishops. Wherefore using the plural, "bishops," we are to understand priests to be included. And nevertheless it is a different order, because in the Gospel after designating the twelve apostles, whose successors are the bishops, the seventy-two disciples are mentioned, whose place is held by the priests. Indeed, Dionysius distinguished bishops from priests. But in the beginning, though the orders were distinct, the names of the orders were not. Wherefore priests are here included with bishops). Aquinas, *Lectura super Philippenses* (hereafter "*In Philip*"), cap. 1, lect. 1.

Commenting on Philippians 1:23–24, where Paul expresses his desire to be "dissolved" and to be with Christ along with his being constrained by the need to stay alive and minister to the faithful, St. Thomas shows that the perfection of charity is not merely reducible to a desire to be with God for one's own personal delight, but it consists, rather, in a more perfect charity that entails loving God and neighbor so that one would forgo the vision of God in order to remain and work for the salvation of one's neighbor.[74] This is significant as it is this very insight of St. Thomas into the kind of love of God that defines the episcopal office, namely, the love of God and one's neighbor for God's sake to the point of delaying one's own beatitude or accepting death on account of one's love for God and neighbor. This insight forms the basis for his arguments on the mendicant controversy, examined below.

Super Evangelium Matthaei (1268–72)

In his commentary on Matthew's Gospel, St. Thomas provides several rich insights into the episcopal office that have been too often overlooked. Commenting on Matthew 4:19, "Follow me, and I will make you fishers of men," Thomas notes (in lect. 2) that it is the greatest dignity for someone to be illumined by Christ in order to illumine others. Such is the call that Christ issues to the apostles and their successors, the bishops. On this point, the Dominican theologian Nicholas Halligan remarks: "This voluntary and complete association with

---

74. "Dicendum est quod duplex est dilectio Dei, scilicet dilectio concupiscentiae, qua vult frui Deo et delectari in ipso, et hoc est bonum hominis. Item est dilectio amicitiae, qua homo praeponit honorem Dei etiam huic delectationi, qua fruitur Deo, et haec est perfecta charitas. Unde Rom. VIII, 38: neque mors, neque vita, neque Angeli, et cetera. Et subdit IX cap., 3: optabam ego anathema fieri pro fratribus meis, et cetera. Et hoc dixit, ut ostendat se esse perfectioris charitatis, quasi sit paratus propter amorem Dei et gloriam carere delectatione visionis Dei; et ideo hoc elegit, et bene, tamquam magis perfectum" (It must be said that there is a twofold love of God, namely the love of concupiscence, by which one desires to enjoy God and to be delighted in him and this is the good of man. The other is the love of friendship, by which a man prefers the honor of God more than his own delight, by which he enjoys God, and this is the perfection of charity, as we read in Rom 8:28, "neither death, nor life, nor angels," etc. and Rom 9:3, "I would choose to be damned for my brethren," etc. And he says this in order to show that he has the perfection of charity, that because of his love for God and his glory he is prepared, as it were, to be deprived of the delight of the vision of God. And so he chooses this, and rightly so, as the greater perfection). Aquinas, *In Philip*, lect. 3.

St. Thomas and His Contemporaries 53

Christ in His mission is the explanation of their [that is, the bishops'] excellence. For, as St. Thomas comments, to be God's cooperator is man's greatest dignity, and to be so enlightened as to enlighten others is to fulfill this dignity most clearly."[75]

Later, commenting on Matthew 6:22–23, "If your eye is single, your whole body shall be lightsome," Thomas provides the following interpretation: "By 'eye' is signified the prelate, who is the eye of his subjects. Wherefore when prelates direct the people to the good, the entire congregation of the people shines with virtue."[76] In applying this passage to the mystical body of Christ, the Church, Thomas has in mind the strict etymology of the term *episkopos*, overseer. Thus begins a series of comments in which Aquinas interprets passages in Matthew which more obviously signify the individual believer, as also signifying the mystical individual or "person" of the Church.

When Christ warns the faithful in Matthew 7:15, "Beware of false prophets," Thomas notes that Jesus is speaking about heretical teachers and prelates in the Church. Since the OT prophetic offices passed away after John the Baptist and the coming of Christ, the prophets of the NT are teachers and prelates in the Church. The term "false prophets" in this passage, then, refers to those bishops in the Church who act as wolves in sheep's clothing.[77] Commenting on Christ's words in Matthew 18:9, "If your eye scandalize you, pluck it out," Thomas argues that since the prelate is, as it were, the "eye" of the Church, this passage indicates that it is better to depose a bad prelate than to scandalize the faithful.[78]

---

75. Nicholas Halligan, "Teaching of St. Thomas Aquinas in regard to the Apostles," *American Ecclesiastical Review* 144 (1961): 34.

76. "Item, per oculum significatur praelatus, qui est oculus subditorum. Unde cum praelati boni dirigunt plebes, tota populi congregatio lucet virtutibus." Aquinas, *In Matt*, cap. 6, lect. 5.

77. "Vestimenta autem eorum sunt ieiunium, eleemosynae, quibus se tegunt; II ad Tim. III, 5: habentes speciem pietatis, virtutem autem eius abnegantes.... Intrinsecus autem sunt lupi rapaces. Hoc principaliter exponitur de haereticis, ex consequenti de malis praelatis" (Their garments are fasting and almsgiving, by which they conceal themselves "having the appearance of piety, but denying its power," 2 Tim 3:5.... "But internally they are ravenous wolves." This is said principally of heretics and afterward about evil prelates). Aquinas, *In Matt*, cap. 7, lect. 2.

78. "Vel potest referri ad totam Ecclesiam, quia oculi sunt praelati, manus diaconi, pes homines simplices. Unde magis est deponendus praelatus, vel diaconus abscinden-

When Christ says, in Matthew 19:21, "If you would be perfect, sell what you have and give it to the poor and come, follow me," Thomas first notes that perfection consists in charity, and above all in the love of God.[79] Then he explains that the state of perfection for religious is for those who seek to acquire the perfection of charity for themselves; whereas the state of perfection for prelates consists in the communication or production of charity in others.[80]

Then, in Matthew 20:25–28, where Christ tells the apostles that their authority is to be exercised in acts of service to the faithful, rather than by dominating them, St. Thomas notes that these words of Christ apply equally to prelates who, if they are to have a primacy in the Church, must be like Christ, who came to serve and not to be served. In this way they must serve the Lord precisely by making themselves the servants of all.[81] In commenting on Matthew 21:2–3, on Christ's

---

dus, quam Ecclesia scandalizetur" (Or this is able to refer to the whole Church, because the eyes are the prelates, the hands are deacons, and the feet are simple men. Wherefore it is better for an evil prelate to be deposed, or a deacon cut off, than the Church to be scandalized). Aquinas, *In Matt*, cap. 18, lect. 1.

79. "Unde si non est in illis perfectio, in quo consistit? Dicendum quod in perfectione caritatis.... Unde dilectio Dei est perfectio" (If perfection is not found in this, in what does it consist? It must be said that it consists in the perfection of charity.... Thus the love of God is perfection). Aquinas, *In Matt*, cap. 19, lect. 2.

80. "Status perfectionis duplex est, praelatorum et religiosorum; sed aequivoce, quia status religiosorum est ad acquirendum perfectionem; unde isti dictum est: si vis esse perfectus.... Status autem praelationis non est ad acquirendum sibi, sed ad habitam communicandam.... Unde talis est differentia inter perfectionem religiosorum et praelatorum, qualis inter discipulum et magistrum. Unde discipulo dicitur: si vis addiscere, intra scholas ut addiscas. Magistro dicitur: lege, et perfice. Unde securior est status religiosorum, quia ignorantia non imputatur eis sicut praelato. Unde sicut ridiculum esset magistro quod nihil sciret, sic et cetera" (The state of perfection is twofold: that of prelates and that of religious, but analogously so because the religious state is for the acquisition of perfection; wherefore it is said "if you want to be perfect."... But the state of prelates is not for the acquisition, but for the communication of perfection.... The difference between the perfection of religious and that of prelates is like the difference between a student and a teacher. Thus to the student it is said: if you want to learn, go to school. To the teacher it is said: lecture and perfect. Thus the religious state is more secure because ignorance is not imputed to them as a flaw as it is to prelates. So just as it would be ridiculous for a teacher to know nothing, so would it be for prelates). Aquinas, *In Matt*, cap. 19, lect. 2.

81. "Si aliquis desiderat habere primatum in Ecclesia, sciat quod illud non est habere dominium, sed servitutem. Servi enim est quod totum se ad servitium domini impendat: sic praelati Ecclesiae totum quicquid habent, quicquid sunt, subditis debent" (If anyone desires primacy in the Church, he knows that this is not to have dominion,

command to the apostles to find the colt, untie it, and lead it to Him, Thomas interprets this loosing of the colt spiritually to signify the prelate's act of loosing the faithful from ignorance by his act of teaching sound doctrine.[82] And interpreting Matthew 24:45, Thomas notes that Christ's sayings about the "faithful and wise servant, whom his lord appointed over his family" provide an admonition for prelates to work for the Lord by serving the faithful and correcting the wicked.[83] Specifically, the prelate gives the flock "food in due time" by teaching true doctrine, giving a good example, and seeing to the provision of their temporal needs.[84]

Finally, in his interpretation of Christ's parable in Matthew 25:27, when the master returns expecting interest on the money he gave his servants, Thomas says that the apostles fulfilled this charge by giving the gift of the Holy Spirit that establishes bishops for the Church.[85] Aquinas's commentary on Matthew is remarkable for the many instances where he provides plausible interpretations of numerous passages, like those cited here, as bearing specifically on bishops and their office—passages that otherwise would not be perceived as evidently bearing such a meaning. He repeats and greatly elaborates upon many of these insights in his commentaries on the PE, as we shall see in subsequent chapters.

---

but servitude. The servant ought to devote his entire self to the service of the Lord: so everything whatsoever the prelates of the Church have, and whatever they are, they owe to their subordinates). Aquinas, *In Matt*, cap. 20, lect. 2.

82. "Solvite a vinculis ignorantiae per doctrinam" (Loosen them from the chains of ignorance by teaching). Aquinas, *In Matt*, cap. 21, lect. 1.

83. "Hic specialiter admonet ad vigilandum praelatos.... Praelati enim est corripere vitia" (Here he urges prelates to be vigilant.... Indeed, the prelate ought to correct vices). Aquinas, *In Matt*, cap. 24, lect. 4.

84. "Item tangit officium praelati ut det illis cibum in tempore: cibum scilicet doctrinae, boni exempli, et temporalis subsidii" (Likewise he touches on the office of the prelate when he says that he ought to give them food in due time, namely, the "food" of doctrine, of a good example, and of temporal assistance). Aquinas, *In Matt*, cap. 24, lect. 4.

85. "Item illi qui multiplicant, ut apostoli, qui aliis dederunt donum spiritus sancti, constituendo episcopos et cetera. Ad Tit. c. I, 5: huius gratia dimisi te Cretae, ut constituas per civitates presbyteros et cetera" (Again, those who increase the investment, as the apostles did, gave to others the gift of the Holy Spirit, by establishing bishops, etc. According to Tit 1:5, "For this cause I left you in Crete, that you should establish priests in every city," etc.). Aquinas, *In Matt*, cap. 25, lect. 2.

Super Epistolam ad Romanos (chaps. 1–8, 1272–73; chap. 9 and following, 1265–68)

In his commentary on Romans, chap. 7, lect. 1 (specifically on Rom 7:3 where St. Paul discusses licit second marriages after the death of the first spouse), Aquinas cites 1 Timothy 3:2 that a bishop must be the husband of one wife only. His remarks on this passage will be treated at greater length below in chapter 4. But here, in his commentary on Romans, Thomas notes that this restriction for bishops is not because second marriages are illicit since they are not so if contracted after the death of the first spouse, but because this would constitute a "defect of the sacrament" (*defectus sacramenti*) for a bishop. Insofar as matrimony is a sign of Christ's union with the Church, and because that union is exclusively and eternally one-to-one, a man who had more than one wife (even licitly after the death of the prior wife) is not suitable to represent Christ to the Church. Just as Christ has one spouse, the Church, so too should the bishop who represents him to the flock and who is, in Christ, the spouse of his local church, have only one spouse.

Later, commenting on Romans 10:14–15 ("how shall they preach unless they be sent?"), Thomas notes that the bishop acts as God's viceroy in sending other clerics to preach the Gospel.[86] And on Romans 12:7, in chap. 12, lect. 2, Thomas notes that the various gifts Paul lists, such as prophecy, ministry, teaching, and the like are *gratiae gratis datae*, also called "charismatic gifts" which are given for the edification of others in the faith. He explicitly states that bishops receive the grace of the office of ministry and are called to this by God, who gives them a "grace freely given"—not for their own edification, but for that of the faithful.

Super 1 ad Corinthios (chaps. 1–7, 1272–73)

Commenting on 1 Corinthians 1:17, "For Christ sent me not to baptize, but to preach the gospel," Thomas affirms that the apostles and their successors, the bishops, are those upon whom the office of preaching

---

86. "Alio modo mittuntur aliqui a Deo mediante auctoritate praelatorum, qui gerunt vicem Dei" (In another way, some are sent by God in a mediated fashion by the authority of prelates, who act in the place of God). Aquinas, *Lectura super Romanos* (hereafter "*In Rom*"), cap. 10, lect. 2, par. 838. See Molloy, "Hierarchy and Holiness," 200.

devolves. Baptizing the faithful can be executed by lesser ministers as this action does not require great wisdom or virtue. Preaching, however, requires a greater capacity, as Nicholas Halligan, OP, remarks: "The effort of the baptizer does not produce the effect of baptism (and so a greater or lesser minister makes no difference for the sacramental effect), whereas the wisdom and power of the preacher act mightily in the effect of his preaching. Thus the Apostles always preached personally."[87]

Then, in commenting on 1 Corinthians 4:1–5, where St. Paul says that the faithful ought to consider the apostles to be "ministers of Christ and dispensers of the mysteries of God," in lect. 1 Thomas remarks that prelates should seek to serve Christ alone in governing their subjects. As mediators between Christ and the faithful, they must dispense the mysteries of God—including both the doctrine of the faith and the sacraments themselves—to the people. It is necessary for the salvation of the flock that they understand their bishop to be acting in the person of Christ and to obey him as they obey Christ.[88]

But in lect. 3, on 1 Corinthians 4:14–21, Thomas insists that the faithful should not follow the evil example of bad prelates; rather, they must imitate their bishop only to the degree that he imitates

87. Halligan, "Teaching of St. Thomas Aquinas in regard to the Apostles," 43. Here he cites Aquinas, *Lectura super 1 Corinthios* (hereafter *"In 1 Cor"*), cap. 1, lect. 2 and *In Rom*, cap. 2, lect. 3.

88. "Pertinet ergo ad officium praelatorum Ecclesiae, quod in gubernatione subditorum soli Christo servire desiderent, cuius amore oves eius pascunt, secundum illud Io. ult.: si diligis me, pasce oves meas. Pertinet etiam ad eos, ut divina populo dispensent, secundum illud infra IX, 17: dispensatio mihi credita est, et secundum hoc sunt mediatores inter Christum et populum, secundum illud Deut. V, 5: ego sequester fui, et medius illo tempore inter Deum et vos. Haec autem aestimatio de praelatis Ecclesiae necessaria est ad salutem fidelium; nisi enim eos recognoscerent ministros Christi, non eis obedirent, tamquam Christo, secundum illud Gal. IV, 14: sicut Angelum Dei excepistis me, sicut Iesum Christum" (It pertains, therefore, to the office of the prelates of the Church, that in governing their subjects they should desire to serve Christ alone, for the love of whom they feed his sheep, as we read in Jn 21:17, "If you love me, feed my sheep." It also pertains to them to dispense divine riches to the people, as we read below in 1 Cor 9:17, "A dispensation is committed to me." And according to this they are mediators between Christ and the people: "I was the mediator and stood between the Lord and you at that time," according to Dt 5:5. This view of the Church's prelates is necessary for the salvation of the faithful, for unless they recognize them as Christ's ministers, they will not obey them as Christ as we read in Gal 4:14, "You received me as an angel of God, as Christ Jesus"). Aquinas, *In 1 Cor*, cap. 4, lect. 1.

Christ, who is the infallible rule of truth.[89] This is significant inasmuch as, for St. Thomas, the ultimate rule of faith is Christ, God the Word incarnate. The Church's teaching is also a rule of faith for Aquinas, but it is only a "secondary" or "derivative" rule, which ought to be subordinate to and in strict conformity with Christ and his teaching. In this regard, if a prelate fails in word or example the faithful must continue to follow Christ's teaching and example.

Super Evangelium Iohannis (1270–72)

In his comments on John 10:11–18, Thomas notes that Christ proclaims himself to be the Good Shepherd, showing that the office of such a pastor entails laying down one's life for his sheep. A good shepherd is a prelate who has become one with Christ by love. Even though only Christ is the True Light (and this latter is *not*, for Aquinas, an office he shares with others in the full sense of the phrase), he does communicate a share in his office of shepherd to others—namely, to Peter, the apostles, and every good bishop.[90] The office of the Good Shepherd consists, above all, in charity. He is willing to suffer for his flock because he desires the good of the flock and not his own private good. The bad shepherd desires his own private good above all. The spiritual pastor must be willing to relinquish his corporeal life for the salvation of the souls of his flock as the latter profoundly outweighs the value of the former.[91]

Thomas then notes three ways in which evil pastors differ from good ones. The first is that the good pastor seeks the benefit of his subordinates while the evil one seeks his own private good.[92] The second is that the good pastor loves his flock whereas the evil one does

---

89. "Intantum ergo debebant eum imitari ut patrem, inquantum et ipse Christum imitabatur, qui est omnium principalis pater. Et per hoc subtrahitur subditis occasio de adhaerendo malis exemplis praelatorum. Unde in hoc subditi solum praelatos imitari debent, in quo ipsi Christum imitantur, qui est infallibilis regula veritatis" (Therefore, they ought to have imitated him as a father, insofar as he imitated Christ, who is the principal father of all. And this removes from subjects the occasion of adhering to the evil examples of prelates. Thus, subjects ought only to imitate their prelates to the extent that they imitate Christ, who is the infallible rule of truth). Aquinas, *In 1 Cor*, cap. 4, lect. 3.

90. Aquinas, *Super evanelium S. Ioannis lectura* (hereafter "*Ioannis*"), cap. 10, lect. 3, par. 1398.

91. Aquinas, *Ioannis*, par. 1399.

92. Aquinas, *Ioannis*, par. 1402.

St. Thomas and His Contemporaries

not.[93] The third is that the good pastor in the face of danger lays down his life for the sake of his flock out of love, while the evil pastor does not. Thomas adds that a good shepherd can flee persecution but only if he provides for the care of his flock.

Commenting on John 21:15–17 (Christ's postresurrection encounter with Peter), Thomas first notes that just as Christ examines St. Peter before raising him to the pastoral office, likewise everyone raised to this office ought to be examined.[94] Then Thomas says that in the course of this exchange Christ reveals three fundamental things absolutely necessary for a prelate, namely, obedience, knowledge (*scientia*), and grace.[95] A candidate for the episcopacy should be examined on these points, but above all, he ought to be examined about his love for Christ since, as Aquinas remarks, many seek this office out of self-love and, as such, are not suitable for the episcopacy. A fit candidate is one who loves Christ above all to the point where he will relinquish all other interests in order to serve him and his flock out of the abundance of his charity which is the hallmark of spiritual perfection.[96] Thomas hastens to add that the fit candidate must not only

---

93. Aquinas, *Ioannis*, par. 1404.

94. "Pastorale autem officium iniungit, examinatione praemissa: et ideo qui ad hoc officium assumuntur, primo examinantur. I Tim. V, 22: manus nemini cito imposueris" (But the Lord imposes the pastoral office on Peter by a prior examination. And thus, those who receive this office are first examined, according to 1 Tim 5:22, "Impose hands lightly on no one"). Aquinas, *Ioannis*, cap. 21, lect. 3, par. 2614.

95. "Modus autem allocutionis ponitur cum dicit dixit Simoni Petro: ubi tria ponuntur quae necessaria sunt praelato. Obedientia, cum dixit Simoni, qui interpretatur obediens, quae est praelatis necessaria: nam qui nescit superioribus obedire, inferioribus nescit imperare" (But the mode of speaking is seen when he says that Jesus called Simon Peter. Three things are given here which are necessary for a prelate. Obedience, when he says to Simon, which means "obedient," which is necessary for prelates. A prelate needs to be obedient because one who does not know how to obey superiors does not know how to govern inferiors). Aquinas, *Ioannis*, par. 2616.

96. "Congruit etiam haec examinatio officio. Multi enim pastorale officium assumentes, utuntur eo sicut seipsos amantes. II Tim. III, 1: instabunt tempora periculosa, et erunt homines seipsos amantes. Et qui non amat dominum, non est idoneus praelatus; sed magis ille qui non quaerit quae sua sunt, sed quae Iesu Christi, et hoc amore eius. II Cor. V, 14: caritas Christi urget nos. Congruit etiam officio quantum ad utilitatem proximorum: ex abundantia enim caritatis est quod aliqui diligentes interdum quietem propriae contemplationis intermittant, ut procurent proximorum utilitatem. Cum enim apostolus diceret, Rom. VIII, 39: certus sum enim, quod neque mors poterit nos separare a caritate Dei, subdit: optabam ego ipse anathema esse pro fratribus meis. Et ideo necessaria est examinatio de dilectione ad praelatum" (This examination was also fitting

love Christ, but love Him "more than these," that is, love Christ in an outstanding way, above that of his fellows. That said, Aquinas recognizes that there are other, secondary, matters to take into account in examining a candidate for the episcopacy such as education, competence, wisdom, and unanimous support of the faithful. But these are ancillary considerations and are conditioned on the fundamental and non-negotiable criterion of the candidate's all-surpassing love of Christ and his Church.[97]

THE MENDICANT CONTROVERSY

The mendicant controversy is a complex historical event. For the purposes of this study, Aquinas's works on this issue are evaluated only insofar as they provide insight into his thought on the nature and duties of the episcopal office. As such, this brief treatment suffers from some awkwardness insofar as Aquinas's principal concern in these works is not, in fact, the episcopacy. Rather, his aim is to defend the newly-founded mendicant orders and their life outside of the cloistered monastery, begging alms so that they may pursue their charism—especially that of teaching and preaching.

In very general terms, the secular clergy and bishops who opposed the new mendicant orders, and in particular the Franciscans and Dominicans, perceived them as movements contrary to the Christian life in which they failed to work for their food, inserting themselves into the spiritual lives of flocks who should rather live under the care of the secular, established clergy and their bishops. Broadly speaking, the mendicants inherited their rule of poverty from the life and teach-

---

for the office. In fact, many who receive the pastoral office use it as self-lovers: "In the last days there will come times of stress. For men will be lovers of self," 1 Tim 3:1. And one who does not love the Lord is not a suitable prelate. A fit prelate is one who does not seek his own things, but those of Jesus Christ, and he does this by his love: "The love of Christ compels us," 2 Cor 5:14. And this is fitting to this office insofar as it is useful for one's neighbors. Indeed, it is from the abundance of charity that those who love will sometimes interrupt their own contemplation in order to procure the advantage of their neighbor. As the apostle said, "I am certain that death will not be able to separate us from the love of God," Rom 8:39, and he added, "Thus I wished that I myself were condemned for the sake of my brethren," Rom 9:3. And so it is necessary that a prelate be examined about his love). Aquinas, *Ioannis*, par. 2618.

97. Aquinas, *Ioannis*, pars. 2619–20.

ings of St. Francis of Assisi (1181–1226) and their involvement in university studies from St. Dominic Guzman (1170–1221). For this they received approbation from the Church and an exemption from local episcopal jurisdiction, granting them rights formerly reserved to the secular clergy, including the right to preach, hear confessions, and teach theology.

The secular clergy's opposition to these orders came to a head at the University of Paris in the thirteenth century. Reacting to some excessive claims of certain mendicants and to the problematic work *Introductorius ad Evangelium aeternum*—falsely attributed to the Dominicans but in fact composed by the wayward "spiritual Franciscan" Gerard de Borgo San Donino—William of St. Amour (ca. 1200–1272) condemned this movement as inspired by the devil and as a harbinger of the antichrist. He and other opponents, especially Gerard of Abbeville (d. 1272), saw these orders as renegades who violated the hierarchical order established by Christ. St. Bonaventure and St. Thomas were the two most articulate defenders of the legitimacy of the mendicant orders and, in the process of their defenses, they eloquently upheld the truth of the nature and duties of the episcopal office. In what follows, I will provide a summary of the essential teachings of Thomas on the episcopacy in his two principal works on the mendicant controversy, *Contra impugnantes* and *De perfectione*. Doing this requires overlooking the riches in these works that bear more precisely on the value of the mendicant way of life in Christ.

It is helpful at this point to recall that, as cited above, in his *STh* II-II, q. 187, a. 1, Aquinas writes: "It is said to be unlawful for monks and other religious to preach, teach, and so forth, because the religious state does not give them the power to do these things [thus, they have no ordinary power to do so]. They can, however, do them if they receive orders, or ordinary jurisdiction, or if matters of jurisdiction be delegated to them."[98] Commenting on this passage from Aquinas, Molloy notes:

St. Thomas replies by acknowledging that preaching pertains to prelates *ex officio* but he maintains that religious can also undertake the office if they re-

---

98. "Et hoc modo dicitur non licere monachis et aliis religiosis praedicare, docere, et alia huiusmodi facere, quia status religionis non dat eis potestatem haec faciendi. Possunt tamen ista facere si ordinem accipiant vel ordinariam iurisdictionem, aut etiam si eis committantur ea quae sunt iurisdictionis." Aquinas, *STh* II-II, q. 187, a. 1, co.

ceive a mission from those competent to give it [citing *STh* II-II, q. 187, a. 4, ad 2].... Hence the right of the local pastor to preach to his flock is a right ultimately derived from the bishop, and since it is a derived power, he himself cannot in turn confer canonical mission on others to exercise the apostolate, above all that of preaching.[99]

St. Thomas was able to mount this argument most likely as a result of his substantive engagement with his opponents on the mendicant controversy. In a. 1, ad 2, Thomas says: "Prelates are competent to preach in virtue of their office, but religious may be competent to do so in virtue of delegation; and thus when they work in the field of the Lord, they may make their living thereby, according to 2 Timothy 2:6."[100]

Contra Impugnantes (1256–59)

In this polemic, St. Thomas is responding principally to the attacks on the mendicant orders mounted by William of St. Amour in his *Tractatus de periculis novissimorum temporum*.[101] St. Thomas's teaching on bishops in *Contra impugnantes* may be summarized as follows: bishops are bound to be versed in sacred learning; preaching (as distinct from scholastic teaching) is the special duty of prelates; bishops represent Christ and each particular church attains its fullness in its own chief priest, the bishop; and, while Christ is the bridegroom of the Church universal, the bishop—who takes the place of Christ—is called the spouse of his diocese because he cooperates with Christ exteriorly in begetting spiritual children for Christ.[102]

---

99. Molloy, "Hierarchy and Holiness," 237; in this passage he references Congar, "Aspects ecclésiologiques," 77.

100. "Ad secundum dicendum quod praelatis competit praedicatio ex officio, religiosis autem potest competere ex commissione. Et ita, cum laborent in agro dominico, possunt exinde vivere, secundum illud II ad Tim. II." Aquinas, *STh* II-II, q. 187, a. 4, ad 2.

101. See Torrell, *Saint Thomas*, 79.

102. "Cum etiam praelationis officium simul habeat et doctrinam adiunctam; non debet inconveniens reputari, si monachus auctoritate eius ad quem spectat, ad praedictum doctrinae officium assumatur" (Indeed, since the office of a prelate also is bound to teaching, it ought not appear unfitting if a monk, by the prelate's authority, receives the office of preaching doctrine), Aquinas, *Cont imp*, part 2, cap. 1; ad 2, "Patet etiam quod Gratianus loquitur in illa quaestione de doctrina praedicationis, quae ad praelatos pertinet; non autem de doctrina scholastica, cui praelati non multum intendunt" (Likewise, Gratian is clear when he speaks on the question of the doctrine of preaching which pertains to prelates; not, however, of scholastic teaching regarding which prelates

In *Cont imp* II, cap. 1, Thomas treats the question whether it is lawful for a religious to teach. In cap. 1, ad 5, Thomas notes that Dionysius never spoke about teaching as a sacred action, yet he attaches this action to the office of bishop and, by extension, to monks and others who are delegated by the bishop or by the pope to teach the faith to others. Here Thomas expostulates a leitmotif of this work: mendicants are able lawfully to preach, hear confessions, and the like when they have received the mandate and jurisdiction to do so either from the local bishop or from the pope himself.

In cap. 3 of the same part, in defending religious who are attacked on account of the journeys they undertake for the salvation of souls, Thomas affirms that bishops have the greatest power in the particular church and that subordinates can do nothing without their permission or that of the pope. In this chapter, Thomas sets for himself the following tasks:

First, we shall show that bishops and superior prelates can preach and absolve those who are under the care of priests, without needing the permission of those priests. Secondly, we shall prove that they can empower others to act in like manner. Thirdly, we shall make clear that religious are, when commissioned by a bishop, capable of exercising these functions. Fourthly, we shall demonstrate that it is expedient for the welfare of souls that others, besides parish priests, should be allowed to preach and hear confessions. Fifthly, it will be shown that a religious order may advantageously be found-

---

do not ordinarily intend to teach); part 2, cap. 3, "Episcopi in Ecclesia tenent locum domini Iesu Christi.... Ut enim omnem hierarchiam videmus in Iesum consummatam, sic unamquamque in proprium divinum summum sacerdotem, idest episcopum" (In the Church, bishops hold the place of our Lord Jesus Christ.... Thus we see every hierarchy perfected in Jesus, so every particular hierarchy is fulfilled in its own high priest, that is, the bishop); ad 22, "Sponsus Ecclesiae, proprie loquendo, Christus est.... Alii autem qui sponsi dicuntur, sunt ministri sponsi, exterius cooperantes ad generationem spiritualium filiorum; quos tamen non sibi, sed Christo generant.... Qui quidem ministri intantum sponsi dicuntur, inquantum vicem veri sponsi obtinent.... Et ideo Papa, qui obtinet vicem sponsi in tota Ecclesia, universalis Ecclesiae sponsus dicitur. Episcopus autem suae dioecesis, presbyter autem suae parochiae" (The spouse of the Church, properly speaking, is Christ.... But others who are called spouses, are ministers of the Bridegroom, who cooperate exteriorly in the spiritual generation of sons not for themselves but for Christ.... Who are indeed ministers, but they are called spouses insofar as they hold the place of the true Spouse.... And so the Pope, who holds the place of the Spouse in the entire Church, is called the spouse of the universal Church. But the bishop is the spouse of his diocese, and a priest of his parish).

ed for the purpose of preaching and hearing confessions, with license from the bishops. Sixthly, we shall reply to the objections of our adversaries.[103]

Aquinas proceeds to affirm that bishops retain their power over the people whom they commit to the care of priests; that bishops are the successors of the apostles; that bishops not only perfect but also illuminate and purge the faithful; that the bishop stands in the place of Christ; that the bishop's power is universal in his diocese whereas the priest's is particular; that the spiritual power held by priests is given to them by their bishops; that bishops ought to imitate Christ in their judgments; and that the office of preaching is most fitting for those who are spiritually perfect.

At the end of cap. 3, in addressing the opposing claims of his adversaries, Aquinas argues (in ad 5) that no one is able to preach unless he is sent by the Lord. Both the twelve and the seventy-two are sent by the Lord along with those who have received their power as their successors. When the subordinate, under the authority of his superior (namely, the bishop) hears confession and preaches, the bishop is understood to be doing this. And, by extension, this also applies to Christ. This fits with Thomas's continual affirmation of the bishop being *in loco Christi* as his vicar.

In ad 10, Thomas shows that bishops can exercise their episcopal powers in other dioceses only with the permission of the bishop (literally, *auctoritate illius episcopi*) in whose diocese they visit. In ad 14, on the need to confess to one's own (proper) priest, Thomas argues that this injunction is fulfilled by confessing not only to one's own parish priest, but also to one's own bishop, to the pope, or to any representative of the bishop. And in ad 19, Thomas notes that when a bishop gives to someone else (for example, a parish priest, a religious priest, etc.) the power and permission to forgive, preach, and consecrate the Eucharist, the bishop himself does not thereby lose his power. In these cases

---

103. "Primo ostendemus quod episcopi et superiores praelati possunt praedicare et absolvere eos qui sacerdotibus subduntur, sine licentia ipsorum sacerdotum. Secundo, quod hoc idem possunt aliis committere. Tertio, quod hoc aliis committi quam parochialibus sacerdotibus expedit saluti animarum. Quarto, quod etiam religiosi ad huiusmodi officia exercenda ex commissione praelatorum sunt idonei. Quinto, quod religio aliqua salubriter institui potest ad haec exequenda de licentia praelatorum. Sexto, respondebimus rationibus quae ad partem contrariam inducuntur." Aquinas, *Cont imp*, part 2, cap. 3.

there is a sharing of power such that they are *in communione potestatis*.

In ad 20, Aquinas shows that the bishop has care of all the people in his diocese. And in ad 21, he notes that bishops have immediate jurisdiction over every person in their diocese as the pope does over the whole world. This is due to the divine ordination of our Lord himself. As noted above, in ad 22 he shows that while bishops are the spouses of their dioceses, priests, bishops, and the pope are all ministers and vicars of Christ. Thus, in essence, there is only one spouse of the Church: Christ himself. Finally, near the end of this chapter (in ad 28), he shows that those in inferior orders are able to exercise a superior office by delegation from a higher authority.

In II, cap. 4, obj. 7 and ad 7, Thomas accedes that "religious, by preaching, exercise an episcopal office." Molloy notes that the preaching office "is so characteristic of [the bishop's] state that if another should preach he is spoken of as exercising an office that is properly episcopal."[104] Finally, in V, cap. 3, Thomas notes that the apostles and their successors, the bishops, are mediators between God and man by preaching the word of God. Because they have received the commission to preach from God and from the Church, bishops are true prelates and, therefore, true apostles.[105]

De Perfectione Spiritualis Vitae (1269–70)

In this work, St. Thomas responds principally to the attacks against the mendicants mounted by Gerard of Abbeville in his *Contra adversarium perfectionis christianae* of 1269 and in his *Quodlibet* XIV of Christmas in the same year. Torrell's claim that in this work Aquinas *begins*, under the influence of Dionysius, to view the episcopal office as one of spiritual perfector is belied by the evidence, given above, that St. Thomas explicitly and approvingly cited Dionysius to this ef-

---

104. Molloy, "Hierarchy and Holiness," 237–38, citing Aquinas, *Cont imp*, part 2, cap. 4, obj. 7.

105. "Prophetae autem et apostoli officium est ut sit mediator inter Deum et populum, verba Dei populo annuntiando" (For the office of a prophet and an apostle is to be a mediator between God and the people by announcing the word of God) and "Veri enim praelati sunt veri apostoli, qui tamen peccatis exigentibus interdum peccatores inveniuntur" (For true prelates are true apostles, although at times by their evident iniquities they may be found among sinners), Aquinas, *Cont imp*, part 5, cap. 3, pars. 519 and 521. Compare this with Molloy, "Hierarchy and Holiness," 238.

fect as early as his *Sentences* commentary.[106] To be fair, Aquinas does not call the episcopacy a *status perfectionis* until later in his career (this is likely what Torrell is referencing).

Bearing this out more precisely, Molloy comments as follows on the development of St. Thomas's doctrine regarding what constitutes the bishop's state of perfection, namely, the love of God or the love of neighbor:

> There seems to have been a clarification of St. Thomas's thought on this point [namely, that the state of perfection of bishops is characterized by the love of neighbor for God's sake] during the course of the controversies of 1269. *Quodl.* I, a. 14, ad 2 (March, 1269) sees both states of perfection in terms of the love of God. Both states are linked with the perfection of this love: that of religious—characterized by the three vows—is preparatory to this perfection; that of bishops—characterized by dedication to one's neighbor—is the effect of this perfection. Hence *both states are called states of perfection in reference to the love of God*. In the *De Perf. V. Sp.*, on the other hand, which dates from the end of 1269, the state of perfection of the bishop is seen *formally in terms of the perfect love of neighbor*: a love perfect with regard to extent, intensity, and efficacy. There is no mention of this perfection of fraternal love in *Quodl.* I, a. 12, ad 2. The position of the *De Perf.* is that found in *Summa Theol.*, II-II, q. 184, a. 5 (dates from 1272). It is quite true that the perfection of fraternal charity can flow only from a perfect love of God; it is quite another thing to define the state of perfection of the bishop formally in terms of this love of God.[107]

St. Thomas's teaching on the episcopacy in *De perfectione* consists in four fundamental points fully consistent with the rest of his *opera*, as summarized above. First, the bishop's office is indeed a state of perfection.[108] Second, in terms of the value of charity, the episcopal office consists essentially in the highest perfection of charity in which the bishop dedicates his entire life to enrich his neighbor in truth, love, and grace for the love of God.[109] Third, with respect to the intensity of perfect charity, the episcopal office demands that bishops

---

106. Torrell, *Saint Thomas*, 86. E.g., "In ordine ecclesiasticae hierarchiae, secundum Dionysium, soli episcopi sunt perfectores" (In the order of the ecclesiastical hierarchy, according to Dionysius, only the bishops are perfectors). Aquinas, *In IV Sent*, d. 7, q. 3, a. 1, qc. 2, s.c. 1–2.

107. Molloy, "Hierarchy and Holiness," 227n103.

108. "Et ideo episcopi statum perfectionis habent, sicut et religiosi" (And so bishops possess the state of perfection, as do religious). Aquinas, *De perf*, cap. 16.

109. "Sunt autem alii qui bona spiritualia et divina supra naturam et rationem exis-

St. Thomas and His Contemporaries 67

be willing to lay down their lives for their neighbor—an act exemplifying the greatest love (see Jn 15:13).[110] Finally, as mediator between God and man, the bishop should be perfect in both the active life and the contemplative life so that he may communicate to the faithful the fruits of his contemplation, received from God, thereby benefitting the people he serves in fraternal charity.[111]

On Aquinas's remarks in cap. 14 on the bishop's duty to be willing to sacrifice his life for the faithful, Molloy notes:

> [This] question is also treated in *Summa Theol.*, II-II, q. 184, a. 5, but here St. Thomas contents himself with mentioning only one aspect of the perfection of fraternal charity: the bishop's obligation of laying down his life for his flock. Since the bishop is obliged to this in virtue of the assumption of the pastoral office, he is constituted in a state of perfection. Note the contrast in this same text between the two states of perfection: the religious are the "*abstinentes*," the bishops are the "*assumentes*."[112]

In cap. 15, Thomas identifies what is required to constitute the state of perfection: "If a person dedicate his whole life to serve God in works of perfection he absolutely embraces the condition or state of perfection."[113] And this must be done by means of a vow.

---

tentia proximis largiuntur: scilicet doctrinam divinorum, manuductionem ad Deum, et spiritualium sacramentorum communicationem.... Huiusmodi autem bonorum collatio ad singularem quandam perfectionem pertinet fraternae dilectionis: quia per haec bona homo ultimo fini coniungitur, in quo summa hominis perfectio consistit" (But there are others who bestow on their neighbor spiritual and divine goods that are above nature and reason: namely, divine doctrine, direction to God, and the communication of spiritual sacraments.... It pertains to a certain perfection of fraternal love to give these goods, because through them man is untied to his ultimate end, in which consists his highest perfection). Aquinas, *De perf*, cap. 14.

110. "Tertius autem gradus dilectionis est ut aliquis animam suam pro fratribus ponat.... Unde in hoc perfectio fraternae dilectionis constituitur" (The third grade of love is that someone would lay down his life for his brother.... Hence in this is established the perfection of fraternal charity). Aquinas, *De perf*, cap. 14.

111. "Cum enim episcopus mediator inter Deum et homines constituatur, oportet ipsum et in actione praecellere, inquantum minister hominum constituitur, et in contemplatione praecipuum esse, ut ex Deo hauriat quod hominibus tradat" (Since, in fact, a bishop is constituted as mediator between God and men, it is necessary that he excel in the active life and especially in contemplation, insofar as he is established as a minister to men, so that he may draw from God what he hands on to men). Aquinas, *De perf*, cap. 18.

112. Molloy, "Hierarchy and Holiness," 227n104. Compare this to Aquinas, *Quodl* I and *STh* II-II, q. 184, a. 5.

113. "Si vero totam vitam suam voto Deo obligavit, ut in operibus perfectionis ei

Thomas shows that the state of perfection is a condition befitting both bishops and religious in cap. 16. Regarding bishops, he identifies three elements in the perfection of brotherly love: (1) that a man love his enemies and assist them (see Mt 10:16; 1 Cor 4:12); (2) that he lay down his life for the brethren either by exposing himself to the danger of death or by devoting his whole life to their service (Jn 10:11); and (3) that he minister to their spiritual needs by dispensing spiritual gifts to his neighbors as their mediator (see 1 Tm 2; Heb 5:1; 2 Cor 2:10 and 13:3; 1 Cor 9:11).

In cap. 17, Thomas shows that the episcopal office is more sacred than the religious state for, as Dionysius says in chap. 5 of his *Ecclesiastical Hierarchy*, the "duty of bishops is to produce perfection." Bishops are obliged to lay down their lives for their flocks; to feed their flocks by word, example, and temporal assistance; to live in chastity (citing Dionysius, *Celestial Hierarchy*, chap. 3: from the abundance of their own chastity, bishops must impart purity to others); and to guide others to God (1 Cor 12:31, "Be zealous for the better gifts"). Thus, as noted above, for Thomas the bishop is to be the servant of all.

In cap. 18, Thomas answers arguments which call into question the perfection of the episcopal state. First, he notes that the secondary perfection of fraternal charity derives from the primary perfection of the love of God (citing 2 Cor 5:13). Second, as mediator the bishop must be preeminent in both the active and the contemplative life. Aquinas argues: "For since the bishop is constituted as a mediator between God and men, he ought to excel in action, insofar as he is constituted a minister of men, and he should be preeminent in contemplation, so that he may draw from God what he gives to men."[114] Lastly, in cap. 19, Thomas warns that the episcopal office, although a state of greater perfection than the religious life, is nevertheless not to be coveted since this likely would involve sinful presumption (see 1 Tm 2:7, on which Thomas remarks that it would be absurd to teach others the way of spiritual perfection without having had previous personal experience of perfection).

---

deserviat, iam simpliciter conditionem vel statum perfectionis assumpsit." Aquinas, *De perf*, cap. 15.

114. Aquinas, *De perf*, cap. 18, par. 664, as cited by Molloy, "Hierarchy and Holiness," 244.

St. Thomas and His Contemporaries

By way of summary, in his seminal essay "Aspects ecclésiologiques," Yves Congar, OP, expresses quite well the development of a theology of the episcopacy in St. Thomas's polemical works on the mendicant controversy:

> In his conflict with the secular Masters St. Thomas constructed a theology of the episcopate which makes of the bishop a successor of the Apostles, not only from the point of view of dignity and powers but also from the point of view of a spiritual upbuilding of the Church by charisms and sanctity. He united, in his idea of the bishop, as in that which he had of the Apostles, juridical structure and grace, the grandeurs of hierarchy and the grandeurs of sanctity.[115]

Congar's claim here is even more apropos to Aquinas's commentaries on the PE.

CONCLUSION

With the context provided by this chapter's overview of the theology of the episcopacy in the writings of St. Thomas Aquinas and his contemporaries, in the following chapters we shall see that Aquinas's PE commentaries contribute not only to the thirteenth-century debate on the episcopacy but also to the contemporary recovery of a fuller theology of the episcopacy—one that treats of the virtues and duties demanded by the office itself. Nothing in Thomas's writings approaches a comprehensive spiritual theology of the episcopacy aside from his PE commentaries. Thomas's predecessors and contemporaries incipiently recognize the unique role of bishops in the ecclesial hierarchy, as identified by Dionysius. But Thomas himself, in his systematic works, biblical commentaries, and polemical works on the mendicant controversy sets forth an increasingly robust theology of the episcopacy and conducts substantive forays into the practical obligations demanded of the bishop. It is only in Aquinas's commentaries on the PE that we find a comprehensive treatment of the intellectual, moral, and spiritual qualifications required of one suited for the episcopal office, along with a nearly exhaustive treatment of the dangers and lofty duties that this office entails.

---

115. Congar, "Aspects ecclésiologiques," 123.

3

St. Thomas's Lectures on the Pastoral Epistles

Aquinas's lectures on the PE are the mature fruit of a career spent commenting on Scripture. Dominican biblical scholar Ceslas Spicq valued these particular commentaries especially for their theological contribution when he wrote: "The commentary on the Pastoral Epistles ... dates from the last years of St. Thomas's life, and it constitutes not only one of the best scriptural works that he had composed, but a masterpiece of medieval exegesis.... Undoubtedly, from a philological and historical point of view it is outdated, but it will always be consulted fruitfully for its psychological observations and above all for its theological elaboration."[1] Before examining the theology Aquinas developed in these lectures, it is first necessary to understand their historical context and methodology. In this chapter, I will discuss the dating of the lectures, the versions of the Bible available to Aquinas, the critical and research tools that he used, the structure and methodology of the lectures, and his account of the principal themes of the PE.

The regent master's lecture on Scripture held a privileged place

1. "Le commentaire des Pastorales ... date des dernières années de la vie de saint Thomas, et constitue non seulement l'un des meilleurs ouvrages scripturaires qu'il ait composé, mais un chef-d'œuvre de l'exégèse médiévale.... Sans doute, au point de vue philologique et historique est-il périmé, mais on le consultera toujours avec fruit pour ses notations psychologiques et surtout pour son élaboration théologique." Ceslas Spicq, *Saint Paul, Les Épitres Pastorales* (Paris: Librairie Lecoffre, 1947), vi.

in the thirteenth-century academy. According to Torrell, who meticulously examined the statues and bylaws of the University of Paris, when Thomas taught there the school year consisted of seventy-nine days of teaching, closing around the end of June.[2] Three main lectures marked the rhythm of each school day at the Dominican theologate of Saint-Jacques, as at all the other theologates of the University of Paris. In the first hour, the master delivered the principal lecture of the day, consisting of a commentary on a text of Scripture read with the standardized gloss, the *Glossa Ordinaria*.[3] As a rule, the master incorporated into his commentary theological questions precipitated by the biblical text at hand. During the second hour, the master's bachelor delivered a lecture on Lombard's *Sentences*, and in the afternoon lecture the master and his bachelor engaged their students in a theological disputation.[4] The themes for this dispute were established by the previous lectures of the day, above all by the master's lecture on Scripture. In this way, a theological dialectic emerged from the academic Scripture commentary at the University of Paris. It was by means of this process that Aquinas produced many of his *quaestiones disputatae*, such as his *De veritate*.[5] His lectures on the PE bear the marks of this same procedure, the scriptural text occasioning the incorporation of theological dispute and reflection into the discussion of its meaning.

Certain questions remain in the contemporary discussion of Aquinas's Pauline commentaries. Did St. Thomas, in fact, give these lectures at the University of Paris or a similarly structured institution? When did he deliver them? Are the lectures merely an inchoate, curso-

2. Torrell, *Saint Thomas*, 62.
3. See Beryl Smalley, *The Study of the Bible in the Middle Ages*, 2nd rev. ed. (Oxford: Basil Blackwell, 1952), 213. The copyists at Paris inserted this gloss either interlinearly or marginally in the texts of Scripture inscribed for the masters and their pupils. The *Glossa Ordinaria* was produced by various scholars who selected comments on Scripture from writings of the Church Fathers and from other commentators. Smalley contends: "Anselm [of Laon] was certainly responsible for the *Gloss* on St. Paul" (Smalley, *The Study*, 60), but recent scholarship calls this claim into question. In any event, this particular gloss was present in the copied manuscripts of the PE from which St. Thomas lectured.
4. Torrell writes: "Thus we can show the development of a day's teaching at Saint-Jacques in the following manner. In the first hour of the day, Thomas gave his lecture; after that came the lecture of his bachelor; in the afternoon, both gathered with their students to 'dispute' on a chosen theme. The three hours of this active pedagogy not being sufficient to exhaust the subject, they continued, article after article." Torrell, *Saint Thomas*, 62.
5. Torrell, *Saint Thomas*, 62.

ry venture into Scripture produced at the beginning of Thomas's academic career, or do they express the mature fruit of a lifetime of theological contemplation?

DATING

In the original catalogues of Thomas's complete works, we find two separate entries for his commentaries on St. Paul. The first lists only Thomas's *expositiones* on Romans and the first part of 1 Corinthians. The second lists his lectures on the rest of the Pauline corpus.[6] To account for these lists, Dominican medievalist and theologian Pierre Mandonnet hypothesized that St. Thomas taught Paul twice.[7] The evidence suggests that Thomas delivered the first set of lectures between 1259 and 1268 beginning in Orvieto where he was conventual lector and finishing in Rome where he was regent master. This accounts for the lectures from 1 Corinthians 11 to the end of Hebrews, which were handed down in the form of *reportationes* recorded by his *socius*, Reginald of Piperno.[8] Mandonnet conjectures that, being unsatisfied with these first lectures, Aquinas began to teach the Pauline epistles again in Naples, where he was regent master from October 1272 to December 1273—his death preventing the completion of this project. Thomas's handwritten *expositiones* on Romans and 1 Corinthians up to chapter 10 originate from this second set of lectures.[9]

---

6. According to Torrell, the two lists, one from Prague and the other from Bartholomew of Capua, "draw a neat distinction between the *Super epistolam ad Romanos* and the *Super primam ad Corinthios capitula XI* (or X), on the one hand, which are ranged in the first category of works attributed to Thomas, and the *Lectura super Paulum a XI capitulo primo ad Corinthios usque ad finem*, on the other hand, which takes its place among the *reportationes* made by Reginald of Piperno" (Torrell, *Saint Thomas*, 250). See the following works cited by Torrell: M. Grabmann, *Die Werke des hl. Thomas von Aquin: Eine literarhistorische Untersuchung und Einführung*, vol. 22 of Beiträge zur Geschichte der Philosophie und Theologie des Mittelalters (Münster in Westfalen: Aschendorffsehen Verlagsbuchhandlung, 1931), and "Fasc. IV, Processus canonizationis S. Thomae, Neapoli," in *Fontes Vitæ S. Thomæ Aquinatis*, ed. M. H. Laurent (Saint-Maximin: Revue Thomiste, 1937): 388–89.

7. Pierre Mandonnet, "Chronologie des écrits scripturaires de saint Thomas [1–3]," *Revue Thomiste* 33 (1928): 222–23.

8. More than merely a collection of class lecture notes, the *reportatio*, taken down by a professional reporter, was an official written record of the master's lecture.

9. The general framework of Mandonnet's theory on dating is adopted by C. Spicq

The Pastoral Epistles

Torrell reworks this hypothesis slightly, noting that Thomas's activities from 1259 to 1261 remain unknown. We do know that during his tenure in Orvieto from 1261 to 1265 Thomas composed his *Expositio in Iob*, completed *SCG*, and began composing the *Catena Aurea*. Torrell notes, too, that Thomas never commented simultaneously on an Old Testament and New Testament text, a fact not recognized by Thomas's biographers until recently. And since he commented on Job at Orvieto, he could not have commented simultaneously on Paul. In any event, it would have been physically impossible for him simultaneously to comment on Job, write the *SCG* and the first part of the *Catena Aurea, and* lecture on all of St. Paul's letters in this relatively short span of time. From this, Torrell concludes that Thomas must have lectured on the Pauline epistles for the first time not at Orvieto but at Rome during his sojourn there as regent master from 1265 to 1268.

Supporting Mandonnet's theory that Thomas began a few years later to lecture once again on Paul's letters during his second regency at Naples, Torrell cites the testimony of Tolomeo of Lucca (1227–1327)—an *auditor* of St. Thomas, one of his confessors, and one of his well-known biographers—who testified at the process of his canonization.[10] In his testimony, Tolomeo recounts the claim of a friar at the Dominican priory in Naples who dreamt that St. Paul appeared in the lecture hall while Thomas was lecturing on his epistles. After commending Thomas's commentary on his epistles, Paul took Thomas by the cape and they departed. Torrell notes: "The premonition in this dream has less importance here than the identification of Thomas as a commentator on Paul by his contemporaries in the last months of his life."[11] This sworn testimony would seem, then, to situate the second set of lectures on Paul in Naples. At that time, Thomas was able to correct rapidly his lectures on the first eight chapters of

---

(*Esquisse d'une Histoire de l'Exégèse Latine au Moyen Age*, vol. 26 of *Bibliothèque Thomiste* [Paris: J. Vrin, 1944]), P. Glorieux ("Essai sur les commentaires scripturaires de saint Thomas et leur chronologie," *Recherches de Théologie Ancienne et Médiévale* 17 [1950]: 237–66), and I. Eschmann, OP ("A Catalogue of St. Thomas's Works," in *The Christian Philosophy of St. Thomas Aquinas*, ed. E. Gilson, trans. L. K. Shook [New York: Random House, 1956], 381–437).

10. "Tolomeo says that he knew Thomas well, that he had lived long with him—at Naples evidently over some eighteen months—that he had been Thomas's *auditor* and frequently heard his confession" (Torrell, *Saint Thomas*, 271).

11. Torrell, *Saint Thomas*, 253.

Romans, which have come down to us in the form of an *expositio*. The lectures on the final eight chapters of Romans are the earlier *reportationes* as his death prevented their revision.

On the other hand, Torrell cites a hagiographical account of Thomas also teaching Paul at Paris provided by William of Tocco, another early biographer of Aquinas.[12] However, the manuscripts for both sets of Aquinas's commentaries on Paul were diffused exclusively from the Italian peninsula. According to Fr. Gilles de Grandpré, OP, chair of the division of the Leonine commission producing the critical edition of Aquinas's commentaries on the Pauline corpus, "The whole [manuscript] tradition comes from Italy, probably Napoli and went to Germany and Austria through Venezia. But the commentary could have been written in Rome. Those are points to be solved."[13] The Italian provenance of the manuscripts and the lack of textual-critical evidence for the claim that Thomas taught Paul at Paris leads Torrell reasonably to dismiss Tocco's account as an error of localization.[14]

Torrell concludes that Thomas's *expositio* on Romans most likely dates from the regency in Naples (1272–73) but that nothing can be said about the dating of his commentary on 1 Corinthians 1–10 with any certainty. Reginald of Piperno's *reportatio*, extending from 1 Corinthians 11 to the end of Hebrews—and this includes Aquinas's lectures on the PE—was recorded in Rome during Thomas's regency there (1265–68). The hypothesis that the first series of lectures on Paul was given during the Roman sojourn would situate these lectures in the beginning of Thomas's mature period—that is, within the last six to nine years of his life.

Torrell addresses several challenges to this theory. First, Thomas explicitly cites by name the *prima pars* of his *STh*, q. 74, aa. 2 and 3 in his commentary on Hebrews (he composed the *prima pars* during his regency in Rome from 1265 to 1268).[15] This citation seems to in-

---

12. He remarks on Guilelmus de Tocco's *Ystoria sancti Thome de Aquino* (Torrell, *Saint Thomas*, 253).

13. Personal communication with the author (June 13, 2003).

14. Torrell, *Saint Thomas*, 254.

15. "Aliter enim accepit Augustinus ab aliis sanctis, sicut patet prima parte Summa, quaest. LXXIV, art. 2 et 3" (For Augustine understands this matter differently from the other saints, as is clear in the first past of the Summa, q. 74, aa. 2 and 3). Aquinas, *Lectura super Hebraeos* (hereafter *In Heb*), cap. 4, lect. 1, [203], 2:380.

dicate either that the lectures on Hebrews were delivered after the composition of q. 74 or that Aquinas subsequently edited Reginald's *reportatio* prior to its publication. Aware of this problem, Torrell suggests the obvious solution that Thomas delivered his lectures on Hebrews (the last epistle in the Pauline corpus) at the same time that he was composing the *prima pars*, namely, at the end of his regency in Rome in the spring of 1268.[16]

Another, more striking difficulty presents itself in a long passage in Thomas's Colossians commentary that is similar in content to propositions 101 and 103 of the *Elementatio theologica* of Proclus (411–85).[17] William of Moerbeke finished translating this work into Latin in May 1268, so it would have been unavailable to Thomas any earlier. Though it is possible for Thomas to have speedily read and incorporated this work into his lectures, Torrell suggests that this passage was most likely inspired, instead, by Thomas's study of Dionysius and the *Liber de causis*.[18] This is all the more plausible since Thomas does not directly cite Proclus, but expresses Neoplatonic claims that harmonize well with those in the *Elementatio*.

Finally, if Torrell's theory is correct, over the course of his three years in Rome Thomas delivered 310 lectures beginning with 1 Corinthians 11 and proceeding through the rest of the Pauline corpus to the end of Hebrews. Add to that number the lectures from Romans 1 to 1 Corinthians 10 and we have Thomas giving no less than 360 lectures over the course of three years, an average of 120 lectures per year. He would have had to deliver *two* lectures a day on Paul if the length of the school year at Rome consisted of seventy-nine days of teaching, as it did at Paris. Though this would permit the needed amount of lectures (158 per year), this could not have occurred at a *studium generale* like the University of Paris, where there was only *one* daily lecture on Scripture. This difficulty is resolved by recognizing, as Torrell indicates, that the *studium* in Rome personally founded by Thomas was neither a *studium generale* nor a *studium provinciale* but rather an "experimental" *studium personale* such that "Thomas could freely ap-

---

16. This would be immediately prior to the composition of *De perf*, which Thomas began writing in 1269 and finished in 1270.
17. Aquinas, *Lectura super Colossenses*, cap. 1, lect. 4, [39–41], 2:133–34.
18. Torrell, *Saint Thomas*, 252.

ply there a study program of his own choosing."[19] Thomas certainly could have structured the curriculum to include two lectures per day on Paul. Interestingly, Torrell does not mention Aquinas's *Roman Commentary*, that is, his second and incomplete commentary on Lombard's *Sentences*.[20] If Thomas lectured on the *Sentences* in Rome then this text, along with the many other works he composed at that time (for instance, his *De Pontentia Dei*), would have to be taken into account.

In a recent essay, "Thomas Aquinas as Interpreter of Scripture," Thomas Prügl provides an untenable counter-theory, arguing that Thomas lectured on the Pauline epistles during his first Parisian regency.[21] That would place the lectures on the PE at the beginning of his academic career. However, Prügl's theory does not take into account the citation of *STh* in the Hebrews commentary. Unless we conjecture that Thomas inserted this reference at a later date while editing the manuscript, he could not have delivered the lectures on Hebrews much earlier than 1268 and certainly not as early as his first Parisian regency. More importantly, his regency at Paris lasted only three years (1256–59), with each school year consisting of seventy-nine days of lecture. Since there was only one lecture on Scripture each day at Paris, Thomas could not have delivered any more than 237 lectures on Scripture over the course of those three years. This reckoning falls quite short of the required total of 360 lectures. Finally, Prügl's theory does not account for the provenance of the manuscripts as being limited exclusively to the Italian peninsula.[22]

Torrell's theory is the most plausible one: Thomas delivered his lectures on the PE as regent master in Rome at the very beginning of his mature period, that is, concomitant with the beginning of his work on the *prima pars* of *STh* in 1265–68. The manuscripts of these

---

19. Torrell, *Saint Thomas*, 144.

20. See John F. Boyle, "Aquinas' Roman Commentary on Peter Lombard" *Annuario Filosófico* 39 (2006): 477–96.

21. Prügl, "Thomas Aquinas as Interpreter of Scripture," 391.

22. Confirming de Grandpré's claim, Torrell remarks: "There is no indication in the manuscript tradition in any case that the texts were diffused from Paris" (Torrell, *Saint Thomas*, 253). In his commentary on 1 and 2 Tm, Luke Timothy Johnson likewise argues for a later dating (*The Anchor Bible: The First and Second Letters to Timothy* [New York: Doubleday, 2001], 35).

lectures were probably diffused from Naples. Unfortunately, we do not yet possess a critical edition of Thomas's lectures on the Pauline corpus. Until that time, de Grandpré recommends the Marietti edition of Aquinas's lectures on Paul as the most reliable.[23] This will be the principal text for the lectures on the PE used in this study.

BIBLES AND TOOLS

Beginning in 1226, the official standard edition of the Bible at the University of Paris was Alcuin's notoriously deficient redaction of the Vulgate commonly known as the "Paris Bible."[24] Both Hugh of St. Cher (1195–1263) and Roger Bacon (1214–94) speak of a committee of university masters assembled at Paris in 1226 that mandated the Paris Bible, along with the *Glossa Ordinaria*, as the standard text for use in the theological schools.[25] Nevertheless, the masters at Paris did not utilize the Paris Bible and the *Glossa* uncritically.[26] The inadequacy of the official Paris Bible was widely recognized and scholars were charged with the task of correcting its errors. As a result, by the time he first began teaching at Paris, Thomas was able to make use of the various *correctoria* that had been issued by the Franciscans and Dominicans

---

23. "In the present state of the edition, I think the best thing should be to stay with the present printed text [viz., the 1953 Marietti edition]" (personal communication with the author, June 13, 2003). The Marietti text is preferred as it takes into account the Piana and Parma editions of the commentaries while expanding on this material with further text-critical scholarship.

24. Raphael Loewe, "The Medieval History of the Latin Vulgate," in *The Cambridge History of the Bible*, ed. G. W. H. Lampe (Cambridge: Cambridge University Press, 1969), 145–52.

25. Loewe, "The Medieval History," 148; see also Smalley, *The Study*, 334–35. Matthew Lamb notes that it was also standard in Paris at that time to incorporate into the lectures material from Peter Lombard's *Magna Glossatura* on the Psalms and Pauline epistles (Lamb, "Introduction," in *Commentary on St. Paul's Epistle to the Ephesians by St. Thomas Aquinas* [Albany, N.Y.: Magi Books, 1966], 20).

26. Richard and Mary Rouse note: "One inescapable 'product' of the Gloss, if we may call it that, was a keen awareness of its inadequacies. Masters 'accepted [the Gloss] as a necessary evil'; basic instruction often requires a textbook. The glossed Bible was the major effort of the schools to order the legacy of the past, biblical and patristic, via juxtaposition; but it was insufficient, and the masters knew this" (Mary A. and Richard H. Rouse, *Authentic Witnesses: Approaches to Medieval Texts and Manuscripts* [Notre Dame, Ind.: University of Notre Dame Press, 1991], 216). To underscore their argument further, they cite Smalley, *The Study*, 226.

earlier in the thirteenth century.[27] In particular, Thomas used the *correctorium* of the Dominican master, Hugh of St. Cher.[28] This unique text, standardized in Thomas's day for use by the Paris Dominicans at Saint Jacques, was not merely a critical and corrected edition of the Vulgate; rather, Hugh incorporated entirely new translations from the best Hebrew and Greek manuscripts available at that time.[29]

Thomas also had some access, direct or otherwise, to the Old Latin Bible and Jerome's two revisions of it, since he mentions textual problems concerning these translations in his commentary on the Psalms. He also cites several redactions of the Septuagint—though it is not clear precisely which editions he had at hand and how much use they were to him. In any event, the official Bible used by St. Thomas and his colleagues at Paris suffered from considerable corruption. Yet this situation precipitated a renewed interest in Greek and especially in Hebrew and that in turn inspired the production of corrected and, relatively speaking, "critical" editions of Scripture.

Regarding his linguistic aptitude, Thomas's comparisons of the Septuagint and the Vulgate demonstrate his familiarity with biblical Greek.[30] But Aquinas was not principally engaged in the philological aspects of exegesis and may have been limited in his knowledge of biblical languages. Even if this had been the case, it should not be thought that Aquinas was entirely inept when it comes to biblical languages and historical research. In his article, "Saint Thomas et l'histoire," Torrell demonstrates that Aquinas was sensitive to historical matters to such a great extent that he may even be called an "historian." Torrell provides numerous examples of Thomas's concern for accurate dates and facts, for the development of the history of ideas, for the verification of the authenticity of sources and texts, for ascer-

---

27. Smalley explains that the *correctoria* were "lists of corrections and alternative readings ... [and they] represent a specialization and systematization of the textual criticism in Stephen Langton's lectures" (Smalley, *The Study*, 335).

28. This *correctorium* is commonly known as the *Correctorium Hugonis* or the *Correctorium Praedicatorum*.

29. Lamb writes that Hugh's *correctorium* "offered variant readings and emendations to the Alcuin Vulgate text used at Paris. St. Thomas relied on these for his textual criticism, not on a direct study of the manuscripts" (Lamb, "Introduction," 21).

30. Biblical scholar Charles J. Callan, OP, notes: "He sometimes elucidates the Latin of the New Testament from the Greek" (Charles J. Callan, "The Bible in the *Summa Theologica* of St. Thomas Aquinas," *Catholic Biblical Quarterly* 9 [1947]: 40).

taining an author's historical context, for identifying the intention of the author of a text, and even for philological and textual-critical accuracy in his biblical interpretations. Aquinas regularly turns to the Hebrew or Greek text in his scriptural commentaries.[31] He also made frequent use of the *correctoria* to account for textual variations.[32]

Besides the critical *correctoria*, Thomas had access to a newly developed research tool, the alphabetical or "verbal" biblical concordance.[33] Not only did Hugh produce the standard *correctorium* for the Dominican order; by 1239, he and some fellow Dominicans had published an alphabetically-ordered biblical concordance.[34] During the thirteenth-century, alphabetical organization eventually replaced the "real" or "rationally-ordered" biblical concordance.[35] Thomas evidently had access to this concordance, "the finest achievement of thirteenth-century toolmaking," as well as to the more common rationally-ordered concordances.[36] This fact can account, in part, for

31. Jean-Pierre Torrell, "Saint Thomas et l'histoire," *Revue Thomiste* 105 (2005): 355–409. Discussing this feature of Aquinas's biblical commentaries, Torrell remarks: "On s'aperçoit, au contraire, que Thomas lit les textes de près et n'hésite pas à remonter au texte original, hébreu ou grec, même s'il n'est pas très bien armé pour cela" (On the contrary, it appears that Thomas reads the texts closely and does not hesitate to return to the original text, Hebrew or Greek, even if he is not well equipped for this). Torrell, "Saint Thomas et l'histoire," 397.

32. See Rouses, *Authentic Witnesses*, chap. 6, "*Statim invenire*: Schools, Preachers, and New Attitudes to the Page" (191), and chap. 7, "The Development of Research Tools in the Thirteenth Century" (221).

33. Of the verbal concordances and *correctoria* as medieval research tools, the Rouses say: "Their very existence has, in general, been overlooked" (Rouses, *Authentic Witnesses*, 222).

34. Rouses, *Authentic Witnesses*, 203. This concordance is commonly known as "Saint Jacques I." See Michel Albaric, "Hugh de Saint-Cher et les concordances bibliques latines (XIIIe–XVIIIe siècles)," in *Hugues de Saint-Cher (+1263): Bibliste et Théologien*, ed. L.-J. Bataillon et al. (Turnhout: Brepols, 2004), 467–79.

35. Thirteenth-century masters were reticent to accept the *verbal* or alphabetically arranged concordance, perceiving it to be a failure to identify the *real*, or rational, structure and sequence of the biblical text. The Rouses show that Hugh's alphabetical concordance was a radical innovation based on the insight that one master's rational order may not be useful to another: "The use of alphabetical order was a tacit recognition of the fact that each user of a work will bring to it his own preconceived rational order, which may differ from those of other users and from that of the writer himself.... Applied, for example, to the Bible itself, this notion produced the verbal concordance" (Rouses, *Authentic Witnesses*, 204).

36. Rouses, *Authentic Witnesses*, 218. A little earlier, the Rouses write: "Concording, relegated to the gloss in the twelfth century, now had a book of its own. At this juncture we

his extraordinary facility in cross-referencing and collating many similar scriptural pericopes from diverse books.

Thus, we can be sure that in his lectures on the PE St. Thomas was commenting on the Paris Bible, making use of the *Glossa Ordinaria* amended by *correctoria* (especially Hugh's), and benefitting from the aid of verbal biblical concordances. A thorough examination of the degree to which his commentary was influenced by the patristic and preceding medieval exegetical tradition would certainly prove to be an invaluable future study.

In his commentary on 1 and 2 Timothy, Luke Timothy Johnson identifies some of the principal commentators in the history of the interpretation of the PE.[37] Ceslas Spicq provides a more comprehensive listing in the introduction to his commentary.[38] Among the patristic commentaries on the PE, the homilies of St. John Chrysostom (347–407) are recognized as some of the best. He delivered eighteen homilies on 1 Timothy, ten on 2 Timothy, and six on Titus.[39] The commentaries of Theodore of Mopsuestia (350–428) supply historical and geographical data, along with information about the life of St. Paul, all of which are absent in Chrysostom's homilies.[40] The anonymous commentary by Ambrosiaster (late fourth century) and the commentary on Titus by St. Jerome (347–420) are also of great value. Jerome's is the only commentary on a pastoral epistle among the Latin fathers.[41] The few remaining commentaries on the PE from the patristic period include those of Pelagius (354–ca. 420/440), Theodoret of Cyrus (393–466), and St. John of Damascus (675–749).

Likewise, there are only a few noteworthy medieval commentaries

---

have come to the type of book that can only be searched, for it cannot be read" (Rouses, *Authentic Witnesses*, 215).

37. Johnson, *The Anchor Bible*, 26–35.

38. Ceslas Spicq, *Les Épîtres Pastorales* (Paris: Librairie Lecoffre, 1947), iii–vii.

39. John Chrysostom, *Homiliae XVIII in Epistolam primam ad Timotheum*, in *Patrologiae Cursus Completus, Series Graeca*, ed. Jacques-Paul Migne (Paris: Garnier and J.-P. Migne, 1862), 62:501–700. See the comments made by Ceslas Spicq on these homilies in *Les Épîtres Pastorales*, iii: "Elles constituent l'une des meilleures élucidations de la pensée paulinienne" (They constitute one of the better elucidations of Pauline thought).

40. See Theodore of Mopsuestia, *In omnes S. Pauli epistolas commentarii*, ed. H. B. Swete (Cambridge: Cambridge University Press, 1882). Also see Spicq, *Saint Paul*, iii.

41. See Ambrosiaster's commentaries in *PL* 17:461–504 and Jerome's in *PL* 26:555–600. See also Spicq, *Saint Paul*, iv–v.

on the PE. The commentary of Alcuin (735–804) was eventually superseded by the collection of patristic glosses commonly attributed to Anselm of Laon (d. 1117) and his school.[42] This collection made its way to the burgeoning schools of Paris by the middle of the twelfth century and continued to be augmented and redacted throughout that century, eventually finding its stable form as the *Glossa Ordinaria* in the early thirteenth century. This text is simply known as the *Glossa* and was standardized for use at the University of Paris.[43] All theology students there heard the master comment on Scripture along with the *Glossa*.[44] Peter Lombard (1100–1160) produced his own gloss on Paul's epistles that, like his *Sentences*, came to be regarded as a principal authoritative source.[45] Spicq notes that Hugh of St. Cher's *Postillae* on the Pauline epistles is "among the most complete and the most precise."[46] The other principal commentators in the medieval period include Haymo of Halberstadt (d. 855), Rabanus Maurus (784–856), Oecumenius of

42. See Alcuin's *Tractatus super sancti Pauli ad Titum epistolam* in *PL* 100:1009–26. In the same time period, Aimon d'Auxerre (d. 855) wrote his *Expositio in divi Pauli epistolas* (*PL* 117:783–814). Regarding this work, Spicq comments, "La richesse de son information autant que la sécurité relative de son jugement lui mériteront un grand crédit dans l'exégèse médiévale" (The wealth of his information along with the relative soundness of his judgment earn him great credit in medieval exegesis). Spicq, *Saint Paul*, v.

43. The prevailing account of the various glossators and of the development of various gloss collections and commentaries into the *Glossa Ordinaria* based on the work of Beryl Smalley is currently being amended in new research by Alexander Andrée and Mark Clark, among others. See, for example, Alexander Andrée, "Anselm of Laon Unveiled: The *Glossa Svper Iohannem* and the Origins of the *Glossa Ordinaria* on the Bible," *Mediaeval Studies* 78 (2011): 217–60, and "Laon Revisited: Master Anselm and the Creation of a Theological School in the Twelfth Century," *The Journal of Mediaeval Latin* 22 (2012): 257–81. This current and revolutionary research is pointing to Peter Lombard as the principal glossator of the entire Bible. I am indebted to Fr. Kevin Augustyn, who had been assisting Mark Clark in research on the *Glossa*, for recommending these references.

44. See *Glossa Ordinaria*, *PL* 114:625–42.

45. See Lombard, *Collectaneorum in Paulum continuatio*, *PL* 192:325–94. Spicq says, "[Lombard] a composé aussi une glose sur les Épîtres qui fit longtemps autorité parmi les Maîtres et les étudiants et pour son texte biblique et pour le commentaire" ([Lombard] also composed a gloss on the Epistles which was held for a long time among the masters and students as authoritative, both for its biblical text and for the commentary). Spicq, *Saint Paul*, vi.

46. "Ces *Postilles* sont parmi les plus complètes et les plus précises." Spicq, *Saint Paul*, vi. See Hugh of St. Cher, "Postilla in epistolas Pauli," in *Opera Omnia* (Vénice: Pezzana, 1703), 7:2–72.

Tricca (tenth century), Theophylact of Bulgaria (d. 1107), and Hugh of St. Victor (d. 1141). In his review of this exegetical tradition, Spicq hails Aquinas's PE lectures as one of the best scriptural commentaries that he had ever written and as a "masterpiece of medieval exegesis" valuable above all for the theological elaborations found therein.[47] Though this study does not trace in further detail the history of interpretation of the PE, several significant points of contact between Aquinas's lectures and the commentaries of his predecessors will be identified.

THE *REPORTATIO* AND ITS RELIABILITY

Aside from Thomas's commentary on the first eight chapters of Paul's letter to the Romans and on the first ten chapters of 1 Corinthians, his lectures on the Pauline corpus were published as *reportationes*—transcriptions of the class lecture produced by his faithful *socius continuus* (constant companion), Reginald of Piperno. How accurate are these transcriptions? In his biography of Aquinas, Torrell describes the duties of the *socius* assigned by the Dominican order: "These 'compan-

---

47. "Le commentaire des Pastorales que nous citerons d'après Marietti ... date des dernières années de la vie de saint Thomas [so he holds for a later dating], et constitue non seulement *l'un des meilleurs ouvrages scripturaires qu'il ait composé*, mais *un chef-d'oeuvre de l'exégèse médiévale*. Admirablement informé des interpreétations traditionnelles, le Docteur Angélique ne laisse pas de donner son jugement personnel; il analyse soigneusement le sens de chaque mot latin, la raison de son emploi; il l'explique en fonction du contexte et de toute la littérature biblique; il a surtout le souci de mettre en valeur l'ordonnance générale des épîtres et la structure de chaque paragraphe. S'il en résulte une composition trop systématique, la vigueur intellectuelle du Maître et son sens scripturaire lui permettent presque toujours de discerner le sens exact du texte sacré; aussi ce commentaire est-il cité encore par les critiques modernes même indépendants.... On le consultera toujours avec fruit pour ses notations psychologiques et *surtout pour son élaboration théologique*" (The commentary of the Pastoral Epistles that we quote from Marietti ... date from the later years of the life of St. Thomas [so he holds for a later dating] and constitute not only *one of the best scriptural works that he composed*, but *a masterpiece of medieval exegesis*. Admirably informed of the traditional interpretations, the Angelic Doctor does not allow himself to give his personal judgment; he carefully analyzes the meaning of each Latin word and the reason for its use; he explains it according to its context and the whole of biblical literature; above all he is concerned to show the value of the general order of the epistles and the structure of each paragraph. If the result is an overly systematic composition, the intellectual force of the Master and his scriptural sense almost always permit him discern the exact meaning of the sacred text; also this commentary is still cited even by independent modern critics.... One will always consult it fruitfully for its psychological notions and *above all for its theological insight*). Spicq, *Saint Paul*, vi; emphasis added.

ions' whom the order put at the service of its lecturers and masters in theology followed them everywhere, on trips as well as in the priory, and helped them personally in the preparation of their lessons. They served not as domestics ... but as assistants and secretaries."[48] The statutes in place at the University of Paris at the time required that all *reportationes* be personally corrected and edited by the master before their publication.[49] Praising the accuracy of Reginald's *reportationes* of Thomas's *Lectura in Iohannem*, Prügl says: "The quality of these notes was so remarkable that they were accepted by the University of Paris as an exemplar, that is, an official copy serving as an authentic text for further copying."[50] We can be confident, then, that Reginald's *reportationes* faithfully express the lectures as Thomas gave them. Though they may lack some of the polish found in his scriptural *expositiones*, they certainly are not lacking in substance.

THE STRUCTURE AND METHOD OF AQUINAS'S BIBLICAL COMMENTARIES

In a recent essay on St. Thomas's approach to biblical interpretation, Thomist theologian John F. Boyle notes: "Throughout his commentaries, Thomas is thoroughly theological; that is, he is first and always concerned with deepening his understanding of the revealed truths of the faith. Scripture always speaks to that faith."[51] Why, then, have his biblical commentaries been so often ignored in theological and biblical studies for much of the twentieth century? There are at least two reasons.

First, in the wake of the specific aims of Pope Leo XIII's scholas-

---

48. Torrell, *Saint Thomas*, 273.

49. "University statutes oblige the master to correct the report personally before it is published." Smalley, *The Study*, 202. This is confirmed by Tolomeo of Lucca, a contemporary of St. Thomas: "All the *reportationes* on Saint Paul were revised by Thomas with the exception of the one on the epistle to the Romans *quam ipse notavit*," cited by Torrell, *Saint Thomas*, 274. See also Lamb, "Introduction," 23.

50. Prügl, "Thomas Aquinas as Interpreter of Scripture," 390. Smalley further corroborates: "We know that St. Thomas Aquinas found it hard to replace Friar Reginald of Piperno, who was a particularly reliable reporter, when his services were no longer available." Smalley, *The Study*, 203.

51. John F. Boyle, "St. Thomas Aquinas and Sacred Scripture," *Pro Ecclesia* 4 (1996): 102.

tic revival, some twentieth-century Thomists did not find Aquinas's biblical commentaries to be useful in their task of adapting and applying his thought for the correction of contemporary philosophical errors that hampered sound theology. Concerned primarily with the apologetic, epistemological, and metaphysical problems of their day, Aquinas's commentaries on Scripture perhaps appeared to them as less relevant than his systematic works. But in overlooking his commentaries, they left untouched a rich strand of theological reflection. Polish theologian and bishop Wacław Świerzawski remarks, "Almost all of the theology called neo-scholastic which was based on Thomas omits from consideration what he had provided in his biblical commentaries."[52] Though their contributions to Christian theology and philosophy are unquestionably of great value, Neo-Thomists too often neglected the biblical foundations of Aquinas's theology.[53]

Second, many twentieth-century Catholic biblical scholars employing historical-critical methods did not find Aquinas's commentaries to be adequate as exegetical works precisely because they are *not* strictly and exclusively "exegetical" according to their admittedly questionable standards. Roland Murphy, for example, issues this warning regarding patristic and medieval allegorical exegesis: "If historical-critical methodology is not brought into play, there is nothing to serve as a control on the reading of the text by Christian imagination."[54] Since his method of interpretation was judged "pre-critical" (a claim heavily qualified if not contradicted by the survey of twelfth- and thirteenth-century critical tools, above), Thomas Aquinas's collection of biblical commentaries, comprising almost one third of the entire corpus of his published works, remained largely unexamined by biblical scholars as well.

52. "Presque toute la théologie dite néoscolastique qui se fondait sur Thomas, ne prend pas en considération ce qu'il a apporté dans ses Commentaires bibliques." Wacław Świerzawski, "L'exégèse biblique et la théologie spéculative de s. Thomas d'Aquin," *Divinitas* 18 (1974): 138.
53. Offering a corrective to this problem, Marie-Dominique Chenu noted that St. Thomas's "*Summa Theologiae*, despite its technical methodology, can only be understood properly as a living emanation from the *pagina sacra* (the sacred page of the Bible)." *Aquinas and His Role in Theology*, trans. Paul Philibert (Collegeville, Minn.: Liturgical Press, 2002), 21; originally published in French in 1959 as *St. Thomas d'Aquin et la théologie*. See also Gilson, *The Christian Philosophy of St. Thomas*, 13.
54. Roland Murphy, "Patristic and Medieval Exegesis—Help or Hindrance?," *Catholic Biblical Quarterly* 43 (1981): 515.

Both groups failed either to recognize or to accept the theological aims of thirteenth-century biblical exegesis. Neo-Thomists often did not recognize Aquinas as principally a biblical commentator rather than as a philosopher or systematic theologian. For their part, many historical-critical scholars rejected the theological purpose of his (or of any) biblical commentaries. And for both parties, their neglect of the overriding theological concerns of the medieval university commentator on Scripture led them to mistaken judgments of the relevance and worth of Aquinas's biblical commentaries. Prügl cautions contemporary scholars to be "mindful of the unified character of medieval theology in approaching Aquinas' interpretation of Scripture, shaped as we are by a rather different, modern, and more specialist understanding of exegesis and biblical theology."[55]

The Theological Purpose of Aquinas's Biblical Commentaries

Thomas Aquinas was, by profession, a biblical commentator. Lecturing on Scripture was the chief occupation of his academic life. Heinrich Denifle demonstrated that the primary theology textbook used by Aquinas and the other thirteenth-century *magistri* at the University of Paris was the Bible.[56] John Boyle underscores this fact, noting that two of the principal duties of a thirteenth-century master of theology were

> to hold periodic public disputations throughout the course of the academic term and to lecture on sacred Scripture. Although Thomas wrote a dozen commentaries on various works of Aristotle, he never taught Aristotle in the classroom. Likewise, the two great summas, the *Summa contra gentiles* and the *Summa theologiae*, were private works of the study; Thomas never taught them. What Thomas taught in his classroom as a master of theology was Scripture.[57]

---

55. Prügl, "Thomas Aquinas as Interpreter of Scripture," 386. For all that, contemporary critical exegesis need not be seen as excluding traditional biblical commentaries, as John Boyle notes: "The traditional exegesis and the modern critical methods need not be necessarily contradictory. But when one considers Thomas one sees how much more there is to the interpretations of Scripture, beyond that which is the focus of the critical methods." Boyle, "St. Thomas Aquinas," 104.

56. Heinrich Denifle, "Quel livre servait de base à l'enseignment des Maîtres en Théologie dans l'Université de Paris?," *Revue Thomiste* 2 (1894): 129–61.

57. Boyle, "St. Thomas Aquinas," 94.

Aquinas's official title during his two regencies at the University of Paris was *Magister in Sacra Pagina*. Throughout his entire career, he expressed a keen awareness of the privileged place of Scripture in the theological discipline. On receiving their office, newly-minted Parisian *magistri* delivered an inaugural lecture, setting the tone for their entire regency. In his inaugural lecture, *De Commendatione Sacrae Scripturae*, Aquinas shows that the foundation of the master's teaching is the *sacra doctrina* revealed in the canonical Scriptures.[58] Likewise, in his mature work, he claims that in the science of theology the authority of Scripture alone provides *proper* arguments from authority furnishing *necessary* conclusions (*STh* I, q. 1, a. 8, ad 2). In this text, Thomas contrasts scriptural authority with arguments from authority appealing to philosophical sources that remain extrinsic to theology and therefore cannot provide *proper*, but only *probable*, argumentation for theology.[59] In this same article of *STh*, he argues that the articles of faith, revealed in Scripture, constitute the first principles of the science of theology. These principles are self-evident to God and the blessed but accepted by the faith of the Church on earth. In practice, Thomas devoted his academic career to the interpretation and explanation of Scripture as the means by which *sacra doctrina* is revealed and understood.

The medieval theological approach to the exegesis of Scripture did not obviate, but rather mandated ascertaining the literal sense of the text. Medieval historian Beryl Smalley (1905–84) underscored the importance of this mandate for Aquinas.[60] However, Aquinas sought

58. Thomas's *De Commendatione Sacrae Scripturae* is the *Breve Principium*, that is, the shorter second part of his *Principia*, or inaugural lectures. It may be found in *Opuscula theologica*, ed. Spiazzi, 1:441–43 (see esp. 442).

59. "Sacra doctrina huiusmodi [*viz.*, philosophical] auctoritatibus utitur quasi extraneis argumentis, et probabilibus. Auctoritatibus autem canonicae Scripturae utitur proprie, ex necessitate argumentando" (Sacred doctrine uses authorities of this kind as extrinsic and probable arguments. But it properly uses the authority of the canonical Scriptures as an argument from necessity). Aquinas, *STh* I, q. 1, a. 8, ad 2. Thomas is not saying that philosophical arguments *as such* cannot conclude with necessity in theology; he is merely saying that philosophical arguments *from authority* cannot be used in this way. In this assertion, Thomas argues for the privileged place of the canonical Scriptures in scientific theology. For a basic study of the role of Scripture in Thomas's theology, see P. E. Persson, *Sacra Doctrina: Reason and Revelation in Aquinas* (Oxford: Blackwell, 1970).

60. Smalley, *The Study*, 300. However, she later came to appreciate the importance

the literal sense of the text in order to discern its deeper meaning or doctrine—to attain a theological insight. Ceslas Spicq observes: "If he applies himself to drawing out the true literal sense, this is only to the degree that these efforts are necessary and fruitful in order to elaborate a biblical theology as a source for his scholastic theology. A master of theology, commenting on Scripture, Saint Thomas perceived exegesis as a science subordinate to theology."[61]

Aquinas's ultimate aim in commenting on Scripture was not merely to discover its literal sense but to arrive at a theological understanding of the literal meaning of revealed doctrine and, ultimately, to provide the fruits of these insights as material for preaching. The literal sense of the text was the foundation for the edifice of Aquinas's theology, for he understood that Scripture itself is theological and that it provides the basis for further theological argumentation and elaboration. In his treatment of the nature and extent of sacred doctrine in the *prima pars* of his *STh*, Thomas argues that Scripture provides the first principles, or sources, of scientific theology, and he insists that all theological argumentation must be drawn from the literal sense of Scripture.[62] In the commentary tradition of the medieval schools that he inherited, we see a firm correlation between the interpretation of the sacred page and the theological inquiry and pastoral preaching that emerge in the very process of discovering its literal meaning.

The theological aim of medieval exegesis was pursued by systematically probing the text to uncover its presuppositions and to develop its further implications, conclusions, or moral imperatives—including even those about which the human author, it would seem, could not have been aware. This systematic examination most often took the form of *quaestiones*: dialectical questioning and rational demonstration used by the master to penetrate the biblical text, producing

---

of the spiritual senses for Aquinas. See her book *The Gospels in the Schools* (London: Hambledon Press, 1985), 265–66.

61. "S'il s'applique à dégager le vrai sens littéral, c'est uniquement dans la mesure où ces efforts sont nécessaires et féconds pour élaborer une théologie biblique source de sa théologie scholastique. Maître en théologie, commentant l'Écriture, saint Thomas voit dans l'exégèse une science annexe de la théologie." Ceslas Spicq, "Saint Thomas d'Aquin Exégète," in *DTC* 15.1, col. 718.

62. See Aquinas, *STh* I, q. 1, aa. 2–3 and 8, where Thomas argues that Scripture provides the first principles of the science of theology, and a. 10, ad 1, on the literal sense of Scripture as the basis for all theological argumentation.

commentaries that are distinctively theological in tone and purpose. With few exceptions, in the thirteenth century hard divisions between the various branches of theology had not yet developed, so this activity—freely moving between literal exegesis and theological argumentation—enjoyed an unfettered expression in the scriptural commentaries of this period.[63]

An example of this type of theological commentary may be found in St. Thomas's remarks on 1 Timothy 1:1, where Paul greets Timothy with wishes for "grace, mercy, and peace." Thomas asks why three gifts are mentioned here, while in his other epistles Paul only wishes two gifts to the recipients, namely, grace and peace. Why would Paul wish Timothy mercy as well? Thomas answers simply that, due to the grave demands of their office, "prelates need more."[64] He then proceeds to interpret "grace" and "mercy" in terms of the needs of bishops and their flocks, providing two alternate theological elaborations. First, *mercy* could signify the remission of the bishop's personal sins and *grace* "the gift of graces that prelates need" to minister to the faithful.[65] Alternately, *grace* could signify sanctifying grace personally needed by the bishop, and *mercy*, "the divine office that raises him to spiritual charisms."[66] In this short theological amplification, Thomas suggests that the greeting in 1 Timothy reveals the greater needs of prelates. A bishop—represented in this passage by Timothy, bishop of Ephesus—personally needs the divine gifts of the forgiveness of his sins and sanctifying grace so that he may be enabled to minister to the faithful by means of spiritual charisms.

There is a contemporary perspective that would view scriptural interpretations like this as overstepping the bounds of legitimate exegesis by assuming presuppositions and drawing conclusions not directly found in the words of the scriptural text itself. To address this

63. The most notable exception to the absence of distinct branches of specialization in theology is the somewhat autonomous development of the study of ecclesial law and its magisterial interpretation by medieval canonists such as Gratian. Yet even their undertakings were not envisaged as entirely distinct from the task of the medieval theologians.
64. "Praelati pluribus indigent." Aquinas, *In 1 Tim*, cap. 1, lect. 1, [6], 2:213.
65. "Gratia vero pro munere gratiarum, quo indigent praelati." Aquinas, *In 1 Tim*, cap. 1, lect. 1, [6], 2:213.
66. "Munere divino in spiritualibus charismatibus exaltante." Aquinas, *In 1 Tim*, cap. 1, lect. 1, [6], 2:213.

concern, it is necessary to understand the historical development of the thirteenth-century theological lecture on Scripture.[67] As masters of Scripture, Thomas and his colleagues at Paris were strictly bound by university statute to perform three primary and interrelated duties: *legere, disputare,* and *praedicare*—to read, to dispute, and to preach.[68] *Legere* meant more than merely "to read" a given text. It signified a sequential, line-by-line reading of a biblical text accompanied by the careful, magisterial commentary of the lecturer. Torrell writes, "'to read' Scripture was the first task for the master in theology, and therefore also for Thomas."[69] The charter of the University of Paris makes it clear that the magisterial lecture on Scripture was the first and, by far, the most important lecture of the day.[70]

These three magisterial duties at Paris—to lecture, to dispute, and to preach—resulted from the transformation in the twelfth century of the monastic *lectio divina*, a prayerful reading of Scripture aimed at promoting spiritual growth. Smalley traces the reception and development of *lectio divina* by the Victorines, especially Hugh of St. Victor (1096–1141), who was greatly influenced by the rules enumerated by Augustine in *De doctrina christiana* for interpreting and teaching Scripture.[71] In his *Didascalicon*, Hugh designs a program of scriptural hermeneutics that entails ascertaining the "letter," its meaning, and

67. The studies of Denifle and Smalley, among others, facilitated the appreciation of the historical context of Aquinas's theology and stimulated research on Thomas's scriptural commentaries and his use of Scripture in his theological syntheses. See also Glorieux, "Essai sur les commentaires"; T. Domanyi, *Der Römerbriefkommentar des Thomas von Aquin* (Bern: Peter Lang, 1979); Wilhelm G. B. M. Valkenberg, *Words of the Living God. Place and Function of Holy Scripture in the Theology of St. Thomas Aquinas* (Leuven: Peeters, 2000).

68. These three labors of the master in theology "were announced at the end of the twelfth century by Peter Cantor and later confirmed in the statutes of the theology faculty [of the University of Paris]." Torrell, *Saint Thomas*, 54.

69. Torrell, *Saint Thomas*, 55. *Legere* may also be construed as "to lecture."

70. Denifle cites this charter in "Quel livre," 150. See also James R. Ginther, "There is a Text in this Classroom: The Bible and Theology in the Medieval University," in *Essays in Medieval Philosophy and Theology in Memory of Walter H. Principe, C.S.B.: Fortresses and Launching Pads,* ed. J. R. Ginther and C. N. Still (Aldershot: Ashgate, 2005), 31–51. 71. Smalley, *The Study*, 196. M.-D. Chenu also describes the evolution of exegetical methodology from the twelfth century to the thirteenth in *Toward Understanding St. Thomas*, trans. A. M. Landry and D. Hughes (Chicago: Henry Regnery, 1964), 58–69 and 249–59.

its *sententia*—that is, its deeper meaning or doctrine.⁷² The theologian Otto H. Pesch summarizes this heuristic model:

> An exposition contains three things: letter, meaning, doctrine. The letter means the fitting order of the words, which we also call construction. The meaning is the obvious and open significance which the letter evidences outwardly. The doctrine is the more profound insight, which is only found through exposition and interpretation. In these three things there is an order, following which first of all the letter, then the meaning, and then the doctrine should be investigated; when that is done, the exposition is completed.⁷³

To discover first the "letter" or "construction" of the text, the commentator "divides" or analyzes it into its constituent parts. By means of this *divisio textus*, he clarifies the mutual relations of the parts, thus uncovering the "literal sense"—that is, the sense or meaning directly signified by the letter. This often spontaneously leads him to uncover the reasons behind what is said in the text and to discover the conclusions that follow from the text. To achieve this purpose, the medieval commentator would integrate *quaestiones* or small systematic chapters into his biblical commentary.⁷⁴ By this method, a doctrinal reformulation of the text is produced in which the literal sense is not abandoned, but is elaborated and built upon by an identification of its presuppositions and further implications.

Hugh's approach to scriptural interpretation was further refined and transmitted by the great twelfth-century Parisian masters: Peter Comestor (d. 1178), Peter the Chanter (d. 1197), and Stephen Langton (1155/56–1228). These three masters established the agenda of medieval scholastic biblical commentary: *legere, disputare*, and *praedicare*. This program found its definitive historical form in the academic life of the theologates in the thirteenth century. Thus was standardized the dialectical and logical *disputatio*, following upon the *lectio*, as the ordinary means to arrive at the deeper meaning of a text. By means of the disputation, the text is worked over with questions until it yields its meaning and the doctrine is discerned. Retaining and amplifying

---

72. Hugh of St. Victor, *The Didascalicon of Hugh of St. Victor*, trans. Jerome Taylor (New York: Columbia University Press, 1991), 6, 8–12, and 147–50.

73. Otto Herman Pesch, "Paul as Professor of Theology: The Image of the Apostle in St. Thomas' Theology," *The Thomist* 38 (1974): 591.

74. Pesch, "Paul as Professor," 592–93.

the spiritual purpose of the monastic *lectio divina*, the scriptural doctrine discovered by the *disputatio* must then be applied pastorally for spiritual growth through *praedicatio*, preaching, which was considered an integral task of exposition or academic biblical study. The duty of preaching has become somewhat foreign to contemporary academic theology; but it was an essential component that crowned and completed the work of the theologian in the thirteenth-century academy. Thus, the interpretation of divine revelation was both an academic and an ecclesial task directed toward a pastoral end for the good of souls. In his *Verbum abbreviatum*, Peter the Chanter employs the image of constructing an edifice of study in order to describe the interrelation of the commentator's three labors: *lectio, disputatio,* and *praedicatio*:

> The practice of Bible study consists in three things: reading, disputation, preaching.... Reading is, as it were, the foundation and basement for what follows, for through it the rest is achieved. Disputation is the wall in this building of study, for nothing is fully understood or faithfully preached if it is not first chewed by the tooth of disputation. Preaching, which is supported by the former, is the roof, sheltering the faithful from the heat and from the whirlwind of vices. We should preach after, not before, the reading of Holy Scripture and the investigation of doubtful matters by disputation.[75]

The action of "chewing" the text by scholarly disputation exemplifies the Chanter's transformation of the monastic *lectio divina*'s "mastication"—repeatedly turning over the text of Scripture in the mind to discern its deeper meaning—into a twelfth-century academic endeavor. Disputation analyzes the text by means of questions posed

---

75. Cited and translated by Smalley, *The Study*, 208: "In tribus igitur consistit exercitium sacrae Scripturae: circa lectionem, disputationem et praedicationem.... Lectio autem est quasi fundamentum, et substratorium sequentium; quia per eam caeterae utilitates comparantur. Disputatio quasi paries est in hoc exercitio et aedificio; quia nihil plene intelligitur, fideliterve praedicatur, nisi prius dente disputationis frangatur. Praedicatio vero, cui subserviunt priora, quasi tectum est tegens fideles ab aestu, et a turbine vitiorum. Post lectionem igitur sacrae Scripturae, et dubitabilium, per disputationem, inquisitionem, et non prius, praedicandum est." Peter the Chanter, *Verbum abbreviatum*, PL 205, col. 25, A–B. Note that the metaphor of "chewing" (a means of breaking down) does not, in this instance, signify the destruction of the edifice (i.e., the biblical text); rather, it indicates that distinctions are made by way of analysis ultimately for the sake of organic growth into a unified understanding of divine revelation. The purpose of making distinctions is not to separate the components of the biblical text, but rather to discern their unity and meaning in order to foster growth to spiritual maturity.

in such a way as to extract the frequently hidden substance. For Peter, the text itself provokes these questions and thus the disputation emerges naturally and organically in the course of a commentary.

Despite the fundamental continuity in this historical development from private monastic contemplation to public academic disputation, several significant monastics—most famously St. Bernard of Clairvaux—strongly resisted the use of scholastic disputation in biblical commentary. Yet Peter the Chanter and the other twelfth-century masters did their part to preserve the medieval academy from an excessive rationalism. These masters viewed human arts and sciences as ordered to knowing Christ, worshiping him, and leading others to the same knowledge and love. Thus, they proposed a scholastic, systematic, and dialectical approach to the interpretation of Scripture with the theological end of arriving at its meaning and doctrine. But they subordinated this theological end to a pastoral one, namely, communicating what has been understood to others by preaching and teaching. The *ratio* of the Dominican order itself reflects this aim. The order has been called "apostolic" since its charism is to bring the fruits of contemplation to others through preaching—hence, the Order of Preachers.

Aquinas and his contemporaries inherited this exegetical approach, and thus they sought to develop a systematic, theological understanding of the biblical text with the explicit purpose of preaching for the salvation of souls and the glory of God. The tasks of the lecture, the disputation, and the university sermon were eventually standardized as official academic duties by the theology faculty at the University of Paris in their statutes.[76] In his inaugural address, *De Commendatione Sacrae Scripturae*, St. Thomas correlates the university mandate of these duties with the command in Titus 1:9 to instruct in sound doctrine and refute those who contradict it.[77] Although these three obligations were not always viewed as distinct in the twelfth century, by the thirteenth century, they were clarified and distinguished. The theological disputations that were formerly incorporated into the lectures on Scripture were shortened, since at that time the disputations themselves began

---

76. Torrell cites the charter of the University of Paris to this effect (*Chartul.* II, no. 1185) in *Saint Thomas*, 54.

77. Aquinas, *De Commendatione Sacrae Scripturae* (also called his *Breve Principium*) in *Opuscula theologica*, [1213], 1:442.

to take on a life of their own in the newly-emerging genres of the *quaestiones disputatae* and the *quaestiones de quolibet*.[78] Smalley writes, "After this change in the syllabus, questions in the lecture [on Scripture] are short and arise directly from the text."[79] The *quaestiones* that continued to be incorporated into the lecture represent a *via media* between literal exegesis on the one hand and the various forms of extended disputation more or less remote from the biblical text on the other.[80] Having a distinct and independent venue for extended disputations, the thirteenth-century biblical commentator was at liberty to keep his *quaestiones* directly focused on the biblical passage in his lectures, producing integrated disputations that did not stray too far from the text itself.[81]

The integration of these medieval disputations into the biblical commentary developed organically as the ordinary means of achieving a deeper understanding of Scripture for spiritual edification. Torrell describes them as "active pedagogy where one proceeded by objections and responses on a given theme."[82] In fact, as with an article in an independent collection of disputed questions or in a theological synthesis like *STh*, they were often distinguished by the standard phrases: *"videtur quod," "sed contra,"* and *"respondeo quod."* Raising and responding to the difficulties elicited by the text itself, the disputations frequently developed argumentation with scriptural premises and theological conclusions. Such disputations or, as Pesch calls them, "short systematical chapters" are incorporated throughout Aquinas's

---

78. Pesch notes, "The ordinary professor, the so-called 'magister,' was alone concerned with continuous commentary on the Holy Scriptures. Only in public debate, the so-called 'quaestiones disputatae,' did the magister teach as systematician. And these 'quaestiones disputatae' had also been developed from the commentary on the Scriptures, both as an academic exercise and as literary form. For in the text of the biblical commentary it had long been customary to deal with 'questions' which arose in the context of the text in the form of a systematic excursus. Thus, the 'magister in sacra theologia' has been produced by the 'magister in sacra pagina,' and not vice versa.... But, except for the debates, his daily courses were concerned with the interpretation of the Holy Scriptures." Pesch, "Paul as Professor," 587–88.

79. Smalley, *The Study*, 209–10.

80. See Torrell, *Saint Thomas*, 60.

81. Theologian Thomas Ryan notes that, besides theological *quaestiones*, Aquinas also includes in his commentaries historical questions and even conundrums regarding apparent scriptural contradictions in *Thomas Aquinas as Reader of the Psalms* (Notre Dame, Ind.: University of Notre Dame Press, 2000), 27.

82. Torrell, *Saint Thomas*, 59.

biblical commentaries.[83] By thus systematically scrutinizing the biblical text, Thomas consistently develops a theology—or a set of theological reflections—in the course of his scriptural commentaries.[84]

Biblical scholar C. Clifton Black discovers in Aquinas's biblical writings "a thoroughgoing theological commentary ... an exegesis whose motive power is *fides quaerens intellectum*."[85] This motive imbues the medieval biblical commentary with a distinctively theological character. It also distinguishes the medieval commentary from contemporary exegesis since the medieval heuristic goal proceeds well beyond uncovering the human author's immediate intention and thus is not limited merely to an interpretation of the direct meaning of the words, even while it is inclusive of it. Though Aquinas moves beyond the text, uncovering its presuppositions and developing further conclusions, he intends to do so without violating the literal meaning. When executed correctly, this procedure in fact illuminates the literal sense.[86] Thus, to appreciate properly Aquinas's biblical commentaries, they should be seen as the *union* of exegesis and theological reflection. Theologian Christopher Baglow sees this fusion as "an extremely valuable exegetical trademark of St. Thomas Aquinas."[87] He likens Thomas to a molder "who works with a pre-existing frame or mesh upon which final materials (such as plaster ...) are applied.... A new model (in the case of Thomas, a new theological model) has emerged from

83. Pesch, "Paul as Professor," 592–93. Conversely, short biblical commentaries are found in portions of his systematic works, for example, in his *STh* see I, qq. 65–74, on the six days of creation; I-II, qq. 98–105, on the Mosaic law; and III, qq. 27–59, on the life of Christ narrated in the Gospels.

84. A. Paretsky notes that the medieval theological examination of the biblical text aimed at doctrinal formulations: "The twelfth and thirteenth centuries reveal the growing tendency of Scripture commentators to insert theological questions into their commentaries, the chief purpose being to extract from the text those teachings relevant to ... theology." Paretsky, "The Influence of Thomas the Exegete on Thomas the Theologian: The Tract on Law (Ia-IIae, qq. 98–108) as a Test Case," *Angelicum* 71 (1994): 549.

85. C. Clifton Black, "St. Thomas' Commentary on the Johannine Prologue: Some Reflections on Its Character and Implications," *Catholic Biblical Quarterly* 48 (1986): 694.

86. Brevard Childs explains the enduring value of Aquinas's Scripture commentaries: "As a master theologian, Thomas struggled in his way with most of the major problems which still confront a serious theological reflection on the Bible." Childs, *Biblical Theology of the Old and New Testaments* (Minneapolis, Minn.: Fortress Press, 1992), 41.

87. Christopher T. Baglow, *"Modus Et Forma": A New Approach to the Exegesis of Saint Thomas Aquinas with an Application to the Lectura Super Epistolam Ad Ephesios* (Rome: Pontificio Instituto Biblico, 2002), 112.

The Pastoral Epistles   95

the molder's labors, one which arises out of the fusion of the work of the two artisans. We can therefore speak of the theology of a particular Thomistic commentary as distinct from Thomas' theology in general."[88] Thus, Thomas's biblical commentaries can and should be examined for their own theological value independent of their possible role as a basis and support for his systematic works.[89] As such, they constitute an indispensable theological source and investigations of his theological work that fail to consider them remain incomplete.

The Prologue and the *divisio textus*

Aquinas customarily introduces his Scripture commentaries with a prologue headed by a passage selected from another book of Scripture. He deploys this passage, often interpreted allegorically, to introduce his reader or auditor to the primary subject matter and purpose of the main text.[90] For this reason, this pericope is called the *accessus* since it provides a point of entry to the main themes or "synchronic categories" by which the rest of the commentary is to be understood.[91] Thomas Ryan, following A. J. Minnis, calls this a "sermon type of prologue."[92] In light of this initial biblical citation, in the prologue Aquinas proceeds to identify the principal elements of the main text, often by structuring his analysis according to the four Aristotelian causes: efficient (the text's author), material (its content or subject matter), formal (its literary mode or genre), and final (its purpose or usefulness). Aquinas, however, did not inflexibly adhere to this model as he ordered his prologues with some variety.[93] In any

---

88. Baglow, *"Modus Et Forma,"* 69.
89. See Pesch, "Paul as Professor," 599, and Baglow, *"Modus Et Forma,"* 78.
90. See Aquinas, *STh* I, q. 1, a. 10, where he says, speaking of the spiritual senses that are founded on the literal sense, that the "allegorical sense" (*sensus allegoricus*) is constituted by the things of the Old Law signifying the things of the New. In his commentaries on Paul, Aquinas more often than not employs an Old Testament passage interpreted in its allegorical sense as the introduction to the principal themes of the scriptural text on which he will be commenting.
91. See Ryan, *Thomas Aquinas*, 17.
92. See Ryan, *Thomas Aquinas*, 13, and A. J. Minnis, *Medieval Theory of Authorship* (London: Scolar Press, 1984), 6 and 64. The lectionary of the *novus ordo Missae* takes this approach in the selection of OT readings that adumbrate or illuminate the NT readings.
93. According to Lamb, sometimes "he borrowed the introductory procedure of

event, the method of procedure in the prologue is a synchronic (as opposed to diachronic) identification of the principal themes, ideas, or arguments of the main text.

In the body of a medieval textual commentary, the principal methodological tool employed is the *divisio textus*—an analysis of the text into its component parts in order to elucidate their interrelationship and unity. This method examines the text's meaning diachronically, following the sequential order of the text itself, explaining its structure and coherence.[94] Aquinas employed this method, according to Matthew Lamb, in order "to define the main theme of a book and then relate each of its parts to this unifying center."[95] The *divisio* was not to be an artificial and extrinsic manipulation of the text. Rather, it was used as a means to discover and express the structure, distinctions, and unity already present in the text itself. Were these divisions merely imposed arbitrarily by the commentator, he would have failed to employ the *divisio textus* properly.

The *divisio* identifies the text's component parts from the most general to the more particular: the arguments or great themes are constituted by sets of propositions or statements, which are in turn constituted by individual terms and notions. Thomas thus often divides the text down to the level of the individual words themselves. This method evidently presupposes a theory of scriptural inspiration that discerns meaning in every part of the text. According to Pesch:

> The text is divided into large, small, and miniscule units, in order to clarify its inner structure, the exact sequence and the connection of the ideas. Nobody at that time was afraid to drain the text of its original vividness and the particular trait of its author. God is a god of order, also in his written word. Therefore, nothing in the text can be by accident or without intention. Analysis, therefore, has to investigate each word right to the last letter.[96]

---

the grammarians and speaks of the matter, intention, and utility of the book." Lamb, "Introduction," 22.

94. "The *divisio textus* method, which highlights thematic *development* . . . represents a diachronic approach." Ryan, *Thomas Aquinas*, 17.

95. Lamb, "Introduction," 26.

96. Pesch, "Paul as Professor," 589–90. In response to criticisms that this process is merely tedious and artificial, Lamb contends, "modern scholarship renders justice to many of Thomas' precisions." Lamb, "Introduction," 26. According to Boyle, "The genius of the commentaries [of Aquinas] is often in the division of the text. It is this divi-

But the analysis achieved by the *divisio* was not an end in itself. It enabled the commentator to perceive and communicate with great precision the sequence of thought and argumentation in the text that leads to its conclusions and, ultimately, to its rational and literary unity. The highly analytical *divisio*, then, is ordered to an ultimate synthesis. The text's distinct components are identified in order to appreciate their relation and resolution in an organic unity.

In this way a meticulous *divisio* is employed in order to arrive at a theological or doctrinal insight.[97] By this method, the commentator begins with a word-by-word consideration of the text to discover its immediate meaning. After determining the literal sense of the text, he then seeks to ascertain the presuppositions and reasons for what the author says.[98] Uncovering these reasons is a source of theological insight and when extended argumentation is warranted, a theological excursus or *quaestio* is incorporated into the commentary itself, as mentioned above.[99]

In terms of methodology, then, the medieval master's lecture on Scripture begins with a synchronic prologue that determines the subject matter and principal themes of the text. The commentary itself proceeds diachronically to discover the inner structure of the text and uncover both the presuppositions of and the conclusions that follow from its literal meaning. St. Thomas employs this method masterfully in his commentaries on the fourteen Pauline epistles. He views them as an integral whole, united by a common theme, specifically, the name (or the grace) of Christ. He sustains this perspective throughout his lectures on the Pauline corpus and it is in this context that he delivers his lectures on the PE.

---

sion that sets every passage in a context, or perhaps better, in a set of nested contexts." Boyle, "St. Thomas Aquinas and Sacred Scripture," 100–101.

97. Pesch describes the process of the *divisio* as follows: "To follow the text word for word and to rise to the 'sententia,' to the doctrine, only on the basis of the 'littera' and the 'sensus,' on the letter and the immediate meaning of the words." Pesch, "Paul as Professor," 590–91.

98. Pesch explains the rationale for this: "The biblical author *must* have reasons in his mind, if in the Scriptures nothing exists by accident." Pesch, "Paul as Professor," 591.

99. On these "small systematical chapters," Pesch remarks: "In an extreme case we meet within the commentary the structure of an 'article' customary in systematic works, i.e., objections, counter-objections, systematic statement, and answers to objections." Pesch, "Paul as Professor," 592–93.

As both Spicq and Torrell indicate, Aquinas consistently displays great skill as an exegete and even as an historian. Despite his alleged philological and critical-historical weaknesses, Thomas incorporates the best of prior exegesis—both patristic and early medieval. He conducts a sustained evaluation of the literal sense and he builds his theology directly upon it. As such, the scholarly consensus noted above is warranted: he is an eminently reliable interpreter of St. Paul.

THEMES OF THE PASTORAL EPISTLES ACCORDING TO ST. THOMAS

In the general prologue to his commentaries on the fourteen epistles of the Pauline corpus, Thomas provides as the *accessus ad auctorem* (the introduction to the text's author and subject matter) Christ's words to Ananias regarding Paul in Acts 9:15: "This man is to me a vessel of election, to carry my name before the Gentiles, and kings, and the sons of Israel."[100] For Aquinas, this verse describes Paul as one who bears the name of Christ in his thoughts, in his affections, and in his whole manner of life. According to Christ's words in this verse, the purpose of this vessel was "to carry the divine name" and Paul did so principally in his preaching, the content of which was the mercy of God toward sinners. This mercy is signified by the name "Jesus" which, according to Matthew 1:21, was given to the Messiah "because he will save his people from their sins." For Aquinas, Acts 9:15 adumbrates the entire work of Paul's life: he taught the gentiles, announced the faith to kings, and disputed with the sons of Israel concerning Christ.[101] He encapsulates these reflections in an analysis of Paul's epistles according to the four Aristotelian causes: the efficient cause (the *author*) of these letters is Paul, who is the vessel; the material cause (or *subject matter*) is the "name of Christ," which fills the vessel; the formal cause (the *mode* in which Christ's name was carried, that is, the literary genre) is epistolary; and the final cause (or *purpose*) of the epistles is the bearing of Christ's name to the gentiles,

---

100. "Vas electionis est mihi iste ut portet nomen meum coram gentibus et regibus et filiis Israel." Aquinas, *Super Epistolas*, prol., 1:1. Unless otherwise noted, all scriptural citations are my translations of the Latin text cited by St. Thomas in his commentaries.

101. Aquinas, *Super Epistolas*, prol., [3–9], 1:1–2.

kings, and the sons of Israel.[102] Since the very name "Jesus Christ" signifies the grace of divine mercy, the underlying theme unifying all of Paul's epistles is, more precisely, the grace of Christ.

Noting that the three groups mentioned in Acts—gentiles, kings, and the sons of Israel—directly correspond to the three groups of people who received Paul's written testimony in epistles, Thomas categorizes the Pauline epistles accordingly:

[Paul] wrote fourteen epistles, nine of which instruct the Church of the Gentiles [Rom through 2 Thes]; four, the prelates of the Church [1 Tm, 2 Tm, and Ti] and her princes, that is, kings [Phlm]; and one instructs the people of Israel, namely the epistle to the Hebrews.

His teaching bears entirely on the grace of Christ, which is able to be considered in three ways.

In one way, this grace is considered as it is in the Head himself, namely Christ, and it is commended thus in the Epistle to the Hebrews [the sons of Israel].

In another way, it is considered as it is in the principal members of the mystical body, and it is commended thus in the epistles to the prelates [the kings].

In a third way, it is considered as it is in the mystical body itself, which is the Church, and it is thus commended in the epistles sent to the Gentiles [the gentiles].[103]

Aquinas thus regards the PE as situated in an integrated Pauline corpus that he considers principally in terms of grace, at once Christological and ecclesiological.[104]

---

102. "Sic igitur ex verbis praemissis possumus accipere quatuor causas huius operis, scilicet epistolarum Pauli, quas prae manibus habemus. Primo quidem auctorem in vase. Secundo materiam in nomine Christi, quae est plenitudo vasis, quia tota doctrina haec est de doctrina Christi. Tertio modum in usu portationis; traditur enim haec doctrina per modum epistolarum, quae per nuntios portari consueverunt.... Quarto distinctionem operis in utilitate praedicta." Aquinas, *Super Epistolas*, [10], 1:3.

103. "Scripsit enim quatuordecim epistolas quarum novem instruunt Ecclesiam Gentium; quatuor praelatos et principes Ecclesiae, id est reges; una populum Israël, scilicet quae est ad Hebraeos. Est enim haec doctrina total de gratia Christi, quae quidem potest tripliciter considerari. Uno modo secundum quod est in ipso capite, scilicet Christo, et sic commendatur in Epistola ad Hebraeos. Alio modo secundum quod est in membris principalibus corporis mystici, et sic commendatur in epistolis quae sunt ad praelatos. Tertio modo secundum quod in ipso corpore mystico, quod est Ecclesia, et sic commendatur in epistolis quae mittuntur ad Gentiles." Aquinas, *Super Epistolas*, prol., [11], 1:3.

104. Remarking on this section of the prologue, Torrell says: "This long text does

A little further on in the same prologue, he identifies with greater specificity the particular themes of the three PE: "[Paul] instructs the prelates of the churches ... on the foundation, construction, and government of ecclesial unity in 1 Timothy, on firmness against persecutors in 2 Timothy, and on defense against heretics in the letter to Titus."[105] Accordingly, in his lectures on 1 Timothy, Aquinas examines episcopal grace, the requisite moral qualifications of the bishop's office, and the specific advice found in that epistle for effectively executing the pastoral duties of this office—for instance, on teaching diverse persons, on correcting presbyters, on ecclesiastical promotion, and the like. He regards 2 Timothy as an exhortation to a pastoral solicitude so complete that the bishop would even endure persecution and martyrdom for the welfare of his flock. In this context, he discusses episcopal grace and the special communication of the Holy Spirit in the bishop's consecration, along with other matters such as the erudition and moral dispositions demanded by the episcopal office and the proper method of correcting and, when necessary, opposing those in error. In his lectures on Titus, he examines the criteria for selecting suitable episcopal successors and the execution of the preaching and teaching office, particularly with regard to the challenges posed by heretics.

Attending to the doctrinal, moral, and spiritual insights that Aqui-

---

not emphasize solely the unity of Thomas's purpose; it also shows to what extent the ecclesial perspective is present in his thinking." Torrell, *Saint Thomas*, 256. Thomas consistently adverts to this same ordering of Paul's epistles at the beginning of his commentaries on each epistle. However, he did not confuse the order of Paul's epistles in the New Testament with the chronological order of their composition. Thus, he says, e.g., "Prius enim videtur scripsisse ad Corinthios" (But it is understood that [Paul] first had written to the Corinthians). Aquinas, prol., [12], 1:3; and in his commentary on Philemon, he writes: "Et epistolae Pauli non ordinatur secundum tempus, quia epistolae ad Corinthios fuerunt ante epistolam ad Romanos, et haec fuit ante ultimam ad Timotheum. Et praemittitur illa propter materiam, quia de digniori" (And the letters of Paul are not ordered chronologically, because the letters to the Corinthians were written before the letter to the Romans, and this was written before the second letter to Timothy. And that [the letter to the Romans] was placed first on account of its content and because of its greater dignity). Aquinas, *Lectura super Philemonem* (hereafter *In Philem*), lect. 2, [30], 2:333.

105. "Praelatos vero ecclesiarum instruit ... de institutione, instructione et gubernatione ecclesiasticae unitatis in prima ad Timotheum, de firmitate contra persecutores in secunda, tertio de defensione contra haereticos in epistola ad Titum." Aquinas, prol., [11], 1:3.

nas provides in his commentaries on the PE will significantly benefit the contemporary recovery of an essential feature of the episcopal office that is infrequently discussed but greatly needed, namely, that of conversion and holiness both for the individual bishop and for his flock.[106] In Thomas's estimation, the bishop, in order to fulfill his role as spiritual perfector of those in his care, must not only be converted to Christ but must also be quite advanced in his intimacy with Christ, in the conformity of his thinking and desiring to the mind and will of Christ so that he may perfect others in holiness. In addition to this, he must also have the wisdom to judge accurately the disposition of his subjects and the skill to lead them to that deeper intimacy with Christ which he should already be enjoying. Yves Congar has shown that the very ontology of the episcopal office has at its core moral uprightness, that is, holiness—fidelity to the gift of the Holy Spirit.[107] In his article, "Authority and Conversion," Joseph Komonchak notes that, for Congar, these "ethical elements" in the episcopacy ought to be understood within the broader context of the holiness of the Church herself:

[Congar] explains this in terms of the Church as a communion of which holiness is a constitutive element and the work of the Spirit is necessary in all members and for all activities. But if the Spirit's assistance is infallibly promised, it does not work *ex opere operato* by some sort of *"automisme de la grâce"* but requires fidelity as a duty and a gift. Perhaps we need a new von Balthasar to write an essay on "Magisterium and Holiness."[108]

Yet by describing the episcopacy as an active "state of perfection," Pseudo-Dionysius and Thomas along with him situate the quintessential element of holiness in the very ontological description of the episcopacy itself. Retrieving this insight will constitute a vital element in the contemporary development of an episcopal theology of holiness for which

---

106. For a recent treatment of the importance of conversion to Christ as constitutive of ecclesial authority and as the ground of the exercise of effective ministry, see Joseph A. Komonchak, "Authority and Conversion or: The Limits of Authority," *Cristianesimo nella Storia* 21 (2000): 207–29.

107. See Yves Congar, "Apostolicité de ministère et apostolicité de doctrine: Essai d'explication de la Réaction protestante et de la Tradition catholique," in *Ministères et communion ecclésiale* (Paris: du Cerf, 1971), 91–92, as cited in Komonchak, "Authority and Conversion," 227.

108. Komonchak, "Authority and Conversion," 227.

Thomas's PE commentaries serve as an indispensable source. However, his thought must not be recovered uncritically or without explanation, lest we risk confusion, facile dismissal, or even a clericalism that would mistake the *mandate* of active spiritual perfection belonging to the bishop's office with the individual bishop's *actual* spiritual perfection or lack thereof.

It should be evident that holiness is not automatic, nor does this term, "holiness," always correctly describe episcopal office-holders at any given place or time. In this vein, Hans Urs von Balthasar has indeed noted (*pace* Komonchak's desire cited above) that Pseudo-Dionysius's identification of the episcopal office with holiness and spiritual perfection is *prescriptive rather than descriptive*: it is the way things *ought to be* but *are not necessarily*. Nor is this identification "a naïve ignorance of the world," as von Balthasar remarks, but it is what the Church's hierarchical structure was intended to be. Von Balthasar in fact insists: "To understand what the episcopal office *really* is, we must think of it as embodied in one who has reached perfection, who possesses the fullness of contemplation, the highest degree of initiation into the mysteries of God."[109] A bishop manifests this holiness only to the extent that he cooperates with grace, ardently striving for profound communion with Christ. When said of the episcopacy the phrase *status perfectionis* does not signify that bishops enter this state to be made perfect (this is the meaning the phrase bears when said of the religious state). Rather, it signifies something too often foreign to our current way of thinking about bishops. As mentioned above, it imports the notion that suitable candidates for the episcopal state ought to already enjoy a high degree of spiritual perfection so that they, in turn, may perfect others spiritually.

Thomas's lectures on the PE might appear to some as merely moralizing ruminations since they are replete with exhortations to virtue and justice in action. That this is not the case becomes clear when the theology of the episcopal *status perfectionis* that animates and informs the PE lectures is uncovered. Aquinas's extended discussions of episcopal virtues and vices lay out in greater detail than in any of his other works the fundamental spiritual dispositions and essential actions

---

109. Hans Urs von Balthasar, *Explorations in Theology*, vol. 1: *Word Made Flesh*, trans. A. V. Littledale and Alexander Dru (San Francisco, Calif: Ignatius Press, 1989), 184.

required of someone in the episcopal *status perfectionis*—one who, replete with fraternal charity, actively assists in bringing about holiness in others. The episcopal theology in his PE lectures must be understood in this light.

According to Thomas, the PE reveal the graces of Christ operative in the Church's principal members.[110] These graces are given in the rite of episcopal consecration and they enable the recipient to serve fruitfully in ecclesiastical office. The bishop is given divine assistance to teach and protect the faithful. He needs these gifts of grace to exercise oversight responsibly on behalf of his flock—without them, he will be ill-equipped to fulfill his charge *ut gubernet populum*, "that he govern the people," which is, for St. Thomas, the subject matter of Paul's first letter to Timothy.[111]

---

110. Aquinas also considers the epistle to Philemon as addressed to a principal member of the Church, though the authority treated in that epistle is temporal in nature, not spiritual.

111. Aquinas, *In 1 Tim*, prol., [2], 2:211.

4

Lectures on 1 Timothy
Ut gubernet populum

This chapter and the two following chapters examine only those portions of Aquinas's PE commentaries that bear more or less directly and theologically on the episcopacy. Nevertheless, some exposition of the prologues and of the overall structure of Thomas's *divisio textus* is needed in order to contextualize his comments on the episcopacy and to establish the guidelines for our investigation of his lectures on 1 Timothy. It is suggested that one read this chapter, and those following, with the PE at hand or, better yet, with a copy of Aquinas's PE commentaries.[1]

THE SUBJECT MATTER AND THEMES OF 1 TIMOTHY

Aquinas introduces and discusses the subject matter and themes of 1 Timothy several times: (1) in his general prologue to the Pauline corpus, (2) in his prologue to 1 Timothy, and (3) at the end of his

---

1. A Latin-English edition of the complete set of Aquinas's Pauline commentaries was recently published: *Commentary on the Letters of Saint Paul: Complete Set* (Lander, Wyo.: Aquinas Institute, 2012). Though not including the Latin text, a superbly readable English translation of Aquinas's lectures on the PE has been produced by Fr. Chrysostom Baer: *Commentaries on St. Paul's Epistles to Timothy, Titus, and Philemon* (South Bend, Ind.: St. Augustine, 2007).

prologue to 2 Timothy. These prologues furnish the synchronic categories by which he orders the content of the epistles. He presents the PE as a set of instructions written by Paul for the bishops Timothy and Titus on the office held by those consecrated to the episcopal state.[2]

In his general prologue to the fourteen Pauline epistles, Thomas states that in 1 Timothy Paul, "instructs the prelates of the Churches ... on the foundation, construction, and government of ecclesial unity."[3] This epistle includes specific instructions on establishing and maintaining the structural and hierarchical aspects of this unity that constitutes the communion of the faithful, that is, the Church. At the end of his lectures on 1 Timothy, Aquinas grounds this ecclesial unity on the proper possession and exercise of the episcopal office, principally with respect to teaching and defending the faith. Ecclesial unity is, fundamentally, a spiritual unity predicated on a shared faith and mutual charity. The epistle instructs bishops on how to secure, safeguard, and promote this communion *by preaching* to bring about faith and *by commanding* to bring about charity. The bishop is to form his people in the true faith, govern them as their servant, establish laws, and impose penalties when necessary. All of his governing activity must conform to the moral law revealed by God. Aquinas thus roots his theology of the episcopacy in an ecclesiology of the Church understood as a hierarchical communion, in which the hierarchy should work to establish, perpetuate, and serve this ecclesial unity.[4]

In the prologue to 2 Timothy, he says: "In the first epistle [Paul] instructed [Timothy] about the Church's structure."[5] Accordingly, the lectures on 1 Timothy focus on the divine calling and grace that establish a bishop in his office, the moral qualifications of bishops, the duty of preaching and its role in establishing the communion of faithful, the way bishops should scrutinize candidates for the pres-

---

2. Thomas understood Paul to be the author of the PE, Timothy the archbishop of Ephesus, and Titus the bishop of Crete. See *In Tit*, cap. 1, lect. 4, [34], 2:309.

3. "Praelatos vero ecclesiarum instruit ... de institutione, instructione et gubernatione ecclesiasticae unitatis in prima ad Timotheum." Aquinas, *prol.*, [11], 1:3.

4. See Y. Congar, "The Idea of the Church in St. Thomas Aquinas," *The Thomist* 1 (1939): 331–59, where he identifies this same notion in Aquinas's other works.

5. "In prima enim instruit eum de ordinatione ecclesiastica." Aquinas, *In 2 Tim*, prol., [2], 2:265.

byterate, and the juridical guidelines for the treatment of accused presbyters in the bishop's ecclesiastical court—all having to do with Church structure. In his lectures on 1 Timothy, Thomas describes this epistle as "a pastoral rule composed by the Apostle for Timothy, instructing him in all matters that regard the rule of prelates."[6]

In his prologue to 1 Timothy, Aquinas remarks that Paul now begins—in 1 Timothy, continuing through 2 Timothy, Titus, and Philemon—to instruct "the rulers of the Church [*rectores ecclesiae*] ... on their establishment and usefulness," that is, on the origins of their office and its purpose.[7] By *rectores ecclesiae*, he here means to include both bishops (who are addressed in the PE) and civil rulers (addressed in Philemon)—both being *prelates* in the sense that they are "placed before" their subjects in a governing role. Whether episcopal or civil, all power originates from or is established in God (*instructio in Deo*) in three ways. First, citing Romans 13:1 ("There is no power but from God"), Thomas recognizes that God is the source of power for all rulers.[8] Second, he argues that the use of this power ought "to be directed" (*regulari*) by God. Supporting this claim by citing Proverbs 8:15, "By me kings reign and lawgivers decree just things," the word *regulari* in his comments signifies "to be guided," "to be regulated," or "to be directed."[9] All power originates in God and God must direct its use. In subsequent lectures on 1 Timothy, Aquinas explains how this power ought to be regulated—for example, in his comments on 1 Timothy 5:21 where the bishop is instructed to judge accused presbyters according to God's own justice. Third, power is established according to God's disposition or plan (*dispositio*), according to Daniel 2:21: "He changes times and ages; takes away kingdoms and establishes them."[10]

6. "Quasi pastoralis regula, quam Apostolus tradit Timotheo, instruens de omnibus, quae spectant ad regimen praelatorum." Aquinas, *In 1 Tim*, cap. 1, lect. 2, [7], 2:214. Thomas's use of the words *"pastoralis regula"* would certainly bring to his students' minds the *Regula Pastoralis* of Gregory the Great on the same topic that Paul treats in these letters.

7. "Hic instruit ipsos rectores ecclesiae.... Circa quod videnda est ista instructio et utilitas." Aquinas, *In 1 Tim*, prol., [1], 2:211.

8. "Non est potestas nisi a Deo." Aquinas, *In 1 Tim*, [1], 2:211. As stated in chapter 3, unless otherwise noted, all scriptural citations are my translation of the Latin text cited by Aquinas.

9. "Per me reges regnant, et conditores legum iusta decernunt." Aquinas, *In 1 Tim*, [1], 2:211.

10. "Et ipse mutat tempora et aetates, transfert regna atque constituit." Aquinas, *In 1 Tim*, [1], 2:211.

Thomas uses the same term, *dispositio Dei*, in his description of divine providence in the *prima pars* of his *STh*, composed around the same time as these lectures (*STh* I, q. 22, a. 1): "*Dispositio* may refer either to the type of the order of things towards an end, or to the type of the order of parts in the whole."[11] Thus, in his prologue to 1 Timothy, Aquinas's description of the episcopal power as being established according to God's *dispositio* signifies God's providential plan to establish the episcopal office as a means of ordering everything to God as the final end. Moreover, the execution of this divine plan establishing bishops as mediators introduces a hierarchical order among the faithful—an ordering of parts in the whole. Hierarchy is, therefore, an essential feature of the ecclesial unity for which the bishop labors. Episcopal power must be seen as originating in God for the purpose of supernatural communion.

The use of this power ought to be directed toward restraining human wickedness and guiding the faithful to virtue. To restrain wickedness, prelates (ecclesial or civil) must sincerely hate evil (interiorly), forbid it, and punish evil deeds.[12] Aquinas mentions the sincere hatred of evil first, since without this interior disposition a prelate will be unable to forbid evil consistently and punish it effectively. Here we have, perhaps, the first adumbration of a notion he develops throughout his lectures on the PE: pastoral effectiveness depends squarely on a proper interior disposition and formation, and on the bishop's own spiritual perfection in charity.

Continuing in the prologue to 1 Timothy, Aquinas mentions three further ways the *rector* (that is, the bishop understood as governor) is useful: "That he support the people by his power ... that he direct the people by his wisdom ... [and] that he restrain the unjust with justice."[13] Though he does not here elaborate on what he means by "support the people by his power," it is clear from his subsequent lectures

---

11. "Dispositio autem potest dici tam ratio ordinis rerum in finem, quam ratio ordinis partium in toto." Aquinas, *STh* I, q. 22, a. 1. In ad 2 of the same article, Thomas uses the words *providentia* and *dispositio* interchangeably.

12. "Item utilitas eorum ostenditur, quia est ad cohibendam nequitiam hominum.... Ea corde odio habeant.... Prohibeant ea ne fiant.... Facta puniant." Aquinas, *In 1 Tim*, prol., [1], 2:211.

13. "Ut gentem sustentet per potentiam ... dirigendo per sapientiam ... ut cohibeat ab iniustis per iustitiam." Aquinas, *In 1 Tim*, [1], 2:211.

on this epistle that he has in mind the episcopal duty to protect the faithful from false doctrine and to care for the temporal needs of the poor. As for directing others wisely, Aquinas often taught that the virtue of wisdom (*sapientia*) enables one to order things rightly and govern them well.[14] Equipped with wisdom, the prelate is empowered to direct his people to their final end and thereby participate in God's providence or plan (*dispositio*) according to which the prelate's power is established in the first place. Finally, the prelate must restrain the unjust. As will be seen, at the end of his lectures on 1 Timothy Thomas argues that bishops must undertake a real and arduous spiritual battle to secure the good of ecclesial unity. Since this unity is founded on the deposit of faith, the bishop's *principal fight* is to defend the faith and oppose false doctrine.

Thomas concludes his prologue to 1 Timothy by identifying that the "material cause" or content (*materia*) of the epistles written to prelates is the instruction of those who shall rule the people of faith (here he uses the phrases *rectores populi fidelis* and *praelati ecclesiarum*).[15] The prelates of the Church who rule in spiritual matters are instructed first, in the PE. Prelates who rule in temporal matters are instructed next, in the epistle to Philemon. St. Thomas identifies the subject matter of 1 Timothy as the bishop's duty *ut gubernet populum*—"that he govern the people."[16] In the lectures that follow this prologue, Aquinas devel-

14. See, e.g., Aquinas, *SCG* I, cap. 1, "Quod sit officium sapientis" (1–2).

15. "Et sic patet materia harum epistolarum, quia est ad instructionem rectorum populi fidelis, in quo quidam praeferuntur in spiritualibus, sicut praelati ecclesiarum, quos primo instruit; quidam vero in temporalibus, quos secundo monet; et hoc in epistola ad Philemonem" (And so the subject matter of these letters is clear, because it is to instruct the rulers of the faithful in spiritual things that ought to be preferred, as in the letters to the prelates of the Church, whom Paul first instructs; and also in temporal matters about which he next warns in his letter to Philemon). Aquinas, *In 1 Tim*, prol., [2], 2:211. It is interesting and significant to note that Y. Congar fails to cite this text in his essay "'Ecclesia' et 'Populus (Fidelis)' dans l'Ecclésiologie de Saint Thomas," reprinted in *Église et papauté* (Paris: Éditions du Cerf, 1994), 211–27.

16. Thomas concludes his prologue to 1 Timothy by introducing the themes of each pastoral epistle: "Tres sunt epistolae, secundum tria quae competunt praelato, quorum primum est ut gubernet populum; secundum, ut pro populo subdito patiatur; tertium, ut malos coerceat. Primum in prima ad Timotheum; secundum in secunda, ubi agit de martyrio; tertium in epistola ad Titum, ubi agit ac docet quomodo vitet haereticos, ut etiam patet in argumentis epistolarum" (There are three letters, according to the three things fitting to prelates, of which the first is that he govern the people; second, that he

ops a pastoral theology of the episcopal office, giving advice for prelates in handling various matters of governance. More importantly, in these lectures he elaborates a spiritual theology of the episcopacy that establishes the primacy and priority of the bishop's interior life as the proper conduit for the spiritual life of his flock. In order to lead others effectively to faith and to the mercy of God's forgiveness, to grace and virtue, and to supernatural union with God, the bishop himself must have already received these benefits and be living the spiritual life fruitfully. In his comments on 1 Timothy 4:14, Thomas remarks that the grace to be this kind of spiritual leader for the faithful, particularly with respect to preaching, comes to the bishop through the imposition of hands in his episcopal consecration. It is not something that can be attained naturally by one who is innately disposed to lead others. The bishop's effectiveness in pastoral ministry has its source in the prior and ongoing fulfillment of his personal spiritual growth and on the flourishing of his spiritual life. Aquinas's spiritual theology of the episcopacy thus forms the basis for his pastoral theology wherein he provides invaluable instruction for the bishop on how to guide the faithful to the same conversion and sanctity that the bishop already ought to enjoy.

In his lectures on 1 Timothy, Aquinas grounds the bishop's pastoral activity of establishing and protecting ecclesial unity in the personal grace and calling that the bishop receives from Christ himself. This activity requires, first and foremost, the bishop's own personal conversion and reception of God's mercy, forgiveness, and grace. Having been called by God to the episcopal office, the bishop supports, guides, and protects the faithful. This pastoral activity includes magisterial acts of preaching, hierarchical acts establishing individuals in the presbyterate, and juridical acts adjudicating cases of alleged heresy or wrongdoing.

---

suffer for his subjects; third, that he correct evildoers. The first he treats in 1 Timothy; the second in 2 Timothy, where he treats of martyrdom; and the third in the letter to Titus, where he teaches how to avoid heretics, which is clear in the argumentation found in these letters). Aquinas, *In 1 Tim*, prol., [2], 2:211.

THE EPISTLE

In his *divisio* of the text, Thomas partitions 1 Timothy into the greeting (1:1–2) and the message (1:3–6:21), and the latter he further divides as follows:

> I. On the management of spiritual affairs (1:3–3:16)
>   A. On faith (1:3–20)
>   B. On worship (2:1–7)
>   C. On appointment to ecclesiastical office (chapter 3)
> II. On the management of temporal affairs (4:1–6:19)
>   A. On food (with an excursus on the correction of presbyters; 4:1–5:25)
>   B. On riches and the different states of men (6:1–19)
>   1. On persons of low estate (6:1–16)
>   a. False doctrine vs. piety
>   b. Fighting evil and doing justice
>   2. On persons of high estate (6:17–19)
> III. Timothy's instruction to guard spiritual unity founded on faith (6:20–21)
>   A. Guard the good
>   B. Avoid evil

After examining Aquinas's comments on the greeting, the remaining sections of this chapter trace the principal themes on the episcopacy and its duties that arise in the context of this division, namely: teaching the faith, regulating divine worship, making appointments to ecclesiastical offices, teaching piety, honoring and correcting presbyters, examining candidates for the presbyterate, and waging "spiritual warfare" on behalf of the flock. It is precisely this comprehensive breadth of topics that led Aquinas to view this epistle as providing "instruction in all matters pertaining to the rule of prelates."[17]

In some instances, Thomas developed theological themes in his lectures on Scripture inchoately. At other times he offered a more substantial treatment that extended into the third lecture in the afternoon. Thus, some of the theology of the episcopacy found in these lectures

---

17. "Instruens de omnibus, quae spectant ad regimen praelatorum." Aquinas, *In 1 Tim*, cap. 1, lect. 2, [7], 2:214.

consists merely of initial theological assertions lacking extensive elaboration. This study primarily examines key portions of these lectures that express his more substantive theological insights. The briefer comments will be mentioned on occasion when useful for enhancing an appreciation of Aquinas's overall thought on the episcopacy.

The Greeting (1:1–2)

In his first lecture on 1 Timothy, St. Thomas comments on the epistle's greeting, "Paul, an apostle of Jesus Christ according to the commandment of God, our Savior, and of Jesus Christ our hope, to Timothy beloved son in the faith: grace and mercy and peace from God the Father and from Jesus Christ our Lord" (1 Tm 1:1–2).[18] In his commentary on this verse, Thomas acknowledges the power and wisdom given to humble prelates, he identifies the episcopal office with the apostolic office in certain respects, he points to the particular needs bishops have for mercy and grace, and he indicates their role as mediators of Christ's peace to the faithful.

Thomas notes that Paul describes himself by his name, by his apostolic authority, and by the divine origin of this authority. Similar to the remarks in his commentaries on the other Pauline epistles, he says here that the name "'Paul' means small."[19] Paul's smallness or hu-

---

18. "Paulus Apostolus Iesu Christi secundum imperium Dei Salvatoris nostri, et Christi Iesu spei nostrae, Timotheo dilecto filio in fide: Gratia, et misericordia, et pax a Deo Patre et Christo Iesu Domino nostro." Aquinas, *In 1 Tim*, lect. 1, 2:213. The Scripture verses Thomas comments on are printed in the Marietti edition at the beginning of each lecture with no paragraph numbers.

19. "Paulus dicitur modicus." Aquinas, *In 1 Tim*, [4], 2:213. See also Thomas's commentary on Galatians, cap. 1, lect. 1, [3], 1:565: "Ex nomine quidem cum dicit 'Paulus,' quod congruit humilitati suae, quia interpretatur humilis" (Also from his name when he says "Paul," which is fitting to his humility because this name is interpreted as "humble"); on Ephesians, cap. 1, lect. 1, [4], 2:3: "Paulus nomen est humilitatis" (The name "Paul" signifies humility); and on 1 Thessalonians, cap. 1, lect. 1, [4], 2:165: "Non facit mentionem de officio suo, sed solum de nomine humilitatis, quod est 'Paulus'" (He does not mention his office, but only the name of humility which is "Paul"). Thus Thomas customarily sees a connection between the name *Paulus* and the Latin adjective *paulus*, meaning "small" and he often extends its meaning to signify "humble." For an initial and extended argument for this interpretation that appeals to the Hebrew, Greek, and Latin origins of this name, see Thomas's commentary on Romans, cap. 1, lect. 1, [16–17], 1:5. Thomas's reflections here are certainly not original. St. Augustine, e.g., noted that the name "Paul" means "small" or "little." For instance, see his *De Spiritu et Littera* 12 and sermon 168.7–8.

mility is the precondition for him profitably to receive his apostolic authority, "for there are two things present in apostleship, namely, lofty power, to which the humble are raised (1 Kings 15:17) ... and the clarity of wisdom that the Lord offers to the very small (Mt 11:25)."[20] As he said in the prologue, the prelate must "direct the people by his wisdom," yet humility is necessary to receive this wisdom and also to receive episcopal power fruitfully.

Paul's authority originates from Christ by divine command: "An apostle of Jesus Christ according to the command of God our savior, and of Christ Jesus our hope" (1 Tm 1:1).[21] Noting that the "command of God" in this verse refers to the basic duty of the episcopal office to preach the Gospel, Aquinas says: "From this it is clear that prelates are obliged, by a necessity of precept, to those things proper to their office: 'Woe unto me, if I preach not the Gospel' (1 Corinthians 9:16)."[22] The primacy of the preaching office for prelates here becomes a theme that Aquinas elaborates throughout his remaining lectures on the PE, arguing that preaching is the preeminent and proper duty of bishops insofar as it brings about the unity of the Church, the unity of faith.[23] Historically speaking, his thoughts on this matter were very likely informed both by his reading of Gratian's *Concordia discordantium canonum* (twelfth century) and by the mandate of the Fourth Lateran Council (1215) requiring bishops to provide for preaching in their dioceses.[24] The Albigensian crisis prompted the

20. "In apostolatu enim duo sunt, scilicet altitudo potestatis, ad quam exaltantur humiles (I Reg. xv, 17) ... item claritas sapientiae, et hanc Dominus praebet parvulis (Matth. xi, 25)." Aquinas, *In 1 Tim*, [4], 2:213.

21. "Apostolus Iesu Christi secundum imperium Dei Salvatoris nostri, et Christi Iesu spei nostrae." Aquinas, *In 1 Tim*, cap. 1, lect. 1, 2:213.

22. "Ex quo patet quod praelati ex necessitate praecepti tenentur ad ea quae sunt proprii officii. I Cor. c. ix, 16: 'Vae mihi enim est, si non evangelizavero.'" Aquinas, *In 1 Tim*, [4], 2:213.

23. In a later lecture, Thomas says that teaching is the "officium proprium praelati" (proper office of the prelate). Aquinas, *In 1 Tim*, cap. 3, lect. 1, [101], 2:233. See also Aquinas, *STh* III, q. 67, a. 2, ad 1, where he calls the bishop's teaching office *"principalissimum"* (most important). *Lumen Gentium* notes that preaching the Gospel is the principal duty of bishops (no. 25).

24. Thomas, in fact, cites Gratian's *Decretum*, cap. 16, q. 1, can. 39, regarding the doctrine of preaching pertaining especially to prelates in *Cont imp*, cap. 1, [32] (*Opuscula theologica*, ed. Spiazzi, 13). See also Fourth Lateran Council, *Constitutions*, chap. 10, "On appointing preachers," in *Decrees*, ed. Tanner, 1:239–40; and Thomas Ryan, *Thomas Aquinas as Reader of the Psalms*, 11.

Church to renew the preaching ministry and led to the establishing of the Order of Preachers.[25] Theologically speaking, Aquinas views preaching as an activity that constitutes the Church as a *congregatio fidelium*. The bishop's preaching ministry is paramount since it brings about and strengthens people's faith, thus both bringing into being and strengthening the Church itself.

In verse 2, Timothy is greeted with wishes of "grace, mercy, and peace." Aquinas remarks that Paul here enumerates three goods instead of the two he usually mentions in the epistles to the Gentiles—grace and peace—because "prelates need more."[26] Grace and mercy are wished "first for [Timothy], and then for the others," and he sees in this an indication that the ecclesial hierarchy is structured such that God's divine gifts are communicated first to prelates and through them to the faithful.[27] A prelate, then, stands in greater need of God's gifts so that he may be a suitable mediator of these same gifts to the faithful.

Aquinas next provides two alternate theological elaborations of "grace" and "mercy." In each instance, he interprets one of these gifts as meeting the bishop's personal needs and the other as supplying what the bishop needs to minister to others. First, "'Mercy' is taken for the remission of sins, because this comes from God's mercy; and 'grace' for the gift of graces that prelates need."[28] Here, he roughly fol-

---

25. M.-D. Chenu describes the historical development of the importance of preaching in the twelfth and thirteenth centuries: "If the *vita apostolica*, in the literal sense of the term, was the decisive force and model of these new groups, it was because the word of God took priority in their thought as in their zeal. Allan of Lille, in his brief tract on the art of preaching, undoubtedly based on his missionary experience among the Cathari (after 1185), placed preaching at the top of his ladder of perfection, as the seventh degree, over the investigation of doubts (fifth degree) and the exposition of sacred scripture (sixth degree), a marked change for those familiar with the usual categories of the classical ladder. [Here Chenu refers to the "ladders" of Benedict, Bernard, and Hugh of St. Victor, for whom the top rung was personal perfection.] This awakening to preaching towards the close of the twelfth century, an awakening that led to the founding of an Order of Preachers, is all the more striking when compared with the deadly silence that prevailed in the church during the previous decades despite pathetic appeals from Rome." Chenu, *Nature, Man, and Society in the Twelfth Century: Essays on New Theological Perspectives in the Latin West*, trans. Jerome Taylor and Lester Little (Toronto: University of Toronto Press, 1997), 247. Chenu proceeds to trace the development in the twelfth century of the idea of preaching as the goal of all theological education.

26. "Praelati pluribus indigent." Aquinas, *In 1 Tim*, cap. 1, lect. 1, [6], 2:213.

27. "Primo sibi, et deinde aliis." Aquinas, *In 1 Tim*, cap. 1, lect. 1, [6], 2:213.

28. "Et sumitur hic misericordia pro remissione peccatorum, quia haec est ex Dei

lows a commentary received as authoritative in the academy at that time, namely, Peter Lombard's *Collectaneorum in Paulum continuatio*: "Note that in this greeting he wishes three things, whereas in the others only two. 'Mercy' here is taken for what in the other epistles is called grace, that is, the remission of sins.... Here he wishes for bishops grace, that is, the gift of the Holy Spirit, with which the ministers of God are equipped."[29] Not content merely to repeat Lombard, Aquinas provides another reason why specifically three gifts are wished: prelates need more divine assistance than do other Christians because their duties are greater.[30]

His alternate interpretation of this pericope is without precedent: "'Grace,' as in the other epistles, stands for justifying grace; but 'mercy' for the divine gift of being raised to spiritual charisms."[31] The gift elevating the bishop to spiritual charisms is called "mercy," in the sense that God mercifully chooses a sinful member of the faithful—one who himself stands in need of sanctifying grace—to become a minister of God's grace and mercy to others.[32]

That the prelate ought to bring God's peace to the faithful is certainly the sense Aquinas gives to the end of verse 2, "peace from God the Father and Christ Jesus our Lord." Citing Psalm 71:3, "Let the mountains receive peace," he says that Paul wishes this peace to be

---

misericordia; gratia vero pro munere gratiarum, quo indigent praelati." Aquinas, *In 1 Tim*, [6], 2:213.

29. "Attende quod in hac salutatione tria ponit quae ei optat, cum in aliis tantum duo posuerit. Misericordia hic accipitur quod in aliis Epistolis dicitur gratia, id est remissio peccatorum.... Gratia vero quam hic addit episcopis optatur, id est donatio Spiritus sancti, quo ministri Dei armantur." Peter Lombard, *Collectaneorum in Paulum continuatio*, "In Epistolam I ad Timothaeum," PL 192, col. 327B. See the *Glossa*, PL 114, col. 623D. This interpretation is also found in *Quaestiones et decisiones in Epistolas S. Pauli*, formerly attributed to Hugh of St. Victor, cap. 10, "In Epistolam I ad Timotheum," PL 175, col. 594D.

30. Aquinas does not incorporate into this lecture Lombard's remarks on the communication of the Holy Spirit, though he mentions a special communication of the Holy Spirit in the ordination of bishops in his comments on 2 Tm 1:6 (see *In 2 Tim*, cap. 1, lect. 3, [13], 2:269).

31. "Vel gratia, sicut in aliis, pro gratia iustificante, sed misericordia pro munere divino in spiritualibus charismatibus exaltante." Aquinas, *In 1 Tim*, cap. 1, lect. 1, [6], 2:213.

32. As these lectures are not systematic treatises, Aquinas does not always provide strict definitions of terms. He deploys the term "mercy" throughout this commentary to signify "a sorrowful heart for another's distress." See Aquinas, STh II-II, q. 30, a. 1: "Dicitur enim misericordia ex eo quod aliquis habet miserum cor super miseria alterius."

"with you and through you to others."[33] Years before delivering this lecture, Thomas wrote the following in his *Sentences* commentary on the mediatorial role of those holding a degree of order in the Church: "The ministers of the Church are not placed over others that they [namely, the subjects] may attribute to them [namely, the ministers] anything by virtue of their own holiness, because this belongs to God alone; but they are placed over others as ministers, and in a certain sense as instruments of the outpouring from the Head to the members."[34]

Implying this earlier notion of mediation here in his lecture on 1 Timothy, Aquinas presents the prelate as the instrument of God's peace for the faithful. In this short theological amplification of verse 2, Aquinas shows that the bishop personally needs the remission of his sins, sanctifying grace, and spiritual charisms in order to meet the spiritual needs of the faithful under his charge.

Teaching the Faith (1:3–20)

According to Thomas, the first chapter of 1 Timothy provides instruction on how to lead people "to the form of true faith."[35] He delivers a total of four lectures on chapter 1: in addition to his first lecture on the greeting (1:1–2) which we just examined, the other three lectures reflect theologically on the priority of the bishop's teaching office for the proper worship of God and for the salvation of the faithful (1 Tm 1:3–20). Then lect. 2 contextualizes the discussion of the teaching office within the historical doctrinal problems recounted in 1:3–4, identifying true doctrine with charity. In lect. 3, Aquinas provides a brief etiology of false doctrine, tracing it ultimately to the loss of charity rather than merely to an error of understanding. And in lect. 4, he ex-

---

33. "Suscipiant montes pacem." Aquinas, *In 1 Tim*, cap. 1, lect. 1, [6], 2:213 (contemporary editions of the Bible list this as Ps 72:3). The latter quotation is "'Et pax,' scilicet tecum, et per te aliis." Aquinas, *In 1 Tim*, cap. 1, lect. 1, [6], 2:213.

34. "Sed ministri Ecclesiae non praeponuntur aliis ut eis ex propriae sanctitatis virtute aliquid tribuant, quia hoc solius Dei est; sed sicut ministri, et quodammodo instrumenta illius effluxus qui fit a capite in membra." *In IV Sent*, d. 24, q. 1, a. 3, qua. 5, sol. 3, ad 2, 7.2:894; in this article, Thomas answers the question, "Whether goodness of life is required for those receiving orders?" In this same article, Aquinas cites chap. 4 of Pseudo-Dionysius's *Ecclesiastical Hierarchy*, showing that he read this work at least as early as his *Sentences* commentary. Compare this with what he says in *In IV Sent*, d. 18, q. 1, a. 1, qua. 1, 7.2:808–10.

35. "Ad formam verae fidei." Aquinas, *In 1 Tim*, cap. 2, lect. 1, [55], 2:223.

plains Paul's description (1 Tm 1:18) of the bishop's duty to teach and guard the true faith as "spiritual warfare."

At the beginning of lect. 2, Aquinas argues that it pertains to prelates first to teach the faith and to safeguard this teaching.[36] In a later lecture (on 1 Tm 2), he contends that salvation itself is not possible without a proper understanding of the truths of the faith.[37] Teaching the faith is ultimately ordered to the supernatural final end of human life, the beatific vision of God. Here in lect. 2 (on 1 Tm 1) he argues that Paul first instructs Timothy on teaching according to the rule of faith before dealing with prelates instructing the faithful in matters of worship (treated later in 1 Tm 2:1–7) because divine worship presupposes right faith.[38]

In 1 Timothy 1:3–4, Timothy is instructed to protect his flock from the false teachings of those who misunderstood the Mosaic law. Thomas notes that the doctrinal question here concerned the extent to which the Mosaic law was to be retained in Christian doctrine, since the false teachers evidently wished to be "teachers of the law" (1:7). Aquinas understands Paul's exhortations to Timothy to "charge them not to teach otherwise" (1:3) and to warn the faithful "not to give heed to fables and endless genealogies" (1:4) as an appeal to a particular historical case in order to provide a general or universal principle for all bishops: "Two things pertain to a prelate: first, that he restrain those who teach what is false. And so Paul says 'not to teach otherwise' .... Secondly, if it should happen that some are teaching what is false, that he [the bishop] forbid the people to pay attention to them."[39] Those whom Timothy was to charge "not to teach otherwise"—that is, not to teach something other than the Gospel of Christ preached by Paul—were false teach-

36. He begins the second lecture: "Item ad praelatum pertinet primo quod doceat de forma fidei, ne fides subditorum corrumpatur" (Likewise it pertains to the prelate first that he teach the form of the faith lest the faith of his subjects be corrupted). Aquinas, *In 1 Tim*, cap. 1, lect. 2, [7], 2:214.

37. "Salus non est nisi per agnitionem veritatis" (Salvation is not possible apart from the knowledge of the truth). Aquinas, *In 1 Tim*, cap. 2, lect. 1, [62], 2:225.

38. "Secundo ut instruat eos de pertinentibus ad cultum Dei, quod non potest esse, nisi fides sit recta" (Second, that he instruct them regarding things pertaining to the worship of God, which is not possible without right faith). Aquinas, *In 1 Tim*, cap. 1, lect. 2, [7], 2:214.

39. "Duo pertinent ad praelatum, ut cohibeat docentes falsa. Et ideo dicit 'ne aliter docerent.' ... Secundo, ut si contingat quod aliqui falsa docerent, prohibeat populum ne eis intendant." Aquinas, *In 1 Tim*, [8], 2:214.

ers confusing the faithful of Ephesus with "fables and endless genealogies." Thomas echoes an older exegetical tradition attributing the source of this doctrinal controversy to certain Jews in Ephesus when he comments that these fables were "handed down orally, namely, in the Talmud ... such as the foolish fable that Adam had another wife, from whom demons were born."[40]

For this study, it is not as important to determine the historical identity of these false teachers as it is to understand that Aquinas, following Paul, uses these verses as a case study to establish the bishop's grave responsibility to preserve the integrity of the true faith for the

40. "Dicit ergo fabulas, non datam legem in scriptis, sed in ore, scilicet Thalmuth ... ut sunt stultae fabulae, scilicet quod Adam habuit aliam uxorem, ex qua dicunt natos daemones." Aquinas, *In 1 Tim*, [9]. Without tracing in detail the transmission of this interpretation, it is possible to identify a few likely sources for Aquinas's comments here. See, e.g., Augustine's *Contra adversarium legis et prophetarum*, book 2, cap. 1, where he says: "Nescit autem habere praeter Scripturas legitimas et propheticas Judaeos quasdam traditiones suas, quas non scriptas habent, sed memoriter tenent, et alter in alterum loquendo transfundit, quas deuterosin vocant: ubi etiam dicere audent et credere, Deum primo homini duas creasse mulieres; ex quibus texunt genealogias, vere, sicut ait Apostolus, infinitas, parientes infructuosissimas quaestiones" (*PL* 42, col. 637). Virtually the same text, with slight alterations, is found in the medieval *Quaestiones et decisiones in Epistolas S. Pauli* attributed to Hugh of St. Victor ("In Epistolam I ad Timotheum," quaest. 4, *PL* 175, col. 594D-595A): "Vel fabulas hic dicit traditiones, quas Judaei non scriptas tenent, et alter in alterum transfundit loquendo, quas deuterosin vocant: ubi dicunt, et credunt duas uxores Deum primo creasse, ex quibus hominum texunt genealogias infinitas parientes infructuosas quaestiones." Perhaps *deuterosin* and what Aquinas here calls "Thalmuth" (the Talmud) refer to the Mishnah (ca. 200 A.D.), one of the principal components of the Talmud codifying the oral law of Judaism. The *Alphabet of Ben Sira* (*Alphabeticum Syracidis*), dated variously between 700 and 1000 A.D., recounts a Talmudic myth virtually identical to that mentioned by Aquinas here: Adam had another wife named Lilith who bore him demon-children. The similarities between this myth and Aquinas's comments are so pronounced that it seems that he must have been either familiar with this work or with the mythos it narrates. See Mark Mirsky and David Stern, eds., *Rabbinic Fantasies: Imaginative Narratives from Classical Hebrew Literature* (New Haven, Conn.: Yale University Press, 1998). Biblical scholar George Knight traces another strand of this tradition: "The idea that the errors in question [in 1 Tm 1:4] have a Jewish background and involve rabbinical speculation began in the commentaries of Ambrosiaster (cf. also on Tit. 1:14) and Chrysostom, and is more or less favored by Kittel.... Jeremias regards the 'myths' as stories of creation and 'genealogies' as the genealogies or generations of the patriarchs (so also Spicq) and appeals to Philo's designation of the history of the patriarchs as 'genealogies.'" Knight, *The Pastoral Epistles, A Commentary on the Greek Text* (Grand Rapids, Mich.: Eerdmans, 1992), 73. Compare this with C. Spicq, *Saint Paul, Les Épîtres Pastorales* (Paris: Librairie Lecoffre, 1947), 20-21, and Luke Timothy Johnson, *The Anchor Bible*, 35.

sake of his flock. The urgency of this responsibility arises both from certain kinds of doctrinal controversies that hinder spiritual growth and from the need for right faith in order to be saved. Aquinas notes that these verses (3 and 4) contain practical advice for prelates on how to distinguish legitimate from illegitimate doctrinal disputes. When doctrinal matters become contentious and "furnish questions rather than the edification of God, which is in faith" (1:4), then the bishop must regulate the teaching in his diocese both by restraining those who teach what is false and by forbidding the people to listen to them.[41] Here, Thomas does not elaborate further on precisely how a bishop should go about restraining and forbidding, but questions regarding false doctrine, debates about the faith, and ecclesial punishment arise many times throughout the course of his subsequent lectures on the PE and he expands on these initial observations in those places.[42]

Regarding 1 Timothy 1:5, "The end of the commandment is charity," Aquinas notes that Paul is identifying true doctrine with true charity and with the virtues necessary to preserve and increase charity. Since the historical and doctrinal matters in question here have to do with the right way for a Christian to be a "teacher of the law" (1:7), verse 5 shows what must be retained of the Mosaic law. In Aquinas's text, this verse reads, "The end of the commandment is charity from a pure heart and a good conscience and an unfeigned faith."[43] Since it is the end of the commandment, the Mosaic law's inculcation of charity in the hearts of the faithful must be upheld as the purpose of all Christian doctrine. He argues: "That toward which all the mandates of the law are ordained is especially to be retained."[44]

At this point, he introduces a *quaestio*: "In what way is charity the end of the commandment?"[45] To answer this, he first underscores the

---

41. "Quae quaestiones praestant magis quam aedificationem Dei, quae est in fide." Aquinas, *In 1 Tim*, cap. 1, lect. 2, 2:214.

42. On legitimate and illegitimate debates about matters of faith, see *In 2 Tim*, cap. 2, lect. 2, [61], 2:279. On excommunication, see *In 2 Tim*, cap. 4, lect. 3, [162–65], 2:298. In addition, a number of Aquinas's lectures on Titus treat the bishop's duty to refute false doctrine.

43. "Finis autem praecepti est charitas de corde puro, et conscientia bona, et fide non ficta." Aquinas, *In 1 Tim*, cap. 1, lect. 2, 2:214.

44. "Illud ergo ad quod ordinantur omnia mandata legis est praecipue tenendum." Aquinas, *In 1 Tim*, [12], 2:215.

45. "Sed quomodo charitas est finis praecepti?" Aquinas, *In 1 Tim*, [13], 2:215.

relationship between the requirements of the law and the acts of the virtues: "All the precepts of the law are concerned with acts of the virtues."[46] All the other virtues serve as means ordered to the one virtue that has the final end as its object. And since the theological virtues have as their object man's final end, God, the other virtues must be ordered, as means, to the theological virtues. However, each of the theological virtues is ordered to God differently. Faith points out the final end and hope makes one tend toward it, but charity actually and concretely unites one to God, since the object of the will animated by charity is not the idea of God conceived in the understanding (as it is with faith) but God as he is in himself.[47]

Charity is the end of the commandment because it is the theological virtue having the ultimate supernatural end of man as its object: concrete and personal union with the triune God. The other virtues, as means, are ordered to charity in various ways. A "pure heart" (1:5), consisting principally in the moral virtues of temperance and meekness, is required in order to be prompt in charity. Otherwise, one would be subject to inordinate passions contrary to charity, such as excessive anger, lust, or fear. Similarly, without a "good conscience" (1:5) God cannot be loved well since a bad conscience produces fear of punishment and causes one to flee from—rather than enter into union with—God.[48] Finally, without an "unfeigned faith" (1:5) charity is impossible because love arises only from what is presented by the intellect as good. On account of a false or feigned faith, one does

---

46. "Omnia praecepta legis sunt de actibus virtutum." Aquinas, *In 1 Tim*, [13], 2:215.

47. Elsewhere, Thomas describes charity as the greatest of the theological virtues since it alone attains God in the concrete in this life: "Fides autem et spes attingunt quidem Deum secundum quod ex ipso provenit nobis vel cognitio veri vel adeptio boni: sed caritas attingit ipsum Deum ut in ipso sistat, non ut ex eo aliquid nobis proveniat" (However, faith and hope indeed attain to God insofar as from Him the knowledge of truth or the acquisition of good comes to us; but charity attains God Himself so that it may rest in Him, not so that something may come to us from Him)." Aquinas, *STh* II-II, q. 23, a. 6. For Aquinas, the object understood (even by faith) remains in the intellect, whereas the object of desire and love is a concrete thing, and in the case of charity, it is God himself. On this, see Aquinas, *In II Sent*, d. 25, a. 2, ad 4, 6:614–15; *In III Sent*, d. 27, q. 1, a. 4, 7.1:296–98; and *STh* I, q. 82, a. 3.

48. Aquinas argues that conscience is a judgment of the intellect regarding the moral goodness or evil of a given action. It is the "application of knowledge to some action." See *STh* I, q. 79, a. 13, and I-II, qq. 19 and 76. As such, someone has a bad conscience when he judges that his own actions are morally evil. Hence, he reasonably fears punishment.

not know God truly and thus one is unable to love God truly: "Consequently, whatever makes for true faith makes for true charity."⁴⁹ To guide the faithful to attain true charity, therefore, the bishop must foster in them the moral virtues (a pure heart), a good conscience, and true faith. True doctrine is of paramount importance for this task because the intellect proposes to the will the object to be loved. One cannot properly love what one does not properly know. Proper reverence and honor of God (*latria*) also moves one to hold the true faith taught by Christ and the apostles.⁵⁰

In lect. 3, discussing 1 Timothy 1:6–7, Aquinas states another reason that the bishop must foster such virtues in the faithful: "Because whoever lacks them runs into the danger of false doctrine."⁵¹ The bishop must not only teach charity, he also must compel others to practice it. To be a minister of the Gospel, then, is to induce and inspire others to virtue. In order to direct the faithful to salvation, a bishop must know and be able to redress the root cause of falling into false doctrine, namely, the departure from charity.⁵² Notably, for Aquinas, the cause of false doctrine is not principally an intellectual error; rather, its source is found in a moral failing. This insight is invaluable for bishops in their exercise of pastoral ministry. Aquinas teaches that those who lose purity of heart become "infected by the passions" and judge everything according to their own affections and not according to God.⁵³ Those who lose a good conscience "cannot

---

49. "Et ideo quae faciunt fidem veram, ordinantur ad charitatem." Aquinas, *In 1 Tim*, cap. 1, lect. 2, [16], 2:215.

50. Aquinas says that the virtue of *latria* (an instance of the virtue of religion which, in turn, is a species of the virtue of justice, whereby we give reverence and honor to God) is ordered to the theological virtue of faith in the sense that *latria* sets a man straight by removing errors and confirming a solid belief in God (see Aquinas, *In 1 Tim*, 2:215). Hence, honoring God in justice also moves one to sound faith. Aquinas's elaborations in this part of the lectures on 1 Timothy provide an interpretive key to his exceptionally brief treatment of the relation of a "pure heart, good conscience, and unfeigned faith" to charity in his *STh* II-II, q. 44, a. 1, co.

51. "Quia quicumque ab his discedit, in periculum falsae doctrinae cadit." Aquinas, *In 1 Tim*, cap. 1, lect. 3, [17], 2:216.

52. "Recessus a charitate, causa est falsae doctrinae, quia qui non amant charitatem, cadunt in mendacium" (Receding from charity is the cause of false doctrine, since those who do not love charity fall into falsehood). Aquinas, *In 1 Tim*, [18], 2:216.

53. "Similiter qui dimittunt cordis puritatem. Habentes enim cor infectum passionibus, iudicant secundum affectum earum, et non secundum Deum" (It is the same

rest in the truth; hence they seek what is false and find their rest in that."⁵⁴ Men in this condition are unable to understand divine revelation and if they "desire to be teachers of the law" (1:7), they pose a particularly urgent problem for a bishop who must serve and protect the faithful.

To deal adequately and effectively with the problem of false teachers, first and foremost the bishop must be a good man himself so that he may "induce others to virtue."⁵⁵ And inasmuch as a bishop induces others to moral goodness by proclaiming and implementing divine law (1:8), Aquinas takes the ninth verse, "The law is not laid down for the just, but for the unjust," as an occasion to explain the purpose and function of God's law enforced by bishops with respect to differently disposed persons.⁵⁶ Here Thomas cites the tenth book of Aristotle's *Nicomachean Ethics* to ground his claim that law is a means to make citizens better. For those disposed to virtue of themselves (*per se*), the bishop need do nothing further to induce them. But for those properly disposed to virtue, not of themselves but by someone else (*non per se sed per alium*) such as a well-respected and beloved superior, "a paternal admonition is enough, and there is no need of force."⁵⁷ However, for those not well-disposed to virtue, neither by themselves nor by another, "it is for such that the law is entirely necessary" and in extreme cases force or coercion ought to be applied.⁵⁸ Though he does not mention here what kind of force he has in mind, he soon makes it clear (as will be seen below) that the ecclesial sanction of

---

for those who abandon purity of heart. For having a heart corrupted by passions, they judge according to their affections and not according to God). Aquinas, *In 1 Tim*, [18], 2:216.

54. "Similiter habentes conscientiam malam, quia non possunt quiescere in veritate. Et inde est quod quaerunt falsa, ut in eis quiescant" (It is the same for those who have a bad conscience, because they are not able to rest in the truth. And so it is that they seek falsehoods that they might rest in them). Aquinas, *In 1 Tim*, [18], 2:216.

55. "Intentio bonorum debet esse, ut alios inducant ad virtutes" (The intention of good men ought to be that they induce others to virtue). Aquinas, *In 1 Tim*, [23], 2:217.

56. "Lex iusto non est posita, sed iniustis." Aquinas, *In 1 Tim*, 2:216.

57. "De istis sufficit paterna monito, non coactiva." Aquinas, *In 1 Tim*, [23], 2:217. Notice Aquinas's use of familial, paternal language to describe the manner in which a bishop ought to correct the faithful.

58. "Eis omnino est necessaria lex." Aquinas, *In 1 Tim*, [23], 2:217. Also see *STh* I-II, q. 95, a. 1.

excommunication is needed in these cases and that this is, in fact, a work of *charity*. In the end, the bishop, charged with the care of souls, must respond with the threat of punishment to those who obdurately teach false doctrine. Thomas notes that in 1 Timothy 1:9–10 Paul lists various types of persons that need and could benefit from this threat: the lawless, the disobedient, the ungodly, sinners, the unholy, the profane, murderers, the immoral, sodomites, kidnappers, liars, perjurers, and "whatever else is contrary to sound doctrine." Aquinas understands the threat and imposition of punishment as a work of charity demanded of a bishop as circumstances might warrant. For him, discipline imposed in justice is not incompatible with Christian charity, but is rather demanded by it when considering the duties of those who hold a hierarchical office established by Christ for the salvation of souls.

Proceeding next to comment on Paul's comparison of his life under the law with his life under the Gospel of grace (1:11–14), Thomas emphasizes that the basic requirement for being a minister of the Gospel is that one be assigned to it by God. Under the law, Paul was subject to sin as a "blasphemer and persecutor," but he obtained "the mercy of God" (1:13).[59] This mercy was necessary for him to be sufficiently strengthened to meet the task to which he was called. The bishop, likewise, urgently needs this divine mercy to be faithful—seeking only the things of God—and "strong enough to follow through."[60]

Next, in lect. 4, Thomas remarks on the manner in which a bishop ought to deliver his message (*sermo*). Commenting on the *sermo* (the "word") described in verse 15 as "faithful and worthy of full acceptance," he says: "Two things are to be commended in a saying, namely that it be true and that it be acceptable."[61] Yet he notes that sometimes sayings can be true yet hard (*durus*), even to the point of arousing hatred (*odia*).[62] Though some Gospel sayings are common-

---

59. "'Qui prius blasphemus fui, et persecutor ... sed misericordiam Dei consecutus sum'" (Who previously was a blasphemer and a persecutor ... but I obtained the mercy of God). Aquinas, *In 1 Tim*, 2:216.

60. "Fortis ad prosequendum." Aquinas, *In 1 Tim*, [32], 2:218.

61. "Duo autem sunt in sermone quod sit acceptabilis, scilicet quod sit verus et quod sit acceptabilis." Aquinas, *In 1 Tim*, lect. 4, [38], 2:219.

62. "Aliquando enim sermo verus est durus, et odia concitans" (Indeed sometimes a word is true and hard, inflaming hatred). Aquinas, *In 1 Tim*, lect. 4, [38], 2:219. Here,

ly recognized as "hard"—that is, susceptible to a hostile reception—the preacher ought to do what he can to present it in an acceptable, attractive light. In any event, the bishop is solemnly bound by an oath to preach the Gospel in its entirety, regardless of how he might anticipate its reception or rejection. To execute this difficult task, the bishop receives Christ's mercy as a sign of divine patience for the salvation of souls and for the honor and glory of God (1:16–17).

In light of this, Aquinas then discusses the bishop's duty to wage spiritual warfare (1:18). Paul knows that he must entrust Timothy with this task on account of prophecy, according to verse 18: "This task I commend to you, Timothy, my son, according to the prophecies in your regard."[63] The Spirit of prophecy guided Paul and the other saints to entrust Timothy with the task of spiritual warfare.[64] Later on, in his third lecture on 1 Timothy 4, Aquinas interprets these prophecies about Timothy as a special revelation of the Holy Spirit designating the person God wants to serve as bishop. Commenting on 4:14, "Do not neglect the grace that is in you, which was given to you through prophecy," he says that episcopal elections in the early Church were conducted purely, for God, and by divine choice (adducing Ambrose and Nicholas by way of example).[65] Thomas points out that, since the time of

---

Aquinas cites Gal 4:16: "Inimicus factus sum vobis, verum dicens vobis" (Have I become your enemy by telling you the truth?). In his commentary on this verse in Galatians, he examines the various ways speaking the truth can be inimical. See Aquinas, *Lectura super Galatas*, cap. 4, lect. 5, [235–37], 1:617–18.

63. "Hoc praeceptum commendo tibi, fili Timothee, secundum praecedentes in te prophetias." Aquinas, *In 1 Tim*, cap. 1, lect. 4, 2:219.

64. "Secundum quod ego et alii sancti de te per spiritum prophetiae cognoverunt tradendum esse tibi" (On account of which I and the other saints learned about you through the spirit of prophecy that it was to be handed over to you). Aquinas, *In 1 Tim*, lect. 4, [50], 2:220.

65. "Noli negligere gratiam quae in te est, quae data est tibi per prophetiam." Aquinas, *In 1 Tim*, cap. 4, lect. 3, 2:244. On this, Aquinas comments: "Nam in primitiva ecclesia, ubi pure et propter Deum electiones fiebant, nullus assumebatur ad episcopatum nisi per electionem divinam, sicut electus est Ambrosius et Nicolaus. Et hanc inspirationem vocat hic prophetiam. Unde Glossa dicit, id est, per sanctorum electionem, quia sancti non eligebant quem a Deo non sciebant electum" (For in the early Church, where elections took place purely and on account of God, no one was accepted into the episcopacy except by divine election, as Ambrose and Nicholas were elected. And here he calls this inspiration prophecy. Wherefore the Gloss says that this was through the election of saints, because the saints did not elect one who was not known to have been chosen by God). Aquinas, *In 1 Tim*, cap. 4, lect. 3, [173], 2:245.

the early Church, episcopal elections have not always been conducted fairly, for upright motives, or by divine choice. Sadly, this was not a controversial claim then nor is it now.

Returning to 1:18, Aquinas explains that the precise "task" (*praeceptum*) commended to Timothy in this verse is "to guard the end of the law"—that is, to guard charity. And this assignment is commended to Timothy and to all bishops (*commendo tibi*), as a "faithful trust."[66] The end of verse 18 likens this task to a military battle: "That you wage in them a good warfare."[67] Accordingly, Thomas identifies relevant similarities between military warfare and the bishop's magisterial office.[68] First, he considers what is required personally on the part of a temporal soldier: "In good warfare two things are expected of the soldiers, namely, that they do nothing contrary to military discipline, and that they not become weak through ease."[69] Second, he examines warfare itself: "And two things are required on the part of the warfare: namely, that [the soldier] conquer those who are acting against the republic and that he subject those who ought to be made subject."[70] Then he compares by analogy these temporal requirements with acts of "spiritual warfare," which are "ordained to the destruction of all who exalt themselves and to the 'bringing into captivity every understanding unto the obedience of Christ,' as it is stated in 2 Corinthians 10 [verse 5]."[71] The first set of requirements is interior to the soldier and to the bishop, the second set bears on their external actions.

---

66. "Dicit ergo 'Hoc praeceptum,' ut scilicet tu custodias finem legis, id est, charitatem conserves semper ... 'commendo tibi,' sicut fidele depositum, quia tibi ideo est commissum" (He says therefore, "This precept," namely that you keep the end of the law, that is, that you preserve charity always ... "I commend to you," as a faithful deposit, because it has been committed to you as such). Aquinas, *In 1 Tim*, cap. 1, lect. 4, [49], 2:220.

67. "Ut milites in illis bonam militiam." Aquinas, *In 1 Tim*, 2:219.

68. Compare this with what Aquinas says in his commentary on Philemon 2: "Et dicit 'Archippo commilitoni,' quia omnes praelati sunt sicut spirituales milites ecclesiae" (And he says, "Archippus our fellow soldier," because all prelates are, as it were, spiritual soldiers of the Church). Aquinas, *In Philem*, lect. 1, [5], 2:329.

69. "In bona militia requiruntur duo ex parte militis, scilicet ut nihil agat contrarium disciplinae militari, ut non marcescat otio." Aquinas, *In 1 Tim*, cap. 1, lect. 4, [50], 2:221.

70. "Item ex parte militiae duo requiruntur, scilicet ut expugnet contrarios reipublicae, et ut subiiciat eos qui debent esse subiecti." Aquinas, *In 1 Tim*, [50], 2:221.

71. "Ordinatur ad destruendum omnes extollentes se, et ad subiiciendum omnem intellectum in obsequium Christi, ut dicitur II Cor. X." Aquinas, *In 1 Tim*, [50], 2:221.

Interiorly, the bishop is to conduct spiritual warfare with "faith and a good conscience" (1:19).[72] Implicit in Aquinas's explanation of verse 19 is a principle he frequently deploys: action follows being. The actions of a thing follow its actual form, that is, its existence as a specific kind of being.[73] For the bishop to act in fulfillment of his commission, he must have a specific intrinsic "form," that is, certain habits of being, powers, characteristics, and attitudes. Thomas's brief discussion of the interior requirements of faith and a good conscience form the rational basis for his comments on the bishop's duty to wage spiritual "warfare." Beyond citing 1 John 5:4, "This is the victory which overcomes the world, faith," he does not explain further the bishop's need for faith for an obvious reason: a bishop must be a believer in order to teach the faith effectively and govern according to its rule.[74] His comments on the bishop's need for a good conscience are equally brief. Repeating the text of verse 19, "Having faith and a good conscience, which, some rejecting, have made shipwreck concerning the faith," he remarks that, without a good conscience, the faith may be lost, and this is tantamount to spiritual death.[75] In this regard, he cites Habakkuk 2:4 and Romans 11:17, to the effect that the just man lives by faith. In order to protect the doctrine of charity from false teachers, the bishop must have faith and a good conscience that comes from an upright life. Faith constitutes the form of Gospel truth, while charity (manifest in a good conscience) preserves the genuineness of the teaching.[76] Once again Aquinas emphasizes that errors in faith are rooted in moral, not intellectual, problems.

---

72. "Habens fidem et bonam conscientiam." Aquinas, *In 1 Tim*, 2:219.

73. For example, in *SCG* Aquinas says: "Cum enim unumquodque agat secundum quod est actu ... est autem unumquodque ens actu per formam: oportet quod operatio rei sequatur formam ipsius. Oportet ergo, si sunt diversae formae, quod habeant diversas operationes" (Since everything acts insofar as it is actual ... [and since] every being is actual through form: it is necessary that the operation of a thing follows its form). Aquinas, *SCG* III, cap. 97, 343–46. He also says: "Agere sequitur ad esse in actu" (To act follows from being in act). Aquinas, *SCG* III, cap. 69, 302–5.

74. "Haec est victoria, quae vincit mundum, fides." Aquinas, *In 1 Tim*, cap. 1, lect. 4, [51], 2:221.

75. "Habens fidem et bonam conscientiam. Quam quidam repellentes circa fidem naufragaverunt." Aquinas, *In 1 Tim*, lect. 4, 2:219.

76. In his commentary on 1 Tm 1:19, J. N. D. Kelly cites Ernest Findlay Scott: "The point Paul is making is the sound one that 'more often than we know, religious error has its roots in moral rather than intellectual causes' (E. F. Scott)." Kelly, *The Pastoral Epistles*

Externally, spiritual warfare is conducted by means of punishment, motivated by charity, with a dual purpose: to protect the faithful and benefit the wrongdoer, saving him from hidden sin. Aquinas interprets verse 20, "I delivered up Hymenaeus and Alexander to Satan, that they may learn not to blaspheme," as describing an act of excommunication.[77] In this instance, the persons "blasphemed" by somehow defecting from the faith. Their penalty was imposed "so that the faithful might avoid [the false teachers] lest they be infected."[78] Excommunication, as a type of spiritual affliction, is a "delivering up to Satan" in the sense that one loses communion with the Church, along with the Church's prayers and God's help—necessary for protection against the devil.[79] However, the "destruction of those who exalt themselves" is not meant to signify literally the annihilation of those who have blasphemed. Here and elsewhere in his lectures, Thomas construes excommunication in terms of shunning or avoiding the heretic. As with his comments on the bishop's preaching office mentioned above, his thoughts on excommunication are influenced in part by the teaching of the Fourth Lateran Council (1215), especially by the following injunction: "Let such persons [namely, the excommunicated] be avoided by all until they have made adequate satisfaction."[80] Bishops ought to imitate the manner and motivation

---

(Peabody, Mass.: Hendrickson Publishers, 1960), 58. See E. F. Scott, *The Pastoral Epistles* (London: Hodder and Stoughton, 1936).

77. "Ex quibus est Hymenaeus et Alexander, quos tradidi satanae, ut discant non blasphemare." Aquinas, *In 1 Tim*, cap. 1, lect. 4, 2:219.

78. "Ut fideles vitent eos ne coinquinent ipsos." Aquinas, *In 1 Tim*, [53], 2:221.

79. "Tamen etiam modo traduntur ad vexandum spiritualiter, quia amittunt suffragia ecclesiae, quae multum iuvant contra diabolum. Et 'tradidi' sicut 'Deus tradidit in reprobum sensum' Rom 1:28, quasi subtrahendo suum auxilium, et communionem ecclesiae, et suffragia" (Nevertheless they are handed over also to be jolted spiritually, since they lose the prayers of the Church, which greatly help against the devil. And "I have handed them over" as "God handed them over to a base mind" (Rom 1:28), as it were, removing His help, and the communion of the Church, and her prayers). Aquinas, *In 1 Tim*, [53], 2:221.

80. "Et usque ad satisfactionem condignam ab omnibus evitentur." Fourth Lateran Council, *Constitutions*, chap. 3, "On Heretics," in *Decrees of the Ecumenical Councils*, ed. Tanner, 1:233. Later in the same chapter of this decree, those who refuse to avoid (*evitare*) heretics are threatened with excommunication. Such persons were to be exiled by civil authority, their property was confiscated and they lost certain civil rights—including the right to work. While the pressure of this historical practice may have helped

of the excommunication imposed by Paul. They should be motivated, Aquinas says, "not by hatred [of those to be excommunicated], but by love and for their progress."[81] Properly imposed, this punishment should benefit both the faithful—by protecting them from corrupt doctrine—and also those who are duly excommunicated.

How can excommunication benefit the punished? Aquinas argues that, when imposed charitably, this penalty teaches the punished to depart from sin. He mentions three ways in which one can learn to flee from sin: "[A man learns to flee sin in three ways:] sometimes from the punishment of sin, when he is afflicted in body, sometimes from the shame of being excommunicated, and sometimes from the fact that, when the Church delivers him over to Satan he falls into public sins. On account of this shame he is humbled and refrains even from hidden sins, which he formerly did not recognize he had."[82] Aquinas's explanation of excommunication as an act of loving correction shows the harmony that ought to obtain between the prevailing political and ecclesiastical discipline of his day and Christ's teaching that those in authority must serve their subordinates in love.[83] The bishop himself, already having personally received the Lord's forgiveness, has an advantage in imposing extreme measures since he is poised to bear witness personally to God's justice, mercy, and generosity by the example of his life and not merely by his teaching and governing.

Thomas is sensitive to the psychology of the excommunicated person, describing his shame and the opportunity to see his hidden sins and repent. This perspective is in continuity with the tradition

---

to form Aquinas's notions of excommunication, he places a premium on charity as the theological principle for all ecclesiastical acts, including punitive ones.

81. "Et hoc non ex odio, sed ex charitate ad profectum eorum." Aquinas, *In 1 Tim*, cap. 1, lect. 4, [54], 2:221. Aquinas discusses excommunication as a last resort in episcopal discipline when commenting on Ti 3:10–12 (*In Tit*, cap. 3, lect. 2, [101–2], 2:325–26).

82. "Quandoque scilicet ex poena, quando corporaliter vexatur; item ex confusione excommunicationis; item ex hoc quod cum ecclesia tradit aliquem satanae ruit in peccata manifesta, unde confusus humiliatur, et abstinet etiam ab occultis, quae prius non cognoscebat se habere." Aquinas, *In 1 Tim*, cap. 1, lect. 4, [54], 2:221.

83. E.g., see Mt 20:25–28 and Mk 10:43–44. As mentioned, the punishments prescribed for heretics by the Fourth Lateran Council included confiscation of all their property, exile, and an injunction prohibiting anyone at all from providing them assistance (see "On Heretics," 1:233–35). Aquinas's remarks here show that these severe punishments are to be imbued with the spirit of charity.

expressed in the documents of the Lateran Council and Aquinas insists that the penalty of excommunication be motivated by love for the faithful and for those being punished. This punishment ought to protect the faithful from spiritual harm and simultaneously work for the spiritual benefit of those being disciplined. It should be used as an instrument of last resort in order to secure ecclesial unity for all parties involved.[84]

Divine Worship (2:1–7)

Aquinas's lectures on the first chapter of 1 Timothy were concerned with the bishop's role in the transmission and regulation of doctrine to cultivate charity in his subjects. His three lectures on the second chapter concern the worship of the faith, which he describes in terms of prayer and obedience (*obsequium*). In these lectures, Aquinas offers further vital insights regarding the relationship of doctrinal truth to salvation.

In his first lecture on 1 Timothy 2, he remarks that Paul "presents the general doctrine on prayer."[85] In verse 1, Timothy is urged to have prayers and supplications offered for all men because, "among all the things necessary for a Christian life the most important is prayer, for it provides powerful aid against temptation and assistance in making progress in good."[86] Aquinas then explains the scriptural text sequentially, identifying the various forms of prayer, the persons for whom prayer should be offered, and the reason for prayer, namely charity (2:2–3, and following).

Discussing verse 4, "God wills all men to be saved and to come to the knowledge of the truth," he further underscores the importance of doctrinal truth proclaimed and guarded by the episcopal office-holder.[87] Lect. 2 on chapter 1, as discussed above, related right doctrine and right worship. Here, in his first lecture on 1 Timothy 2:4,

---

84. See Aquinas's remarks on this in *STh* II-II, q. 11, a. 3.

85. "Ponit doctrinam orationis in communi." Aquinas, *In 1 Tim*, cap. 2, lect. 1, [55], 2:223.

86. "Inter omnia necessaria ad vitam christianam praecipua est oratio, quae valet contra pericula tentationis et ad proficiendum in bono." Aquinas, *In 1 Tim*, cap. 2, lect. 1, [56], 2:223.

87. "Qui omnes homines vult salvos fieri, et ad agnitionem veritatis venire." Aquinas, *In 1 Tim*, 2:223.

he says, "[Paul] adds, 'and come to the knowledge of the truth,' because salvation depends on knowing the truth: 'You shall know the truth and the truth shall make you free'" (Jn 8:32).[88] For Aquinas, salvation is not merely metaphysical and moral, but also intellectual since eternal life consists essentially in the personal knowledge of a supernatural vision—the beatific vision of the triune God.[89] This destiny is initiated and adumbrated in this life, beginning with God's grace reaching those who are called when they hear the sound doctrine of the true faith preached. Thus Thomas insists that salvation itself, man's greatest good and final end, depends on knowing the truth. He could hardly accord the office of preaching the faith a higher place among the episcopal duties since it is precisely by preaching that knowledge of the truth of Christ, the one Mediator who ransoms all, is engendered (2:5–6).

Then, in lect. 2, Aquinas likens Paul's apostolic office to the episcopal office of preaching in his comments on verse 7: "For this I have been appointed a preacher and apostle (I speak the truth, I am not lying)."[90] He says, "The work of this office is to preach the truth; for this is the duty of preachers, namely, to preach the truth ... and this is the duty of [Paul's] office, namely, to preach the truth without lying."[91] Since Paul serves as an exemplar for Timothy and for all prelates, the episcopal office is likewise an office of preaching truth. The preacher of the Gospel teaches truth and, precisely as a teacher, he "produces knowledge in the soul of his disciple."[92] The remaining verses of chapter 2 specify the respective roles for men and women

88. "Et subdit 'ad agnitionem veritatis,' quia salus non est nisi per agnitionem veritatis. Io. VIII, 32: 'Agnoscetis veritatem, et veritas liberabit vos.'" Aquinas, *In 1 Tim*, cap. 2, lect. 1, [62], 2:225.

89. Later, in his third lecture on 1 Tm 3, Thomas cites Augustine's description of beatitude in his *Confessions* X, chap. 23, n. 34: "Unde Augustinus dicit, quod beatitudo est finis hominis, quae nihil aliud est quam gaudium de veritate" (Wherefore Augustine says that beatitude is the end of man, which is nothing other than delight in the truth). Aquinas, *In 1 Tim*, cap. 3, lect. 3, [128], 2:237.

90. "In quo positus sum ego praedicator et Apostolus (veritatem dico, non mentior)." Aquinas, *In 1 Tim*, cap. 2, lect. 2, 2:226.

91. "Usus autem officii est praedicare veritatem, et hoc est officium praedicatorum, ut veritatem dicant.... Et hic est usus officii, scilicet veritatem sine mendacio praedicare." Aquinas, *In 1 Tim*, cap. 2, lect. 2, [69], 2:226.

92. "Doctor autem generat scientiam in anima discipuli." Aquinas, *In 1 Tim*, [69], 2:226.

in divine worship (2:8–15). Verses 12 through 15, in particular, touch on the prohibition of women teaching and holding authority in the Church. Aquinas handles this question, one which is currently quite controversial, by making precise distinctions between public and private instruction and authority. While some may consider his views to be antiquated, a responsible and scholarly resolution of this matter must be remanded to a study that proceeds well beyond the limits of this present work.

Appointments to Ecclesiastical Office (3:1–15)

In his lectures on the third chapter of 1 Timothy, Aquinas treats three matters bearing on the nature of the episcopal office: (1) the distinction among the hierarchical orders in the Church, (2) whether it is lawful to desire the episcopal office for oneself, and (3) the moral character required of bishops. These lectures lie at the very heart of his theology of the episcopacy. He begins his first lecture on this chapter by posing a short *quaestio* arising from the division of the subject matter in chapter 3 into the teaching on bishops (3:1–7) and the teaching on deacons (3:8–13). Why, he asks, are priests (*presbyteri*) not mentioned? Is this because the early Church made no distinction between the orders of priest and bishop? He appeals to the teaching of Pseudo-Dionysius (whom he took to be an apostolic father) that there are three distinct hierarchical orders in the Church and he provides a creative solution to the problem of the apparent lack of distinction in the New Testament between the presbyteral and episcopal orders. Though "priest" (*presbyter*) signifies "elder" (*senior*) and "bishop" (*episcopus*) signifies "overseer" (*superintendens*), bishops are also elders and priests overseers.[93] Thus, he argues that no *linguistic* distinction was made in the early Church between the orders of priest and bishop—and this is, in fact, reflected in New Testament usage (for example, in Acts 20:28 and 1 Tm 5:17).[94] In his subsequent lectures on 1 Timothy, Aquinas argues that there is, nevertheless, a *real* hierarchical distinction among priests since some of them, such as Timothy himself, held authority over other priests: appointing

---

93. Aquinas, *In 1 Tim*, cap. 3, lect. 1, [87], 2:231.
94. Thomas treats this same question in more detail in *STh* II-II, q. 184, a. 6, ad 1.

them to the ministry, honoring some and censuring others. Other priests did not possess such authority.

Then, in lect. 2, when commenting on the list of qualifications for deacons, Aquinas says something rather puzzling: "In the early Church there were *only three orders*, as Dionysius says: bishops, priests, and ministers [that is, deacons], and these were not divided into various grades, but *all were in one order* because of the scarcity of ministers and the newness of the Church."[95] At first glance, this statement might appear to be internally inconsistent, not to mention partially inconsistent with what he says in response to the *quaestio* in lect. 1 (mentioned above). The text as we have it seems, in one sentence, both to affirm three hierarchical orders and then to insist immediately that there was only one.

What is the reason for this apparent discrepancy? Reporter error can be excluded reasonably, since Reginald was publicly praised as an expert recorder, even by Thomas himself. Moreover, as discussed in the previous chapter of this book, Thomas personally reviewed these texts before they were copied and disseminated. In this light, we must conclude that his assertion here—that, in the early Church, there were "only" (*solum*) three orders, bishop, priest, and deacon—specifies that it was exclusively this last order, that of deacons, which was not divided into various "grades" (*gradus*). Aquinas is referring to the historical fact that in the early Church the grades of ecclesial order lower than deacon (namely: porter, exorcist, acolyte, lector, and subdeacon) had not yet been introduced. Twice in his *Sentences* commentary, he mentions that the ecclesial duties of all grades of ecclesial orders inferior to deacons were subsumed by the diaconate in the early Church for precisely the same reason he adduces here, namely, on account of the scarcity of ministers.[96] The lesser orders in which ecclesial and liturgical

---

95. "In primitiva enim ecclesia *solum erant tres ordines*, ut dicit Dionysius, scilicet episcoporum, presbyterorum et ministrorum; et non dividebantur per diversos gradus, sed *omnia erant in uno ordine* propter paucitatem ministrorum et propter novitatem ecclesiae" (emphasis added). Aquinas, *In 1 Tim*, cap. 3, lect. 2, [109], 2:234.

96. "Dionysius sub ministris comprehendit omnes ordines inferiores; et ideo ministris qui diaconi dicuntur, attribuit omnia quae sunt inferiorum ordinum: quia forte in primitiva ecclesia nondum erant illi ordines ita distincti propter paucitatem ministrorum" (Dionysius included all the inferior orders under "ministers"; and so he attributes everything which belongs to the inferior orders to the "ministers" who are called deacons, since

duties were distributed developed later in the Church's history. Thus, the second part of his assertion—that "these [namely, *deacons*] were not divided into various grades, but *all* were in one order because of the scarcity of ministers and the newness of the Church"—refers to this lack of distinction among lesser orders, all of the duties of which were originally subsumed in the one order of *ministri* or deacons.[97] In other words, Aquinas is not saying that the episcopacy, presbyterate, and diaconate were all in one order. Rather, he is indicating the historical fact that the various lesser orders were not yet distinguished—the duties of these orders being executed entirely by the one order of the diaconate. Thus, the lack of the division of orders mentioned in this text has as its immediate grammatical referent the term for deacons (*ministri*).

Desiring the episcopacy

Commenting on 1 Timothy 3:1, "If a man desires the office of a bishop, he desires a good work," Aquinas notes, "From these words some have taken occasion to aspire to the office of the episcopacy and prelacy, but they do not rightly understand what is said here."[98] Verse 1 does not say that the *desire* for the episcopacy is good; rather, it says that to desire *the episcopacy* is to desire a *good work*. This passage says nothing directly on whether it is good or licit to desire the episcopacy itself; rather, the Paul's concern here is to show the good work that is essential to the episcopacy. Analyzing the Greek word *episkopos* into *epi*, "above," and *skopos*, "watcher," Aquinas says: "Two things must be considered in the bishop, namely, his higher station and his beneficial actions on behalf of his subjects."[99] The episcopal office may be

---

in the early Church those orders were not yet distinguished because of the lack of ministers). Aquinas, *In IV Sent*, d. 6, q. 2, a. 3, qua. 3, sol. 3, ad 1, 7.1:565. See also Aquinas's remarks to this effect in *In IV Sent*, d. 24, q. 2, a. 1, qua. 2, ad 2, 7.2:896.

97. Furthermore, see *In IV Sent*, d. 24, q. 2, a. 1, qua. 3, 7.2:895–97: "Utrum debeant plures ordines distingui?" (Whether many orders ought to be distinguished?). Aquinas argues that the distinction of orders is among members of a potential whole in which the fullness of order (i.e., the nature of the whole) is found complete in the highest member, viz., the priesthood. So, there is *only one order* in the sense that all the orders share in the one priestly order, yet there are *three orders* in the sense that there are duties and prerogatives exclusive to some.

98. "Ex hoc sumpserunt aliqui occasionem ambitionis episcopatus et praelationis, sed non recte intelligunt quod hic dicitur." Aquinas, *In 1 Tim*, cap 3., lect. 1, [88], 2:231.

99. "Duo ergo sunt consideranda in episcopo, scilicet gradus superior, et actio plebi utilis." Aquinas, *In 1 Tim*, [88], 2:231.

desired under either one or both of these aspects. To desire this office principally on account of the honor and power that accompany this higher station, however, is to seek circumstances that attend, but that do not define, the essence of the episcopacy. This is why Aquinas says, "One who desires the episcopate for these reasons does not know what a bishop is."[100] But what *is* the episcopacy, in Thomas's estimation? Following Augustine, he argues that in verse 1 Paul describes the office of bishop as "a good work" in order to make known what is actually desired when one aspires to it. This "good work" of the episcopal office is procuring "the welfare of [the bishop's] subjects."[101]

Others, correctly understanding the nature of the episcopal office as a good work of service, might desire this work as such. But is it ever licit to desire the episcopacy in this fashion? Here Aquinas initiates a discussion of the qualifications for a suitable episcopal candidate. Explaining Augustine's position (expressed similarly in the *Glossa*) that it is neither licit nor becoming to desire this office, he says: "No one should desire something that exceeds his powers and is not proportionate to them; otherwise he would be a fool. Horace says: 'One who does not know how to play refrains from taking up the weapons used in the martial games.'"[102] If one is capable of fulfilling the demands of the episcopacy, then one can properly desire it. However, it is *never* appropriate to consider oneself equal to the demands of this office. Aquinas explains: "A prelate by reason of his lofty station and duties should exceed all others in his manner of life and in his contemplation, so that in comparison to him the others are as a flock of sheep. And to presume oneself fit for this is of the greatest pride."[103]

---

100. "Qui propter ista desiderat episcopatum, nescit quid sit episcopus." Aquinas, *In 1 Tim*, cap. 3, lect. 1, [88], 2:231.

101. "Utilitatem plebis." Aquinas, *In 1 Tim*, [88], 2:231. Compare this with Augustine: "Propter quod ait Apostolus, 'Qui episcopatum desiderat, bonum opus desiderat' (I Tim III, 1). Exponere voluit quid sit episcopatus; quia nomen est operis, non honoris" (On account of this the Apostle says, "He who desires the episcopacy desires a good work" [1 Tim 3:1]. He wants to explain what the episcopacy is; because the name is of a work, not of an honor). Augustine, *De civitate Dei*, book 19, chap. 19, PL 41, col. 647.

102. "Nullus debet appetere aliquid supra vires suas non sibi proportionatum, alias esset stultus. Horatius: 'Ludere qui nescit campestribus abstinet armis.'" Aquinas, *In 1 Tim*, cap. 3, lect. 1, [89], 2:231.

103. "Praelatus secundum gradum et convenientiam debet omnes alios excedere in conversatione et contemplatione, ita ut in respectu sui alii sint grex. Et hanc idoneitatem de se praesumere est maximae superbiae." Aquinas, *In 1 Tim*, [88], 2:231. In *STh* II-II,

Since it would be presumptuous in the extreme to consider oneself above all others in manner of life and contemplation, he concludes, "Therefore, [an episcopal appointment] is not to be accepted, unless it is imposed."[104] A little later, he states more succinctly, "The episcopal state presupposes perfection; consequently, unless one is perfect he should not seek the office of bishop."[105]

Excursus on seeking the episcopacy and on the episcopal state of perfection

Aquinas posed the question whether it is lawful to desire the episcopacy several times during his career, as discussed in chapter 2 above.[106] The following remarks supplement the brief conspectus of chapter 2. The question of the morality of seeking the bishop's office—raised both by Aquinas and by his questioners in the *quodlibetal* format—included a concern regarding those who would seek the episcopacy for the sake of the temporal *regalia* that attended the episcopal office, something peculiar to medieval Christendom. This kind of ambition ineluctably moves the prelate to abandon his episcopal mandate to labor spiritually on behalf of the faithful in order to pursue the temporal power, titles, and holdings attached to a given episcopal post.[107]

---

q. 182, a. 1, ad 1, Thomas says: "Ad praelatos non solum pertinet vita activa, sed etiam debent esse excellentes in vita contemplativa" (To prelates pertains not only the active life, but also they ought to excel in the contemplative life). Also, see Aquinas's commentary on Jn 21:15, where he interprets Christ's question—"Do you love me more than these?"—as an indication that the suitable candidate for the episcopacy must have a love of Christ that exceeds that of others, arguing that this is required if the bishop is to fulfill his duty to lead others to a loving union with Christ, Aquinas, *Ioannis*, cap. 21, lect. 3, [2614–27], 481–83.

104. "Et ideo non est accipiendum nisi impositum." Aquinas, *In 1 Tim*, cap. 3, lect. 1, [89], 2:232. See *De perf*, cap. 19 (*Opuscula theologica*, ed. Spiazzi, 2:139–40) and *STh* II-II, q. 185, a. 1.

105. "Status episcoporum praesupponit perfectionem, et ideo nullus appetere debet nisi habeat eam." Aquinas, *In 1 Tim*, cap. 3, lect. 1, [90], 2:232.

106. He treats this question in the following places: *Quodl* II, q. 6, a. 1 (33), "Utrum peccatum sit appetere praelationem" (Whether it is a sin to seek the prelacy?); *Quodl* III, q. 4, a. 1 (46); *Quodl* V, q. 11, a. 2 (112); *Quodl* XII, q. 11, a. 3 (230), "Utrum liceat appetere episcopatum" (Whether it is lawful to seek the episcopacy?); *De perf*, cap. 19 (*Opuscula theologica*, ed. Spiazzi, 2:139–40); *STh* II-II, q. 185, a. 1.

107. More subtly, perhaps, such ambition pressures the prelate to acquire and retain

In *Quodl* III, q. 4, a. 1, dating between 1268 and 1272, Aquinas contrasts the seeking of a magisterial chair (*cathedra magistralis*) in a university with the seeking of a pontifical chair (*cathedra pontificalis*). Receiving a magisterial chair in a university does not bestow upon the recipient any eminence that he did not previously have; rather, this recognition merely provides the opportunity to communicate knowledge. However, with the reception of the episcopal chair (*cathedra episcopalis*) comes an eminence of effective power over others. He calls this power a perfection of man, not in relation to himself (like the knowledge of a *magister*), but in relation to others. And whereas a sufficiency of knowledge makes one fit for the magisterial chair, it is through an excelling charity (*caritas excellens*) that one becomes fit for the pontifical chair. In support of this last point, he cites John 21:15, where Christ asks Peter if he loves him *more than the others do* prior to his pontifical appointment. In this passage Christ insists that an excelling love of him is the essential prerequisite for pastoral office. However, since one cannot know with certitude that one has charity (let alone an excelling degree of it), it would be presumptuous and even vicious to think oneself fit for episcopal office.[108]

Aquinas argues similarly in chapter 19 of his treatise *De perfectione* (1270). Whoever receives the pontifical dignity assumes a "spiritual magisterium" (*spirituale magisterium*) by which he is to lead others to the perfection of charity. However, he notes, "It is ridiculous for one to become a teacher of perfection who does not know perfection from experience."[109] As in *Quodl* III, q. 4, a. 1, he again cites John 21:15 to ground his claim that the spiritual perfection of charity is a necessary

---

good graces and standing in the eyes of his contemporaries who wield temporal power and with whom he interacts, professionally and personally, on a regular basis. In Aquinas's estimation, this is a rather dangerous situation for a bishop.

108. In light of this, he says seeking the episcopacy is "shameful" (*turpe*), adding, "Appetitus autem potestatis super alios est vitiosus: quia, ut Gregorius dicit, 'contra naturam superbire est hominem homini velle dominari.' ... Et ideo semper est vitiosum pontificatum petere" (But the desire for power over others is vicious because, as Gregory says, "it is contrary to nature to be so proud that a man would wish to rule over another man." ... And for this reason it is always vicious to seek the pontificate). Aquinas, *Quodl* III, q. 4, a. 1, [47]. Note that he does not say, "*Power* over others is wicked." Rather, he calls the *seeking* of power over others *vitiosus*, "vicious."

109. "Ridiculum autem est perfectionis magistrum fieri qui perfectionem per experimentum non novit." Aquinas, *De perf*, cap. 19, [674], 2:139.

prerequisite for the suitable episcopal candidate. Since it is manifestly presumptuous for someone to consider himself spiritually perfect, it is not licit to seek this office. In a pointed remark on episcopal appointments in his day, Aquinas adds, "Those who assume the pontifical dignity are usually intent upon temporal goods rather than eternal."[110]

As noted in chapter 2, above, in his *STh* II-II, q. 185, aa. 1–2, Aquinas takes up this question with greater precision. He distinguishes three aspects of the episcopacy: (1) the bishop's work for the good of his neighbor (this is the principal and final aspect of the episcopacy), (2) the height of degree (*altitudo gradus*), and (3) the reverence, honor, and temporal goods which result from the first two. To seek the episcopacy on account of the honor and temporal goods that accompany (but are incidental to) the office is patently covetous and ambitious and hence immoral. To seek the office on account of the height of degree would be presumptuous. And though desiring the good of one's neighbor is no doubt laudable, because episcopal acts are necessarily accompanied by the height of degree, it would be similarly presumptuous. However, in q. 185, a. 2, he argues that if a superior appoints one to the episcopacy, it should be received on account of charity for one's neighbor and out of humble obedience to that superior.[111]

On account of his elevated station and duties, the prelate must be perfect spiritually, that is, he must live an exemplary, virtuous life and enjoy lofty contemplation. The good work of his office, to benefit the faithful, requires a superior grasp of the faith and an excelling holiness of life. In the very beginning of his academic career, Aquinas articulated in his *Sentences* commentary the bishop's need for spiritual (that is, both moral and intellectual) perfection:

> The active life serves as a disposition for the contemplative life.... And hence, as long as a man has not reached perfection in the active life, the contemplative life cannot be present, except imperfectly and in an incipient way:

---

110. "Qui vero pontificalem dignitatem assumunt, plerumque magis temporalia bona considerant quam aeterna." Aquinas, *De perf*, [676], 2:140.

111. Aquinas, *STh* II-II, q. 185, aa. 1–2. These remarks have greater weight in light of the fact that Thomas himself was tapped for the episcopacy, from which he fled and successfully avoided in the end.

for this person the acts of the moral virtues cause him difficulty and he must devote all his attention to them, so that he is drawn away from the exercise of contemplation. But when the active life is already perfect, then the acts of the moral virtues come easily, so that he can freely give himself to contemplation without being impeded by them.... And since it pertains to prelates to be perfect in both lives, insofar as they are mediators between God and the people, receiving from God through contemplation and passing on to the people through action, they ought to be perfect in the moral virtues, as should preachers be as well.[112]

This perfection must be moral—in one's "manner of life"; yet it must also be intellectual—in one's "contemplation." The bishop's mediatorial role demands that he be (or strive to be) perfect both morally and in contemplation. He must not only pass on to his subjects the doctrine of charity, he must copiously work to produce charity in their souls. Later in his *Sentences* commentary, Aquinas argues that any priest who has received the *cura animarum* must have a basic knowledge of faith and morals, but bishops, entrusted with the care of their churches, should have a more perfect knowledge of the law: "To the higher priests, namely the bishops, it belongs to know even those points of the law which may offer some difficulty, and to know them better insofar as they are placed in a higher grade."[113] This loftier knowledge comes from a profound contemplation that is impossible to attain without possessing a high degree of moral perfection in virtue.[114]

Thomas's account of the episcopacy as a life of charitable service to the faithful envisions hierarchical office in light of Christ's teaching

112. "Vita autem activa est dispositio ad contemplativam.... Et ideo quamdiu homo non pervenit ad perfectionem in vita activa, non potest in eo esse contemplativa vita, nisi secundum quamdam inchoationem imperfecte: tunc enim difficultatem homo patitur in actibus virtutum moralium, et oportet quod tota solicitudine ad ipsos intendat, unde retrahitur a studio contemplationis. Sed quando jam vita activa perfecta est, tunc operationes virtutum moralium in promptu habet, ut eis non impeditus libere contemplationi vacet.... Et quia praelatorum est in utraque vita perfectos esse, utpote qui medii sunt inter deum et plebem, a deo recipientes per contemplationem, et populo tradentes per actionem; ideo oportet eos in moralibus virtutibus perfectos esse; et similiter praedicatores." Aquinas, *In III Sent*, d. 35, q. 1, a. 3, qua. 3, sol. 3, 7.1:405.

113. "Sed ad superiores sacerdotes, scilicet episcopos, pertinet ut etiam ea quae difficultatem in lege facere possunt, sciant: et tanto magis quanto in maiori gradu collocantur." Aquinas, *In IV Sent*, d. 24, q. 1, a. 3, qua. 5, sol. 2, ad 1, 7.2:893. The matter at hand in this *quaestiuncula* is whether those with the *cura animarum* ought to know all of Scripture.

114. Compare this with Aquinas's remarks in *STh* II-II, q. 15, a. 3, and q. 153, a. 5.

that those set in authority must be the servants of their subjects (see Mt 20:25–28 and 23:11–12). His thoughts on this are also informed by the Dionysian principle of hierarchy: the lowest are led to the highest by intermediaries. Bishops in authority, out of love for their flock, should be moved to lead them to the perfection of supernatural union with God. In the fifth chapter of his *Ecclesiastical Hierarchy*, Pseudo-Dionysius calls the episcopacy the office of spiritual "*perfector*."[115] The holder of this office is required to perfect spiritually his subjects by leading them to a greater assimilation with the divine nature, to a greater *theosis*—a *theosis* that the episcopal office-holder already enjoys.[116] The perfection in question here is the spiritual perfection of love of God and neighbor.

In both *De perfectione* and *STh* II-II, qq. 184–85, Thomas cites Dionysius's identification of the episcopacy as the office of spiritual perfector, calling it a "state of perfection." As mentioned in chapter 2, other medievals recognized the bishop as a spiritual perfector of the faithful, though they did not formally recognize the episcopacy as a *state* of perfection, nor did they describe the bishop's perfecting activity as consisting principally in teaching and preaching. In discussing both the religious and the episcopal states of perfection, Aquinas notes that, although charity constitutes the essence of spiritual perfection (*STh* II-II, q. 184, a. 1), the perfect in this life do commit venial sins (a. 2, ad 2). And with regard to the episcopacy, it is essential to keep in mind that Thomas is speaking about it as a *status perfectionis* prescriptively not descriptively—he has a realistic grasp of the fact that there have been many legitimate bishops who were notably im-

---

115. Pseudo-Dionysius, "The Ecclesiastical Hierarchy," in *Complete Works*, 235 and 243.

116. In his *Sentences* commentary, Aquinas cites chap. 3 of *Ecclesiastical Hierarchy* to the effect that the bishop must be deiform and godlike in order to dare lead others to goodness of life: "In omni divino non est audendum aliis dux esse, nisi secundum omnem habitum suum factus deiformissimus et Deo simillimus" (In every divine matter a man ought not dare to be the ruler of others, unless in his entire character he is most deiform and most similar to God). Aquinas, *In IV Sent*, d. 24, q. 1, a. 3, qua. 5, sol. 1, 7.2:893. Likewise, in his commentary on Eph 4:12, he mentions this as one of the proximate effects of the episcopal office of preaching: "Etenim specialiter debent intendere praelati ad subditos suos, ut eos ad statum perfectionis perducant; unde et ipsi perfectiores sunt, ut dicit Dionysius in *Ecclesiastica Hierarchia*" (And indeed for their subjects prelates ought to work in particular to lead them to the state of perfection; wherefore they themselves are more perfect, as Dionysius says in *Ecclesiastical Hierarchy*). Aquinas, *Lectura super Ephesios* (hereafter "*In Eph*"), cap. 4, lect. 4, [214], 2:53.

moral.¹¹⁷ In *STh* II-II, q. 184, a. 4, Aquinas distinguishes between an ecclesial state constituted by interior actions directed to God and an ecclesial state constituted by exterior actions directed to the Church. The episcopacy is an instance of the latter: the bishop binds himself to the pastoral care of the faithful by a solemn vow accompanied by a public consecration. The episcopal "state of perfection" is thus an *external* state. While those entering this condition are bound to serve the faithful, they may lack the interior perfection (charity) and wisdom to succeed.¹¹⁸ To avoid the absurdity of holding an ecclesial office consisting of an external state of perfection while lacking internal perfection, the bishop's task, then, demands nothing less than a personal commitment to strive for the interior perfection of charity along with the determination and skill to lead others to this same interior state. Accordingly, Aquinas deploys the phrase *status perfectionis* to describe the episcopacy in order to signify directly an external state obliging the bishop to perfect the faithful. Indirectly, yet no less importantly, this state demands an interior spiritual perfection on the part of the bishop—a perfection he may or may not enjoy but for which he must strive ardently. Without this interior perfection, a bishop will be ill-equipped to fulfill the demands of his external state of perfection, that is, helping to bring about this perfection in others. Studying this teaching of Aquinas should become standard fare for candidates to the episcopacy, bishops-elect, and all prelates.

The moral perfection required of a bishop

Returning to St. Thomas's commentary on the moral qualities required of a bishop listed in 1 Timothy 3:2–7, he states: "[Paul] shows

117. Aquinas says that there are some in the *status perfectionis* who lack charity altogether, thus indicating that the state principally signifies something external, regardless of the interior state of soul. See *STh* II-II, q. 184, a. 4, s.c.: "Aliqui sunt in statu perfectionis qui omnino caritate et gratia carent, sicut mali episcopi et mali religiosi" (Some are in the state of perfection who entirely lack charity and grace, such as evil bishops and evil religious). In fact, in the next article, he goes so far as to say that there are "many" prelates who lack the interior perfection of charity: "Sed multi sunt praelati vel religiosi qui non habent interiorem perfectionem caritatis" (But there are many prelates or religious who do not have the interior perfection of charity). Aquinas, *STh* II-II, q. 184, a. 5, obj. 2.

118. Aquinas, *STh* II-II, q. 184, a. 4. Here Aquinas notes that one may bind himself to something he fails to keep and another may fulfill something to which they have not bound themselves.

what sort of person a bishop ought to be when he says, 'It is necessary for a bishop to be,' et cetera."[119] First, a general requirement is listed: a bishop must be "blameless" (3:2).[120] The remaining items in the list then specify particular moral qualities which Aquinas divides into those bearing on the bishop's interior life and those bearing on his relations with others. In relation to himself, a bishop should be "the husband of one wife, sober, distinguished, prudent, and chaste" (3:2).[121] In his interior dispositions toward others (as distinct from his external actions toward them), a bishop should be "hospitable and a teacher" (3:2).[122] Verse 3 lists the vices from which a bishop should be free: "Not given to wine, no striker, but modest, not quarrelsome, not covetous" (3:3).[123] The remaining items in this pericope describe how a bishop ought to be and act in relation to others: he should rule his family well, he should instruct his children well, he must not be a neophyte, and he must have a good reputation among unbelievers (3:4–7).

Aquinas explains that the obligation for a bishop to be "blameless" (similar to his obligation to be "perfect") should not be interpreted as a requirement that he be entirely sinless. In support of this, he cites 1 John 1:8: "If we say that we have no sin, we deceive ourselves." Nor should this be understood as requiring a bishop to be free of all mortal sin after baptism, otherwise, he says, "there would be so few"![124] In fact, the episcopal state of perfection can and does include rather imperfect individuals. Thomas explains: "What is required is that he be 'blameless,' that is, not subject to any sin for which he could be blamed by others, because it is unbecoming for one who

---

119. "Sed qualis debeat esse episcopus, ostendit, cum subdit 'Oportet episcopum,' etc." Aquinas, *In 1 Tim*, cap. 3, lect. 1, [91], 2:232.

120. "Irreprehensibilem." Aquinas, *In 1 Tim*, 2:231.

121. "Unius uxoris virum, sobrium, ornatum, prudentem, pudicum." Aquinas, *In 1 Tim*, 2:231.

122. "Hospitalem, doctorem." Aquinas, *In 1 Tim*, 2:231.

123. "Non vinolentum, non percussorem, sed modestum, non litigiosum, non cupidum." Aquinas, *In 1 Tim*, 2:231.

124. Thomas's complete statement is as follows: "Nec est dicendum, sicut aliqui dixerunt, quod quicumque peccavit mortaliter post baptismum, non est idoneus, quia pauci essent tales" (Nor should it be said, as some would have it, that whoever has sinned mortally after baptism is not suitable, since there would be so few). Aquinas, *In 1 Tim*, [92], 2:232.

should be blameless to be blameworthy."¹²⁵ It seems that Aquinas has in mind here public, scandalous sins for which the individual has not repented. Such persons would not make suitable episcopal candidates. Yet for all that, as Aquinas himself understood, some notorious sinners became great and holy bishops. These individuals repented and repudiated their former lives, found forgiveness in Christ, and thus they *became* blameless and indeed well-suited for the episcopal office. Their witness serves as a profound testimony of Christ's great mercy, love, and power.

Aquinas next discusses the virtues with which the bishop should be adorned internally: "Every moral virtue is concerned primarily with the passions and there are two which make for sanctity [*sanctitas*], namely chastity and sobriety; because the soul is mainly disturbed by the pleasures of the flesh."¹²⁶ He sees the demand for chastity in the requirement that the bishop be the "husband of one wife" (3:2). The reason for this requirement is not only the potential intemperance involved in having had multiple wives in succession, but also the integrity of the sacramental signification of marriage: the union between Christ and the Church. Because there is only one Church, the bishop, who represents Christ, ought to be the husband of one wife only.¹²⁷ At this juncture, in order to avoid a critical misunderstanding it must be noted that the Church historically has mandated that all married clergy of any rank or order live in complete continence with their wives. It has been recently demonstrated by Christian Cochini, SJ, and several other scholars that this practice forms an essential part of the received apostolic tradition and is therefore unable to be changed licitly regardless of particular historical and localized departures from this

125. "Irreprehensibilis, id est, non subiectus alicui peccato, unde ab aliis reprehendi posset, quia indecens est si reprehensibilis sit reprehensor." Aquinas, *In 1 Tim*, [92], 2:232. See Aquinas's comments on Ti 1:6, where he more explicitly distinguishes between mortal sin and public crimes (*In Tit*, cap. 1, lect. 2, [13], 2:305).

126. "Omnis autem moralis virtus est primo circa passiones; et sunt duo quae faciunt sanctitatem, scilicet castitas et sobrietas, quia per delectationem vel delectabilia carnis, maxime inquietatur anima." Aquinas, *In 1 Tim*, cap. 3, lect. 1, [94], 2:232.

127. "Dicendum quod hoc fit non propter incontinentiam tantum, sed propter repraesentationem sacramenti, quia sponsus ecclesiae est Christus, et una est ecclesia" (It should be said that this is not only on account of incontinence, but also on account of the signification of the sacrament, because Christ is the spouse of the Church and the Church is one). Aquinas, *In 1 Tim*, [96], 2:232.

discipline. Cochini's study was hailed by Henri de Lubac as a work of paramount importance for the Church.[128]

Sobriety, mentioned next, is particularly important for the bishop since his duty is to watch over his flock. Aquinas comments: "Here [Paul] is stating that a bishop, who is called an overseer, should watch.... And drunkenness is an obstacle to watchfulness."[129] Finally, the bishop's intellect ought to be regulated by prudence "because prudence rules all the virtues, and a bishop is chosen to rule others."[130] Here he cites Matthew 24:45: "Who, do you think, is a faithful and wise servant, whom his lord has appointed over his family, to give them meat in season?"[131] Drawing this familial terminology from Scripture, he portrays the bishop as a servant who watches over the Lord's family, feeding them and caring for their needs. To succeed in this, the bishop needs prudence both to direct his own actions and those of his subjects.

The next quality listed, "distinguished" (*ornatum* in 3:2), signifies "proper composure in actions and words."[132] More than a matter of mere etiquette, *ornatum* "suggests beauty, which depends on proportion."[133] Proper proportion manifests itself in suitable words and actions that the prelate exhibits in order to present a good image of himself to others. Aquinas knew well that people judge the interior from what they see and hear, for better or worse. Since a bishop is in a public position of authority, he must have the habit or quality of being distinguished—speaking and acting in a winsome and appealing fashion.

---

128. See Christian Cochini, *Origines Apostoliques du Cèlibat Sacerdotal* (Paris: P. Lethielleux, 1981). Other studies supporting this conclusion include: Stefan Heid, *Zölibat in der Frühen Kirche: Die Anfänge einer Enthaltsamkeitspflicht für Kleriker in Ost und West* (Paderborn: F. Schöningh, 1997); Thomas McGovern, *Priestly Celibacy Today* (Downers Grove, Ill.: Midwest Theological Forum, 1997); and Alfons Stickler, *Der Klerikerzölibat: Seine Entwicklungsgeschichte und seine theologischen Grundlagen* (Abensberg: Kral Verlag, 1993).

129. "Hic enim docet episcopum qui dicitur superintendens, ut vigilet.... Et ebrietas obstat vigiliis." Aquinas, *In 1 Tim* [97], 2:232.

130. "Quia haec est regitiva omnium virtutum, et episcopus eligitur ut alios regat." Aquinas, *In 1 Tim* [98], 2:232.

131. "Matth. c. XXIV, 45: 'Quis, putas, est fidelis servus et prudens,' etc." Aquinas, *In 1 Tim* [98], 2:232.

132. "Bene componitur in actibus et dictis." Aquinas, *In 1 Tim* [100], 2:232.

133. "Ornatus enim importat pulchritudinem quae consistit in proportione." Aquinas, *In 1 Tim*, [100], 2:232.

One who is to form others in charity, to perfect them spiritually, must not be repulsive. He remarks that Ambrose refused to ordain certain men because their gait was dissolute. A distinguished composure requires a response of "modesty" (*pudicum*) when the bishop observes something indecent (*aliqua turpia*) in another's words or actions.[134]

Toward others, a bishop must be "hospitable" (*hospitalis* in 3:2). Thomas says, "A bishop is required to feed his sheep (John 21:15 and 1 Peter 5:2)."[135] He interprets these passages as requiring the bishop to provide his flock with both corporal and spiritual alms; but he assigns priority to the spiritual. "Spiritual alms" is equivalent to doctrine and so the bishop must also be an apt "teacher" (*doctor*). Once again placing a premium on the magisterial duties of the bishop, he notes: "Concerning spiritual alms, he says, 'a teacher': 'Some should be pastors and teachers' (Ephesians 4:11). And this is the *proper office of a prelate* (*officium proprium praelati*), 'I will give you pastors according to my own heart, and they shall feed you with knowledge and doctrine' (Jeremiah 3:15)."[136] He frequently deploys this passage from Jeremiah to explain that the image of the shepherd feeding his flock (see the citations from Jn 21 and 1 Pt 5) signifies the bishop teaching the faithful. In the passage cited, Aquinas uses the word *proprium* to underscore the fact that the magisterial duty defines the episcopal office itself, distinguishing a bishop essentially and functionally from other offices in the Church. He does not elaborate any further here on precisely how

---

134. The contemporary use of the word "modesty" makes it difficult to understand Aquinas's meaning. *Pudicum*, for Aquinas, is an interior disposition of aversion to some indecency. Aquinas's juxtaposition of the virtues of *ornatus* and *pudicum* with *turpia* surely invoked for his students the idea that a bishop ought to be possessed of a manly strength of character free from an effeminate softness unbecoming of a fatherly bishop. It was well known that in antiquity, Furius and Aurelius accused Catullus of being "parum pudicum," the clear import of their invective being to impugn Catullus for being "unmanly." Given the classical liberal arts formation of his thirteenth-century auditors in theology, this point was not lost on Aquinas's attentive students. For more on the *locus classicus* of this use of the term *pudicum*, see Robinson Ellis, *A Commentary on Catullus* (Oxford: Clarendon Press, 1889) and Julia Haig Gaisser, *Catullus* (Oxford: Wiley-Blackwell, 2009).

135. "Imponitur autem episcopo ut pascat oves. Io. Ult. [XXI, 15] et I Petr. Ult. [V, 2]." Aquinas, *In 1 Tim*, [101], 2:233.

136. "Quantum ad secundum [viz., spiritual alms (*spiritualis eleemosyna*)] dicit 'doctorem.' Eph IV, 11: 'Alios pastores et doctores,' etc. Et hoc est *officium proprium praelati*. Ier. III, 15: 'Dabo vobis pastores iuxta cor meum, et pascent vos scientia et doctrina,' etc." (emphasis added). Aquinas, *In 1 Tim*, [101], 2:233.

the teaching office is distinctive to the episcopacy—since priests, deacons, and even laity also teach—though he does develop this line of thinking with more precision in several other works, particularly *STh*. In III, q. 71, a. 4, ad 3, he argues that the kind of teaching distinctive of the episcopal magisterium is a *perfective* type of teaching—not initial catechesis or rudimentary instruction, but teaching for those becoming proficient in the contemplation of divine mysteries. On the part of the bishop, to teach in this way evidently requires a lofty contemplation, which is both a gift of grace and the fruit of natural mental acumen developed by intense study. In addition to this, the task of teaching demands great skill on the part of a bishop to communicate the fruits of his contemplation to others and, in fact, to lead them to attain the same interior perfection he enjoys.[137]

Paul goes on to list (in 1 Tm 3:3) three vices that would disqualify a candidate for the episcopacy: concupiscence, anger, and avarice.[138] Since these vices pose particular dangers especially for bishops, they must exercise greater caution than others in order to avoid them. First, Aquinas interprets "not given to wine" (*non vinolentum*) as pertaining to concupiscence, remarking, "He [that is, Paul] says little but means more," and then he cites Ephesians 5:18 to the effect that drunkenness leads to sexual immorality.[139] Next, regarding anger, two vices are proscribed by the scriptural text: striking (*non percussorem*) and quarrelsomeness (*non litigiosum*).[140] First, regarding the outward act of anger, striking is forbidden and mildness enjoined. Striking is appropriately listed after drunkenness, "for the drunk very easily come to blows."[141] He takes mildness (*modestum*) to mean patience and notes that Christ, undergoing his suffering, did not strike back.[142] A bishop, like Christ his master, will encounter opposition

---

137. See Aquinas, *In IV Sent*, d. 24, q. 1, a. 3, qua. 5, cited above (7.2:893–94); *De veritate*, q. 9, a. 3, where he describes the perfecting duty of bishops in terms of uncovering the spiritual riches concealed in the mystical symbols of Scripture; *STh* III, q. 67, a. 2, ad 1, where he argues that the principal duty of the episcopacy is preaching; but see esp. *STh* III, q. 71, a. 4, ad 3, mentioned here.

138. Aquinas, *In 1 Tim*, cap. 3, lect. 1, [102], 2:233.

139. "Minus dicit, et plus significat." Aquinas, *In 1 Tim*, [102], 2:233.

140. *Percussor* may also be translated "murderer."

141. "Quia ebrii de facili percutiunt." Aquinas, *In 1 Tim*, [102], 2:233.

142. "Christus passus non percutiebat (Christ suffered but did not strike). Aquinas, *In 1 Tim*, [102], 2:233.

and personal attacks, and he should bear them as the Lord bore his: with meekness rather than vengeful anger. Secondly, with regard to angry words, the bishop is charged not to be "quarrelsome" (*non litigiosum*) since he is commanded to announce peace: "And this, because bishops are successors of the apostles, whom Christ instructed to announce peace."[143]

Finally, regarding temporal things (*res temporales*), the bishop must not be "covetous" (*non cupidum* in 3:3, sometimes rendered as "no lover of money"). Aquinas underscores the importance of this scriptural warning, showing how covetousness easily sways bishops from the fulfillment of their duties through an inordinate attachment to temporal goods. The temptation of bribes is particularly acute for prelates: "[The bishop is] appointed judge and governor [*ordinator*] of the church. If he is covetous, it will be easy for him to fall away from justice: 'Neither shall you take bribes, which blind the wise and pervert the words of the just,' (Exodus 23:8)."[144] *Ordinator* also includes being in charge of church finances, a duty imperiled—and in the end altogether thwarted—by covetousness. In a cutting social commentary, Aquinas poignantly ends his first lecture on 1 Timothy 3 by inveighing: "But alas! 'From the least of them even to the greatest, all are given to covetousness' (Jeremiah 6:13)."[145] At the end of the list of virtues that the ideal bishop should possess and vices from which he should be immune, Aquinas laments the state of the episcopacy before his students. Deploying Jeremiah 6:13 in this context is tantamount to a bold and deft indictment of avaricious persons and, in particular, of those particular prelates of his day who were enamored with temporal gain in its many forms.

In lect. 2, on 1 Timothy 3, Thomas discusses the qualities a bishop should have in relation to others, specifically, his family, his church,

---

143. "Et hoc quia episcopi sunt successores apostolorum, quos Christus instruxit ut pacem annuntiarent." Aquinas, *In 1 Tim*, [102], 2:233.

144. "Ponitur iudex et ordinator ecclesiae, qui, si sit cupidus, de facili declinat a iustitia. Ex. XXIII, 8: 'Ne accipias munera, quae exaecant etiam prudentes et subvertunt verba iustorum.'" Aquinas, *In 1 Tim*, [102], 2:233. In his commentary on 2 Cor, Aquinas argues that the faithful are to give temporal goods to bishops not for the benefit of the bishops themselves, but only insofar as they are the distributors of those goods to the poor. Aquinas, *Lectura super 2 Corinthios*, cap. 12, lect. 5, [499], 1:551.

145. "Sed heu! Ier. VI, 13: 'A maiore usque ad minorem omnes avaritiae student.'" Aquinas, *In 1 Tim*, cap. 3, lect. 1, [102], 2:233.

and unbelievers. With respect to his family, he should "rule his own house well" (3:4). Good domestic government involves the acquisition of goods not as ends, but as means to the end of living an upright life.[146] Obedient children are often a sign of good governance: "Having his children in subjection" (3:4). This consists in the father ruling the children "without being softened by the tenderness of affection, which he sometimes offers his children."[147] The bishop should not let gentleness for his children obscure his judgment on their behalf. Disobedient children, on the other hand, are potentially a sign of ineptness in ruling. The scriptural text indicates that a bishop will not be able to rule the church of God if he is unable to rule his own house well. His children ought to be obedient "with all chastity" (3:4) for two reasons. First, a lack of chastity in his children would be a witness against the prelate's capacity to govern. Second, since many people flock to the bishop's home, his children should be chaste lest they corrupt the visitors.[148] Though the episcopal candidate's success in governing his own house gauges the likelihood of his success in governing his church, Aquinas claims a broad exception: "Yet it frequently happens that some do not govern well in small domestic matters, who nevertheless rule well in greater [matters]."[149] With this remark, he clarifies the injunction in verse 5 (that those who do not know how to rule their own house well cannot rule the church of God well) by acknowledging that someone less adept at—though not neglectful of—smaller household matters is not thereby disqualified from the episcopacy, as long as that candidate is capable of handling serious matters.

146. "Bona autem gubernatio non solum est acquisitio divitiarum, quia hae non sunt finis oeconomiae, sed instrumenta; sed finis eius est recta vita" (However, good management is not merely the acquisition of riches, because riches are not the end of the domestic economy, but the instruments thereof; but the end is an upright life). Aquinas, *In 1 Tim*, cap. 3, lect. 2, [104], 2:233.

147. "Non emollitus ex teneritudine amoris, quam quandoque extendit ad filios." Aquinas, *In 1 Tim*, [105], 2:233.

148. "Ideo subditur 'cum omni castitate,' quia mala eorum vita esset testimonium contra parentem et praelatum.... Secunda ratio est, quia ad domum episcopi concurrit populus, ideo oportet eos esse castos" (And so he adds "with all chastity," because their evil life would be a testimony against the parent and the prelate.... The second reason is that, since people assemble at the house of the bishop it is necessary that the children be chaste). Aquinas, *In 1 Tim*, [105], 2:234.

149. "Contingit tamen frequenter quod aliqui non sunt bene regitivi in parvis domesticis, qui tamen bene regunt in maioribus." Aquinas, *In 1 Tim*, [106], 2:234.

Regarding the bishop's relation to his local church community, he should not be a "recent convert" (3:6). Aquinas mentions the obvious historical exception to this, Ambrose of Milan, remarking that sometimes new converts have such an abundance of grace and spiritual maturity that they should be dispensed from this requirement. Thus, he argues that this prohibition should be understood as applying to those who are neophytes *in virtue*. Nevertheless, as a general rule, the newly converted should not be appointed to the episcopacy, "for when someone new in the faith is promoted to some state, he may think himself better than others and regard himself as indispensable; as though without him the Church could not function."[150] Though the bishop ought to be elevated above the flock in his moral character and lofty contemplation, he must not be "puffed up with pride" (3:6) and consider himself superior and vital to his church. Aquinas implies here that no individual is indispensable to the life of the Church or, at least, that no one should consider himself such.

Finally, a bishop must have a good reputation in the eyes of unbelievers (3:7). Thomas says: "This is required of a prelate, because the character of the entire congregation is judged from the prelate."[151] The credibility of the faithful and of the Gospel message that constitutes their identity is at stake. He distinguishes between someone with an unwarranted bad reputation based on falsehoods spread by a malicious detractor, on the one hand, and someone with a bad reputation arising from a true report about actual sins that the person committed, on the other. In the latter case, there are two dangers in such a one being made bishop. First, he will fall into "reproach" (*opprobrium*) (3:7) among the people and thereby fail to govern effectively. The moral authority of the bishop to teach and command hinges in large part on his reputation as a faithful disciple of Christ. Second, he will fall "into the snare of the devil" (*in laqueum diaboli*), which Aquinas interprets as the danger of "impatience in enduring difficulties, by which the bishop gains a bad reputation and this leads to hatred [of him] and he despairs. That a prelate is hateful to the laity

---

150. "Quando enim aliquis de novo veniens ad fidem et ad conditionem aliquam promovetur, reputat se aliis meliorem et valde necessarium, quasi nisi ipse esset, non haberent unde provideretur ecclesiae." Aquinas, *In 1 Tim*, [107], 2:234.

151. "Et hoc necessarium est praelato, quia conversatio totius congregationis iudicatur ex praelato." Aquinas, *In 1 Tim*, [108], 2:234.

happens if he neglects the worship of divine praise."¹⁵² Losing moral authority and inciting the people to hatred by his irritability, intolerance, and negligence renders the prelate impotent. The following verses (3:8–13) identify the essential moral qualities demanded of deacons. This list is evidently helpful for bishops in examining ("testing," verse 10) candidates for ordination to the diaconate.¹⁵³

Finally, in lect. 3, Thomas provides the theological and ecclesiological basis for all of the moral exhortations and teachings given in this epistle. His insight is occasioned by verses 14 and 15 of chapter 3, where the purpose of the epistle's instructions is given: "I write these things to you, hoping that I shall come to you soon. But if I am hindered, [I write these things] in order that you may know how you ought to conduct yourself in the house of God, which is the Church of the living God, the pillar and foundation of the truth."¹⁵⁴ He comments: "The Church is called a kind of assembly, because in the

152. "Impatienter sustinendo, per quod infamis concitetur ad odia, et desperet, et huiusmodi. Et quod prelatus sit odiosus laicis, contingit, si negligit cultum divinae laudis." Aquinas, *In 1 Tim*, [108], 2:234.

153. It should be briefly noted that in his comments near the end of this lecture, on the advice for deacons given in 3:9, "Habentes mysterium fidei in conscientia pura" (Holding the mystery of faith in a pure conscience) (Aquinas, *In 1 Tim*, 2:233), Aquinas remarks that deacons ought to know not only what the people know about the faith, but also its hidden mysteries since they are required to instruct others: "Mysterium enim idem est quod occultum, quia ministri debent scire non tantum ea de fide quae et populus intelligit, sed et mysteria, quia debent alios instruere" (For a mystery is the same as what is hidden, because the ministers ought to know not only those things of the faith that the people understand, but even the mysteries, since they must instruct others). Aquinas, *In 1 Tim*, [113], 2:235. Though these comments directly address a requirement for deacons, they can be applied *a fortiori* to bishops. Again, at the very end of lecture two, Aquinas makes a passing remark on the question whether women can be ordained to the diaconate (1 Tm 3:11). The argument of the Cataphrygians, as he expresses it, states that women are able to receive sacred orders since female deacons often ministered to women. He replies that those women were called *diaconissae* not because they had holy orders, but on account of some ecclesial ministry that they provided: "Sed sciendum est quod in iure aliquae mulieres aliquando vocantur diaconissae, non quia habeant huiusmodi ordinem, sed propter aliquod ministerium ecclesiae, sicut in Graeco dicitur diaconus quilibet minister" (But it ought to be known that in law some women are sometimes called deaconesses, not because they have this kind of order, but on account of some ministry of the Church, as in the Greek whoever is a deacon is a minister). Aquinas, *In 1 Tim*, [118], 2:235.

154. "Haec tibi scribo, sperans me ad te venire cito. Si autem tardavero, ut scias quomodo oportet te in domo Dei conversari, quae est Ecclesia Dei vivi, columna et firmamentum veritatis." Aquinas, *In 1 Tim*, lect. 3, 2:236.

Church is [found] the assembly of the faithful [*adunatio fidelium*]: 'Whom he called, them he also justified' (Romans 8:30). And they are assembled in God."[155]

Here, Aquinas once again identifies the Church as the communion of faithful, whose union is constituted by a shared faith and a holy life. These verses commend the Church as the place where people come to a justifying faith, thereby entering into supernatural communion with God and other believers. Because the Church belongs to the living God, "it is, thus, that we should dwell in it, so that we may live spiritually."[156] He adds that the Church is called "the pillar and foundation of truth" (*columna et firmamentum veritatis*), because it provides firm knowledge of the truth, unavailable through philosophy alone, along with confident security in this truth thanks to the sacraments. Aquinas is arguing here that *sacramental grace* itself provides a firm grasp of Gospel truth so that it may be held with conviction, free both from the insecurity that attends mere opinion and from the significant limitations of natural reasoning or philosophy.[157] Bishops perform a special function for the Church as they work to constitute and preserve spiritual communion in the truth of faith and charity. The upshot of the epistle's exhortations is, simply, that the Church's identity as the communion of faithful is established and reflected by the actions of her prelates, entrusted as they are with the special mission of preaching the truth of the Gospel.[158] The Church's preaching of and belief in the "mystery of our religion," which is the

---

155. "Ecclesia dicitur quasi adunatio, quia in ecclesia est adunatio fidelium. Rom. VIII, 30: 'Quos vocavit,' etc. Et adunantur in Deum." Aquinas, *In 1 Tim*, [127], 2:237.

156. "Est ergo sic in ea conversandum, ut spiritualiter vivamus." Aquinas, *In 1 Tim*, [127], 2:237.

157. "Sed in ecclesia est firma cognitio et veritas.... 'Et firmamentum,' scilicet quantum ad alios, quia non possunt firmari in veritate, nisi per ecclesiae sacramenta" (But in the Church is firm knowledge and truth.... "And foundation," namely regarding others, since they are not able to be firm in the truth except through the sacraments of the Church). Aquinas, *In 1 Tim*, [128], 2:237.

158. J. N. D. Kelly, commenting on these same verses (1 Tm 3:14–15), notes that this passage "provides the theological basis for the rules and regulations, as well as for the onslaught on false teaching, which make up the body of the letter. The gist of Paul's message is that order, in the widest sense of the term, is necessary in the Christian congregation precisely because it is God's household, his chosen instrument for proclaiming to men the saving truth of the revelation of the God-man, Jesus Christ." Kelly, *The Pastoral Epistles*, 86.

essence of the Gospel message, centers on Christ's manifestation in the flesh and his being "taken up in glory" (3:16).

How to Teach *Pietas* (4:6–5:2)

St. Thomas begins his comments on 1 Timothy 4 by noting that in the first three chapters of this epistle, Paul instructs Timothy on spiritual and internal things regarding the teachings of faith, the worship of God, and the qualities required of ministers. In chapter 4, we have instructions on the Church's attitude toward external things such as food, riches, and the different states of men. In lect. 1, on 1 Timothy 4:1–5, Aquinas understands Paul to be issuing a warning about errors contrary to the faith in latter times. These errors specifically regard the prohibition of food and marriage, both of which are created and established by God and, as such, are good. In passing, it should be noted that Aquinas identifies these errors as distinctive of the Manichean heresy. Moreover, inasmuch as these things are consecrated "by the word of God and prayer," they are to be "received with thanksgiving" (4:5).

In lect. 2, on 1 Timothy 4:6–10, Aquinas comments on the bishop's duty to seek and teach piety (*pietas* in verse 7), explaining why it is valued so highly for prelates in these verses. As a proper effect of charity, piety is intrinsically ordered to eternal salvation. Since the doctrine of piety includes both things to be done and things to be believed, in the next lecture (lect. 3, on 4:11–5:2), he discusses how a bishop becomes fit for commanding and teaching. The prelate's goal in fulfilling these duties is the salvation of souls, including his own. Again, Aquinas affirms that the bishop must first attend to his own needs in order to provide well for the spiritual needs of his flock.

He interprets verse 6, "Proposing these things to the brethren, you will be a good minister of Christ Jesus, nourished with the word of faith and good doctrine," as an indication that both Timothy's office and his education require him to pass on his knowledge and faith to his people.[159] Timothy possessed the office of preaching and ruling (*officium praedicandi et regendi*) because he was constituted "in the of-

---

159. "Haec proponens fratribus, bonus eris minister Christi Iesu, enutritus verbis fidei et bonae doctrinae." Aquinas, *In 1 Tim*, cap. 4, lect. 2, 2:241.

fice of Christ's ministry" (*in officio ministerii Christi*) and this office requires him to teach and govern. Moreover, on account of his "spiritual nourishment" (*spirituale nutrimentum*), that is, his education in the doctrine of God's word, he was required to instruct others regarding what is to be believed (*credenda*) and what ought to be done (*agenda*).[160]

Commenting on verse 7, "Train yourself in piety," Thomas describes piety both as a species of the virtue of justice prompting us to "pay the debt of good will to our parents and native land" and to worship God.[161] *Pietas* as such conveys the notion of affection directed to those from whom one originates (*affectionem ad suum principium*), whether those persons be earthly or heavenly. Earthly piety extends both to parents and to country in the person of one's compatriots. Christian piety extends this same good will even further to include all humans since "we are all of the same country" (*omnes sumus eiusdem patriae*)—*patriae* meaning here the eternal fatherland or heaven—and Aquinas remarks that "in this sense, piety is taken for mercy."[162] Insofar as piety most fully signifies affection for one's ultimate source (*principium*), *pietas* extends beyond parents and country, and ultimately to God. This affection is expressed by acts of worship. Thus, the piety enjoined upon the bishop in verse 7 entails both performing acts of mercy for others and offering divine worship. Mercy, like hospitality, includes providing for bodily needs, but above all it moves the bishop to provide for spiritual needs and this is done principally by preaching and teaching.

Thomas next explains the greater value of piety in contrast to abstinence as expressed in verse 8: "For bodily discipline is useful for little but piety is profitable *in every respect*."[163] Having taken piety to signify both mercy toward others and divine worship, he interprets its universal profitability in terms of earthly grace and heavenly glory. In the present life, the virtue of piety removes all sins, fosters what

---

160. Aquinas, *In 1 Tim*, [150–51], 2:241.
161. "Exerce autem teipsum ad pietatem." Aquinas, *In 1 Tim*, 2:241. "Pietas est, per quam parentibus patriaeque benevolentiae officium impendimus." Aquinas, *In 1 Tim*, [154], 2:242. Compare this with *STh* II-II, q. 101, a. 1.
162. "Et ideo pietas sumitur pro misericordia." Aquinas, *In 1 Tim*, [154], 2:242.
163. "Nam corporalis exercitatio ad modicum utilis est, pietas autem *ad omnia* utilis est" (emphasis added). Aquinas, *In 1 Tim*, 2:241.

is good, and merits God's special mercy.[164] In one of several *quaestiones* on this verse, Aquinas argues that piety is to be preferred to abstinence especially because it merits eternal life *by its very nature*. Questioning whether bodily discipline might also hold a special promise of heavenly reward, his response rests on this principle: "When two virtues are such that one contains the other, then the *per se* characteristics of the higher virtue belong accidentally to the lower."[165]

Now the virtue of charity contains the virtue of piety, which he describes as charity's proper and immediate effect (*proprius et immediatus effectus*), for a genuine love of God and neighbor necessarily includes gratitude and honor for those who give and foster one's very life. And since it is the *per se* characteristic of charity to merit eternal life, piety, as its proper and immediate effect, has this same characteristic *per accidens*. He concludes: "Therefore, it belongs to the very nature [of piety] to merit eternal life" (interpreting verse 8, which states that piety "holds promise for the present life and also for the life to come").[166] However, with respect to "bodily discipline," it is possible, for example, to fast and yet not to merit eternal life if the fasting is devoid of or contrary to the love of God. Abstinence, thus, is not ordered to charity *per se*, though it can be ordered in this way accidentally.[167] The point here is that, in his life and in his teaching, the bishop should not place as high a priority on bodily discipline as on piety—that is, on acts of mercy toward one's neighbor and acts of the worship of God. These latter he should cherish and promote above all as the way to eternal life.

Aquinas understands the advice given in verses 8–10 (namely, to prefer *pietas* to abstinence) as addressing Timothy's tendency to be too hard on his flock. He remarks: "It should be known that Timothy was a very abstemious person."[168] With profound psychologi-

---

164. "Et 'est ad omnia utilis,' quia ad omnia peccata delenda.... Item ad bona promovenda.... Item promeretur specialem Dei misericordiam" (And "it is useful for all things," because it removes all sins.... Again, it impels to good.... Likewise, it merits the special mercy of God). Aquinas, *In 1 Tim*, [157], 2:242.

165. "Quando duae virtutes sunt et una continet aliam, illud quod est superioris virtutis per se, competit per accidens inferiori." Aquinas, *In 1 Tim*, [160], 2:243.

166. "Et ideo secundum propriam rationem attingit ad merendam vitam aeternam." Aquinas, *In 1 Tim*, [160], 2:243.

167. See Aquinas, *STh* II-II, q. 146, a. 1.

168. "Et sciendum est quod Timotheus erat homo valde abstinens." Aquinas, *In 1 Tim*, cap. 4, lect. 2, [153], 2:242.

cal sensitivity, Thomas notes that Paul advised Timothy to be more merciful, "because those who are hard on themselves are likely to be hard on others. Consequently, he advises him to prefer piety to abstinence."[169] A little later in this same lecture, he remarks: "A person is not merciful, if he is not merciful to himself," reinforcing this point by citing Sirach 30:24, "Have pity on your own soul, pleasing God."[170] But he adds that being merciful to oneself is only possible, "if a man is united to God in love, otherwise he cannot be merciful."[171]

In lect. 3, he notes that verse 11, "Command and teach these things," provides advice on the way piety ought to be taught.[172] Since piety is essential in meriting eternal life, the bishop must not only possess it himself, but he must also teach it to his flock. According to verse 11, teaching piety consists both in commanding things to be done and in teaching things to be believed.[173] Note that the bishop must not merely *propose* the things to be done; rather, he also must *command* that they be done and for this, he needs authority (*auctoritas*).

Being fit for commanding

Aquinas interprets verse 12 as giving advice on how a prelate should forestall contempt of his authority: "Let no one despise your youth, but be an example to the faithful in word, in behavior, in charity, in faith, in chastity."[174] The bishop must be respected if he is to command piety successfully. This respect is grounded on the authority of the one commanding—if the authority is scorned, the com-

---

169. "Quia qui non parcunt sibi, frequneter nec aliis parcunt. Et ideo inducit eum ut pietatem praeferat abstinentiae." Aquinas, *In 1 Tim*, [153], 2:242.

170. "Non est misericors qui sibi non miseretur." Aquinas, *In 1 Tim*, [161], 2:243. Aquinas cites this same passage from Sirach again in his comments on 1 Tm 4:16, where he says: "Aliqui sic attendunt doctrinae, quod sui curam negligunt; sed Apostolus dicit quod primo attendat sibi, et postea doctrinae. Eccli. xxx, 24: 'Miserere animae tuae placens Deo'" (Some so attend to doctrine that they neglect their own care; but the apostle says that first he should attend to himself and then to doctrine. "Be merciful to your own soul, pleasing God" [Eccl 30:24]). Aquinas, *In 1 Tim*, cap. 4, lect. 3, [176], 2:245.

171. "Si homo coniungatur Deo per amorem, alias non est misericors." Aquinas, *In 1 Tim*, [161], 2:243.

172. "Praecipe haec et doce." Aquinas, *In 1 Tim*, cap. 4, lect. 3, 2:244.

173. Aquinas, *In 1 Tim*, [166], 2:244.

174. "Nemo adolescentiam tuam contemnat, sed exemplum esto fidelium in verbo, in conversatione, in charitate, in fide, in castitate." Aquinas, *In 1 Tim*, [166], 2:244.

mand is frustrated and likely will be flouted.¹⁷⁵ In the case of Timothy—whom Thomas understood to be a youth (4:12) and, therefore, not generally considered prudent—it was even more imperative that he establish his authority. Any prelate, however, establishes authority by way of good example ("in behavior," 4:12).

To the faithful, the bishop should exemplify virtue in word and deed (4:12). His speech ought to be well thought out, well arranged, and cautious.¹⁷⁶ His behavior must also be exemplary so that he excels in good deeds just as he excels in place and dignity. In his relationship with God, he must display exemplary charity and a faith that, as Thomas notes, "is peculiarly suited to prelates who are the guardians of the faith."¹⁷⁷ In his own person, the bishop is to be an example of chastity, which conforms one to Christ in a particular way and "orders life and the mind."¹⁷⁸ The reason for this is that it is unbecoming (*indecens*) that the life of the minister should disagree with that of the Lord.¹⁷⁹

Excelling in virtue, the bishop is equipped to execute the duties of his office and to serve the faithful as a concrete example of Christian faith and charity. He secures his moral authority to command others by the public witness of his life: attaining excellence in virtue in his own person and in his relationships with others and with God.

Being fit for teaching

Prelates are advised on how to become fit for teaching in verse 13: "Until I come, attend to reading, exhortation, and doctrine."¹⁸⁰ The

---

175. "Praeceptum efficaciam non habet nisi per auctoritatem praecipientis, et ideo quando auctoritas contemnitur, praeceptum frustratur" (A precept does not have efficacy except through the authority of the one commanding, and so when his authority is disdained, the precept is rejected). Aquinas, *In 1 Tim*, [168], 2:244.

176. "Ponderato, ordinato, et circumspecto" (Pondered, ordered, and circumspect). Aquinas, *In 1 Tim*, [169], 2:244.

177. "Quod specialiter competit praelatis, qui sunt custodes fidei." Aquinas, *In 1 Tim*, [169], 2:244.

178. "Vitam et mentem ordinat castitas." Aquinas, *In 1 Tim*, [169], 2:245.

179. "Indecens est nimis, ut vita ministrorum discordet a vita Domini" (It is exceedingly unfitting that the life of ministers should disagree with the life of the Lord). Aquinas, *In 1 Tim*, [169], 2:245.

180. "Dum venio, attende lectioni, exhortationi et doctrinae." Aquinas, *In 1 Tim*, 2:244.

bishop's personal preparation for teaching is twofold: reading and gaining the experience of teaching. By reading Scripture, the bishop acquires knowledge of divine revelation and prepares himself to bear God's word to the faithful. For Aquinas, this preparation is signified allegorically in Exodus 25:14, about which he says: "It is stated that in the ark of the Lord there must always be poles in the rings that are on the sides, so that it may always be ready for carrying."[181] This signifies the bishop's obligation constantly to be immersed in Scripture so that he will always be prepared to carry or bear God's word to the faithful. Teaching itself also prepares the bishop for this task by furnishing experience in giving "exhortations" regarding what is to be done and "doctrine" regarding what is to be believed.

Thomas argues that Paul had two reasons for warning Timothy to prepare himself to command and teach: first, the grace Timothy received at his episcopal consecration enjoined these duties upon him; and, second, his reward for the faithful execution of these duties is nothing less than eternal life. On verse 14, "Neglect not the grace that is in you, which was given you by prophecy, with the imposition of the hands of the presbyter," Aquinas comments that the recipient of episcopal grace is expected to bear fruit.[182] He cites the parable in Matthew 25:24 of the lazy servant who hid his master's money in the ground as a warning to prelates that they will be punished if they neglect to bear fruit with the grace they have been given. The episcopal "grace" mentioned in verse 14 is to be understood as "either episcopal dignity or the gift of knowledge or prophecy or miracles, none of which ought to be neglected."[183]

In these remarks, Aquinas calls both the gratuitous gifts mentioned and the dignity of the episcopacy itself a "grace," conferred "by prophecy" and "by the imposition of hands." "Prophecy" signifies the inspiration of the Holy Spirit given to the members of the early Church to identify the person God wants to fill the bishop's office.

---

181. "Et hoc significatur Ex. XXV, 12 s., ubi dicitur, quod semper in arca Domini debebant esse vectes in circulis, et circuli in angulis: quasi semper parati ad portandum." Aquinas, *In 1 Tim*, [171], 2:245.

182. "Noli negligere gratiam quae in te est, quae data est tibi per prophetiam, cum impositione manuum presbyteri." Aquinas, *In 1 Tim*, cap. 4, lect. 3, 2:244.

183. "Per hoc intellige, vel dignitatem episcopalem, vel donum scientiae, vel prophetiae, vel miraculorum, quorum nihil debet negligi." Aquinas, *In 1 Tim*, [173], 2:245.

He comments: "For in the early Church where elections were conducted *purely* and *for God's sake*, no one was selected for the episcopacy except by divine choice, as Ambrose and Nicholas were chosen."[184] According to Aquinas, this method of election, grounded in the prophetic revelation of divine choice, was much more beneficial for the people than other methods of episcopal appointment. He cites Proverbs 29:18, lamenting the loss of this custom and the subsequent disarray of the Church in his day: "'When prophecy shall fail,' that is, this manner of electing, 'the people shall be scattered.'"[185]

Regarding the last part of verse 14, "the imposition of the hands of the presbyter," he interprets "presbyter" to signify "bishop" (noting that the two terms were used interchangeably, as mentioned above) and then he asks why the word *presbyteri* is used since it is in the singular (genitive case), whereas bishops are to be ordained by three. He offers several interpretations. First, it might have been the case that other bishops were indeed present, but as assistants to the principal prelate, who is the only one mentioned in this verse. He also notes that the arrangement of three ordaining prelates was not required by the early Church, since the scarcity of bishops (*episcopi*) prevented them from assembling easily. Secondly, *presbyteri* can be interpreted not as specifying a particular prelate, but to signify the *office* of prelates, thereby distinguishing the laying on of hands by prelates from that done by others in the Church.[186] According to this second inter-

---

184. "Nam in primitiva ecclesia, ubi *pure* at *propter Deum* electiones fiebant, nullus assumebatur ad episcopatum nisi per electionem divinam, sicut electus est Ambrosius et Nicolaus" (emphasis added). Aquinas, *In 1 Tim*, [173], 2:245. He then cites the *Glossa* to the same effect: "Per sanctorum electionem, quia sancti non eligebant quem a Deo non sciebant electum" (Through the election of the saints, because the saints did not elect someone who was not known to be elected by God). Aquinas, *In 1 Tim*, [173], 2:245.

185. "'Cum prophetia defecerit,' id est, talis modus electionis, 'dissipabitur populus.'" Aquinas, *In 1 Tim*, [173], 2:245. This warning applies just as well to the condition of the Church in our day.

186. Aquinas provides this second interpretation based on another version of verse 14 of this biblical text. He says: "Alia littera habet 'presbyteri,' id est, illorum qui sibi imposuerunt manus non inquantum homines, sed inquantum presbyteri.... Et ideo dicit 'presbyterii,' vel 'presbyteri,' quia manus impositio, alia est quae fit a diaconibus, et alia quae fit a presbyteris" (Another text has "of the priesthood," that is, of those who imposed their hands not insofar as they were men, but insofar as they were priests.... And so he says "of the priesthood" or "of the priest," because there is one imposition of hands

pretation, it is precisely the bishop's laying on of hands that confers grace in virtue of his ministerial office: "This [imposition of hands] signifies the conferring of grace: not that the ministers give grace, but that they signify the grace given by Christ. Hence it is only given by those who are Christ's ministers."[187]

This second interpretation (along with Thomas's remarks on 2 Tm 1:6) led Lécuyer to conclude that Aquinas's thought developed from his *Sentences* commentary—where he denies that the episcopacy is a sacramental order—to the affirmation that episcopal consecration is a sacrament.[188] It is important to note that in his earlier writings, such as his *Sentences* commentary, Aquinas neither affirms nor denies that episcopal consecration confers grace. Rather, in those works he is principally concerned with the question whether the office is a sacramental grade of holy orders (which he denies). With due respect for the value of Lécuyer's work, the development of the discussion in Thomas's later works regarding the communication of the Holy Spirit and grace given in episcopal consecration does not indicate that he began to consider the episcopacy a sacrament. For instance, in *STh* II-II, q. 184, a. 5, he holds that consecration to the religious life also imparts grace to the recipient, and yet he denies its sacramentality. Likewise, the fact that episcopal consecration cannot be repeated does not require that it be considered a sacramental order. As Lécuyer himself acknowledges, the reasons Aquinas gives against its repetition are grounded not in its sac-

---

by deacons and another by priests). Aquinas, *In 1 Tim*, [174], 2:245. Here the Marietti edition of Aquinas's text is problematic. "Presbyteri" is not an "alia littera" but is identical to the first version of the text on which he remarked. At the end of his remarks, Aquinas says "dicit presbyterii." Moreover, his comments on this alternate reading discuss the laying on of hands characteristic of the prelate's *office* (hence, "presbyterii") as distinct from the laying on of hands done by a particular prelate (which would be "presbyteri"). Currently, the Latin Vulgate has the corrected version in verse 14: "presbyterii" (not "presbyteri"). In any event, and though Thomas does not mention this here, firm evidence that Paul was the principal presbyter who consecrated Timothy as a bishop is given in 2 Tm 1:6.

187. "Et haec impositio significat collationem gratiae, non quod ministri dent gratiam, sed quod significant gratiam datam a Chrsito. Unde illorum est solum, qui sunt ministri Christi." Aquinas, *In 1 Tim*, [174], 2:245. Aquinas's efforts both to be historically accurate and to provide a number of possible interpretations supports Torrell's claim in his article "Saint Thomas et l'histoire" (*Revue Thomiste* 105 [2005]: 355–409) that he was more concerned with historical questions than is commonly acknowledged.

188. See Lécuyer, "Aux origines," 84, and "Les étapes," 35–37.

ramentality, but in the fact that the bishop receives his *potestas ordinis* from a sacred consecration imparting a relatively permanent condition to the person or thing consecrated. Such an act places the recipient in a *status*, a stable "state." In fact, as stated above in chapter 1, Stenger has shown that, even in his more mature works such as *De perfectione*, written in 1270, Aquinas continues explicitly to deny the sacramentality of the episcopal order: "With regard to the true body of Christ that is contained in the sacrament [of the Eucharist], a bishop does not have an order higher than the presbyterate."[189] In any event, the Church's doctrine has now developed to the point where episcopal consecration is recognized as the fullness of the sacrament of holy orders.

Even though Aquinas makes no explicit claim that this ordination is sacramental in his comments on 1 Timothy 4:14, at the very least his comments on this pericope represent a development in his theology of the episcopacy, specifically, that the imposition of hands signifies the communication of grace to the episcopal candidate. The bishop's obligations to teach and command, along with the strength to fulfill this obligation, come from his episcopal consecration and the grace it bestows.

The prelate is enabled to fulfill the obligation to teach piety by "continually meditating upon the things that pertain to his office."[190] The advice in verse 15 to "meditate upon these things" is meant to prompt the bishop frequently to consider his duty to care for his people. If he consistently directs his thoughts and behavior to this end, others will see his usefulness, that is, the good he affords the community. Thus, the people will listen to the prelate, being inclined to believe his words and to obey his commands.

If the grace of episcopal consecration is the beginning of the prelate's obligation to teach piety by word and example, then the reward of

189. "Sed quantum ad corpus Christi verum, quod in Sacramento continetur, [episcopus] non habet ordinem supra presbyterum." Aquinas, Aquinas, *De perf*, cap. 24, [715], 2:150. Stenger remarks: "This text is important, for it was written in January of 1270; the position which Saint Thomas here maintains is exactly what he had written earlier when he commented on the Sentences." Stenger, "Development," 170–71. All of this is noted without prejudice to the fact that the official development of the Church's doctrine has resulted in the affirmation that episcopal consecration is the fullness of the sacrament of holy orders. See Vatican Council II, *Lumen Gentium*, no. 22.

190. "Continue meditetur ea quae spectant ad officium suum." Aquinas, *In 1 Tim*, cap. 4, lect. 3, [175], 2:245.

eternal life serves as the end (or final cause) of teaching piety. Thomas says that this reward will be abundant (*copiosus*) because, "in doing this you shall save yourself and them that hear you" (verse 16).[191] The reward for such a bishop is twofold: bringing his flock to salvation and saving his own soul. The bishop must vigorously pursue the duties of his office, especially that of teaching piety (love of God and mercifulness toward neighbor), and this for the sake of his neighbor's salvation. In linking the bishop's own salvation with the proper execution of this duty to the faithful, Aquinas underscores the gravity of the demands of this office: episcopal duties must be fulfilled in order for the bishop himself to be saved. He notes that the converse is implied in this verse: failing to fulfill these duties will exclude the bishop from everlasting life. The bishop who successfully lives and works for the salvation of others deserves a commensurate reward, and thus he concludes: "Hence teachers ought to receive a golden crown."[192]

Nevertheless, in verse 16, "Take heed to yourself and to doctrine," he sees a warning for the bishop to take care of himself *first*: "For some attend to doctrine so much that they neglect themselves; but the Apostle tells him to attend to himself first, and afterwards to doctrine."[193] The bishop's personal needs that follow from the demands of his office have both a chronological and a causal priority over the needs of his flock since apart from their fulfillment, the duties of the prelate's office cannot be executed properly.

He concludes his third lecture with some brief comments on 1 Timothy 5:1–2. Since different persons must be taught in diverse ways according to age and gender, bishops ought to know the members of their church personally. Thomas issues to bishops a particular warning to treat young women as sisters, that is, "with the love of charity—and this 'in all chastity' because spiritual love toward women, unless one is cautious, degenerates into carnal love. Therefore, in matters pertaining to young women, chastity must be applied."[194]

---

191. "Hoc enim faciens et teipsum salvum facies, et eos qui te audiunt." Aquinas, *In 1 Tim*, 2:244.

192. "Unde doctoribus debetur praemium aureolae." Aquinas, *In 1 Tim*, [176], 2:246.

193. "Attende tibi et doctrinae." Aquinas, *In 1 Tim*, 2:244. "Aliqui sic attendunt doctrinae, quod sui curam negligunt; sed Apostolus dicit quod primo attendat sibi, et postea doctrinae." Aquinas, *In 1 Tim*, [176], 2:245.

194. "Ex amore charitatis. Et hoc, 'in omni castitate.' Quia amor spiritualis ad mu-

The first two full lectures on 1 Timothy 5 do not bear on the episcopacy as directly as the previous lectures. In them, he comments on the instructions found in 1 Timothy 5:1–16 to teach widows to pursue good and abstain from evils.[195]

Honoring and Correcting Presbyters and the Criteria for Promotion (5:17–24)

In his third lecture on 1 Timothy 5, Thomas discusses three matters of episcopal governance: honoring presbyters, correcting them, and promoting individuals to the presbyterate. He interprets "presbyters" (*presbyteri*) in verse 17—"Let the presbyters who rule well be esteemed worthy of a double honor, especially they who labor in the word and doctrine"—to signify both bishops and priests.[196] The prelates who "rule well" are those who rule *prudently*, that is, those who act "for the honor of God and not their own advantage."[197] The double honor they deserve includes both the satisfaction of their needs (*ministratio necessariorum*) and a display of respect for them (*exhibitio reverentiae*). They merit this honor "by their labors, namely, 'they who labor in the word of preaching.' … 'And in doctrine,' that is, in teaching."[198]

---

lieres, nisi cautus sit, degenerat in carnalem, ideo in his, quae ad iuvenculas pertinent, adhibenda est castitas." Aquinas, *In 1 Tim*, [179], 2:246.

195. See Aquinas, *In 1 Tim*, cap. 5, lect. 1, [187] and [190], 2:248. Aquinas makes an interesting statement in his comments on 1 Tm 5:9 ("Let a widow be chosen of no less than sixty years of age, who has been the wife of one husband") that reveals his independence from the exegetical tradition represented by the *Glossa* which he considers mistaken: "Haec Glossa est magistralis et partum valet" (Here the Gloss is magisterial and of little value). Aquinas, *In 1 Tim*, lect. 2, [195], 2:249. The *Glossa* on this passage claims that widows must be the wife of only one husband "because of the sacrament"; yet Aquinas says that no sacrament would require women to have had only one husband. Rather, the admonition in verse 9 applies, in Aquinas's estimation, to those women who have a continual intention to persevere in the status of "widowhood."

196. "Qui bene praesunt presbyteri, duplici honore digni habeantur, maxime qui laborant in verbo et doctrina." Aquinas, *In 1 Tim*, cap. 5, lect. 3, 2:251. He says: "Et ideo praelati ecclesiae, scilicet episcopi et sacerdotal, vocantur presbyteri" (And so the prelates of the Church, namely bishops and priests, are called presbyteri). Aquinas, *In 1 Tim*, cap. 5, lect. 3, [212], 2:251–52.

197. "Ad Dei honorem, et non ad propriam commoditatem." Aquinas, *In 1 Tim*, [212], 2:252.

198. "Hoc merentur suo labore, scilicet 'qui laborant in verbo praedicationis.' … Item 'in doctrina,' id est, in eruditione." Aquinas, *In 1 Tim*, [213], 2:252. Again, Aquinas

Thomas explains that the reason verse 18 cites Deuteronomy 25:4 ("You shall not muzzle the ox") and Luke 10:7 ("The laborer is worthy of his wages") is to show how this honor ought to be understood: "Teachers and preachers are not to be prevented from having their honoraria [*sumptus*]."[199] The passage from Luke, "The laborer is worthy of his wages," prompts him to introduce a *quaestio*: "Are those [honoraria] to be considered wages?"[200] He replies that they are "wages" only in a broad sense (*modo large*). If "wage" means a "final reward," then the honoraria are not wages since the final reward for the preacher's labors in teaching the Gospel is neither temporal sustenance nor human respect. He remarks: "Far be it that the wages of preachers be that sort of honorarium."[201] An honorarium is not to be considered a final reward but something temporal that the preacher deserves for his labor.

Next, verse 19 instructs prelates on judging and correcting presbyters: "You should not receive an accusation against a presbyter, except under two or three witnesses."[202] First, he argues that the interpretation found in the *Glossa*, "A person in such a lofty order should not be easily accused, for he is Christ's representative," does not sufficiently explain verse 19's instruction, since even accusations against the laity customarily require two or three witnesses to be admitted as evidence.[203] Aquinas's resolution of this difficulty hinges on the traditional difference in jurisprudence between an indictment and a conviction. *Accusations* against the laity can be admitted for indictment even if only one person levels them; but the accused layperson should not be condemned without two or three witnesses. Howev-

---

explicitly identifies the role of the *doctor* with the office of the *episcopus*: "Iungit pastores et doctores, quia hoc est officium episcopi" (He joins pastors and teachers because this is the office of a bishop). Aquinas, *In 1 Tim*, [213], 2:252.

199. "Ergo non sunt prohibendi praedicatores et doctores quin sumptus habeant." Aquinas, *In 1 Tim*, [215], 2:252.

200. "Sed numquid isti sumptus sunt merces?" Aquinas, *In 1 Tim*, [217], 2:252.

201. "Absit quod praedicatorum merces sint huiusmodi sumptus." Aquinas, *In 1 Tim*, [217], 2:252. Compare this with Gaines Post, Kimon Giocarinis, and Robert Kay, "The Medieval Heritage of a Humanistic Ideal: *Scientia donum Dei est, unde vendi non potest*," *Traditio* 11 (1955): 195–234.

202. "Adversus presbyterum accusationem noli recipere, nisi sub duobus aut tribus testibus." Aquinas, *In 1 Tim*, 2:251.

203. "Non est facile accusanda tam alti ordinis persona, quae sit vice Christi." Aquinas, *In 1 Tim*, [219], 2:252.

er, with respect to the clergy, no accusation should even be *admitted* for indictment "unless it is evident."[204] Instead of insisting absolutely on two or three accusers in order to indict a clergy member, he interprets this passage to mean that the charge against the presbyter must at least be "evident" (*evidens*). Implicit in this account is the recognition that, since the bishop has juridical power over other presbyters who are particularly vulnerable to false accusations, he must exercise this power responsibly and with greater solicitude.

In Aquinas's estimation, verse 20, "Those that sin, reprove before all that the rest also may have fear," instructs bishops to correct presbyters publicly who are found guilty—but not without proper discrimination.[205] He distinguishes procedurally between instances of simple fraternal correction, which should be conducted in private, and instances in which a prelate conducts a formal trial of an accused presbyter, which he calls "judicial cases" (*iudiciaria*). Since the judge is a public person (*personam publicam*), "he must intend the common good, which is harmed by a public sin, because many are [thereby] scandalized."[206] Thus, the judge must act not only for the good of the one found guilty by imposing a penalty for his correction, but also he must act for the edification of the people. Such actions bear upon public acts (in this case, of a presbyter), what is now commonly called the external forum. In support of public punishment in such cases, he cites Ecclesiastes 8:11: "Because sentence is not speedily pronounced against the evil, the children of men commit evils without any fear." But here he raises another *quaestio*: punishing the presbyter "before all" seems contrary to Matthew 18:15: "If your brother offends you, go, and rebuke him between you and him alone." He resolves the tension between these passages with another distinction, this time, between private and public sins. Private sins should be corrected privately and this is what the Lord had in mind in the text from Matthew. However, commenting on 1 Timothy 5:20, he says: "The Apostle is speaking of a public sin, which calls for a public remedy."[207]

204. "Nisi sit evidens." Aquinas, *In 1 Tim*, [219], 2:252.
205. "Peccantes coram omnibus argue, ut et caeteri timorem habeant." Aquinas, *In 1 Tim*, 2:251.
206. "Ideo debet intendere bonum commune, quod laeditur per peccatum publicum, quia multi scandalizantur." Aquinas, *In 1 Tim*, [221], 2:253.
207. "Sed Apostolus loquitur de peccato publico, quod publica poena indiget."

Commenting on verse 21, "I charge you before God and Christ Jesus, and the elect angels, that you observe these things without prejudice, doing nothing by inclining to either side," Aquinas remarks that the prelate must judge justly because "the ecclesiastical judge acts in the person of God in a special way when he judges."[208] He must judge, then, according to God's own justice. The phrase "observe these things without prejudice" is taken as a warning against rash judgment. He gives two complementary interpretations of "without prejudice" (*sine praeiudicio*): first, the bishop should not proceed rashly, but with deliberation (*deliberatione*); second, the bishop should not proceed "without previous discussion" (*sine praecedenti discussione*).

He next comments on the warning in verse 22, "Impose not hands lightly upon any man, neither be a partaker of other men's sins."[209] He had already explained this passage in his *Sentences* commentary: "[The bishop] is required to take the greatest care, in proportion to the order or office to be enjoined, to be certain of the qualifications of those to be promoted, at least from the testimony of others. This is the meaning of the Apostle when he says, in 1 Timothy 5:22: 'Impose not hands lightly.'"[210] Here in lect. 3, he interprets this verse similarly. Just as the bishop should not be quick to condemn a presbyter, neither should he be quick to promote someone to the presbyterate. Citing the admonition in 1 Timothy 3:10, "Let these also first be proved," Aquinas interprets the second part of 5:22 ("neither be a partaker in another man's sins") as the very reason for Timothy's warning: "If you promote indiscriminately and, as a result, they sin with themselves or

---

Aquinas, *In 1 Tim*, [222], 2:253. This same question is raised in *Quaestiones et decisiones in Epistolas S. Pauli* (formerly attributed to Hugh of St. Victor), mentioned above (see footnote 40): "Publica enim offensa publica indiget satisfactione" (For a public offense requires a public satisfaction). *Quaestiones et decisiones in Epistolas S. Pauli*, PL 175, col. 600D, though the Latin in Aquinas's conclusion is worded much more cleverly: "Publicum peccatum publice puniendum" (A public sin is to be punished publically). Aquinas, *In 1 Tim*, cap. 5, lect. 3, [222], 2:253. Compare this with Aquinas, *STh* II-II, q. 33, a. 7.

208. "Iudex ecclesiasticus maxime gerit in iudicando personam Dei." Aquinas, *In 1 Tim*, [223], 2:253.

209. "Manus cito nemini imposueris, neque communicaveris peccatis alienis." Aquinas, *In 1 Tim*, 2:251.

210. "Sed etiam exigitur amplius ut, secundum mensuram ordinis vel officii iniungendi, diligentior cura apponatur ut habeatur certitudo de qualitate promovendorum, saltem ex testimonio aliorum. Et hoc est quod Apostolus dicit, I Tim 5, [22]: 'Nemini cito manum imposueris.'" Aquinas, *In IV Sent*, d. 24, q. 1, a. 3, qua. 5, sol. 4, ad 3, 7.2:894.

among the people you will be held responsible."[211] Then, he proposes an alternative interpretation for this verse, not limited to the examination of candidates for the presbyterate: "Or he 'partakes in other's sins' who does not correct when he is able."[212] Citing Romans 1:32, "They are worthy of death not only they that do them, but they also that consent to them," Aquinas notes that a bishop, by failing to correct another's sins when he is able, *de facto* consents to those sins and shares both in their guilt and in their punishment.

Since verse 22 does not strictly limit the warning not to partake in "other men's sins" to candidates for priestly office, this broader interpretation is clearly warranted by the text. As such, Aquinas sees in this verse a very stern warning for bishops. In no sense are prelates at liberty to refuse or otherwise fail to correct those in their particular church who teach or act contrary to the faith. In his opinion, failure on this score renders the bishop liable to a rather severe judgment (deserving of "death," whether temporal or, even worse, everlasting). The bishop must correct such sinners under his charge not only by teaching but also by imposing due juridical sanctions—up to and including excommunication, with just consideration of all relevant circumstances. Such action is demanded of him by the episcopal office, all the more when it comes to the correction of those who teach the faithful—and above all, of priests or presbyteral candidates.

Aquinas interprets verse 24, "Some men's sins are manifest," to mean that the sins of some candidates for the presbyterate are so notorious that they need no further examination.[213] Other offenses, however, are "hidden and require probing."[214] However, if such sins of a candidate are revealed through private examination, those "must not then be made public," since they were not manifest and therefore are not susceptible to public correction.[215] These cases call for private fraternal correction. In any event, Aquinas argues that such an individual should not be promoted to an ecclesial office.

---

211. "Si inordinate promoveas, et ex hoc contingat peccatum eis, vel in plebe, hoc tibi imputabitur." Aquinas, *In 1 Tim*, cap. 5, lect. 3, [225], 2:253.
212. "Vel 'communicat alienis,' quia non corripit cum potest." Aquinas, *In 1 Tim*, [225], 2:253.
213. "Quorumdam hominum peccata manifesta sunt." Aquinas, *In 1 Tim*, 2:251.
214. "Quaedam occulta, et haec indigent [examinatione]." Aquinas, *In 1 Tim*, [230], 2:254.
215. "Non tunc publicandam." Aquinas, *In 1 Tim*, [230], 2:254.

Spiritual Warfare (6:11–20)

After his comments on 1 Timothy 6:1–10, in which Aquinas remarks on the virtues required of persons in low estate ("slaves"), in lect. 2 and lect. 4 on 1 Timothy 6, Thomas discusses the bishop's duty to wage spiritual warfare, how to execute this task, and the purpose of such warfare. He also discusses Timothy's instructions for dealing with persons of high estate. Finally, he explains in more detail the bishop's task of guarding the Church's unity, which is grounded in faith.

Verse 11 warns the bishop to avoid fastidiously the sins mentioned in the previous verses (6:4–5), specifically, avarice, envy, and false doctrine. Thomas takes the words addressed to Timothy in this verse, "You, however, O man of God, flee these things," as an occasion to remark that the bishop, dedicated to the service of God, should do as Christ did when he fled from those seeking to make him king (Jn 6:15).[216] In other words, the bishop should not seek after the dignities and honors of his office. Rather, in the person of Timothy, he is told, "Pursue justice, piety, faith, charity, patience, and meekness" (6:11).[217] In light of the following verse (6:12), "Fight the good fight," Aquinas characterizes the obligation to "pursue justice" as a mandate to conduct spiritual warfare.[218] The bishop should, "first, seek after spiritual arms and, secondly, do battle in them."[219] Spiritual arms are useful for doing good or enduring evil. Internally, the bishop ought to be oriented to do good for his neighbor by means of the virtues of "justice" and "piety" (6:11), the latter being interpreted once again by Aquinas as mercy. He must act both justly and mercifully toward the flock. Justice is "fitting to prelates," but without mercy, the bishop's justice is undue severity (*severitas*); yet without justice, the bishop's mercy is remiss (*remissio*).[220] Thus, there is no true justice without mercy (or piety); nor is there true mercy without justice.

Regarding the virtues listed next in verse 11, prelates are oriented to good for God, first, by *faith*, "which perfects the intellect" and

---

216. "Tu autem, o homo Dei, haec fuge." Aquinas, *In 1 Tim*, cap. 6, lect. 2, 2:258.
217. "Sectare vero iustitiam, pietatem, fidem, charitatem, patientiam, mansuetudinem." Aquinas, *In 1 Tim*, 2:258.
218. "Certa bonum certamen fidei." Aquinas, *In 1 Tim*, 2:258.
219. "Primo scilicet ad sectandum arma spiritualia; secundo ad certandum in eis." Aquinas, *In 1 Tim*, [255], 2:259.
220. "Quae competit praelatis." Aquinas, *In 1 Tim*, [256], 2:259.

second, by *charity*, "which perfects the affections."²²¹ Next, two virtues are mentioned for withstanding evils in spiritual warfare: "patience and meekness" (6:11). Patience (*patientia*) counters an inordinate sadness in the face of evil while meekness (*mansuetudinem*) counteracts the anger that results from that sadness. Thomas makes these comments in lect. 2 rather briefly, without elaboration. Nevertheless, they express his perception of an orderliness in the scriptural text (6:11) that may not be immediately evident. The verse may appear at first as a concatenation of virtues that Timothy should cultivate. Aquinas, however, understands it as an ordered set of directions on donning spiritual armor and using spiritual weapons (his use of the word *arma* in this part of the lecture bears the double meaning of both "armor" and "weapons"). To do good to his neighbor, the bishop must pursue both justice and mercy. Toward God, he must pursue faith and charity. To withstand evil, he must clothe himself in patience and meekness. Adorning himself with these virtues, the prelate is then well equipped for "spiritual warfare."

He interprets verse 12 as issuing a charge to do spiritual battle along with instructions on how to wage this warfare: "Fight the good fight of faith, lay hold of eternal life, to which you were called and to which you professed a good confession before many witnesses."²²² Temporal soldiers fight, he notes, either to defend what is possessed or to acquire what is lacking, "and this holy persons also should do."²²³ Accordingly, bishops are to guard their possessions, namely, "faith and the virtues."²²⁴ He gives three complementary interpretations to the phrase "the good fight *of faith*": it could mean a battle to defend the faith; or it could be a fight against sin by means of faith (citing 1 Jn 5:4, "This is the victory which overcomes the world: our faith"); or it could signify the struggle to convert others to the faith by preaching. Bishops also must fight to acquire what they lack, mentioned in the next part of verse 12: "Take hold of the eternal life to which you were called." The bishop must struggle to acquire eternal

---

221. "Quod perficit intellectum"; "Quod perficit affectum." Aquinas, *In 1 Tim*, [256], 2:259.
222. "Certa bonum certamen fidei, apprehende vitam aeternam, in qua vocatus es, et confessus bonam confessionem coram multis testibus." Aquinas, *In 1 Tim*, 2:258.
223. "Et hoc imminet sanctis." Aquinas, *In 1 Tim*, [258], 2:260.
224. "Fidem et virtutes." Aquinas, *In 1 Tim*, [258], 2:260.

life for two reasons. First, he has been called to this reward by God: "To which you were called." Second, he is duty-bound to struggle for eternal life by the profession he confessed "before many witnesses." For Aquinas, this refers to the solemn vow professed by the episcopal candidate: "At your consecration you promised to fight the good fight when you were ordained a bishop."[225] In virtue of this promise the bishop is not at liberty to relinquish this fight; he must strive for eternal life and preserve the faith by his preaching. And he is solemnly obligated to persevere in this battle until the coming of Christ in glory (1 Tm 6:13–16).

In lect. 4, Thomas comments on the instructions for Timothy on how to deal with the rich and how to preserve ecclesial unity. On verse 17, "Charge the rich of this world not to be high-minded," he remarks, "This is virtue, that a man use his authority toward superiors, not toward inferiors. Hence he says, [in effect]: Do not fail to issue orders through respect for their riches or high estate."[226] Timothy is to charge them "not to be high-minded," that is, "not to feel anything important about themselves."[227] This advice supplements the warnings against avarice and bribes in 3:3 and for similar reasons. The prelate should be courageous in preaching and impartial in judgment, not acting for temporal gain or money, but rather for the common good and the salvation of the faithful. Therefore, he should not be swayed either by a desire for money or by undue respect for the power of those of high estate among his flock. He must not allow the fear that the wealthy might withdraw their financial support to dissuade him from correcting or rebuking them. It is virtuous, Aquinas says, for bishops to exercise authority over the rich and powerful. On the other hand, it is not virtuous for them to do so over servants or slaves; hence, "when [Paul] treated of servants, he did not issue a command," but rather advised that they be encouraged.[228]

---

225. "In consecratione bonum certamen professus es, quando ordinatus es in episcopum." Aquinas, *In 1 Tim*, [259], 2:260.

226. "Hoc est virtus, quod homo utatur auctoritate ad maiores, non ad minores. Et ideo dicit: Non dimittas propter divitias et propter altum statum eorum, quin praecipias." Aquinas, *In 1 Tim*, cap. 6, lect. 4, [273], 2:263.

227. "Non sentire aliquid excelsum de se." Aquinas, *In 1 Tim*, [274], 2:263.

228. "Quando de servis egit, non posuit praeceptum." Aquinas, *In 1 Tim*, [273], 2:263. See his comments on 1 Tm 6:1–2 in cap. 6, lect. 1, [232–34], 2:255–56.

He explains that verses 18–19, "Do good, be rich in good works, give easily, communicate to others, lay up a good foundation for the future, that they may attain eternal life," instruct Timothy to lead the rich to acquire spiritual riches by using their material resources to obtain the end to which they should lead.[229] True riches consist in good works and these ought to be pursued eagerly. As for temporal goods, they ought to be given away easily, "that is, without interior heaviness of heart.... And without delay."[230] Recognizing that their possessions are goods that can be of service to the community, the rich should readily share them with others. Verse 19 indicates the goal of laying up spiritual riches: eternal life. Thomas explains: "Spiritual treasure is a storehouse of merits, which are the foundation of a future edifice prepared for us in heaven; because the entire preparation for future glory is through merits, which are acquired by grace, the principle of meriting."[231]

Finally, in verse 20, Timothy is ordered: "Guard the deposit, avoid the profane novelties of words and oppositions of knowledge falsely so called."[232] Here Aquinas provides two interpretations of "deposit" (*depositum*). First, it signifies the grace of God that the bishop should work to preserve and increase. In addition, he interprets it thusly: "Prelates especially are entrusted with the deposit, namely, the care of their neighbor and of the faithful, 'Feed my sheep' (John 21:17)."[233] The warning in verse 20 directs prelates to guard against evils that are apt to defile the faith. He comments: "Just as a worldly prince is appointed to guard the kingdom's unity, so the spiritual prince must guard spiritual unity.... But the unity of the Church is founded on the faith; therefore, he especially advises him to guard the faith."[234]

---

229. "Bene agere, divites fieri in bonis operibus, facile tribuere, communicare, thesaurizare sibi fundamentum bonum in futurum, ut apprehendant bonam vitam." Aquinas, *In 1 Tim*, 2:263.

230. "Sine gravitate cordis interius.... Et sine tarditate." Aquinas, *In 1 Tim*, [277], 2:264.

231. "Thesaurus spiritualis est congregatio meritorum, quae sunt fundamentum futuri aedificii, quod nobis praeparatur in caelo, quia tota praeparatio futurae gloriae est per merita, quae acquirimus per gratiam, quae est principium merendi." Aquinas, *In 1 Tim*, [277], 2:264.

232. "Depositum custodi, devitans profanas vocum novitates, et oppositiones falsi nominis scientiae." Aquinas, *In 1 Tim*, 2:263.

233. "Et specialiter praelati habent depositum, scilicet curam proximorum et fidelium. Io. ult. [XXI, 17]: 'Pasce oves meas.'" Aquinas, *In 1 Tim*, [279], 2:264.

234. "Sicut princeps saecularis ponitur ad custodiendam unitatem regni, ita spiritualis

The bishop has an essential role in establishing and preserving the spiritual unity of the Church: the common assent of faith. Thomas remarks here that the bishop must guard the faith specifically against fallacies (*fallacia*) and sophistical reasoning (*rationes reales sophisticae*).[235] Failing this, the bishop has "missed the mark as regards the faith" (verse 21).

Thus, Thomas's comments on this epistle end where they began, with the importance of the bishop's duties to preach the Gospel, to safeguard the faith, and to secure ecclesial unity—thereby establishing the Church, understood as the communion of the faithful. Since these actions of the bishop for the sake of ecclesial unity cooperate with God's actions of perfecting and saving souls—actions that exceed the innate powers of human nature—the bishop must be both called and empowered by God for this ministry. He needs supernatural grace to serve as a minister of revealed truth and to rule wisely over the faithful, leading them to union with God. Aquinas grounds the bishop's role in establishing and guarding Church unity on the proper possession and exercise of the episcopal office, with a particular concern for teaching and defending the deposit of faith. The bishop's efforts to secure this unity depend on the quality of his interior life of grace, faith, and virtue.

CONCLUSION

In his lectures on 1 Timothy, St. Thomas elaborates a pastoral theology of the episcopacy that is based upon a robust spiritual theology of the episcopal office. He grounds the bishop's pastoral work for the spiritual life and well-being of the faithful on the quality of his interior life. In Aquinas's theology, the bishop is like a father, an older brother, or a mentor who has personally attained the excellence to which he directs others by his governing, teaching, and example.

---

ad servandam unitatem spiritualem.... Sed unitas ecclesiae est in fide, et ideo principaliter monet ad custodiam fidei." Aquinas, *In 1 Tim*, [280], 2:264.

235. See also Aquinas, *In Eph*, cap. 4, lect. 2, [197–203], 2:49–50, where he discusses the elements that establish unity in the Church. Elsewhere, he discusses ecclesial unity in treating schism (*STh* II-II, q. 39, aa. 1–2) and the Eucharist (*STh* III, q. 67, a. 2)—note that he composed these articles after he delivered the PE lectures.

The prelate is, thus, a divinely appointed mediator, guiding his people to a conversion and supernatural union with God in Christ that he himself already enjoys. By doing this, he establishes, promotes, and guards ecclesial unity, constituted by a common assent to the deposit of faith—the content of which is encapsulated by the doctrine of charity, which is "the end of the law" (1:18). To fulfill this task, he must attain a spiritual perfection consisting in an excelling contemplation of divine revelation, a life of exemplary virtue, and above all a life of outstanding charity.[236] The reason for this requirement is twofold. First, as the mediator of faith and virtue, he must *have* faith and virtue, along with the resolve and moral authority to impose laws, punish vice, and promote virtue. Second, as the representative of Christ to the people, he must be a living example of the Christian perfection of contemplation, charity, and mercy that he preaches in order to lead the faithful more efficaciously to the same spiritual perfection and, ultimately, to eternal life. In all of these considerations, Aquinas consistently recognizes that the bishop's moral authority is rooted in the quality of his personal example as a follower of Christ.

The bishop must not only enjoy profound contemplation and holiness, but also be able to guide others to the same. Thus, he ought to be a gifted and appealing speaker and leader, capable of communicating the faith eloquently and persuasively, able to attract others to union with God in faith—the essence of ecclesial unity. In the ceremony of episcopal consecration, the imposition of the ordaining prelate's hands establishes the candidate in the episcopal office by a consecration that communicates grace and ratifies his divine calling. For Aquinas, this episcopal grace is the principal theme of the PE and he goes so far as to call the episcopacy itself a grace. In his consecration, the episcopal candidate binds himself with a solemn vow to work tirelessly for ecclesial unity in the common assent to the faith. Guarding this unity requires, among other things, that the prelate carefully scrutinize candidates for the presbyterate. He must also take action to protect the flock from dangers to the faith by forbidding false teach-

---

236. Several years after these lectures, Aquinas described the episcopal state as "mixed." It is both active and contemplative insofar as bishops should contemplate not only for their own good, but also that they may teach others. See Aquinas, *STh* II-II, q. 184, a. 7, ad 3.

ers to preach or to be heard and, if necessary, by imposing the sentence of excommunication out of a loving concern both for the good of the flock *and* for the one being punished. He should be cautious in receiving accusations against his presbyters. When he does so, he is to judge them impartially and impose public punishments only when it is clearly established that a public offense has been committed. He must not precipitously elevate an untested candidate to orders and he is charged with the grave duty to correct not only such candidates, but also (and especially) those teachers and presbyters who preach or act contrary to the faith. Failure to do so renders the bishop liable to the most severe divine judgment.

By his sacred vow, the bishop dedicates his entire life to the common spiritual good of his people, as a loving father who guides his children. Strengthened by episcopal grace, he governs his subjects by *serving* them with authority. In this, he is to be motivated by piety: the love of God and neighbor. The fruit of his labors for unity is the eternal life of his flock. In fact, his very salvation depends on the fulfillment of his episcopal duties to preach and command. Many obstacles can impede the bishop's efforts to satisfy these demands. In his lectures on 2 Timothy, Aquinas discusses the principal difficulties faced by bishops and the special communication of the Holy Spirit that prelates receive at their consecration designed to help them overcome these difficulties so that they may persevere in bearing witness to Christ, even when facing the threat of martyrdom.

5

Lectures on 2 Timothy
Ut pro populo subdito patiatur

THE SUBJECT MATTER AND THEMES OF 2 TIMOTHY

Returning now to his general prologue to the Pauline epistles, Aquinas says that 2 Timothy instructs prelates "on firmness against persecutors."[1] In his prologue to 1 Timothy he observes that 2 Timothy discusses one of the three things appropriate for a prelate, namely, "that he suffer for the people," noting that martyrdom is the principal theme of this epistle.[2] Finally, in the prologue to his commentary on 2 Timothy, he states that this epistle commends pastoral solicitude, even to the point of death.

In this latter prologue, he employs Genesis 31:40 as an *accessus*: "Day and night was I burned with heat and with frost, and sleep departed from my eyes."[3] He interprets this verse spiritually to introduce the principal theme of 2 Timothy: "These words, spoken by Jacob, show and commend pastoral care and the pastoral office."[4] In Jacob's complaint to Laban (Gn 31) that he endured extreme temperatures (heat by day and cold by night) and sleepless nights while tending

---

1. "Firmitate contra persecutores in secunda." Aquinas, *Super Epistolas*, prol., [11], 1:3.
2. "Ut pro populo subdito patiatur." Aquinas, *In 1 Tim*, prol., [2], 2:211. He goes on to say (*In 1 Tim*, 2:211) that in this epistle Paul "agit de martyrio" (treats of martyrdom).
3. "Nocte et die aestu urebar et gelu, etc." *In 2 Tim*, prol., 2:265.
4. "Verba sunt Iacob ostendentis et commendantis curam pastoralem, ac pastorale

Laban's flocks, Aquinas sees a figurative representation of three attributes that ought to characterize those in episcopal office: the phrase "day and night" signifies constant attention or assiduousness (*assiduitas*), "burned with heat and frost" signifies patience (*patientia*), and "sleep departed from my eyes" signifies anxiety or solicitude (*sollicitudo*). The prelate must assiduously attend to the faithful, that is, without pausing for a break (*sine intermissione*). Aquinas then gives two alternate allegorical interpretations for the phrase "day and night." On one reading, the prelate must diligently serve the faithful, teaching them by day and praying for them at night. Alternately, he must continuously serve them both in times of prosperity ("day") and in adversity ("night"). Citing Proverbs 17:17, "He that is a friend loves at all times," Aquinas describes the assiduous bishop as a true *friend* to his people.[5] *Patience* indicates that he is to endure all things, even death, for the salvation of the faithful (and here he cites Jn 10:11, "The good shepherd gives his life for his sheep"). This endurance is signified by Jacob being burned by the heat and by the cold while caring for his flock. This is a vivid metaphor for the bishop's duty to patiently endure the heat of present persecution and the chilling fear of future troubles. Finally, *solicitude* drives away from the bishop the "sleep" of negligence. Aquinas concludes his prologue by identifying the subject matter of 2 Timothy: "Rightly, then, do these words [Gn 31:40] suit the subject matter of this epistle. For in the first epistle [Paul] instructs [Timothy] about the Church's structure; here in this second one he treats of pastoral solicitude so great that he would endure martyrdom for the care of the flock, as is clear in the [general] prologue."[6] This synchronic analysis of 2 Timothy reflects the exegetical

---

officium." Aquinas, *In 2 Tim*, [1], 2:265. He interprets this verse "spiritually" as opposed to literally. The particular spiritual sense Aquinas discerns in this passage is either allegorical, as he uses the term (*sensus allegoricus*) in *STh* I, q. 1, a. 10, viz., that something in the Old Law is used by God to signify something in the New. Or it is moral (*sensus moralis* in the same article of *STh*), as things done in Christ or things that signify Christ are signs of what we ought to do.

5. "Prov. XVII, 17: 'Omni tempore diligit, qui amicus est.'" Aquinas, *In 2 Tim*, [1], 2:265.

6. "Recte ergo haec verba materiae huius epistolae conveniunt. In prima enim instruit eum de ordinatione ecclesiastica. In hac autem secunda agit de sollicitudine tanta pastorali, ut etiam martyrium sustineat pro cura gregis, ut patet in prologo." Aquinas, *In 2 Tim*, [2], 2:265.

tradition in the West, though Aquinas is unique in emphasizing *martyrdom* above the other themes of this epistle. Other commentators merely list martyrdom without distinction along with the themes of pastoral solicitude and redressing dangers to the faith.[7] For Aquinas, the martyrdom of the bishop is the main theme around which all the other matters treated by 2 Timothy are organized.

In his lectures on 2 Timothy, Thomas discusses various obstacles that can impede both the bishop's preaching office and his duty to endure tribulations for Christ and the faithful—above all, the fear of death (a genuine concern for bishops both in the early Church and throughout the Church's history). The prelate must prepare for a martyr's death by growing in virtue and he must identify suitable candidates to succeed him in the event of his death. As in his comments on 1 Timothy, these lectures include a discussion of the excommunication of heretics, examining the specific ways a bishop should resist unbelievers—a subject to which he returns again in his lectures on Titus. In light of the strict stance toward unbelievers and heretics adopted by the Church in his day, it is all the more striking that Aquinas unhesitatingly insists that prelates show mercy and charity to those persons.

THE EPISTLE

The diachronic analysis of 2 Timothy given by Thomas in his *divisio* partitions the text into the greeting (1:1–1:2) and the message (1:3–4:22). He further divides the epistle as follows:

7. Compare Aquinas's prologue with *Quaestiones et decisiones in Epistolas S. Pauli*: "Et est intentio Apostoli in hac epistola exhortari Timotheum ad sui officii diligentem exsecutionem, et ad palmam martyrii, et quaedam adhuc addit de episcopali officio" (It is the intention of the Apostle in this epistle to exhort Timothy to the diligent execution of his office, and to the honor of martyrdom, and, in addition, to certain things associated with the office of bishop). *Quaestiones et decisiones*, cap. 11, "In Epistolam II ad Timotheum," *PL* 175, col. 602D–603A; and with Lombard: "Item Timotheo scribit de exhortatione martyrii, et omni regula veritatis, et quid futurum sit temporibus novissimis, et de sua passione, scribens ei ab urbe Roma" (Again he wrote to Timothy regarding an exhortation to martyrdom, and on everything regarding the rule of truth, and on what concerns the future regarding the last things, and on his passion, writing to him from the city of Rome). Lombard, *In Epistolam II ad Timothaeum*, *PL* 192, col. 363A.

I. Fortifying Timothy against present persecutions (1:3–2:26)
   A. Exhortation to continue preaching (1:3–1:18)
   B. Exhortation to endure tribulations for Christ (2:1–2:26)
II. Fortifying Timothy against future dangers for the Church (3:1–4:22)
   A. Prediction of dangers to come (3:1–3:9)
   B. How a bishop becomes fit to resist future dangers (3:10–3:17)
   C. How to resist the evils of the last days (4:1–4:22)

After examining the greeting, the rest of this chapter will investigate the following principal themes on the episcopacy and its duties as they arise diachronically in the context of this *divisio*: overcoming obstacles to preaching, enduring tribulations for Christ and the faithful, preparing for martyrdom, opposing heretics, and becoming fit to resist spiritual dangers.

Paul's Greeting (1:1–2)

Commenting on the greeting in verse 1, "Paul, an apostle of Christ Jesus by the will of God according to the promise of life itself in Christ Jesus," Aquinas notes in his first lecture on 2 Timothy that the proper end of the episcopacy is not anything earthly (*terrenum*); rather, the fruit of the episcopacy is eternal life.[8] He perceives St. Paul as the prototype of a good prelate and, as such, the eternal life promised to him extends to all bishops. However, unlike his comments on 1 Timothy 4:16, here he says that life everlasting "*should* be the end of prelates."[9] Eternal life is not, categorically, the result of accepting this office; rather, prelates must deliberately order all their labors to this end for themselves and their people, encouraged by the promise of Christ.

He interprets the "grace" (*gratia*) and "mercy" (*misericordia*) that Paul wishes for Timothy in verse 2 differently than he does in his comments on the greeting in 1 Timothy, where he interprets it alternately as sanctifying grace or the gift of graces prelates need. Here,

---

8. "Paulus apostolus Iesu Christi per voluntatem Dei, secundum promissionem vitae, quae est in Christo Iesu." Aquinas, *In 2 Tim*, cap. 1, lect. 1, 2:267.
9. "Hic *debet* esse finis praelatorum" (emphasis added). Aquinas, *In 2 Tim*, [4], 2:267.

"grace" signifies the means for the remission of sins (*remissio peccatorum*). And here he takes God's "mercy" to signify the means by which the final good of eternal life (mentioned in verse 1) is obtained. Again, this contrasts with his comments in 1 Timothy where "mercy" signifies either the remission of sins or being raised to spiritual charisms.[10] He interprets "peace" (*pax*), along with the *Glossa*, as "'tranquility of mind,' which befits a prelate, who is appointed to produce peace."[11] In support of this reading, he cites Matthew 10:12, where Christ advises those entrusted with the preaching ministry to confer peace on the houses they enter. These comments on "grace," "mercy," and "peace" build on the promise of eternal life mentioned in verse 1. The connection between these remarks and his subsequent lectures on 2 Timothy may not be readily apparent since he does not mention the remission of sins or "peace" again in these lectures. However, he does discuss mercy in terms of the charity prelates should extend to others and he elaborates upon the special communication of grace and of the Holy Spirit given at episcopal ordination.

Obstacles to Preaching (1:5–18)

After remarking on Paul's prayers for Timothy and his desire to be reunited with him (1:3–4), Thomas begins a lengthy treatment of the various obstacles to preaching that bishops can expect to encounter. But first, in lect. 2, Aquinas remarks briefly on 2 Timothy 1:5, "Calling to mind that faith which is in you unfeigned."[12] The episcopal ministry presupposes that the bishop has faith since he is called not only to preach, but also to guard the faith. His faith must be "unfeigned" (*non ficta*), the clear sign of which being that such a faith produces the fruit of good works.[13]

---

10. In his interpretations of *gratia* and *misericordia*, he also departs from the exegetical tradition expressed by Lombard in his commentary on 2 Tm: "*Gratia*, scilicet donatio Spiritus sancti qua ministri armantur, *et misericordia*, scilicet remissio peccatorum" ("Grace," namely the gift of the Holy Spirit with which ministers are equipped, "and mercy," namely the remission of sins). Lombard, *PL* 192, col. 363D (emphasis added).

11. "'Pax,' Glossa: 'Id est, tranquilitas mentis'; haec competit praelato, qui ad hoc ponitur ut pacem procuret." Aquinas, *In 2 Tim*, cap. 1, lect. 1, [6], 2:267.

12. "Recordationem accipiens eius fidei, quae est in te non ficta." Aquinas, *In 2 Tim*, lect. 2, 2:268.

13. "Fides necessaria est praelato, qui est fidei custos. Hebr. XI:6: 'Sine fide impossibile est placere Deo.' Et dicit 'non ficta,' vera enim per opera bona est" (Faith is neces-

In his third and fourth lectures, Aquinas interprets the rest of the first chapter (1:6–18) as providing a set of exhortations delivered personally to Timothy—but applicable to all bishops—to persevere courageously in proclaiming the Gospel, when preaching frequently occasioned the persecution of bishops in the early Church. In lect. 3 he argues that, through the imposition of hands in episcopal ordination, the bishop receives the special assistance of God to fulfill his magisterial duties during such times of trouble.

Beginning in verse 6, "For this reason, I admonish you that you rekindle [*resuscites*] the grace of God which is in you by the imposition of my hands," Paul urges Timothy to make use of what Aquinas understood to be Timothy's "gratuitously given gifts" (*bonae gratuitae*), chiefly by preaching the Gospel.[14] Thomas gives two possible explanations for why God's grace in Timothy is likened to smoldering embers that need to be rekindled into flames. In Timothy, God's grace was weakened either on account of his sloth (*torpor*) or because of human fear (*humanus timor*). Reconstructing the historical context of this epistle, Aquinas supposes that Timothy must have been afraid of suffering repercussions similar to those suffered by Paul, who was persecuted and imprisoned in Rome for preaching the Gospel. For instance, in discussing verse 8, "Do not be ashamed of the testimony of our Lord, nor of me his prisoner," he says that Timothy was tempted to be ashamed of his association with Paul, who was publically and officially identified as a criminal.[15] Aquinas interprets verse 6 as reminding Timothy to make use of the grace he received in his ordination to overcome this fear and shame: "In the imposition of hands the grace of the Holy Spirit was given to him."[16] As he mentioned in his

---

sary for a prelate, who is the guardian of faith. Heb 11:6: "Without faith it is impossible to please God." And he says "unfeigned," for it is true through good works). Aquinas, *In 2 Tim*, [11], 2:268. Compare this with Aquinas's comments on 1 Tm 1:5 (*In 1 Tim*, cap. 1, lect. 2, [16], 2:215).

14. "Propter quam causam admoneo te, ut resuscites gratiam Dei, quae est in te per impositionem manuum mearum." Aquinas, *In 2 Tim*, lect. 3, 2:269.

15. "Noli itaque erubescere testimonium Domini nostri, neque me vinctum eius." Aquinas, *In 2 Tim*, 2:269.

16. "In qua manus impositione data est ei gratia Spiritus Sancti." Aquinas, *In 2 Tim*, [13], 2:269. Lécuyer argues that these comments represent the beginning of Thomas's mature thought on the sacramentality of episcopal ordination. See "Aux origens," 84, and "Les étapes," 35–37.

comments on 1 Timothy 6:12, episcopal ordination imposes upon the recipient the mandate and the power to preach the Gospel. Now, in 2 Timothy 1:6, we have a reaffirmation that the grace to fulfill this duty is given in the bishop's consecration when he receives the Holy Spirit to help him overcome the fear of reprisal and any other obstacle to his duties that may arise.

The reason Timothy should revive this grace is given in verse 7, "For God has not given us a spirit of fear, but one of power, and love and sobriety."[17] This exhortation follows from the nature of the divine gifts (*ex conditione divinorum munerum*) given to the bishop: "One who accepts an office [*munus*] should act in accordance with its gifts [*muneris*]."[18] Aquinas interprets "spirit," in verse 7, to signify love, "because the name 'spirit' suggests an impulsion and love impels."[19] The spirit of fear is an inordinate love of the world inspired by the spirit of the world. Contrary to the spirit or impulses of grace given in episcopal ordination, this spirit "makes one love the good things of the world and fear temporal evils."[20]

Opposed to this is the Spirit of God, present in the bishop as a "spirit of power" (1:7), which Aquinas interprets as the virtue of courage (*fortitudo*) to confront temporal adversities. By means of this gift, the Holy Spirit protects the bishop from the evil of relinquishing his preaching ministry. In addition, God's Spirit is in the bishop moving him to do good both as a "spirit of love" or charity (*caritas*), by which all other loves are ordered, and as a "spirit of sobriety," that is, temperance (*temperantia*) by which the bishop moderates his use of this world's goods. Aquinas thus establishes a pneumatological basis not only for the episcopal duties themselves (see his comments on 1 Tm 6:12, treated in chapter 4 above) but also for the strength to fulfill them.

In verse 8, "Do not be ashamed of the testimony of our Lord nor of me his prisoner, but labor in the Gospel according to the power

17. "Non enim dedit nobis Deus spiritum timoris, sed virtutis, et dilectionis et sobrietatis." Aquinas, *In 2 Tim*, 2:269.
18. "Qui enim accipit munus, debet operari secundum congruentiam muneris." Aquinas, *In 2 Tim*, [14], 2:269.
19. "Quia nomen spiritus impulsionem importat, et amor impellit." Aquinas, *In 2 Tim*, [14], 2:269.
20. "Facit amare bona mundi, et timere mala temporalia." Aquinas, *In 2 Tim*, [14], 2:269.

of God," Paul mentions two kinds of shame that can prevent a bishop from preaching.[21] First, when compared with the wisdom of this world, preaching Christ seems to be folly (here he cites 1 Cor 1:25, "We preach Christ crucified ... foolishness to the Gentiles") and is, thus, a potential source of shame for the preacher. Second, he argues that in Timothy's case, shame arose because his associate, Paul, was accused of criminal behavior.[22] Along with Timothy, the bishop is exhorted to "labor in the Gospel according to the power of God," that is, by God's grace he must overcome shame and preach boldly, "with confidence not in himself, because 'we are not sufficient to think anything of ourselves' [2 Cor 3:5], but 'according to the power of God,' that is, trusting in God's power."[23] Shame can interpose a barrier so great that a special grace is required to overcome it. Verse 9a expresses two ways the power of God's grace succeeds in overcoming this obstacle: by freeing the faithful from evils ("Who has delivered us ...") and by calling them to goodness through sanctification ("... and has called us by his holy calling").[24] The bishop's calling is in virtue of God's providential plan and has been made manifest by Christ who conquered death and who offers eternal life through the Gospel (1:10).

In lect. 4, Aquinas says that in verses 11–18 Paul presents himself to Timothy and to all bishops as an example of how to suffer for Christ. Paul was appointed to his office by Christ (verse 11) and he suffers (*patior*, verse 12) "chains and weariness for the faith of Christ," that is, his suffering directly results from the faithful execution of his duties.[25] For Aquinas, although suffering as such is not intrinsically good, it is nevertheless praiseworthy when endured willingly for a just cause.[26]

21. "Noli itaque erubescere testimonium Domini nostri, neque me vinctum eius, sed collabora evangelio, secundum virtutem Dei." Aquinas, *In 2 Tim*, 2:269.

22. "Quod si latro videt aliquem suspensum, erubescit se confiteri socium eius" (If a thief sees someone hung, he is ashamed to admit that he is his companion). Aquinas, *In 2 Tim*, [16], 2:270.

23. "Et hoc cum fiducia, non propria, quia non sufficientes sumus cogitare aliquid a nobis quasi ex nobis, etc. [2 Cor 3:5]; se 'secundum Dei virtutem,' id est, habendo fiduciam de virtute Dei." Aquinas, *In 2 Tim*, [19], 2:270.

24. "Qui nos liberavit et vocavit vocatione sua sancta." Aquinas, *In 2 Tim*, 2:269.

25. "Ostendit quae patitur pro sui officii executione" (He shows what he suffers for the execution of his office). Aquinas, *In 2 Tim*, [26], 2:271.

26. "Pati simpliciter non est laudabile, sed propter iustam causam" (Suffering, simply speaking, is not laudable, except for a just cause). Aquinas, *In 2 Tim*, [26], 2:271.

Paul bears persecution without shame and with a great degree of confidence. In verse 12 he continues: "For I know whom I have believed, and I am certain because he is able to preserve my deposit until that day."[27] The assurance of his hope in God forms the basis for his freedom from shame.[28] The "deposit" (*depositum*) could refer, on the one hand, to Paul entrusting his salvation to God by an unconditional commitment. Alternately, the "deposit" is the "office" (*officium*) God entrusted to Paul: that of evangelizing.[29] Timothy and all prelates ought to imitate Paul's example, expecting to suffer some adversity for preaching the Gospel. Their confidence in God's promise prevents or removes shame, enabling them to persevere confidently in evangelization and thus attain the reward of heaven.

Verse 13, "Hold the form of sound words, which you have heard from me in faith and in love in Christ Jesus," refers to the doctrine Paul learned from Christ.[30] The words are "sound" (*sana*) both because they are true and because they make their hearers spiritually healthy (*sani*). Aquinas explains the implications of this verse: "He says, therefore: You cannot excuse yourself, if you are not prepared to suffer even unto chains, even as I suffer, because you 'hold the form of sound words,' namely, which do not contain the corruption of falsehood."[31] The bishop must imitate Paul's virtue, holding fast to these sound words heard "in faith and in love." A prelate must not only know sound words but he must also believe them with faith in a spirit of love; otherwise, "he would not be fit [for preaching], nor would he love, since he would easily retreat from teaching either because of ad-

---

27. "Scio enim cui credidi, et certus sum quia potens est depositum meum servare in illum diem." Aquinas, *In 2 Tim*, 2:271.

28. "Deinde cum dicit 'scio,' ponitur certitudo spei, quae facit eum non confundi" (Then when he says "I know," he asserts the certitude of hope, which prevents him from being confounded). Aquinas, *In 2 Tim*, [27], 2:271.

29. "Et sic homo deponit apud Deum salutem suam, quando se Deo totum committit.... Vel 'depositum,' id est, quod penes me positum est officium, scilicet officium evangelii" (And thus man deposits his salvation before God, when he commits himself totally to God.... Or "deposit," that is, what it placed in my power is the office, namely, of evangelization). Aquinas, *In 2 Tim*, [28], 2:272.

30. "Formam habe sanorum verborum, quae a me audisti in fide et in dilectione in Christo Iesu." Aquinas, *In 2 Tim*, 2:271.

31. "Dicit ergo: Non potes te excusare, si patienter te non habeas usque ad vincula sicut ego, quia tu es 'habens formam sanorum verborum,' scilicet quae non continent falsitatis corruptionem." Aquinas, *In 2 Tim*, [30], 2:272.

versity or prosperity."[32] As discussed in the prologue, the bishop must be assiduous, preaching in good times and in bad. To do this, he must first receive the Gospel of Christ lovingly in faith. However, neither faith nor love is possible apart from Christ, "because the true faith is concerned with the things Christ taught, and true love is found in Christ, who gave the Holy Spirit through whom we love God."[33] Lacking the unselfish motives of faith and charity, a bishop will fail to sustain the resolve he needs to continue preaching in times of "adversity," when threatened with persecution, or in times of "prosperity," when presented with the opportunity of private, personal gain.

Thomas interprets the "good deposit" mentioned in verse 14: "Guard the good deposit by the Holy Spirit, who dwells in us," to be "the office of preaching."[34] Bishops must receive strength from the indwelling of the Holy Spirit, who was given to them in their consecration, in order to guard the preaching office. The power of the Spirit prevents this office from being neglected or altogether abandoned. Verses 15–18 briefly describe the way certain persons betrayed Paul and others supported him as he endured trials and persecution for preaching the Gospel.

Enduring Tribulations for Christ and the Faithful (2:1–26)

In four lectures on 2 Timothy 2, Thomas discusses two hardships that bishops might likely face: martyrdom and threats to the faith posed by unbelievers. The injunction in verse 3, "Share in suffering as a good soldier of Christ Jesus," encourages bishops both to endure tribulations (even martyrdom) and also to labor in spiritual warfare for the sake of Christ and the faithful.[35]

Preparation for martyrdom

The second chapter of 2 Timothy specifies three ways a bishop should prepare to undergo martyrdom. Even if this threat is not immi-

---

32. "Non esset idoneus, nec etiam diligeret, quia de facili recederet a doctrina, vel per adversa, vel per prospera." Aquinas, *In 2 Tim*, [30], 2:272.
33. "Quia vera fides est eorum, quae Christus docuit, et vera dilectio est in Christo, quia dedit Spiritum Sanctum, per quem Deum diligimus." Aquinas, *In 2 Tim*, [30], 2:272.
34. "Officium praedicationis." Aquinas, *In 2 Tim*, [31], 2:272.
35. "Labora sicut bonus miles Christi Iesu." Aquinas, *In 2 Tim*, 2:275.

nent, a bishop must be prepared for suffering since the Gospel message counters worldly concerns in any day and age. First, suffering martyrdom requires strength of soul to face the dangers of death: "You, therefore, my son, be strong in the grace which is in Christ Jesus" (2:1).[36] Aquinas remarks that, in contrast with the prelate's personal weakness, the grace "in Christ Jesus" enables him to face death with courage.[37]

Second, a bishop prepares for martyrdom by providing for the proper distribution of his spiritual goods after his death—principally by selecting successors. In verse 2, "And the things which you have heard from me by many witnesses, the same commend to faithful men who will be fit to teach others also," Paul directs Timothy to prepare, as it were, a last will and testament to dispose of his spiritual riches.[38] Just as a person provides for the distribution of temporal goods before death, bishops must prepare to transfer their spiritual goods: "When a person is about to die, he disposes of his goods. But the saints should be no less solicitous about the spiritual goods entrusted to them, lest they be scattered after their death; rather, they should entrust them to others."[39] Their successors must be "faithful men able to teach others" (2:2)—that is, those "who will not seek temporal gain but God's glory."[40] To be fit to teach, in their intellect (*intellectu*) they must be "wise in understanding" (*sapientes ad intelligendum*), in language (*lingua*) they must be "eloquent in teaching" (*facundi ad docendum*), and in work (*opere*) they must follow the example of Christ who "began to do and to teach (Acts 1:1)."[41] In these brief remarks, Aquinas presents the transmission of doctrine and the selection of successors in a highly personal fashion. He does not conceive of Christian teachings as merely a set of abstract propositions.

---

36. "Tu ergo, fili mi, confortare in gratia, quae est in Christo Iesu." Aquinas, *In 2 Tim*, 2:275.

37. "'Quae est' non in te, scilicet cuius fortitudo est vana, sed 'in Christo Iesu'" ("Which is" not in you, certainly such fortitude is in vain, but "in Christ Jesus"). Aquinas, *In 2 Tim*, [36], 2:275.

38. "Et quae audisti a me per multos testes, haec commenda fidelibus hominibus, qui idonei erunt et alios docere." Aquinas, *In 2 Tim*, 2:275.

39. "Quando aliquis adducitur ad mortem, disponit de suis. Non ergo minus debent esse solliciti sancti de bonis spiritualibus sibi creditis, quod non dispereant post eorum mortem, sed aliis credant." Aquinas, *In 2 Tim*, [37], 2:275.

40. "Non quaerant lucrum temporale, sed gloriam Dei." Aquinas, *In 2 Tim*, [37], 2:275.

41. "Coepit Iesus facere et docere (Act. I, 1)." Aquinas, *In 2 Tim*, [37], 2:276.

Rather, he presents them as the personal possessions of the bishop, who receives them as spiritual goods from his predecessors and, ultimately, from Christ. Thus he construes the act of succession as the handing on of the patrimony of spiritual goods (personally possessed) from one bishop—spiritual father and teacher—to another.

Verse 3 gives the third requirement for martyrdom, "Labor as a good soldier of Christ Jesus," that is, labor lawfully in spiritual warfare.[42] Here, Aquinas evaluates spiritual warfare, discussing its lawful execution, its fruits, wages, and reward. He states: "Someone is a soldier of Christ in three ways," specifically, a soldier of Christ fights three things: sin, error, and tyrants.[43] The bishop must fight against *sin* in its sources: the flesh, the world, and the devil. Citing 2 Corinthians 10:4, "The weapons of our militia are not carnal, but powerful to God, for pulling down fortifications, destroying counsels," Aquinas describes refuting *error* as a spiritual battle. But the bishop's "more laborious" (*laboriosior*) task is to take part in "the military campaign of martyrs against tyrants."[44]

The meaning of "against tyrants" is illuminated by a similar use of the phrase in Thomas's commentary on Philippians (lect. 1), where he interprets 1:7b, "You are all partakers with me of grace in the defense and confirmation of the Gospel," as a description of the early Christians, "preaching boldly against tyrants and heretics, and confirming the Gospel in the hearts of the faithful."[45] These "tyrants" were the pagan rulers before whom early Christians were accused and often executed. Thus, the spiritual warfare conducted by bishops (discussed in his comments here on 2 Tm 2:3) is "more laborious" because bold preaching "against tyrants" will surely provoke acute persecution—whereas combating sin and error usually will not. And the spiritual soldier "should not rest" from this labor, hence the use of the word *miles* (soldier) in verse 3, which Aquinas thinks is derived from *militia sustinenda* (constant warfare).[46] In this struggle, the bishop

---

42. "Labora sicut bonus miles Christi Iesu." Aquinas, *In 2 Tim*, 2:275. Aquinas calls this labor *militia spiritualis* in [41], 2:276.

43. "Est autem tripliciter aliquis miles Christi." Aquinas, *In 2 Tim*, [39], 2:276.

44. "Militia martyrum contra tyrannos." Aquinas, *In 2 Tim*, [39], 2:276.

45. "Audacter praedicando, contra tyrannos et haereticos, et confirmando Evangelium in cordibus fidelium." Aquinas, *In Philip*, cap. 1, lect. 1, [13], 2:92.

46. "Non debet quiescere." Aquinas, *In 2 Tim*, cap. 2, lect. 1, [39], 2:276.

gains experience in remaining faithful to his ministry when opposed by the threats of temporal or secular authority.

Verse 4 describes the correct or "lawful" way to conduct this warfare: "No person, being a soldier to God, entangles themselves with secular businesses."[47] Aquinas comments: "The end of spiritual warfare is to obtain the victory over those who are against God. Therefore, they must refrain from everything that distracts from God. These are secular businesses, because the cares of the world choke the Word."[48] However, did Paul not entangle himself in temporal affairs when he supported himself by manual labor?[49] In a short systematic excursus, Aquinas replies to this challenge with the following clarification: Paul does not prohibit bishops from being "engaged" (*exercitus*) in temporal affairs as he was. Moreover, the text does not say a bishop may not "be entangled" (*implicatur*) since he can be entangled in secular affairs against his will. Rather, this verse specifically prohibits the prelate from "entangling himself" (*implicat se*), which happens, "when [a bishop] undertakes a business without piety and necessity calling for it."[50] However, "when the duty of piety and authority demand it, he does not entangle himself, but is entangled by such requirements."[51] Aquinas provides the criterion of *pietas* to assist a bishop in evaluating a given situation: if the duty of piety, that is, the worship of God and mercy toward neighbor, requires it, then he is free—and may even be obliged—to be entangled by secular affairs. Note, too, that in coordinating the terms "piety" and "authority" (in the preceding citation) Aquinas indicates that the authority or power of the bishop is to be exercised for the worship of God and mercy to-

47. "Nemo militans Deo implicat se negotiis saecularibus, ut ei placeat cui se probavit." Aquinas, *In 2 Tim*, 2:275.

48. "Sed militiae spiritualis finis est, ut victoriam habeant ab hominibus, qui sunt contra Deum; et ideo oportet, quod abstineant ab omnibus, quae distrahunt a Deo. Haec autem sunt negotia saecularia, quia sollicitudo huius saeculi suffocat verbum." Aquinas, *In 2 Tim*, [41], 2:276.

49. "Sed contra: Negotia saecularia sunt temporalia, hoc autem Apostolus fecit, quando vixit labore manuum suarum" (On the contrary: secular businesses are temporal things. This, however, the Apostle did, when he lived by the labor of his own hands). Aquinas, *In 2 Tim*, [42], 2:276.

50. "Quando sine pietate et necessitate assumit negotia." Aquinas, *In 2 Tim*, [42], 2:276.

51. "Quando necessitas officii pietatis et auctoritatis exercetur, tunc non implicat se, sed implicatur huiusmodi necessitate." Aquinas, *In 2 Tim*, [42], 2:276.

ward neighbor—that is, for the sake of charity. In any event, he proposes *piety* as the measure of the bishop's choices and actions with respect to worldly engagements. Verse 4b supplies the reason for the prohibition against secular entanglements: "That he may please him to whom he has engaged himself."[52] In such legitimate imbroglios, the bishop must strive to please God above all since he has "vowed to do battle for God" at his ordination.[53]

Thomas expands on the metaphors of "soldier" in verse 4 and "farmer" in verse 6, likening the episcopal preaching office to both. In verse 5, the metaphor of an "athlete" is interposed and similarly deployed. On verse 4, Aquinas comments: "For the office of preachers and teachers is a military office, inasmuch as they do battle against enemies and vices."[54] And in verse 6, the preaching office is likened to "a farmer's [work] inasmuch as [prelates] produce fruit by exhorting others to [be] good."[55] The field is the Church and the chief farmer is God because he works both exteriorly and interiorly on souls. For their part, the bishops are merely "exterior farmers" (*exteriores agricolae*), working only from the "outside"—that is, without direct access to souls—by the offerings of their ministry.[56]

Because of their participation in this labor, bishops should share in its fruits. They do this, first, by rejoicing in "the works of the virtues" (*opera virtutum*) performed by the Christians that they helped form and inspire. Second, bishops should receive from the faithful "temporal subsidies" (*subsidia temporalia*), though prelates must never seek or receive these subsidies as the main reward for preaching, but only "as a stipend" (*stipendio*).[57] But even in this, "discretion is

52. "Ut ei placeat cui se probavit." Aquinas, *In 2 Tim*, 2:275.
53. "Devovit se ad militandum Deo." Aquinas, *In 2 Tim*, [43], 2:276.
54. "Officium enim praedicatorum et doctorum est officium militum, inquantum insurgunt contra hostes et vitia." Aquinas, *In 2 Tim*, [46], 2:276. Compare this with Aquinas, *In Heb*, cap. 13, lect. 3, [757], 2:503, where he insists that prelates vigilantly guard the flock from enemies.
55. "Agricolae, inquantum fructum faciunt promovendo ad bona." Aquinas, *In 2 Tim*, [46], 2:276.
56. "Huius ager est ecclesia, et principalis agricola est Deus, interius et exterius operans.... Homines autem exterius adhibent ministerium.... Item sunt exteriores agricolae" (This field is the Church, and the principal farmer is God, working interiorly and exteriorly.... Men, however, conduct an exterior ministry.... Again, they are the exterior farmers). Aquinas, *In 2 Tim*, [46], 2:276.
57. "Secundo de subsidiis temporalibus, non pro praemio principali, sed stipendio"

necessary" (*est necessaria discretio*), since it is sometimes obligatory for a bishop to live by the labor of his own hands, like Paul did, instead of by a stipend received from the faithful. Aquinas establishes a general criterion to determine which course of action is most fitting: "[Stipends] are not to be accepted where they are the occasion of avarice contrary to the Gospel, either on account of covetousness or leisure."[58] If a stipend leads the bishop to greed or a life of ease, he must refuse it and work to support himself. This practical advice accords with his insistence that the prelate's work should be directed by piety rather than by a desire for earthly prosperity. These remarks harmonize with Aquinas's comments on 1 Timothy 5:17–18 to the effect that a bishop must not seek any *honoraria* as the final reward for his labor. Aquinas issues some of his sternest warnings to prelates in his lectures on 1 Timothy concerning the dangers of avarice.[59] In verse 7, Paul urges Timothy to consider carefully this teaching, assuring him that the Lord will grant him understanding.

In lect. 2, Aquinas returns to the topic of martyrdom, discussing its reward, Paul's example, the purpose of martyrdom, and the consequences for enduring it—or for refusing to do so. To find encouragement in enduring martyrdom, the bishop should focus on its reward, given in verse 8: "Be mindful that the Lord Jesus Christ has risen from the dead, from the seed of David, according to my Gospel."[60] In verse 9, "In which I labor in chains, as an evildoer, but the word of God is not bound," Paul presents himself as an example to encourage Timothy and all prelates to persevere courageously in their duties.[61] The pain of martyrdom and the shame suffered from unbelievers who consider the preacher an "evildoer" will compel the prelate either to find the resolve necessary to continue preaching or relinquish the task altogether. By considering Paul's words and example,

---

(Second, from temporal relief, not as their principal reward, but as a stipend). Aquinas, *In 2 Tim*, [46], 2:277.

58. "Ibi non sunt accipienda ubi est occasio avaritiae contra evangelium, vel propter cupiditatem, vel propter otium." Aquinas, *In 2 Tim*, [47], 2:277.

59. See his comments on 1 Tm 3:3, discussed in chapter 4 of this book, where he laments the pervasiveness of this vice.

60. "Memor esto Dominum Iesum Christum resurrexisse a mortuis, ex semine David, secundum evangelium meum." Aquinas, *In 2 Tim*, lect. 2, 2:277.

61. "In quo laboro usque ad vincula, quasi male operans, sed verbum Dei non est alligatum." Aquinas, Aquinas, *In 2 Tim*, 2:277.

the bishop will realize that "although the body is bound, the word of God is not bound, because preaching was from the will of the Apostle, which is free [that is, unbound], especially on account of the efficacy of charity, which fears nothing."[62] In this verse, then, Aquinas discerns words of great encouragement for a bishop: whatever may be done to his body, nothing can be done to prevent a bishop from earnestly willing to share the Gospel. Christian history affords countless examples of such evangelical heroism among bishops from apostolic times to the present.

Commenting on verse 10, "Therefore, I endure everything for the elect, that they may acquire salvation, which is in Christ Jesus, with heavenly glory," Aquinas says, "It is not the pain, but the cause, that makes a martyr."[63] The final cause of martyrdom is the honor of God and the salvation of one's neighbor. Here, he introduces another *quaestio*, asking whether Christ's pain was not sufficient for the salvation of the neighbor. If so, how can a bishop's suffering and death contribute anything to the salvation of the faithful? He replies that Christ's suffering was indeed sufficient, and efficaciously so (*effective*); but the martyr's death helps to save others by providing them with "an example of perseverance in the faith" (*exemplum persistendi in fide*) and by confirming them in their faith, "and by this they were brought to salvation."[64]

If the bishop remains faithful and "dies with Christ" (verse 11), he will be rewarded with a glorious resurrection and enter the eternal kingdom of Christ in order to "reign with him" (verse 12a). However, verse 12b warns, "If we deny him, he also will deny us."[65] Aquinas explains that for Christ, "To deny is not to know them to be members of his flock," that is, to exclude such persons from the Kingdom.[66] Since the penalty for failure is rejection by Christ, when confronted with martyrdom the bishop must endure it as the fruition of his love

---

62. "Licet enim corpus sit alligatum, tamen verbum Dei non est aliigatum, quia praedicatio fuit ex voluntate Apostoli, quae libera est, praecipue propter efficaciam charitatis, quae nihil timet." Aquinas, *In 2 Tim*, [51], 2:278.

63. "Martyrem non poena facit, sed causa." Aquinas, *In 2 Tim*, [52], 2:278.

64. "Et ex hoc inducebantur ad salutem." Aquinas, *In 2 Tim*, [52], 2:278.

65. "Si negaverimus, et ille negabit nos." Aquinas, *In 2 Tim*, 2:277.

66. "Negare est non cognoscere eos esse de ovibus suis." Aquinas, *In 2 Tim*, [57], 2:278.

and his labors for the salvation of the faithful. Fulfilling this charge, when unavoidable, is inextricably woven into his own eternal destiny. He must not give up his preaching office, even when threatened with death on its account. These verses help the bishop persevere in his ministry. Aquinas interprets Paul as insisting that the bishop will find the needed strength to undergo martyrdom by reflecting on his episcopal vow to preach, his duty to work for the salvation of his neighbor, the reward of glory, the threat of punishment, and the heroic example of Paul himself. To acquire and maintain this resolve, the bishop is given grace and a special communication of the Holy Spirit at his episcopal consecration. Animated and strengthened by this episcopal gift of the Holy Spirit, he participates in the salvation of the faithful by serving as an example of the ultimate perfection of charity by enduring martyrdom for Christ and for his neighbor. Verse 13 ("If we do not believe, he remains faithful, he cannot deny himself") encourages the bishop, reminding him that Christ will continue to remain faithful to him despite his failings.

Resisting unbelievers

The remaining lectures on chapter 2, namely, the end of lect. 2 through lect. 4, discuss "how to resist unbelievers."[67] Aquinas treats improper and proper methods of resisting them, the criteria for determining whether a bishop should enter into public disputes about the faith with them, why they should be avoided, and the reasons for taking action against them.

First, Paul precludes unjust methods of resisting unbelievers in verse 14: "Contend not in words, it is useful for nothing but the subversion of the hearers."[68] This admonition prohibits "contention" (*contentio*) understood by Aquinas as "a conflict of words" (*concertationem in verbis*), which is perverse if it favors falsity, such as "when a person, trusting in shouts, attacks the truth."[69] It is also inordinate when the person of one's adversary is attacked in an *ad hominem* argu-

---

67. "Quomodo resistat infidelibus." Aquinas, *In 2 Tim*, [59], 2:279.
68. "Noli contendere verbis, ad nihil enim utile est, nisi ad subversionem audientium." Aquinas, *In 2 Tim*, 2:277.
69. "Quando quis cum confidentia clamoris impugnat veritatem." Aquinas, *In 2 Tim*, [60], 2:279.

ment. Such contentions bring about the "subversion of the hearers" by raising doubts among the faithful regarding matters they previously held as certain. However, if a dispute is conducted moderately, in the right context, and for the sake of truth, "it is not a sin" (*non est peccatum*). Aquinas argues: "If this is done not with words only but with true reasons, then it is a dispute [*disputatio*], not a contention," and "a moderate dispute, conducted reasonably, is useful for instruction."[70]

Nevertheless, not every dispute about matters of faith should be conducted before the people; several other factors must be taken into account. First, on the part of the listeners: if they are troubled by what they have heard from unbelievers, then public debate is useful and even necessary "because the simple thereby become more learned when they see those in error refuted."[71] But if they are not troubled by unbelievers, debating would be dangerous, and though Aquinas does not explicitly say why, he surely implies that such debates would undermine the faith by calling it into question without cause. Second, on the part of the disputant: if the disputing person, that is, the bishop, is prudent (*prudens*), "such that he can manifestly refute his opponent, he should debate publicly; but if not, then he should *in no way* debate."[72] Note that this would be a contingency plan. Ideally, the bishop ought to be well equipped to engage in necessary debates, since the truth of the faith and the salvation of souls are at stake. If he is not in a position to engage in such debates, he ought to strive expediently to remedy this flaw.

In verse 15, "Be careful to present yourself commendable to God, a laborer unashamed, rightly treating the word of truth," Paul describes the proper manner of resisting unbelievers in a dispute.[73] First, to present himself as "commendable to God," the bishop must examine his intention to confront unbelievers in order to ensure that his motivation

---

70. "Si hoc fit non verbis tantum sed veris rationibus, hoc est disputare, non contendere.... moderata disputatio quando cum ratione fit, est utilis ad instructionem." Aquinas, *In 2 Tim*, [60–61], 2:279.

71. "Quia per hanc simplices efficiuntur magis instructi quando vident errantes confutari." Aquinas, *In 2 Tim*, [61], 2:279.

72. "Sic quod manifeste confutet adversarium, tunc debet publice disputare: si vero non, *nullo modo*" (emphasis added). Aquinas, *In 2 Tim*, [61], 2:279.

73. "Sollicite cura teipsum probabilem exhibere Deo, operarium inconfusibilem, recte tractantem verbum veritatis." Aquinas, *In 2 Tim*, 2:277.

is borne from "good zeal" (*bono zelo*). Next, a "laborer unashamed" is one whose words match his exemplary behavior: "He must confirm in his deeds the doctrine he preaches with his mouth; if he does not, he deserves to be embarrassed."[74] Finally, the bishop rightly handles the "word of truth" in a dispute "by teaching true and useful things to his hearers ... not seeking gain and glory."[75]

In lect. 3, Thomas discusses what a bishop should resist in particular, namely, the "profane and vain babblings" (2:16a) of unbelievers. The bishop must "avoid" (*vitet*) the "profane," that is, things that are far from the sanctuary (*procul a fano*)—far from divine worship. These are "heretical teachings" (*documenta haeresum*) and statements "contrary to the faith" (*fidei repugnant*), which are particularly dangerous because "they bring about much impiety" (2:16b).[76] False doctrine impedes the growth of piety. "Hence," Thomas explains, "the doctrine of the faith is a doctrine of piety, but impiety is a doctrine against the faith; hence he says, 'for they bring about much impiety,' that is, they lead to error or to erroneous doctrine. But this is done abusively [*abusive*]."[77] Aquinas here uses the late Latin adverb, *abusive*, which bears the meaning of an "improper use of language," as in catachresis or a simple verbal error. In the case of impious doctrine, the abuse consists in mixing error with truth. Verse 17 describes this threat figuratively: "Their speech creeps like a cancer."[78] Aquinas comments on the progression of this diseased pedagogy: "For heretics say true and useful things in the beginning; but when they are heard they mix in deadly doctrines, which they vomit out."[79] And verse 18 provides as an example of this kind of toxic teaching the claim that the general resurrection has already occurred, an error that might sound odd to con-

---

74. "Doctrinam quam praedicat ore, stabiliat per opera, quod nisi faciat, est confusione dignus." Aquinas, *In 2 Tim*, [62], 2:279.

75. "Vera docendo et utilia audientibus ... non quaerens lucrum et gloriam." Aquinas, *In 2 Tim*, [62], 2:279.

76. "Multum enim proficiunt ad impietatem." Aquinas, *In 2 Tim*, cap. 2, lect. 3, 2:280.

77. "Unde doctrina fidei est doctrina pietatis. Impietas vero est doctrina contra fidem; unde dicit 'multum enim proficiunt ad impietatem,' id est, perducunt ad errorem sive ad erroneam doctrinam. Sed hic profectus est in malis abusive." Aquinas, *In 2 Tim*, [66], 2:280.

78. "Et sermo eorum ut cancer serpit." Aquinas, *In 2 Tim*, 2:280.

79. "Haeretici enim dicunt a principio quaedam vera et utilia, sed cum audiuntur, immiscent quaedam, quae evomunt, mortifera." Aquinas, *In 2 Tim*, [67], 2:280.

temporary believers but one that was familiar to Christians in earlier generations. Charged with guarding ecclesial unity which is founded in faith, the bishop must avoid whatever stifles piety and subverts that faith, even though the faith cannot be subverted altogether: "But the firm foundation of God stands" (2:19).[80] The "foundations" (*fundamenta*) mentioned in this verse are not the teachings, according to Aquinas, but the teachers themselves who have been given the special grace of predestination (2:20–21) to help them stand immoveable so that the faith will not be entirely corrupted.[81] Then, closely following verses 22 and 23, Aquinas briefly enumerates (with little to no commentary) specific things the bishop must avoid, namely, the defilement of bad company, "youthful desires," and "senseless controversies," and specific things he ought to pursue: "righteousness, faith, hope, charity, and peace."[82]

When the bishop engages in disputes with unbelievers or in exchanges with others, he needs to be equipped with particular virtues so that the meeting is able to bear fruit. In verses 24 and 25, the bishop (in the person of Timothy) is advised "to be mild toward all, docile, patient, modestly admonishing those who resist the truth, lest God give them repentance to know the truth" (2:25).[83] Aquinas explains: "The general advice is that anyone who desires to dispute must be mild.... For meekness is a virtue that restrains anger, which disturbs the [sound] judgment of reason, which [judgment] is necessary in questions and judgments of truth."[84] Moreover, the bishop should be docile (*docibilis*), "that is, prepared to be corrected by anyone. And this is heavenly wisdom."[85] He should patiently endure

80. "Sed firmum fundamentum Dei stat." Aquinas, *In 2 Tim*, 2:280.
81. "Haec enim fundamenta sunt illa, quibus datur gratia immobiliter standi" (For these are the foundations, by which the grace of standing firm is given). Aquinas, *In 2 Tim*, [70], 2:281. Aquinas goes on to say that their firmness depends, first, on God's predestination and, second, on their free response to God's grace. See *In 2 Tim*, [71], 2:281.
82. Aquinas, *In 2 Tim*, lect. 4, [75–80 and 82], 2:282–83.
83. "Mansuetum esse ad omnes, docibilem, patientem, cum modestia corripientes eos qui resistunt veritati, nequando Deus det illis poenitentiam ad cognoscendam veritatem." Aquinas, *In 2 Tim*, 2:282.
84. "Generale quod debet habere qui vult disputare, est quod sit mansuetus.... Est enim mansuetudo virtus compescens ab ira, quae perturbat iudicium rationis, quae necessaria est in quaestione et iudicio veritatis." Aquinas, *In 2 Tim*, [84], 2:283.
85. "Id est, paratum corrigi a quocumque. Et haec est sapientia caelestis." Aquinas, *In 2 Tim*, [84], 2:283.

"persecutions"—that is, the difficulties presented by unbelievers—and he should correct false teachers "with modesty" (*cum modestia*). Verses 25 and 26 express the reason for this advice: "That God may give [unbelievers] repentance to know the truth, and they may recover from the snares of the devil"—the snares being the causes of error both in the intellect ("false imaginations," for example) and in the will ("envy," "pride," and the like).[86] Obviously, on the part of the bishop this requires profound humility, prudence, patience, and courage.

Becoming Fit to Resist Spiritual Dangers (3:1–17)

The second division of the body of the message (3:1–4:22) concerns a warning about future dangers for the Church: "In the last days dangerous times will approach" (3:1).[87] Hazards will arise from the sins of those with inordinate self-love (*seipsos amantes*), which Aquinas calls "the root of all iniquity."[88] The vices of this disorder, listed in 3:2–5a, pose serious pastoral problems for prelates: "Men will be lovers of self, greedy, haughty, proud, blasphemous, disobedient to parents, ungrateful, wicked, without affection, without peace, slanderers, incontinent, cruel, without kindness, traitors, violent, swollen with conceit, and lovers of pleasure more than lovers of God, having the appearance of a certain piety, but denying its power."[89] The sins of those who are "greedy" (*cupidi*) and "haughty" (*elati* and *superbi*) consist in the abuse of external things.[90] The next three adjectives describe those who relate improperly to their superiors: "blasphemous" (*blasphemi*) toward God, "disobedient" (*non obedientes*) to parents,

---

86. "Dicit 'et resipiscant a diaboli laqueis,' id est, ab occasionibus errorum ex parte intellectus, sicut falsae phantasiae, et ex parte affectus, sicut sunt invidia, superbia, et huiusmodi" (He says "and they recover from the snares of the devil," that is, from the occasions of error on the part of the intellect, such as false imaginations, and on the part of the affection, such as envy, pride, and things of this kind). Aquinas, *In 2 Tim*, [87], 2:284.

87. "In novissimis diebus instabunt tempora periculosa." Aquinas, *In 2 Tim*, cap. 3, lect. 1, 2:285.

88. "Radix autem totius iniquitatis." Aquinas, *In 2 Tim*, [92], 2:285.

89. "Erunt homines seipsos amantes, cupidi, elati, superbi, blasphemi, parentibus non obedientes, ingrati, scelesti, sine affectione, sine pace, criminatores, incontinentes, immites, sine benignitate, proditores, protervi, tumidi, et voluptatum amatores magis quam Dei, habentes speciem quidem pietatis, virtutem autem eius abnegantes." Aquinas, *In 2 Tim*, 2:285.

90. Aquinas, *In 2 Tim*, [94], 2:286.

and "ungrateful" (*ingrati*) to benefactors.[91] Toward equals, some will be "wicked" (*scelesti*) in their deeds, some will be "lacking affection" (*sine affectione*)—that is, they will be, "without the feelings of charity 'and without peace'"—and some will be "slanderers" (*criminatores*) in word.[92] The bishop will also encounter those who are improperly disposed toward themselves. Some will be "incontinent" (*incontinentes*), manifesting the degeneration of their concupiscible appetite which, according to Aquinas, consists in those passions that regard simple sensory goods and evils, such as love, hate, desire, aversion, joy, and sorrow. Others will be "unmerciful" (*immites*) in their irascible appetite which consists in passions that regard complex goods and evils (that is, difficult to attain or to avoid), for instance: hope, despair, fear, daring, and anger. And others will be "without kindness" (*sine benignitate*) in their rational appetite, which is the will.[93] Simply put, Aquinas takes verses 2–5a as a list of vices that harm every area of human life (bodily, emotional, spiritual) and human relations (to external things, God, superiors, benefactors, equals, and themselves). In verse 5b, Paul instructs the prelate very simply: "Avoid such people."[94]

In lect. 2, Thomas notes that vicious persons not only will appear in the last days, but are already present and the bishop must avoid them and help the faithful do the same so that they do not fall into similar vices. However, he adds a critical qualification for prelates that is not explicitly stated in the scriptural text: "Although you must avoid them under some aspects, you must not neglect to persuade them."[95] Though the bishop must guard against these dangers because they subvert the faith, he must also care for those subject to such disorders. In other words, the prelate must not merely avoid these persons without qualification, but seek to expose their folly to themselves and to the faithful (see verse 9); this is both for their benefit and that of others. The bishop's office and charity itself demands this of him. But in this he must exercise great caution, as verses 6 and 7 warn that such in-

91. Aquinas, *In 2 Tim*, [96], 2:286.
92. "Sine affectu charitatis, et sine pace." Aquinas, *In 2 Tim*, [97], 2:286.
93. Aquinas, *In 2 Tim*, [99–100], 2:286. On the concupiscible and irascible appetites, see *STh* I-II, qq. 22–48.
94. "Et hos devita." Aquinas, *In 2 Tim*, lect. 2, 2:287.
95. "Et licet quantum ad aliqua vitandi sunt, sed non quantum ad sermonem exhortationis." Aquinas, *In 2 Tim*, [103], 2:287.

dividuals strive to persuade anyone who will give them a hearing, preventing others from arriving at the truth of the faith.

Aquinas does not say here whether the bishop's avoidance of those persons necessarily entails excommunication. He does, however, characterize the difficulty such persons pose for bishops as a manifestation of the perennial struggle between truth and falsehood.[96] The magicians who resisted Moses mentioned in verse 8, Jannes and Jambres (see Ex 7:10–12), serve as an ancient example of this strife and of the problem false teachers present for prelates (*praelatis*), specifically, the harm of rejecting the prelates' doctrine.[97] Commenting on verse 9, "But they shall proceed no farther, for their foolishness will be manifested to all," Aquinas notes that God limits the amount of damage such persons cause by giving the bishop (*praelatus*) the duty to restrain them: "The way they are to be hindered is by [the bishop] taking from them their *pallium* and their concealment because by them they inflict harm.... Therefore, he says, 'their folly shall be made manifest' (3:9b), God exposing them when 'he lights up things hidden in the dark and manifests the counsels of hearts,' as is said in 1 Corinthians 4:5."[98] The Latin word *pallium* has a double meaning and, as such, Aquinas uses it here to indicate either the "teaching authority" of office-holders in the Church (namely, of prelates) or the "concealment" used by false teachers (or both). While the danger they pose is hidden (*occultatio*), God will expose "their foolishness" (*insipientia*) in and through the bishop removing either their authority in the Church or their camouflage. And in fact these may be one and the same, such as when authority is used as camouflage (such as the "wolves in sheep's clothing" in Mt 7:15). In any case, the bishop's

---

96. "A principio mundi semper fuit pugna inter veritatem et falsitatem" (From the beginning of the world there was always a fight between truth and falsehood). Aquinas, *In 2 Tim*, [108], 2:288.

97. "Deinde cum dicit 'Quemadmodum,' ostendit nocumentum quod afferunt praelatis, et nocumentum resistendi eorum doctrinae (Then when he says, "in this way," he sows the harm which they pose to prelates and the harm of resisting their teaching). Aquinas, *In 2 Tim*, [108], 2:288.

98. "Modus impediendi est, ut tollatur eorum pallium et occultatio, quae sunt tollenda, quia nocent.... Et ideo dicit, 'insipientia eorum manifesta erit,' Deo detegente, quando *illuminabit abscondita tenebrarum*, etc., ut dicitur I Cor. IV, 5." Aquinas, *In 2 Tim*, [112], 2:288. I intentionally did not translate *pallium* since it can bear the dual meaning of "concealment" and "mantle [of authority]."

role is to be the one through whom God unmasks, publicly identifies, and deposes dangerous teachers in order to protect the faithful even—or especially—when those false teachers are other prelates.

A bishop prepares himself to handle these difficulties by receiving instruction in faith and morals, by considering the outstanding example of individuals like Paul, and especially by studying Scripture. Timothy was instructed by Paul in the knowledge of truth and in the doing of righteousness, as verse 10 says, "but you have known my doctrine, instruction, purpose, faith, forbearance, love, patience."[99] Aquinas notes that the beginning of this verse shows how Timothy was prepared to resist false teachers: "'But you have known my doctrine,' [3:10a] that is, you have been instructed in the Catholic faith, so it should be easy for you to avoid them."[100] Paul's teaching includes both "doctrine" (*doctrina*), interpreted by Aquinas as the truths of faith, and "instruction" (*institutio*), interpreted as "knowledge about things to be done, which fall under human activity," that is, knowledge about doing what is "just" (*iustitia*).[101] Timothy was also instructed in doing good by the example of Paul's behavior, witnessing his intended end, that is, his "purpose" (*propositum* means both "conduct" and "purpose"), and Paul's attainment of that end by good works flowing from three virtues: "faith" (*fidem*), hope (derived by Aquinas from *longanimitatem*, "forbearance"), and "love" (*dilectionem*). Finally, with respect to enduring evil, the prelate must imitate Paul's "patience" (*patientiam*) by relying on divine help to endure evil and persecution. In verse 11, Paul mentions the specific sufferings and persecution he endured at Antioch, Iconium, and Lystra, boldly proclaiming that the Lord rescued him from them all.

In this, Paul does not consider himself unique since all faithful bishops are to expect difficulties, as stated in verse 12: "All who want to live piously in Christ Jesus will suffer persecution."[102] Interestingly,

99. "Tu autem assecutus es meam doctrinam, institutionem, propositum, fidem, longanimitatem, dilectionem, patientiam." Aquinas, *In 2 Tim*, 2:287.
100. "'Tu autem assecutus es meam doctrinam,' id est, instructus es in fide catholica; ideo bene potes vitare eos." Aquinas, *In 2 Tim*, [114], 2:288.
101. "Eruditio, quae est de aliquibus agendis, quae subduntur operationi humanae." Aquinas, *In 2 Tim*, [114], 2:288.
102. "Et omnes qui pie volunt vivere in Christo Iesu, persecutionem patientur." Aquinas, *In 2 Tim*, lect. 3, 2:289.

Thomas interprets "piously" (*pie*) in this verse as signifying the manner of life of those who desire to worship God in the liturgy of the Christian religion.[103] Those who observe the liturgy, including but not limited to those in the early Church, will suffer persecution. In line with his prior remarks on piety, Thomas provides an alternative interpretation in which living piously in Christ signifies those "who wish through Christ's faith to show mercy to their neighbor."[104] According to this reading, a pious bishop will undergo an *interior* "persecution" or suffering when he feels sorrow upon seeing the guilt and punishment of his neighbors, sympathizing with their shortcomings.[105] And while evil men and imposters progress in their corruption, Timothy is told to hold fast to his belief in salvation through faith in Christ, about which he had been instructed by his lifelong study of the sacred page (verses 13–15).

In fact, Thomas observes, all prelates become fit to resist these dangers by remaining true to their training, above all to their education in Scripture (3:16–17). Though every Christian learns the truths of the faith, "the documents [*documenta*, which term also bears the meaning 'instructions'] of faith are entrusted *in a special way* to prelates, inasmuch as they ought to dispense them to others."[106] Thus, it is paramount that the bishop be well-versed in *all* of the sacred writings ("all Scripture," verse 16) since they are "the way to salvation" for him and the faithful.[107]

This knowledge is necessary and useful for prelates because of its divine source—it is "inspired of God" (3:16). Here, Aquinas introduces a *quaestio*: are not all writings that contain truth divinely in-

103. "'Omnes ergo qui pie volunt vivere in Christo,' etc., id est, volunt observare cultum religionis Christianae" ("Therefore, all who wish to live piously in Christ," that is, who want to observe the worship of the Christian religion). Aquinas, *In 2 Tim*, [117], 2:289.
104. "Volunt per fidem Christi servare misericordiam ad proximum." Aquinas, *In 2 Tim*, [117], 2:289.
105. "Quando scilicet compatiuntur defectibus proximorum, quorum culpas et poenalitates vident" (When they suffer the defects of their neighbors, whose guilt and punishments they see). Aquinas, *In 2 Tim*, [117], 2:289. Once again, Aquinas interprets piety as both the worship of God and as the offering of mercy to one's neighbor.
106. "Sed specialiter documenta fidei sunt credita praelatis, inquantum debent aliis ea dispensare." Aquinas, *In 2 Tim*, [120], 2:290.
107. "Rationem autem manifestat, dicens 'omnis.' Ubi ostendit quod sacrae litterae sunt via ad salutem" (And he manifests the reason, saying "all Scripture." Here he shows that the sacred writings are the way to salvation). Aquinas, *In 2 Tim*, [124], 2:290.

spired since every truth proceeds from the Holy Spirit? He replies: "God works in two ways: either immediately, as his own work, such as miracles; or mediately, by using secondary causes, as in the works of nature, 'Your hands have made me' (Job 10:8), though they were brought about by the operation of nature. And so in humans [God] instructs the intellect both immediately by the sacred writings, and mediately by other writings."[108] He values the knowledge of Scripture for bishops so highly because he acknowledges both the divine authorship of the sacred books and their didactic potential as actualized by God's action working *directly* and *immediately* on the human intellect. Though it would be a mistake to think, from this passage alone, that Aquinas denies the subordinate causality either of human agents in working miracles or of human authors in composing Scripture, since throughout his writings he unequivocally affirms and explains the role of the creature in both instances. Rather, here he is pointing out the difference between God working through creatures who act to produce an effect solely according to their nature, on the one hand (such as purely natural acts of procreation or of writing a book), and God working through creatures to produce an effect that exceeds their natural capacities as such (such as performing miracles or composing Scripture), on the other.[109]

Thus, in a singularly divine fashion—preeminently reliable and certain—Scripture produces knowledge of the truth and exhorts to works of justice and "therefore it is useful for knowing the truth and for directing us in our actions."[110] Closely following the text of this verse (3:16), Aquinas introduces a fine distinction between the speculative mode of reasoning (knowledge of what is the case) and the practical mode (knowledge of what ought to be done). In both

---

108. "Dicendum est quod Deus dupliciter aliquid operatur, scilicet immediate, ut proprium opus, sicut miracula; aliquid mediantibus causis inferioribus, ut opera naturalia, Iob X, 8: 'Manus tuae, Domine, fecerunt me,' etc. Quae tamen fiunt operatione naturae. Et sic in homine instruit intellectum et immediate per sacras litteras, et mediate per alias scripturas." Aquinas, *In 2 Tim*, [126], 2:290–91.

109. See, e.g., the study of Aquinas's treatment of this matter as it relates to the authorship of Scripture by Paul Synave, OP, and Pierre Benoit, OP, *Prophecy and Inspiration. A Commentary on the Summa Theologica II-II, Questions 171–178*, trans. T. L. Sheridan and A. R. Dulles (New York: Desclée, 1961).

110. "Et ideo utilis est ad cognoscendam veritatem, et utilis est ad dirigendum in operatione." Aquinas, *In 2 Tim*, cap. 3, lect. 3, [127], 2:291.

modes, the wise person acknowledges the truth and rejects what is false.[111] The wise prelate uses Scripture to teach what is to be believed as factually true—the object of the intellect in its speculative mode. This is indicated in verse 16, where Paul states that Scripture is useful "for teaching" (*ad docendum*). It is also useful "for reproving" (*ad arguendum*), that is, for refuting errors in speculative matters. In the moral or practical mode of reasoning which regards what ought to be done, Scripture is useful "for correcting" (*ad corripiendum*), that is, for showing what should not be done. Taking his cue from the etymology of the term *corripiendum*, Aquinas says that Scripture is useful "to snatch [*corripere*] someone from evil."[112] Finally, the prelate should find Scripture useful "for instructing in justice" (*ad erudiendum in iustitia*), that is, for guiding the practical intellect toward the recognition of good works that ought to be done.

The ultimate fruit of this instruction is "that the man of God may be perfect, prepared for every good work" (3:17).[113] Thomas concludes that Scripture is useful "to lead humans to perfection" and the bishop is to employ it accordingly.[114] As spiritual *perfector* of the faithful, he instructs their speculative reason, teaching truth to be believed and refuting errors which should be avoided. Likewise, he instructs their practical reason, persuading the faithful to do works of justice and dissuading them from bad behavior by means of correction. In these reflections on the mandate for bishops to study Scripture, Aquinas presupposes that bishops cannot presume an extraordinary understanding of divine revelation as a grace of their office, but must labor with the sacred text—by the help of grace—to understand it and preach it to others. Bishops can fail in their preaching

---

111. "Est enim ratio speculativa, et est etiam ratio practica. Et in utroque sunt duo necessaria, scilicet quod veritatem cognoscat, et errorem refellat. Hoc enim opus est opus sapientis, scilicet non mentiri, et mentientem refellere" (For there is the speculative reason and the practical. And in each two things are necessary, namely, that he know the truth and refute errors. This, indeed, is the work of the wise man, namely, not to lie and to refute the liar). Aquinas, *In 2 Tim*, [127], 2:291. As mentioned above, a recurring theme in Aquinas's works is that the office of the wise person is to teach the truth without lying and to refute errors. See, e.g., *SCG* I, cap. 1.

112. "Corripere a malo." Aquinas, *In 2 Tim*, cap. 3, lect. 3, [127], 2:291.

113. "Ut perfectus sit homo Dei ad omne opus bonum instructus." Aquinas, *In 2 Tim*, 2:289.

114. "Perducat homines ad perfectum." Aquinas, *In 2 Tim*, [128], 2:291.

and governing duties either by teaching falsehoods or by neglecting to correct speculative or practical errors.

Instruction on Preaching (4:1–16)

In his third and fourth lectures on the first chapter of 2 Timothy, Thomas discussed the grace of the Holy Spirit assisting bishops to remain steadfast in their resolve to preach. In his first two lectures on 2 Timothy 4, he discusses how bishops ought to resist the many dangers of the last days by preaching in a way that respects the various predispositions of their hearers. In this context, he also treats the purpose of preaching and the reward to be expected for fidelity to the preaching ministry.

Verse 1 (4:1) specifies the subsequent commands as a charge laid on Timothy and all bishops in the presence of Christ, the judge of the living and the dead. Paul's order, "Preach the word" (4:2a) exhorts bishops to be urgent in teaching.[115] Aquinas reiterates the two elements (speculative and practical) that form the content of preaching, "the announcement of truth and instruction in morals," and insists that "the preacher must do both."[116] Regarding the next part of verse 2, "be urgent in season [and] out of season," he poses a *quaestio*.[117] Why should a bishop preach "out of season" since Scripture itself seems to call this foolish (for instance, Sir 20:22, "A parable coming out of a fool's mouth is rejected; for he speaks it not in due season"; and Prv 15:23, "A word in due time is best")? He replies: "It must be said that a preacher of truth should preach in season; but according to the false opinion of his hearers, he should preach out of season, because it is always in season for the preacher of truth, but out of season for the wicked."[118] In other words, the bishop must preach not only to those willing to hear the Gospel, but also to those unwilling, so that

---

115. "Praedica verbum." Aquinas, *In 2 Tim*, cap. 4, lect. 1, 2:293.

116. "Denunciatio veritatis, et instructio ad mores. Et haec duo debet praedicator facere." Aquinas, *In 2 Tim*, [133], 2:294.

117. "Insta opportune, importune." Aquinas, *In 2 Tim*, 2:293.

118. "Dicendum est quod praedicator secundum veritatem, semper debet praedicare opportune, sed secundum existimationem falsam audientium, debet praedicare importune, quia praedicator veritatis semper est bonis opportunis, et malis importunus semper." Aquinas, *In 2 Tim*, [134], 2:294. The words *opportune* and *importune* may also be translated "conveniently" and "inconveniently."

they may come to the truth. Aquinas says: "If one were to take advantage of an opportunity to speak only to those who are willing to hear, he would benefit the just alone; but it is necessary to preach also to the wicked, that they may be converted, that is why he adds, 'out of season.'"[119] The phrase, "out of season," signifies the unfavorable reception of preaching. Because of this, the bishop's resolve to teach may diminish because instructing unbelievers in faith and morals likely will result in harassment. Therefore, he needs encouragement to remain constant in his determination to preach: "Preach the word in season and out of season."

Verse 2b gives advice on how to instruct variously disposed hearers: "Reprove, entreat, rebuke in all patience and doctrine."[120] The bishop must respect the differences among his hearers, adapting his instruction to their condition. He must "reprove" in order "to teach truth and remove error."[121] When speaking to persons of good will, especially those who are in higher stations (*superiorem*)—for instance, those of advanced age—he must "entreat" them, that is, calmly and gently exhort them to moral goodness. This is especially the case if the hearers are evidently not sinning out of malice.[122] However, he ought to "rebuke" any individual who does not have a good will; but the mode of rebuke ought to be "in all patience" (4:2b). Aquinas gives the reason for this: "Lest you appear angry and you rebuke out of anger."[123] The bishop ought to rebuke such persons calmly, moved by genuine love and not anger, retribution, or jealousy.

The prelate must continue preaching courageously because "There will come a time when they will not endure sound doctrine" (4:3).[124] The perversity and wickedness of the times will affect people so that "they desire to hear not what is useful, but what is curious."[125] The

---

119. "Si homo enim vellet hanc servare opportunitatem, ut solum diceret his qui volunt audire, prodesset tantum iustis; set oportet quod aliquando etiam praedicet malis ut convertantur. Et ad hoc additur 'importune.'" Aquinas, *In 2 Tim*, [134], 2:294.

120. "Argue, obsecra, increpa in omni patientia et doctrina." Aquinas, *In 2 Tim*, 2:293.

121. "Doceat veritatem, et removeat errorem." Aquinas, *In 2 Tim*, [136], 2:294.

122. "Et specialiter si non peccat ex malitia" (And especially if one is not sinning from malice). Aquinas, *In 2 Tim*, [136], 2:294.

123. "Ne iratus appareas, et ex ira instruas." Aquinas, *In 2 Tim*, [137], 2:294.

124. "Erit enim tempus cum sanam doctrinam non sustinebunt." Aquinas, *In 2 Tim*, 2:293.

125. "Utilia nolint audire, sed curiosa." Aquinas, *In 2 Tim*, [139], 2:294. Compare this

bishop needs courage to preach to this audience because his doctrine will be "hateful" (*odiosa*) to them. They will "not endure" his teaching; instead, they will prefer to hear "strange and harmful things" (*curiosa et noxia*), turning away from the truth to seek after myths (4:4). And thus, he is told, "Be vigilant" (4:5a), for his own sake as well, since he was entrusted with the duty of preaching to all when he received the episcopal office.[126]

He is to be solicitous and to "labor in all things" (4:5b), that is, to watch and rule with caution and also to labor universally, "that is, among every race of humans."[127] Though the previous admonitions to avoid heretics may seem to strictly limit the bishop's evangelization, Aquinas interprets this part of verse 5 as extending the preaching duty universally and without discrimination. He perceives in this biblical text a mandate for the bishop, based on his love of God and neighbor, to work tirelessly for the salvation of every person without exception. He must do this even if it costs him his life, as it did for Paul who was nearing the point of his own martyrdom, having "fought the good fight" (verses 6 and 7).

In lect. 2, commenting on verse 8, "As for the rest there is laid up for me a crown of justice," Thomas remarks that there is a twofold reward for Paul and for every faithful bishop.[128] "The primary crown is the essential reward, which is nothing less than joy in the truth.... In this sense God is our crown."[129] The second reward is bestowed for good works. He mentions martyrs, virgins, and teachers—all of whom shall receive a golden crown—citing Proverbs 4:9, "She shall give to your head the increase of graces and protect you with a glorious crown."[130]

---

with Aquinas on the vice of curiosity in *STh* II-II, q. 167, where he identifies this as the vice of seeking to know truth so as to take pride in that knowledge.

126. "Deinde cum dicit 'Tu vero,' ponitur necessitas ex parte Timothei, cui erat officium commissum; et ideo necessarium erat quod praedicaret" (Then when he says "you truly," he gives the necessity on the part of Timothy, to whom this office was entrusted; and so it was necessary that he preach). Aquinas, *In 2 Tim*, [141], 2:295.

127. "Id est, in omni genere hominum." Aquinas, *In 2 Tim*, [143], 2:295.

128. "In reliquo reposita est mihi corona iustitiae." Aquinas, *In 2 Tim*, cap. 4, lect. 2, 2:295.

129. "Prima [corona] est praemium essentiale, quae nihil est aliud quam gaudium de veritate.... Deus est ergo corona nostra." Aquinas, *In 2 Tim*, [151], 2:296.

130. "Prov. IV, 9: 'Dabit capiti tuo augmenta gratiarum, et corona inclyta proteget te.'" Aquinas, *In 2 Tim*, 2:296.

But this crown, he adds, will be given for charity alone (*solum charitati*).[131] In verses 9–13, Paul gives Timothy specific instructions, hoping that Timothy will be able to visit Paul in prison soon.

Throughout his remarks on the bishop's preaching office, Aquinas construes episcopal teaching as an act of fraternal charity. Desiring the salvation of his neighbors, the prelate dedicates himself by a solemn vow to serve them by instructing and perfecting them in Christ's doctrine of love. In his episcopal ordination he is empowered by the grace of the Holy Spirit to fulfill this vow. Thus, the preaching ministry of the bishop is a result of grace and charity, even (or especially) when it is exercised with respect to "unbelievers" or "heretics." The bishop ought to preserve God's gifts, especially faith, moved by his desire for God's glory and his neighbor's salvation.[132] Almost every time Aquinas mentions avoiding or punishing heretics, he qualifies his comments by insisting that they be loved and that the bishop not neglect them in his ministry. For example, discussing Alexander, who had harmed Paul (4:14–15), Aquinas notes that he will be punished in the future by the Church, and not by Paul himself: "Although his punishment is being reserved for the future, the Church should punish him by excommunication. Hence he adds, 'Avoid him,' that is, as a heretic. 'A man that is a heretic, after the first and second admonition, avoid' (Titus 3:10). He gives the reason for this advice, saying, 'He has greatly withstood our words.'"[133] Using the language of the scriptural text, here and elsewhere in the PE lectures he describes excommunication as "avoiding" the heretic for the protection of the faithful. However, he interprets verse 16, "May it not be laid to their charge," as Paul begging for the pardon of others who refused to defend him in

---

131. "Quia corona solum charitati debetur" (Because the crown is owed only for charity). Aquinas, *In 2 Tim*, [153], 2:297.

132. "Bonus usus donorum Dei est duplex, scilicet conservatio fidei et ideo dicit, 'fidem servavi,' quod facit qui utitur donis Dei ad gloriam Dei et salutem proximorum" (The good use of the gifts of God is twofold, namely for the preservation of the faith and so he says, "I have kept the faith," which he does who uses the gifts of God for the glory of God and the salvation of his neighbors). Aquinas, *In 2 Tim*, [149], 2:296.

133. "Tamen cum hoc quod reservatur ei poena in futurum, Ecclesia debet etiam eum punire excommunicando. Unde subiungit, 'Quem et tu devita,' scilicet tamquam haereticum. Tit 3:10," 'Haereticum hominem post unam et secundam correctionem devita.' Cuius etiam dicti reddit rationem, dicens, 'valde enim restitit verbis nostris.'" Aquinas, *In 2 Tim*, lect. 3, [161–62], 2:298.

court: "Because they did this out of weakness, he prays for them and does not excommunicate them."[134] In verses 17 and 18, Paul reaffirms his confidence in the Lord, glorifying him who will not fail to rescue him, but not from temporal evils; rather, from sin and for everlasting life. Verses 19–22 provide further directives and details to Timothy as Paul prepares for his death.

In the next chapter, we shall see the further criteria Aquinas establishes for excommunication, particularly in his discussion of Titus 3:10. His comments on 2 Timothy 4:16 indicate that the bishop should forestall excommunication in cases of weakness, but not necessarily in cases of malice. In either case, the bishop must act in fraternal charity for all involved.

CONCLUSION

According to St. Thomas, 2 Timothy advises prelates on how to remain faithful to their preaching ministry while under the threat of persecution or martyrdom—a problem relevant especially for leaders in the early Church but easily applicable to prelates in our day (or in any age) who labor to evangelize in contexts hostile to Christianity. Prelates are instructed on handling difficulties presented by unbelievers or heretics who harm the faith of the flock. In addressing these problems, the bishop must have the right aim: the salvation of all the souls in his care and the glory he owes to God. The bishop should be motivated to this end by piety and Christian friendship—love of God and neighbor. Thus, his prelacy ought to be directed ultimately to everlasting life, not to earthly goods. As a genuine spiritual father and friend to his neighbors, the bishop binds himself by a solemn vow at his ordination to work assiduously for their good by preaching the Gospel. Because preaching is often dangerous, he needs a special grace to face the prospect of suffering for his people and to stand firm against persecutors.

Aquinas establishes a pneumatological basis for the bishop's pastoral ministry. Through the imposition of hands at his ordination, the

---

134. "Sed quia fecerunt ex infirmitate, orat pro eis, et non excommunicat." Aquinas, *In 2 Tim*, [165], 2:298.

bishop receives a special communication of the Holy Spirit giving grace and power. By this assistance, the Holy Spirit guards the bishop from relinquishing the preaching ministry by offering him the spirit of courage. He is thus empowered to do good works by the spirit of charity and temperance. Episcopal ordination thus affords the power both to evangelize courageously because of the love he bears for his neighbors and also to use the world's goods in moderation.

In spite of the disgrace that a bishop may suffer on account either of the Gospel (whose message may seem foolish to many) or of his association with other persecuted Christians, his trust in God's power will strengthen him to overcome this shame and continue preaching. He must follow Paul's example, confidently relying on God to sustain him on earth and reward him in heaven. For this, he needs to cultivate the virtues of faith and love, without which he cannot truly be assiduous—easily falling away from preaching when confronted with adversity or tempted by prosperity.

Preparing for the possibility of martyrdom, the bishop must develop strength of soul by those graces of the Holy Spirit given at his ordination. Knowing his time is short, he disposes properly of his spiritual goods by choosing worthy successors. A large part of his undertaking includes conducting spiritual warfare, accomplished by faithfully executing his preaching duties and defying tyrants who threaten the faithful. He must help the faithful resist unbelievers by avoiding contentious arguments, yet by welcoming public disputes when conducted meekly, before the right audience, and with a proper and vigorous preparation. For his labors, the bishop is entitled to collect stipends, but they are not to be received as final rewards—he must not make material gain the purpose of his ministry. And he should resolutely refuse stipends if receiving them presents him with an occasion for avarice. In that case, he should support himself materially like St. Paul did. If he remains steadfast in executing his duties in the face of martyrdom, he can confidently expect the reward of a glorious resurrection. By his martyrdom, he will help to save others by instructing and inspiring them with an example of heroic charity. However, if he fails in his duties in the face of persecution, he is threatened (in 2 Tm 2:12) with ultimate rejection by Christ.

In response to the problems caused by false teachers, Aquinas insists on the bishop's duty to remove the concealment of their fraud and take away their *pallium*, that is, the cover of their teaching authority, correcting them with modesty and patience so that they may be converted. He must consistently provide a good example, treat unbelievers fairly, accept correction—even from subordinates—with docility, and offer instruction mildly. In this way, he will lead others to repentance and knowledge of the truth. His concern with the spiritual welfare of others must extend to all humans, both to his subjects and to unbelievers alike. In his lectures, Aquinas's discussion of the mercy bishops should extend to unbelievers and heretics is integrated remarkably well with his strict stance on these matters.

Finally, a prelate is prepared to confront all of these dangers by the diligent study of Scripture, the fruits of which he must use to instruct and correct those under his charge in both speculative and practical/moral matters. All the while, he must be sensitive to the condition of his hearers, adopting different approaches for people in diverse conditions. The ultimate reward of the bishop's labors is twofold: the supernatural vision of God and a "golden crown" bestowed upon the bishop who teaches the truth and even suffers martyrdom, persevering in charity despite the deleterious opposition he must face from tyrants and from gainsayers within the Church. In his lectures on Titus, Aquinas discusses in greater detail the bishop's duty to defend the faith against heretics.

6

Lectures on Titus

Ut malos coerceat

In his general prologue to the Pauline epistles, Aquinas says that the epistle of Titus concerns the defense of the church against heretics.[1] In the prologue to his lectures on 1 Timothy, in his list of prelate's duties, Aquinas says that the third duty, namely, "that he restrain the wicked" (*ut malos coerceat*) is treated in the epistle to Titus, "where [Paul] teaches how to avoid heretics."[2] In his *Quaestiones et decisiones in Epistolas S. Pauli* Hugh of St. Victor says, "It is the intention of the Apostle in this epistle to instruct Titus on the episcopal office, and to warn him to manage the office powerfully and to avoid heretics."[3] Peter Lombard understood this epistle to be an instruction to Titus on the constitution of the presbyterate, on spiritual conduct, and on avoiding heretics.[4]

---

1. "De defensione contra haereticos in epistola ad Titum" (On the defense against heretics in the epistle to Titus). Aquinas, *Super Epistolas S. Pauli*, prol., [11], 1:3.

2. "Ut malos coerceat ... ubi agit ac docet quomodo vitet haereticos." Aquinas, *In 1 Tim*, prol., [2], 2:211.

3. "Est ergo intentio Apostoli in hac Epistola instruere Titum de episcopali officio, atque monere, ut id imperiose tractet, et haereticos vitet." *Quaestiones et decisiones in Epistolas S. Pauli*, cap. 12, "In Epistolam ad Titum," *PL* 175, col. 605C.

4. "Titum commonefacit et instruit de constitutione presbyterii, et de spirituali conversatione, et de haereticis vitandis, qui traditionibus Judaicis credunt, scribens ei a Nicopoli" ([Paul] writing to Titus from Nicopolis, warns and instructs him on the ordaining of presbyters, and on the spiritual life, and on avoiding heretics, who believe

AQUINAS'S PROLOGUE TO HIS LECTURES ON TITUS

In his lectures on Titus, Aquinas presents the bishop as the principal defender of the faith for his flock. In his prologue, he employs Luke 12:39 as an *accessus*: "If the householder had known at what hour the thief was coming, he would have been awake and would not have left his house to be broken into."[5] He interprets this description of the householder as signifying the three duties prelates must perform: "the begetting of the faith, instruction for salvation, [and] protection for security."[6] As in his previous lectures, Aquinas draws an analogy between a natural parent and the bishop, a spiritual parent, both of whom engender, instruct, and guard their children. The bishop begets the spiritual life of the soul by helping to bring about faith in his hearers: "Just as bodily life depends on the soul, so spiritual life depends on faith. 'My righteous one lives by faith' (Habakkuk 2:4). And just as one is engendered into physical life by the emission of bodily seed, so [one is engendered] into spiritual life by the infusion of a spiritual seed, which is the word of God (Matthew 13:3–17): 'I have begotten you through the Gospel' (1 Corinthians 4:15)."[7]

---

in the traditions of the Jews). Lombard, *In Epistolam ad Titum*, PL 192, col. 383B. In the prologue to his commentary on Titus, St. Jerome explains that this epistle instructs Titus on how to uproot the seeds of idolatry from the faithful in Crete (see *In Epistolam ad Titum*, PL 26, col. 556B). For representative examples of the exegetical tradition that developed from Jerome, see Rabanus Maurus (780–856), *Expositio in Epistolam ad Titum*, PL 112, col. 653C–D; Alcuin (735–804), *Explanatio in Epistolam Pauli ad Titum*, PL 100, col. 1009B; Walafrid Strabo (808–49), *Epistola ad Titum*, PL 114, col. 637D; Florus of Lyon (d. 860), *In Epistolam ad Titum*, PL 119, col. 409B; Lanfranc (d. 1089), *Epistola B. Pauli Apostoli ad Titum cum Interjectis B. Lanfranci Glossulis*, PL 150, col. 367A–368A; and St. Bruno the Carthusian (1030–1101), *In Epistolam ad Titum*, PL 153, col. 473. Lombard's introduction to the subject matter of Titus essentially restates the formula developed by this tradition. While Aquinas reflects this tradition, he is original in his organization of all the various themes of the epistle around the treatment of heretics.

5. "Si sciret paterfamilias, etc. Lc XII, 39." Aquinas, *In Tit*, prol., 2:301.

6. "Generationem ad fidem, eruditionem ad salutem, custodiam ad securitatem." Aquinas, *In Tit*, [1], 2:301.

7. "Sicut est vita corporalis per animam, ita spiritualis per fidem. Ab. II, 4: 'Iustus autem meus ex fide vivit.' Et sicut ad vitam carnalem generatur quis per emissionem seminis corporalis: ita ad vitam spiritualem per infusionem seminis spiritualis, quod est verbum Dei, Matth. XIII, v. 3–17 et I Cor IV, 15: 'Per evangelium ego vos genui.'" Aquinas, *In Tit*, [1], 2:301.

The bishop, as a spiritual father, communicates his spiritual "seed" by proclaiming and explaining the word of God, the reception of which engenders supernatural faith—characterized here as the substantial form of the spiritual life. Aquinas describes the transmission of faith in very personal terms, likening it to an act of physical procreation that both brings about a new human being and constitutes a natural family. Physical begetting naturally bears with it the responsibilities of the instruction and protection of offspring. The supernatural familial relationship in faith, begotten by God working through the bishop's ministry, similarly constitutes the basis for the bishop's responsibility, as a spiritual father, to provide for and to protect the spiritual lives of the faithful.

Thus the bishop's other two duties, "instruction for salvation, protection for security," follow from the first duty and Aquinas notes: "This engendering requires knowledge."[8] In order to teach, the bishop himself must possess knowledge. This teaching both begets and instructs his spiritual offspring. Then, in order to protect the "house" (that is, the Church) from the "thief" (that is, the heretic) the bishop must be erudite, knowing not only what to teach the flock he engendered, but also how to care for and guard his subjects.

Though he describes the bishop in paternal terms, he also calls him a servant in the household of God and not the master, "This house belongs to God as its Lord, and to prelates as to servants."[9] They are entrusted with the responsibility to guard this household against the thief:

> [The heretic] is called a thief because he comes secretly and walks in the darkness. Hence, "thief" [*fur*] is named from an "oven" [*furno*], which is dark, as the heretic is named from his obscure dogmas.... Heretics are called thieves also from a perverse intention because they intend to kill. "The thief comes only to steal and slaughter and destroy" (John 10:10). Likewise, they are so called from their mode of entry, because it is not by the door.[10]

---

8. "Sed ad hanc generationem requiritur scientia." Aquinas, *In Tit*, [1], 2:301.

9. "Haec domus est Dei, sicut domini, et praelati sicut famuli." Aquinas, *In Tit*, [1], 2:301.

10. "Qui dicitur fur, quia occulte venit, et graditur in tenebris. Unde fur a furno dicitur, quod est obscurus; sic isti per obscura dogmata.... Item ex perversa intentione, quia intendunt occidere.... Item ex modo intrandi, quia non per ostium." Aquinas, *In Tit*, [1], 2:301.

The heretic poses a lethal threat to the spiritual lives engendered by the bishop, whose paternal duty compels him to protect and defend the faithful. Thomas's lectures on Titus relate the many topics treated in this epistle to the question of how a bishop should respond to false teachers. He concludes his prologue on Titus by identifying the purpose of this letter: to instruct Titus on how to govern his church in Crete.[11]

THE EPISTLE

After partitioning the epistle into the greeting (1:1–4) and the message (1:5–3:15), Thomas further divides the message of Titus diachronically as follows:

I. Admonition to instruct others to oppose heretics (1:5–16)
   A. Advice on appointing bishops to withstand heretics (1:5–8)
   B. The need for this advice: false teachers and wicked hearers (1:9–16)
II. How to oppose heretics (2:1–3:15)
   A. The general plan (2:1)
   B. The specifics (2:2–3:15)
     1. Sound doctrine against perverse living (2:2–3:8)
     2. Sound doctrine against errors in teaching (3:9–15)

Along with the greeting, there are two other themes in Aquinas's lectures on Titus that relate directly to the episcopacy: the need for promoting suitable candidates to the episcopacy and advice for opposing heretics.

The Greeting (1:1)

Commenting on the greeting, Thomas notes that Paul's suitability for preaching is indicated in verse 1 by the fact that he is appointed an apostle "according to the faith of God's elect and the knowledge of

---

11. "Sic ergo ex praemissis trahitur convenienter intentio huius epistolae, in qua Apostolus instruit Titum, quomodo regat Ecclesiam, ut patet in argumento" (So, therefore, from the things having been set forth the intention of this epistle is suitably derived, in which the Apostle instructs Titus how he should rule the Church, as is clear in the argument). Aquinas, *In Tit*, [2], 2:301.

the truth which is according to piety" (1:1).[12] This verse establishes two qualifications for preachers and teachers: a foundation in doctrine ("the faith of God's elect") and perfection in it ("knowledge of the truth ... according to piety"). While the foundation of faith can belong to anyone, the perfection of doctrine pertains in a special way to preachers and teachers.[13] The articles of faith constitute the foundation: "And just as in the other sciences there are principles, so in this science there are principles, namely, the articles of faith which are known to every believer in virtue of an infused light, and these articles are the foundation of the faith."[14]

For Aquinas, understanding the faith is a *scientia*, that is, a habit of the speculative intellect whereby an object is known through its causes by means of demonstration. And in the case of *sacra doctrina*, the principles of this science are received by supernatural faith and further conclusions are drawn forth by demonstration.[15] Thus, *sacra doctrina* or theology has a much wider signification than merely an academic discipline or branch of study. It is the very nature of the act of faith that it be "scientific" in this broader sense as a habit of mind. This knowledge is possessed not only by the "experts" but also by all the faithful in a fundamental and basic mode, but the teacher of doctrine must be perfected in this knowledge in order to communicate, explain, and defend it. Verses 2–4 state that this faith leads to eternal life and is made known by preaching, the mandate for which Paul received from God and passed on to Titus, to whom he wishes "grace and peace" from God the Father and from Christ.

12. "Secundum fidem electorum Dei, et agnitionem veritatis, quae secundum pietatem est." Aquinas, *In Tit*, cap. 1, lect. 1, 2:303.

13. "Doctor autem debet habere fundamentum doctrinae, et perfectionem. Primum pertinet ad quemlibet, secundum vero pertinet ad praedicatores, et ad doctores" (A teacher, however, ought to have a foundation and perfection in doctrine. The first [a foundation] pertains to all, but the second [perfection] pertains to preachers and teachers). Aquinas, *In Tit*, [5], 2:303.

14. "Et sicut in aliis scientiis sunt principia, sic in hac sunt articuli fidei, qui innotescunt cuilibet fideli secundum lumen infusum, et articuli sunt fundamenta fidei." Aquinas, *In Tit*, [5], 2:303. Around the same time he delivered these lectures, Aquinas wrote in *STh* I, q. 1, a. 7: "Quod etiam manifestum fit ex principiis huius scientiae, quae sunt articuli fidei, quae est de Deo" (Which, indeed, is manifest from the principles of this science [of sacred doctrine, or theology], which are the articles of faith, and [faith] is about God).

15. See Aquinas's elaboration on *sacra doctrina* as a science in *STh* I, q. 1.

Appointing Bishops to Oppose Heretics (1:5–13)

Lect. 2–4 discuss the instructions given to Titus on what kind of ministers should be appointed in order "to ward off heretics" (*ad arcendum haereticos*).[16] Thomas's comments are similar to those he made on the moral qualifications of bishops in general listed in 1 Timothy 3; however, here he relates these qualifications specifically to the episcopal candidate's ability to confront heretics adequately. In lect. 2, he discusses what kind of person ought to be considered for the episcopacy with respect to family life and public reputation, the vices from which he should be immune, and the virtues by which he might "shine" (*luceat*).[17] In lect. 3, Aquinas discusses the necessity and usefulness of the diligent study required of bishops. He also comments on the reasons such bishops had to be appointed, namely, because of false teachers and the corrupt condition of the faithful in Crete. Finally, in lect. 4 he remarks briefly on Paul's advice to remedy this condition by rebuking the Cretans "sharply" so that "they may be sound in faith" (1:13).

Qualifications for bishops

For the defense of the Church against heretics, in verse 5 Titus is told: "On account of these things I left you in Crete, that you may correct what is defective and appoint presbyters [*presbyteros*] for the cities as I appointed you."[18] Aquinas argues that *presbyteros* in this verse ought to be understood precisely as signifying bishops (*episcopos*)

---

16. Aquinas describes this section of Titus retrospectively in his initial comments on Ti 2: "Superius Apostolus instruxit Titum quales ministros instituat ad arcendum haereticos" (Above, the Apostle instructed Titus on what kind of ministers he should institute to ward off heretics). Aquinas, *In Tit*, cap. 2, lect. 1, [47], 2:313. The overall intention of this epistle is to defend the Church against heretics: "Accedit ad narrationem; et, sicut dictum est [n. 3], intendit munire Ecclesiam contra haereticos" (He arrives at the narrative; and, as was said, he intends to strengthen the Church against heretics). Aquinas, *In Tit*, cap. 1, lect. 2, [10], 2:305.

17. "Deinde cum dicit, 'Non superbum,' ostendit a quibus debet esse immunis: et primo ostendit a quibus criminibus; secundo quibus virtutibus luceat) (Then, when he says, "Not proud," he shows from what he ought to be immune: and first he shows from what crimes; second, in what virtues he ought to be resplendent). Aquinas, *In Tit*, [18], 2:306.

18. "Huius rei gratia reliqui te Cretae, ut ea quae desunt corrigas et constituas per civitates presbyteros, sicut et ego disposui tibi." Aquinas, *In Tit*, 2:305.

because verse 7, which provides instructions on what kind of "presbyters" to appoint, reads, "a bishop [*episcopus*] must be blameless."[19] Further, it is the duty of superiors to appoint bishops, even though it is the canons that elect him.[20] They are to be appointed in the towns, "for just as in a republic kings are only in the cities, so in the spiritual kingdom with bishops."[21] Insofar as the city is the epicenter of a given region, it is natural that the temporal and spiritual leaders would reside and conduct their ministry there. Further, bishops should be mature (*presbyteros* in verse 5, taken here to mean "elders"), not only in years but also in morals and they should be appointed "according to the form of the Church."[22]

Verses 6–16 specify the kind of person suitable for the episcopal task of opposing heretics.[23] First, a candidate must be "blameless" (*sine crimine*) (1:6). Aquinas carefully distinguishes "blame" (*crimen*) from "sin" (*peccatum*). While a sin can be great, small, or hidden, "blame" or a "crime" always signifies something "great" (*magnum*) and "notorious" (*infame*).[24] Aquinas concludes: "This does not mean that a person who has sinned mortally after baptism cannot be chosen, but that the chosen person not be notorious [*infamis*]."[25] These

---

19. "'Et constituas presbyteros,' id est, Episcopos, unde inferius dicit, 'Oportet Episcopum,' etc. Et utitur indifferenter nomine Episcoporum et presbyterorum" ("And establish presbyters," that is, bishops, wherefore he says below, "For a bishop must be." And he uses the name of bishops and presbyters indifferently). Aquinas, *In Tit*, [12], 2:305.

20. "Item, quia pertinet ad superiores Episcopum constituere, licet eum canonici eligant" (Again, because it pertains to superiors to establish a bishop, though the canons elect him). Aquinas, *In Tit*, [12], 2:305. Aquinas's comment here is anachronistic since episcopal election by canons, strictly speaking, did not develop until the early Middle Ages. Nevertheless, this point underscores the importance in any historical context of soliciting the opinion of a reigning bishop regarding who might be a suitable candidate for the episcopal office.

21. "Sicut enim in republica reges sunt tantum in civitatibus, sic in spirituali regimine Episcopi." Aquinas, *In Tit*, [12], 2:305.

22. "Item secundum formam Ecclesiae; unde dicit, 'sicut ego disposui tibi'" (Similarly according to the form of the Church, wherefore he says, "as I also appointed you'"). Aquinas, *In Tit*, [12], 2:305.

23. Compare Aquinas's comments on Ti 1:6–9 with those on 1 Tm 3:1–7 (Aquinas, *In 1 Tim*, cap. 3, lect. 1 and 2, [86–108], 2:231–34).

24. *Infamis* is a specific legal term signifying convicted criminals from whom rights and privileges are removed. In the Middle Ages such persons were prohibited from testifying in court.

25. "Non quod qui mortaliter peccat post baptismum, non possit eligi; sed quod

comments are similar to those on 1 Timothy 3:2, but here he provides a precise basis—absent in his commentary on 1 Timothy—for distinguishing crime from sin. In this vein, commenting on verse 7, he adds that the bishop must be blameless "because he must dispense divine things."[26]

A suitable episcopal candidate must also be "the husband of one wife" (1:6).[27] After dismissing the interpretation of the "Easterners" (*Orientales*) on this pericope, namely, that the candidate must not have two wives simultaneously (since this would be redundant as Roman law already prohibited polygamy), he mentions the conflicting interpretations of verse 6 by St. Jerome on the one hand, and by Saints Augustine and Ambrose on the other. Jerome says that the bishop must have had only one wife *after* his baptism, but he may have had more before.[28] Augustine counters that baptism removes sins, but it does not wash away matrimony which is not a sin but a dignified state. Accordingly, this verse should be interpreted as an injunction requiring a bishop to have had only one wife ever.[29] Thomas is aware that ecclesial tradition has adopted Augustine's position (with a provision for dispensations), mentioning this practice in his *Sentences* commentary.[30] Though he accepts this tradition, he grounds his argument on the sacramental ministry of the bishop and on the signification of marriage (as he did in his comments on 1 Tm 3:2), arguing:

> But there is a loftier reason, namely, because [the bishop] dispenses the sacraments, and no sacramental defect [*defectus sacramentorum*] should be present in him; but the sacrament of matrimony signifies Christ's union with the Church. Therefore, in order that the sign correspond to the thing signified,

---

eligendus non sit infamis." Aquinas, *In Tit*, cap. 1, lect. 2, [13], 2:305. Aquinas mentions both this verse and St. Jerome's commentary on it in his *Sentences* commentary. See *In IV Sent*, d. 24, q. 1, a. 3, qua. 1, 7.2:892, "Utrum in sucipientibus ordines requiratur bonitas vitae" (Whether the reception of orders requires goodness of life).

26. "Quia debet dispensare divina." Aquinas, *In Tit*, cap. 1, lect. 2, [17], 2:306.
27. "Unius uxoris vir." Aquinas, *In Tit*, cap. 1, lect. 2, [17], 2:306.
28. Jerome, *In Epistolam ad Titum*, PL 26, col. 564A–B.
29. Augustine, *De bono conjugali*, cap. 18, PL 40, col. 387.
30. Aquinas, *In IV Sent*, d. 27, q. 3, a. 2, 7.2:955–56. Gratian cites Augustine's interpretation in his *Decretum magistri Gratiani*, ed. Aemilius Ludwig Richter (Graz: Akad. Druck- und Verl.-Anst., 1959), part 2, case 28, q. 3, can. 1, "Oportet episcopus," I, 1090 (hereafter "*RF*"). See also Gratian, *Decretum*, part 1, dist. 26, can. 2, "Actius" (*RF* I, 95) and can. 4, "Una tantum" (*RF* I, 97).

as Christ is one and the Church is one, so also in a bishop's case. However, this signification would be lacking if the bishop had more than one wife.[31]

Though having more than one wife in succession is not a sin, for Aquinas it presents a "sacramental defect" (*defectus sacramentorum*) that impedes the reception of episcopal orders. He does not elaborate further on whether this is an absolute impediment, though this seems likely from the tenor of his remarks. In light of the bishop's duty to dispense the sacraments, having had multiple wives in succession constitutes a sacramental defect with respect to holy matrimony. The theological presupposition here is that the sacramental signification of the one Christ and his one Bride, the Church, is properly and most completely manifested by those who have had only one spouse.

Verse 6 continues: "His children are believers and not open to the charge of being profligate or insubordinate."[32] Since a bishop is appointed to oversee the faithful, a good episcopal candidate must be prudent and skilled in ruling. A sign of this skill is his success in governing his children, evident in their virtue and faithfulness.[33] This verse identifies three characteristics of his children that indicate the candidate's potential for success in three parallel areas of pastoral responsibility. First, a bishop is required to teach the faith and so his children must be "believers." Second, he is required to instruct the

---

31. "Sed est alia ratio altior significato, scilicet quia ipse est dispensator sacramentorum, et ideo nullus defectus sacramentorum debet esse in eo; sed sacramentum matrimonii est significativum coniunctionis Christi et Ecclesiae; ergo ut signum respondeat signato, sicut Christus est unus, et Ecclesia una, sic et hic; quod quidem deficeret, si Episcopus plures uxores habuisset." Aquinas, *In Tit*, cap. 1, lect. 2, [14], 2:306. This argument is essentially identical to the one he deploys in his comments on 1 Tm 3:2. See Aquinas, *In 1 Tim*, cap. 3, lect. 1, [96], 2:232. Note, too, that the Church's tradition from apostolic times has been to enjoin on married bishops a life of strict continence (see the discussion of this in chapter 4, above, in connection with Aquinas's comments on 1 Tm 3:2).

32. "Filios habens fideles, non in accusatione luxuriae, aut non subditos." Aquinas, *In Tit*, cap. 1, lect. 2, 2:305. His comments here are similar to those on the parallel passage, 1 Tm 3:4. See Aquinas, *In 1 Tim*, cap. 3, lect. 2, [105], 2:233–34.

33. "Episcopus enim constituitur, ut superintendat: et qui constituitur ad aliquid debet esse exercitatus in illo, alias non prudenter institueretur. Praesumitur autem esse bene exercitatus, si bene alios rexit" (For a bishop is established as an overseer, and he who is established for something ought to be experienced in it, otherwise he would not be appointed prudently. He is presumed to be well-experienced if he ruled others well). Aquinas, *In Tit*, cap. 1, lect. 2, [15], 2:306.

people in virtue and since sins of lasciviousness destroy virtue, his children must not be "profligate." Third, since he must correct the obstinate, his children must not be "insubordinate."³⁴ According to Aquinas, this text builds on paternal and familial relationships: a bishop's care for the faithful is so similar to a father's care for his children that success in the latter may be used as a reliable basis to expect success in the former.

Verse 7a reiterates that a bishop must be "blameless" (*sine crimine*) and the reason Aquinas gives for this is "because he ought to dispense divine things."³⁵ The verse continues, "not arrogant or hot-tempered or drunk or violent or greedy for base profit."³⁶ He discerns that this verse enumerates vices corresponding to three of the seven deadly sins (leaving out envy, sloth, gluttony, and lust). Gluttony and lust are omitted from this verse "because [bishops] ought to be entirely cleansed of those."³⁷ And two of the spiritual sins, envy and sloth, "have no place among prelates" and thus they are also absent from the list.³⁸ To wit, envy is a "sin of the unimportant" (*peccatum parvulorum*) and, as such, it is not mentioned since a prelate is in the highest place (*in summo*). And sloth is omitted because the ruling prelate would have no occasion for torpor "since everything advances for him according to his wishes."³⁹ Accordingly, Aquinas coordinates the five vices mentioned in verse 7b with pride, anger, and avarice as follows. Because of his lofty station among the faithful, a bishop must not be "proud"

34. "Episcopus autem constituitur ad tria. Primo ut fidem doceat.... Et ideo dicit 'fideles.' Secundo requiritur quod populum instruat ad virtutes.... Peccata autem lasciviae magis abstrahunt a virtute.... Et ideo dicit 'non in accusatione luxuriae.' I Reg. III, 13: Heli condemnatur, quia filios de hoc non correxit. Tertio oportet, quod pertinaces corrigat. Unde dicit 'aut non subditos,' id est, non obedientes" (And a bishop is instituted for three things. First, that he teach the faith.... And so he says, "faithful." Second, it is required that he instruct the people in the virtues.... But sins of lasciviousness greatly move one away from virtue.... And so he says, "not accused of lust." 1 Kgs 3:13: "Heli is condemned because he did not correct his sons." Third, it is necessary that he correct the obstinate. Wherefore he says, "not unruly," that is, not obedient). Aquinas, *In Tit*, [15], 2:306.
35. "Quia debet dispensare divina." Aquinas, *In Tit*, [17], 2:306.
36. "Non superbum, non iracundum, non vinolentum, non percussorem, non turpis lucri cupidum." Aquinas, *In Tit*, 2:305.
37. "Quia omnino debent mundi esse ab eis." Aquinas, *In Tit*, [19], 2:306.
38. "Non habent locum in praelatis." Aquinas, *In Tit*, [19], 2:306.
39. "Quia omnia ei ad votum succedunt." Aquinas, *In Tit*, [19], 2:306.

(*superbum*). To amplify this he cites Sirach 32:1: "Have they made you the ruler? Do not exalt yourself."[40] The prelate should not regard himself as better than the other members of the faithful. He should also be free of anger—"not hot-tempered." He must avoid getting drunk, which Aquinas calls the "fire of anger" (*incendium irae*), resulting in physical violence ("not drunk or violent"). Finally, the prelate must not be avaricious ("not greedy for base profit"), since he is the steward of temporal things.[41] In a sharp commentary similar to the one he makes on 1 Timothy 3:3, Aquinas here cites Wisdom 15:12, "But they considered our existence an idle game, and life a festival held for profit, for one must get money however one can, even by base means."[42] Suitable candidates for the episcopacy must be immune from such an ignoble perversion of the bishop's office.

Verse 8 lists virtues pertaining to the bishop's manner of life: "Hospitable, kind, sober, righteous, holy, and continent."[43] These virtues, in Thomas's estimation, are so evident that they need no further explanation.[44] Verse 9 lists virtues pertaining to the truth of doctrine: "Embracing the faithful word that is taught, so that he may be able to give exhortations in sound doctrine and refute those who contradict it."[45] This verse proposes for bishops the virtue of diligent study (*diligentia studii*), describing what they should study and the use that should be made of their studies.[46] Commenting on the first part of this verse (1:9a), "Embracing the faithful word that is taught," he remarks that

---

40. "Rectorem te posuerunt? Noli extolii, etc." Aquinas, *In Tit*, [19], 2:306.

41. Compare this with Aquinas's comments on 1 Tm 3:3 (*In 1 Tim*, cap. 3, lect. 1, [102], 2:233).

42. "Sap. XV, 12: 'Sed aestimaverunt lusum esse vitam nostram, et conversationem vitae compositam ad lucrum, et oportere undecumque etiam ex malo acquirere.'" Aquinas, *In Tit*, cap. 1, lect. 2, [19], 2:306. See his comments on 1 Tm 3:3, especially his citation of Jer 6:13 (*In 1 Tim*, cap. 3, lect. 1, [102], 2:233).

43. "Hospitalem, benignum, sobrium, iustum, sanctum, continentem." Aquinas, *In Tit*, cap. 1, lect. 2, 2:305.

44. "Et patent omnia" (And all the rest is clear). Aquinas, *In Tit*, [20], 2:306.

45. "Amplectentem eum qui secundum doctrinam est, fidelem sermonem, ut potens sit exhortari in doctrina sana, et eos qui contradicunt arguere." Aquinas, *In Tit*, cap. 1, lect. 3, 2:307.

46. "Primo ostendit quod ad ipsum requiritur diligentia studii; secundo ponit materiam studii; tertio eius utilitatem" (First, he shows that he is required to be diligent in study; second, he states the matter of this study; third, its usefulness). Aquinas, *In Tit*, [21], 2:307.

embracing (*amplectens*) involves holding something carefully (*diligenter*) moved by love (*ex dilectione*).⁴⁷ The bishop must not merely know doctrine. "It is necessary that he cling to science [*scientia*] with his embrace, that is, with a firm adhesion of mind and love of heart."⁴⁸ Much is implied in this verse and Aquinas's comments on it. A bishop with knowledge of the truth of the faith but who lacks love for it is in a dangerous condition. What then could possibly move him to serve his neighbor and work for his salvation? The remedy for this can be nothing other than "embracing" the faith with an ardent love.

As for the subject matter to be studied, the bishop ought to avoid fables (*fabulae*) and temporal subjects (*temporalia*), dedicating himself to the contemplation of the "faithful word." Some persons are interested in study for both learning and doing, "but this is not enough for a bishop, for he must instruct others."⁴⁹ His study must be more profound and diligent, his contemplation more lofty, and he must perfect his skill in teaching since he is required not only to understand and embrace the Gospel and to live by its precepts, but also to explain it fruitfully to others.

The purpose of the bishop's laborious study is given in verse 9b, "so that he may be able to give exhortations in sound doctrine and refute those who contradict it." Thus, the prelate will be able to fulfill two chief obligations of his office, which Aquinas compares to the two basic duties of a shepherd: to feed his flock and to hold off the wolf.⁵⁰ A bishop must feed the faithful with "sound doctrine"—that is, doctrine without any falsehood—and be ready to "give exhorta-

---

47. "Aliquid enim amplectens, illud diligenter constringit, et amplexus ex dilectione fit" (For one who embraces something diligently holds it, and it becomes an embrace of love). Aquinas, *In Tit*, [22], 2:307.
48. "Oportet enim eum scientiae inhaerere cum amplexu, id est firma adhaesione animi et cordis dilectione." Aquinas, *In Tit*, [22], 2:307.
49. "Sed hoc non sufficit episcopo, sed oportet ut et alios instruat." Aquinas, *In Tit*, [23], 2:307.
50. "Utilitas est facultas exequendi officium suum. Officium autem praelati est sicut pastoris.... Pastor vero duo habet facere, scilicet pascere gregem ... item arcere lupum" (The usefulness is the ability to execute his office. But the office of a prelate is, as it were, that of a shepherd, namely to feed the flock ... and to ward off the wolf). Aquinas, *In Tit*, [24], 2:307. Aquinas draws this metaphor from the following texts he cites in this portion of his lecture: Jn 21:17, "Feed my sheep"; 1 Pt 5:2, "Feed the flock of God which is among you"; and Jer 3:15, "I will give you shepherds close to my heart, and they will feed you with knowledge and doctrine."

tions" when necessary. Likewise, he must guard his flock against heretics (*contra haereticos*), refuting those who contradict sound doctrine. He is enabled to do this principally by his copious study of Scripture.[51] These two duties correspond to the work of the wise man, articulated by Aristotle and frequently adduced by Aquinas: not to lie about things known and to expose liars.[52] In correlating the episcopal duties mentioned in Titus 1:9 with Aristotle's description of the task of the wise man, Aquinas portrays the bishop as a "philosopher" in the broadest sense: one who *lovingly* embraces to his science—a lover of wisdom. The prelate ought devoutly to possess the divine science, meditating on the divinely revealed first principles, the articles of faith. His meditation is for the sake of others, to teach them the truth and to refute the errors of those who oppose sound doctrine.[53]

---

51. "Sic et episcopus pascere debet per doctrinam veram.... Item ut custodiant contra haereticos. Et ideo dicit 'et eos qui contradicunt arguere,' id est, convincere. Et hoc per studium sacrae scripturae" (Thus a bishop ought to feed with true doctrine.... Likewise, they are to guard against heretics. And so he says, "and to convict the gainsayers," that is, to refute. And this through the study of Sacred Scripture). Aquinas, *In Tit*, [24], 2:307.

52. "Et haec duo secundum Philosophum pertinent ad opus sapientis, scilicet non mentiri de quibus novit, quantum ad primum; et mentientem manifestare posse, quantum ad secundum" (And these two pertain to the work of the wise man, according to the Philosopher, namely not to lie about what he knows, regarding the first; and to be able to expose the liar, according to the second). Aquinas, *In Tit*, [24], 2:307. The exact reference to Aristotle is missing in the text, but Aquinas is referring here to Aristotle's *Sophistical Refutations*, section 1, part 1, where Aristotle says that the task of the wise man is to avoid fallacies and to refute those who commit them.

53. In several significant places, Aquinas invokes this very doctrine on the task of the wise man to teach truth and refute falsehood. E.g., introducing the project of his *SCG*, he writes: "Unde sicut sapientis est veritatem praecipue de primo principio meditari et aliis disserere, ita eius est falsitatem contrariam impugnare" (Hence, as it belongs to the wise man to meditate especially on the truth belonging to the first principle and to explain it to others, so it belongs to him to fight against the opposing falsehood). Aquinas, *SCG* I, cap. 1. Likewise, in his inaugural lecture, he says: "Secundo modo sapientiam docendo, et hoc dupliciter, secundum duplex opus sapientis; quorum unum est mentientem manifestare posse: et quantum ad hoc est liber Iob.... Alius opus eius est non mentiri de quibus novit" (In another way, by teaching wisdom, and this in two ways according to the twofold work of wisdom; of which the first is to be able to expose the liar and the book of Job exhibits this.... His other work is not to lie about what he knows). Aquinas, *Principium*, pars 2, "Partitio sacrae Scripturae."

The need for such bishops

The mandate to appoint prelates able to exhort in sound doctrine and correct errors was necessary both because of the proliferation of false teachers (1:10–11) and on account of the corrupt condition of the Cretans (1:12–14). In verse 10, "For there are many disobedient, empty talkers and seducers, especially of the circumcision party," Paul describes the false teachers with respect to their large number, their disobedience, their speech, and their position (*ex loco*).[54] Verse 11 explains that these persons, motivated by a desire for temporal gain, were harming entire families in Crete with their false doctrine. About such persons, Aquinas says, "They are not to be tolerated, because the people would become corrupt, and the shepherd would be blamed.... Therefore, he says, 'they must be refuted.'"[55] The phrase "not to be tolerated" is interpreted by Aquinas as signifying a skilled refutation of false teachers by the bishop. Aquinas continues to portray the prelate in this lecture as a "philosopher"—a lover of wisdom—charged with the task of instructing in truth and refuting fallacious arguments.

The disposition of the Cretans also occasioned Titus's commission. They were easy to seduce and their corruption is described in verse 12, "One of themselves, a prophet of their own, said, 'Cretans are always liars, evil beasts, lazy gluttons.'"[56] The prophet Epimenides is the one who laid this charge in his poem, *Cretica*. Aquinas approvingly cites the *Glossa* on this passage, saying, "Through this we understand that the teacher of sacred Scripture accepts the testimony of truth wherever he may have discovered it."[57] Thomas is quick to note that this does not entail approval of everything Epimenides wrote, but that the truth must be recognized wherever it is found, "because all truth, no matter by whom it is spoken, comes from the Holy Spirit."[58]

---

54. "Sunt enim multi etiam inobedientes, vaniloqui et seductores, maxime qui de circumcisione sunt." Aquinas, *In Tit*, cap 1, lect. 3, 2:307. See also Aquinas, *In Tit*, [26], 2:307–8.

55. "Non enim sunt tolerandi, quia corrumperetur populus et imputaretur pastori.... Et ideo dicit, 'quos oportet redargui.'" Aquinas, *In Tit*, [27], 2:308.

56. "Dixit quidam ex illis proprius ipsorum propheta: 'Cretenses semper mendaces, malae bestiae, ventres pigri.'" Aquinas, *In Tit*, 2:307.

57. "Per hoc intelligimus quod doctor sacrae scripturae accipit testimonium veritatis, ubicumque invenerit." Aquinas, *In Tit*, [32], 2:308.

58. "Quia verum a quocumque dicatur, est a Spiritu sancto." Aquinas, *In Tit*, [32], 2:308.

The advice in verse 13, "Therefore rebuke them sternly, that they may be sound in the faith," contrasts with the guidance given in 2 Timothy 4:2, "In all patience."[59] Aquinas gives two reasons for this difference. First, on the part of the persons being rebuked: "The Cretans were cruel and obstinate; consequently he orders that they be rebuked sharply."[60] Whereas this was not the case with the Ephesians, "whose archbishop was Timothy."[61] Second, on the part of the one rebuking, because Titus was gentle and mild (*lenis et mansuetus*), whereas Timothy was stern (*rigidus*) and therefore was told to be patient.[62] A bishop must discriminate when choosing the manner of teaching and correcting, basing his approach on a correct understanding of his own dispositions and those of his hearers. It is a difficult and often painful task to arrive both at this kind of self-knowledge and at an understanding of the temperaments of one's flock. Grace, honesty, humility, ongoing self-examination, and conversion are indispensable for this endeavor. The purpose for Titus in rebuking his flock was "that they may be sound in the faith" (verse 13), since their faith was vitiated by heretics (*fides vitiabatur per haereticos*).[63] A "sound faith" is one that is not corrupted, which Thomas likens to a sound body free of corruption.[64] Verses 14–16 provide further details regarding the specious nature of false teaching and the intractable character of those who peddle it.

Opposing Heretics (2:1–3:11)

St. Thomas remarks that appointing other bishops in Crete did not free Titus from his responsibility to care for souls and his responsibil-

---

59. "Quam ob causam increpa illos dure, ut sani sint in fide." Aquinas, *In Tit*, lect. 4, 2:309.

60. "Cretenses enim duri et pertinaces erant, et ideo dure eos reprehendi iubet." Aquinas, *In Tit*, [34], 2:309.

61. "Quorum archiepiscopus erat Timotheus." Aquinas, *In Tit*, [34], 2:309.

62. "Alia ex parte reprehendentium, quia et Titus fuit lenis et mansuetus, et ideo inducitur quasi ad contrarium; sed Timotheus erat rigidus, et ideo inducitur ad patientiam" (The other is on the part of the ones rebuking, because Titus was gentle and mild, and so he is led as it were to the contrary; but Timothy was rigid, and so he was led to patience). Aquinas, *In Tit*, [34], 2:309.

63. Aquinas, *In Tit*, [35], 2:309.

64. "Nam homo est sanus, in quo non est corruptio. Et sic sanus est in fide, qui in nullo habet eam corruptam" (For a man is healthy in whom there is no corruption. And so he is healthy in faith who in no way has it corrupted). Aquinas, *In Tit*, [35], 2:309.

ity to oppose false teaching, as if he could relegate these duties to his successors. Rather, he should be all the more careful to instruct the faithful personally.[65] In his three lectures on Titus 2 and two lectures on Titus 3, Aquinas explains the guidance given to prelates on how they are to oppose the work of heretics by the example of their *life* and by *teaching* "a sound doctrine against perverse living and against heretics and errors."[66]

In manner of life

Thomas understands Titus 2:1–8 to be distinguished into two sections: one on the prelate's duty to instruct by his words those in various states of life (2:1–6) and another on instructing others by his example (2:7–8). He comments on instruction by word in lect. 1, noting that the bishop is given guidelines there on how to teach different classes of persons. This lecture repeats the directives given by the scriptural text regarding particular problems faced by men and women, both old and young (2:1–6). However, Aquinas does not mention anything further about what, specifically, a bishop should do when instructing these persons beyond citing the guidance of the scriptural text. Since this lecture is concerned more with examining the psychology of persons of differing ages and genders and less with specific guidance for the bishop's ministry to those persons, an examination of this section must be left for a different study. Yet this passage and Aquinas's comments on it imply something rather relevant for the bishop, namely, that he should come to know the faithful personally and accommodate his manner of teaching and exhortation to respect the various states and conditions of his hearers.

Lect. 2 discusses the duty of prelates to instruct by example. On verse 7, "In all things present yourself a model of good works: in doctrine, in integrity, and in gravity," Aquinas remarks, "A prelate should

---

65. "Dicit ergo: Ita dixi quod oportet episcopos constituere, sed ne credas quod tu sis propter hoc alienus a cura, imo maior debet esse tibi sollicitude ad instruendum" (He says, therefore: I have said that it is necessary to establish bishops, but lest you believe on account of this that you are free from care, rather you ought to be more solicitous in teaching). Aquinas, *In Tit*, cap. 2, lect. 1, [48], 2:313.

66. "Doctrina sana contra perversitatem vitae; secundo contra haereticos et errores." Aquinas, *In Tit*, cap. 2, lect. 1, [49], 2:313.

be a living model for his disciples."[67] He should serve as an example especially in his teaching since magisterial activity is distinctive of the episcopacy.[68] Since Titus also held authority over other bishops, he had to provide them with a good example "in doctrine" by teaching others well.[69] In his manner of life, the bishop must also provide an example "in integrity" (*integritas*) and "in gravity" (*gravitas*). He displays integrity by avoiding evil and the corruption of sin in three principal ways: "In a prelate there is integrity of the senses by prudence, of the affection by charity, and of the body by chastity."[70] As an example of *gravitas*, the prelate shows that he is resolute in performing good deeds done out of charity. Such a prelate is stable and firm, unable to be dissuaded easily from doing good.[71]

Verse 8a, "Sound words not liable to reproof," describes the quality of the bishop's doctrine and speech.[72] His words must be "sound," that is, not corrupted by falsehoods. And he must cultivate his delivery so that he speaks "at the right time, and in a manner entirely fitting, moving [others] to the amendment of their lives."[73] Verse 8b gives the reason for this advice, namely, "that an opponent be put to shame, having nothing evil to say of us."[74] Aquinas remarks, "If ev-

---

67. "Praelatus enim debet esse quasi forma existens discipulis." Aquinas, *In Tit*, cap. 2, lect. 2, [60], 2:316.

68. "Primo ostendit quis debeat esse eius actus, scilicet in doctrina; unde dicit 'in doctrina.' *Hoc enim est proprium praelati*" (First, he shows what ought to be his action, namely teaching; wherefore he says, "in doctrine"). Aquinas, *In Tit*, [61], 2:316; emphasis added.

69. "Et ei maxime convenit, ut qui habet alios episcopos sub se.... Ideo debet alios docendo, eis exemplum doctrinae praebere" (And this is most fitting to him who has other bishops under him.... So that by teaching others, he ought to provide them an example of instruction). Aquinas, *In Tit*, [61], 2:316.

70. "In praelato autem est integritas sensus per prudentiam, affectus per charitatem, corporis per castitatem." Aquinas, *In Tit*, [61], 2:316.

71. "Quod sit gravis quantum ad bona quae cum charitate fiunt.... [Grave] est stabile et firmum. Et ideo illi dicuntur graves, qui non de facili moventur a bono" (That he be grave when it concerns goods which come through charity.... To be grave is to be stable and firm. And so they are called grave who are not easily moved from the good). Aquinas, *In Tit*, [61], 2:316.

72. "Verbum sanum, irreprehensibile." Aquinas, Aquinas, *In Tit*, 2:316.

73. "Tempore suo, et cum omni decentia et provocatione ad correctionem." Aquinas, *In Tit*, [61], 2:316.

74. "Ut is qui ex adverso est, vereatur, nihil habens malum dicere de nobis." Aquinas, *In Tit*, 2:316.

eryone acts well, namely prelates and their subjects, your adversaries cannot harm you."[75]

In lect. 3, Aquinas remarks on verses 9–14, which detail the content of the bishop's preaching, chiefly the grace and teachings of Christ as set forth in verses 11–14 (instructions on the proper relationship between slaves and their master are given in verses 9 and 10). At the end of lect. 3 Aquinas reflects on verse 15, "Declare these things, exhort, reprove with all authority. Let no one disregard you."[76] This verse directs the bishop to "declare" things to be believed, to "exhort" things to be done, and to "reprove" those who do evil. And the bishop is to do these things "with all authority," Thomas explains, "because he speaks as an instrument [*instrumentum*] or minister of God, and therefore with confidence in divine authority."[77] The plenary authority of the bishop (verse 15) is an extension and instantiation of God's plenary authority and, recognizing that he is to be an instrument of the divine, the bishop must trust God in this as in all things. Nevertheless, he should not always speak with authority. Sometimes he must exhort "with an entreaty" (*cum prece*), especially when he considers his own weakness.[78] To those who are good he must speak with gentleness (*cum mansuetudine*), but he should address the obstinate "with authority" (*cum imperio*). As Titus was meek by nature, Paul had to exhort him to speak with authority.[79] Thus, in his commentaries on the letters to Timothy and to Titus, Aquinas explains the scriptural advice found therein for bishops of varying temperaments: the rigid (like Timothy) must take care to acquire and apply a gentle approach to themselves and their flock, whereas those who are naturally meek (like Titus) must develop an authoritative voice. In each case, the end is the same: to bring the

---

75. "Si omnes bene se habeant, scilicet praelati et subditi, adversarii non possunt vobis nocere." Aquinas, *In Tit*, [62], 2:316.

76. "Haec loquere, et exhortare, et argue cum omni imperio. Nemo te contemnat." Aquinas, *In Tit*, cap. 2, lect. 3, 2:317.

77. "Quia loquitur ut instrumentum, vel minister Dei. Et ideo cum fiducia divinae auctoritatis." Aquinas, *In Tit*, [76], 2:319.

78. "Est tamen loquendum in exhortando quandoque cum prece, considerando infirmitatem propriam" (And yet he ought to speak in encouragement with requests, considering his own infirmity). Aquinas, *In Tit*, [76], 2:319.

79. "Habet autem moneri, et cum imperio arguat, quia naturaliter fuit mitis" (However, he had to be warned to convict with authority, because he was naturally meek). Aquinas, *In Tit*, [76], 2:319.

faithful to the profound knowledge of revealed truth and to the perfection of the love of God and neighbor.

Following this, Thomas devotes a large part of his first lecture on the third chapter of Titus to a discussion of the general admonitions for all the faithful given in verses 1 through 7. These verses enjoin believers to be kind and gentle to all, being mindful of their former sins and of the great mercy that God extends to them in Christ so that they might be justified and attain eternal life. At the end of this lecture Aquinas considers Titus 3:8: "This saying is sure. I want you to declare these things, so that those who have believed in God may hasten to excel in good deeds. These things are good and profitable for men."[80] On this verse, Thomas remarks that the bishop is commanded to preach "these things," namely, those things that pertain to God's blessings of grace, the reform of sinners, and instruction in faith and morals.[81] The purpose of his preaching is to prompt *bishops* so that they "may hasten to excel in good works." He interprets verse 8 as an instruction for Titus about the bishops he supervises, explaining: "This can be understood of prelates, as if he were saying: I desire that you [Titus] strengthen the travelers, that is, the prelates 'so that' they 'hasten to excel' those 'who believe in God,' namely, the faithful, in good works."[82] Lacking this excellence, how could a bishop lead his flock to further perfection in holiness?

In doctrine

Titus 3:9–11 addresses what the bishop should avoid in his teaching and provides instruction on how to handle heretics.[83] Verse 9

---

80. "Fidelis sermo est. Et de his volo te confirmare, ut current bonis operibus praeesse qui credunt Deo. Haec sunt bona et utilia hominibus." Aquinas, *In Tit*, cap. 3, lect. 1, 2:321.

81. "Dicit ergo 'et de his,' scilicet quae ad Dei beneficia, reprehensionem peccatorum, documenta fidei et morum" (He says, therefore, "and these things," namely the blessings of God, the censuring of sinners, the instructions on faith and morals). Aquinas, *In Tit*, [97], 2:324.

82. "Quod postest intelligi de praelatis; quasi dicat: Volo quod confirmes viatores, id est, praelatos, 'ut,' ipsi, 'curent praeesse' his 'qui credunt Deo,' scilicet fidelibus in bonis operibus." Aquinas, *In Tit*, [97], 2:324.

83. "Nunc ostendit quae vitet in doctrina.... Item prima in duas, quia primo ostendit quomodo vitet inutilia et aliena dogmata; secundo quomodo vitet haereticos, ibi [n. 101], 'Haereticum'" (Now he shows what to avoid in teaching.... And the first is in two

specifies those things from which he should refrain in teaching: "Avoid foolish inquiries, genealogies, dissensions, and quarrels over the law, for they are unprofitable and futile."[84] In lect. 2, Aquinas comments on this verse: "For him who professes the doctrine of any science, it pertains, first, that he give satisfaction to questions raised in that science; second, that he treat some things *per se*; third, that he dispute with those who resist; and fourth, that he teach what should be avoided in that science."[85] The bishop ought to answer questions of doctrine; but, like someone who is wise and learned in a given science, he is not expected to answer questions that fall outside the purview of that discipline. He is not, then, obliged to answer every question and in particular he must avoid those queries that fall outside the scope of revealed truth. Further, since the doctrine of the faith is wisdom, "foolish inquiries" that run contrary to the intentions of this doctrine should not be addressed.[86] Such include questions regarding matters that he calls *indisciplinabilia* (literally, "unteachable"), that is, those claims that are either patently absurd or not subject to verification or refutation by the scientific knowledge of *sacra doctrina*.

As an example of the first (the patently absurd), Aquinas gives the following: "When the evident, such as whatever is to be held *per se* in a science, is proposed as doubtful. These are things that are considered for the instruction in faith and morals."[87] It is foolish to doubt the *per se* propositions of a science because they are such that the predicate belongs to the very nature of the subject, or the subject pos-

---

parts, because first he shows how to avoid useless and hostile dogmas; second, how to avoid heretics, where he says, "a heretic"). Aquinas, *In Tit*, lect. 2, [98], 2:325.

84. "Stultas autem quaestiones, et genealogias, et contentiones, et pugnas legis devita. Sunt enim inutiles et vanae." Aquinas, *In Tit*, 2:325.

85. "Ad eum, qui profitetur doctrinam alicuius scientiae, primo pertinet, ut satisfaciat quaestionibus quae moventur in illa; secundo ut per se aliqua tractet; tertio ut disputet cum resistentibus; et quarto quod doceat quid circa eam sit vitandum." Aquinas, *In Tit*, [99], 2:325.

86. "Stultitia enim sapientiae opponitur. Haec autem doctrina est sapientiae.... Ideo dicit 'stultas quaestiones.' Quaestiones ergo adversantes intentionibus doctrinae istius, stultae sunt" (For foolishness is opposed to wisdom. But this is the doctrine of wisdom.... So he says, "foolish questions." Thus, the questions opposing the intentions of this doctrine are foolish). Aquinas, *In Tit*, [99], 2:325.

87. "Item quando manifestum proponitur ut dubium, scilicet quaecumque debet aliquis per se tenere in scientia. Et haec sunt quae spectant ad instructionem fidei et eruditionem morum." Aquinas, *In Tit*, [99], 2:235.

sesses the predicate as an essential property, or because some other similar *per se* relation obtains between predicate and subject. For instance, in the proposition: "All of God's judgments are just" the predicate is a (necessary) property of the subject. To deny this is simply foolish and such contentions should not be addressed at any length. With respect to *sacra doctrina*, the *per se* nature of its principles is directly grasped by God and the blessed and indirectly grasped by the assent of the believer through faith.[88] "Genealogies" (3:9) are examples of things not subject to scientific knowledge and questions about them should be avoided in this science since they are given in Scripture as revealed mysteries in order to illuminate historical, contingent events which are unsuitable as objects of scientific inquiry.[89] Since historical knowledge only regards contingent singulars, it inescapably falls short of the standard of science which strictly concerns universal and necessary truths.

Though the bishop should certainly argue against those who gainsay his teaching, nevertheless he ought to avoid "dissensions and quarrels over the law, for they are unprofitable and futile" (9b). The basic criterion used to determine if a dispute is merely a pointless conflict is to judge whether the debate is conducted in order to uncover the truth. Such disputes are certainly worthwhile.[90] Other debates, such as "quarrels over the law," arise from apparently conflicting assertions in Scripture. However, according to Aquinas, since there cannot be genuinely contrary statements in Scripture, such passages must either *seem* contrary "because they are incorrectly understood," or, in fact, really *be* contrary "because a copyist has transcribed them incorrectly. This is especially true concerning numbers and genealogies. Consequently, since these matters cannot be settled, they should be avoided."[91] Since

---

88. Although some *per se* propositions in a given science are self-evident or primary, not all are. See Guy Mansini, OSB, "Are the Principles of *Sacra Doctrina per se nota*?," *The Thomist* 74 (2010): 429–30.

89. "Unde dicit 'genealogias.' Ponuntur enim genealogiae in scripturis propter mysteria, et propter intellectum historialem" (Wherefore he says, "genealogies." Since genealogies are placed in Scripture on account of mysteries, and for the sake of historical understanding). Aquinas, *In Tit*, [99], 2:325.

90. "Quando enim est disputatio ad inquisitionem veritatis, est laudabile" (For when there is a disputation to investigate the truth, it is laudable). Aquinas, *In Tit*, [99], 2:325. Compare this with Aquinas's comments on 2 Tm 2:14.

91. "Quia non intelligitur, vel quia corrupta sunt vitio scriptorum, quod patet spe-

no profit can be gained from such debates, they should be eschewed as useless, contributing nothing solid to doctrine.[92] Aquinas explains: "The knowledge of singulars, such as genealogies, does not improve the intellect or strengthen morals or faith. And they are 'futile,' [3:9] because they have no solid truth."[93] For all that, St. Thomas does not consider scriptural genealogies themselves to be of no account. It must be kept in mind that here he is discussing Paul's directive in verse 9 to avoid fruitless disputes over them.

Verse 10 implies certain criteria for determining who is a heretic and lays out the course of action a bishop should take with respect to such persons: "After admonishing a heretic once or twice, avoid him."[94] Aquinas makes an important distinction: though every heretic is in error regarding doctrine, not everyone who errs in faith or morals is a heretic.[95] To qualify as a heretic, the person first must be in *material* error about something pertaining to the end of human life or about faith and good morals.[96] But second, he must be obstinate and, as such, in *formal* error, not accepting correction by the Church; otherwise, his error arises not from malice but from ignorance.[97]

---

cialiter in numeris et genealogiis. Et ideo haec, quia determinari non possunt, vult quod vitentur." Aquinas, *In Tit*, [99], 2:325. Aquinas was keenly aware of the copyists' errors that commonly crept into manuscripts of Scripture. See Torrell, "Saint Thomas et l'histoire," *Revue Thomiste* 105 (2005): 355–409.

92. "Non est ergo intromittendum se de inutilibus, et quae non habent solidam veritatem" (He is not, therefore, to introduce useless things which do not have the unalloyed truth). Aquinas, *In Tit*, cap. 3, lect. 2, [100], 2:325.

93. "Scire enim singularia, ut sunt genealogiae, non est ad perfectionem intellectus, nec ad instructionem morum, nec fidei. Et sunt 'vanae,' quia non habent solidam veritatem." Aquinas, *In Tit*, cap. 3, lect. 2, [100], 2:325.

94. "Haereticum hominem post unam et secundam correctionem devita." Aquinas, *In Tit*, 2:325.

95. "Unde sciendum est, quod omnis haereticus est errans, et non e converso" (Wherefore it should be known that all heretics are erring, but not vice versa). Aquinas, *In Tit*, [102], 2:326.

96. "Primo, ex parte materiae circa quam errat, puta si non est circa finem vitae humanae, vel circa id quod ad fidem pertinet et bonos mores. Talis enim sic errans non est haereticus" (First, on the part of the matter regarding which he errs, if he does not consider the end of human life or what pertains to faith and good morals, such a person in error is not a heretic). Aquinas, *In Tit*, [102], 2:326.

97. "Secundo ex parte electionis, quia eligens, si non est pertinax, sed est paratus corrigi secundum ecclesiae determinationem, et sic non est ex malitia, sed ex ignorantia, non est haereticus" (Second, on the part of choice, since the one choosing, if he is not obstinate but prepared to be corrected according to the determination of the Church,

If one is obdurate and is repeatedly admonished with no good result, and if he is causing significant harm to the faithful, he must be avoided as a heretic. If, however, someone does evil (even significant harm) out of weakness, yet accepts correction, he is not a heretic and the bishop should not excommunicate him. In other words, those in material error regarding faith and morals ought to be avoided only if sincere attempts to reason with them fails.

Even though persons in formal error (heretics) should be avoided, they must not be despised. Commenting on verse 11 ("Knowing that such a person is subverted and delinquent, he is condemned by his own judgment"), Aquinas cites Matthew 9:12, "Those who are well have no need of a physician, but those who are sick," indicating that heretics should be viewed as "sick" and in need of healing.[98] And on account of his spiritual sickness, the heretic "should not be dismissed, until it is seen whether he can be cared for; but if he cannot be healed, then he should be dismissed."[99] He notes that this is the way the Church proceeds in dealing with teachers of false doctrine.[100] The bishop should attempt to correct him three times, signifying thoroughness, because "the numbering of everything involves a beginning, a middle, and an end. Consequently, it is taken as an expression of thoroughness."[101]

Failing this, the bishop is duty-bound to excommunicate and avoid heretics for three reasons: (1) the danger they pose for the faithful (Aquinas cites 2 Tm 2:17, "Their speech creeps like a canker"), (2) the scandalous appearance of the bishop or the Church consenting to their false teaching (citing 2 Jn 10, "If anyone comes to you and does not bring this doctrine, do not receive him into the house or give him any greeting"), and (3) the threat of punishment (citing Nm 16:26, "Depart

---

and so not from malice but from ignorance, he is not a heretic). Aquinas, *In Tit*, [102], 2:326.

98. "Sciens quia subversus est, qui eiusmodi est, et delinquit, cum sit proprio iudicio condemnatus." Aquinas, *In Tit*, 2:325.

99. "Non est dimittendum quousque videatur si curari poterit; sed si non potest sanari, tunc est dimittendus." Aquinas, *In Tit*, [103], 2:326.

100. "Sic enim fit in ecclesia in excommunicationibus" (So, indeed, it happens in the Church in excommunications). Aquinas, *In Tit*, [102], 2:326.

101. "Numerus omnis rei habet principium, medium, et finem. Ideo accipitur ut sufficiens ad omnia." Aquinas, *In Tit*, [102], 2:326. Compare this with Mt 18:15–17 and Thomas's comments on these verses.

from the tents of the wicked and touch nothing of theirs, lest you be swept away with all their sins"). The epistle to Titus closes with specific instructions regarding the requisite preparations for Titus to visit Paul as detailed in verses 12–15.

CONCLUSION

In the prologue to his lectures on Titus, Aquinas likens the bishop to a supernatural father, a householder who begets spiritual children by preaching the word of faith, who instructs them in this doctrine, and who guards them from the "thief," that is, the teacher of false doctrine. Commenting on the greeting (1:1), he calls the "knowledge of faith" a *scientia*, understood as an intellectual habit whereby one possesses a body of knowledge with a certitude based on the understanding of (or, in the case of *sacra doctrina*, belief in) first principles. The bishop must not only have a foundational grasp of this science of faith, but he must be perfected in it in order to explain it to others and defend it from attacks.

Paul charged Titus with the task of appointing bishops who are virtuous and capable not only of handing on sacred teaching, but also of engaging and refuting those who detract from that doctrine. Although many of Aquinas's comments are similar to his remarks on 1 Timothy 3, he expands upon several items. The mandate that a suitable episcopal candidate be "blameless" does not preclude even mortal sinners from the office. Rather, Aquinas takes "blameless" to mean "not infamous" and, thus, only the notoriously wicked must be absolutely excluded from the episcopacy. As the principal dispenser of the sacraments, the bishop ought to be free from the sacramental defect of having had more than one wife in succession, since matrimony signifies the relationship between the one Christ and his one Spouse, the Church. A potential bishop's aptitude for administration can be surmised from how well or poorly he has formed his children in the faith and in virtue. And a suitable candidate for the episcopate must be free from the particular sins of pride, anger, and greed—any of which will devastate his ministry and greatly harm the faithful.

The bishop must also study Scripture most diligently in order to fulfill the work of his pastoral office, which Aquinas likens to the shepherd's duties to feed his flock and guard them from the wolf. He notes that these duties are similar to the work of a philosopher understood in the broad sense as a "lover of wisdom," insisting that the bishop lovingly embrace his "science" (that is, the understanding of the faith) in order to benefit others wisely by not lying about what he knows to be true and by refuting liars. The good prelate possesses this divine science by meditating on the divinely revealed first principles, the articles of faith; but his meditation is for the sake of others, so that he may teach them the truth and refute the errors of those who oppose it. Nevertheless, a bishop must carefully discriminate when choosing the rhetorical manner of his teaching and correcting, basing his decision on a penetrating and possibly painful insight into his own dispositions and those of his hearers.

He must be a living example, especially to his fellow bishops, of teaching sound doctrine, avoiding vice, and persevering in good works. In his teaching activity, he must avoid questions and debates that do not concern the faith or that inquire into matters where no certitude is possible, either on account of some obscurity in the scriptural text or because the matter deals with unresolvable contingent particulars. He must not be quick to judge his opponents to be heretics, even if they are teaching error. Such persons are to be approached with compassion as persons suffering from a spiritual sickness. Only after determining that their false teaching bears on a matter of faith or morals *and* after trying unsuccessfully to convince them of their error, can the bishop rightly identify those persons as manifest and obdurate in their error, that is, as formal heretics who must be avoided by the faithful.

7

Conclusion

Chapter 1 began with a reference to Thomas O'Meara's criticisms of the lack of an adequate treatment of episcopal grace in contemporary theological studies of the episcopacy. O'Meara advises: "Evidently the theology of the ordinary magisterium is only in its beginnings, and in each moment of its progressive realization and understanding the guide should be Paul's advice cited by Vatican II: 'Do not extinguish the Spirit' (1 Thessalonians 5:19)."[1] This study of Aquinas's lectures on the PE is offered as a work of Thomistic *ressourcement* and is intended to contribute to the development for which O'Meara hopes. We find in Aquinas's commentaries a rather robust treatment of the episcopacy and episcopal grace. He calls the episcopacy itself a grace and he considers episcopal grace to be the principal theme of the PE. In his lectures on these epistles, he develops a systematic, spiritual, and pastoral theology of the episcopacy, one that is remarkably sensitive to the psychology of the individual bishop, the high demands of his office, the temptations he can expect to confront, and his acute need for grace and moral virtue. Aquinas underscores the special communication of the Holy Spirit received by the bishop at his consecration, given so that he may execute the duties of this office in the face of many difficulties. St. Thomas offers a comprehensive theological treatment of the essential elements of the episcopacy and its duties. Accordingly, this conclusion provides a systematic

1. O'Meara, "Divine Grace," 706.

summary of Aquinas's theology of the episcopacy in his PE lectures, treating: (1) the manner in which the office is bestowed (its efficient cause), (2) what kind of person should hold it (its material cause), (3) the nature of the episcopacy itself (its formal cause), and (4) its ultimate purpose (or final cause). Following this, a few remarks will indicate some ways Aquinas's insights may prove useful for the contemporary discussion of the episcopacy.

AQUINAS'S THEOLOGY OF THE EPISCOPACY IN HIS PE LECTURES

Aquinas's account of the way the episcopal office is bestowed (the *efficient cause*) emphasizes the role of God, bishops, and members of the particular church in the process of election.[2] In his comments on Titus 1:5, he notes that bishops are to assist the Church in identifying suitable candidates for the episcopacy. This selection process is to be guided by the criteria given in 1 Timothy 3:1 and Titus 1:7. Though the candidate is necessarily drawn from among sinners, he must be notable for living an exemplary and virtuous Christian life and he must possess great erudition along with the ability to teach and govern others skillfully and charitably. In the PE, the divine charism of prophecy is central and exemplary for this process: episcopal election occurred in the early Church and should be conducted, as Aquinas says, purely and for God's sake (see his remarks on 1 Tm 4:14). For this reason, discerning suitable candidates should be attended with assiduous prayer and fasting.

After the candidate is designated, at least one prelate is to consecrate him with prayer and the laying on of hands. During this rite, the recipient binds himself by a solemn vow to spend the rest of his life in loving service to his neighbor by teaching piety (that is, the love of God above all else and his neighbor as himself) through his preaching and example. This vow admits of very little exception, so that the bishop is bound to fulfill it even if persecution and a martyr's death seem the likely outcome. In his ordination, the candidate receives a

---

2. In his remarks on Ti 1:5, Thomas mentions "canons." The anachronistic nature of this remark was noted in chapter 6, above.

special outpouring of grace and the Holy Spirit, establishing him in the episcopal office and in the external state of active perfection with its attending duties to teach and govern. This grace assists the bishop in fulfilling his obligations since, especially under extreme duress, it is unlikely or impossible that anyone could do so were he to rely merely on his own natural powers. In interpreting the exhortation to "stir up the grace of God which is in you by the imposition of my hands" (2 Tm 1:6), Aquinas teaches that this grace, given initially in episcopal consecration, perdures and is available throughout the entire duration of the bishop's ministry.

Aquinas develops a spiritual theology of the episcopacy that situates the excelling love of God and neighbor at the heart of this hierarchical office. Interpreting the "good work" (1 Tm 3:1) of the episcopacy as an active state of perfection in which the bishop perfects the faithful in charity, Thomas understands the list of virtues to attain and vices to avoid (1 Tm 3) as enumerating those things required personally and spiritually of the bishop-elect in order to fulfill this role (the *material cause*—those suitably disposed for this office). To produce spiritual perfection in others, the bishop himself must be spiritually perfect both in contemplation and in charity. Recognizing that bishops often fall short of this, Aquinas is concerned with establishing the ideal of a good bishop as set forth in the text of the PE.

All of the bishop's activities should flow from this spiritual foundation. Aquinas's treatment of the bishop's actions arises from his understanding of the *formal cause* or nature of the episcopacy which is, to put it simply: the active, hierarchical state of perfection. The specifying feature of this state is an excelling love of God and neighbor moving the bishop to dedicate his life to bringing his flock to the maturity of charity. Episcopal acts flow from the nature of the episcopal state. And since love follows understanding, Aquinas argues that the bishop's duty to preach is the act distinctive of his office (1 Tm 3:2). The episcopal "magisterium of perfection" consists principally in preaching with its twofold modality: speculative and practical (2 Tm 3:16).[3] Speculatively, preaching produces faith finding its fruition in a profound contemplation of the divinely revealed mysteries. Practically,

---

3. See Aquinas, *STh* II-II, q. 185, a. 8, and *De perf*, cap. 19, [674], 2:139.

the bishop's preaching and governing acts inculcate and deepen charity. This twofold operation of the episcopal magisterium brings about the supernatural union of faith and love that is the Church—the communion of the faithful (1 Tm 6:20). It is in precisely this way that the prelate secures and promotes ecclesial unity.

St. Thomas explains the bishop's teaching and governing duties in the light of Christ's own teaching (Mt 20:25–28 and Mk 10:43–44), namely, that they ought to be expressions of loving service and not of a domineering spirit. From the spiritual core of supernatural charity, the bishop undertakes to correct, avoid, and discipline heretics (see Aquinas's comments on 1 Tm 1:20, 2 Tm 2:17, and Ti 1:9). Aquinas construes the administering of punishment as a charitable act, protecting the faithful and working for the benefit of the heretic (1 Tm 1:20 and Ti 3:10–11). When challenges to the Gospel arise, the bishop needs prudence to determine when and before whom he ought to engage in public disputes (2 Tm 2:15). It is obvious that, for this, the prelate must have a commanding and penetrating knowledge of Scripture, acquired by study and contemplation.

The bishop also needs wisdom to determine which persons are suitable candidates for the presbyterate—he must not "impose hands lightly on any man" (1 Tm 5:22). In hearing accusations against presbyters and in disciplining them, the bishop likewise needs prudence to avoid precipitous judgment and also charity to administer fitting penalties, public or private (1 Tm 5:19). He must not fail to correct prelates and other teachers who speak or act contrary to the faith, lest he incur a severe divine judgment. And he should readily honor worthy presbyters.

The ultimate goal of the bishop's vocation, the purpose of all his activity and that to which his office is finally directed (namely, the *final cause* of the episcopacy) is nothing less than the glory of God and the salvation of his neighbors (1 Tm 5:17, 1 Tm 6:12, and 2 Tm 4:7). The bishop's own salvation depends squarely on his fidelity to his duties. Such faithful prelates will be rewarded with a "golden crown" (2 Tm 4:8).

Conclusion

FURTHER AVENUES OF STUDY

Recovering and integrating into the life of the Church a theology of episcopal holiness like that developed by Aquinas will have the effect of restoring the theological categories of the episcopal powers of order and jurisdiction to their foundation: the nature of the episcopacy properly understood as an active *status perfectionis* animated by supernatural charity. There are several promising ways Aquinas's theology can be used to achieve this and to stimulate contemporary theological discourse on the episcopacy, despite the fact that Aquinas's work might seem outdated and surpassed. Certainly, there has been a good bit of development, theologically, pastorally, and administratively with respect to the episcopacy in the last seven centuries, none of which should be summarily dismissed. Nevertheless, the essential elements of Aquinas's reflections merit attention and application to our own historical circumstances.

One of the most striking elements of his spiritual theology of episcopal grace and holiness is its penetration into the psychological condition of those in the episcopal state. His meditations bring into focus the particularly serious difficulties and temptations faced by the episcopal office-holder. Aquinas meticulously explains the many passages in the PE that bear on the qualifications and personal needs of a bishop in order for him to be effective in his pastoral ministry. He elaborates upon the attitudes and dispositions that the faithful prelate must seek to cultivate. The fit prelate never considers himself worthy for the office, but accepts it as imposed. He is acutely aware of his own sinfulness and of his need for God's mercy and forgiveness. Not considering himself irreplaceable, he knows well that the source of his episcopal office and power is the Holy Spirit who is constantly working in his life and office by means of the grace given him at his ordination. He strives for erudition in sacred doctrine, for an upright moral character, and for the heights of prayerful contemplation of God so that he may provide his faithful with guidance both by his teaching and the example of his life. He needs and seeks from God the courage to protect his flock from false doctrine and corruption—correcting heretics and even being willing to forfeit his life as a martyr. Finally, he pursues all of this knowing that his eternal salvation rests on his fidelity in cooperating with the Lord in the execution of his duties, the chief one being preaching. To be sure, many bishops live and die as examples of this kind of prelate. And yet all bishops would benefit from meditating on the riches of St. Thomas's reflections on their office for he provides much more than pious ruminations for daily spiritual reading. His carefully articulated considerations follow from his precise theological understanding of the nature of the episcopacy as a state of perfection.

Aquinas's spiritual and pastoral theology of the episcopacy in these commentaries can serve as a reliable handbook for those in the episcopal state and for those who are about to enter it. His theology is useful not so much because it is particularly innovative, but because it faithfully follows and elucidates the instructions St. Paul gives to bishops in the PE. For this reason, St. Thomas's work possesses a perennial value. He articulates the episcopal ideal that must be sought so that the Church may succeed in her mission to bring eternal salvation to all and glory to God.

Aquinas's PE lectures provide a robust account of the ideal prelate directing doctrine and regulating praxis among the faithful, ranging from preaching and theological activity (such as disputes) to liturgical discipline. This prelate is, evidently, concerned above all with the supernatural life of the soul and with serving Christ. Everything else—the administrative duties, the diocesan budget, schools, hospitals, fundraising—is secondary and ordered to the salvation of souls and the glory of God. The common expectation that a bishop must be politically savvy and an expert in fiscal matters too often eclipses awareness of the supernatural purpose of the exercise of his authority in the doctrinal and liturgical life of the diocese. Aquinas's theology of the episcopacy can serve as a guide for prelates to revive, strengthen, and affirm the true understanding of their office and the exercise of their authority as a solemn work of piety, mercy, and fraternal charity.

In addition to this, the criteria Aquinas develops for selecting suitable candidates for the episcopacy ought to be critically evaluated for what they can offer the contemporary Church. While being an apt administrator and possessing diplomatic suavity resonates to some degree with the criteria Aquinas identifies for the bishop-elect, holiness of life, a mature and abundant charity, erudition, wisdom, purity of motives, courage, and generosity of soul play a far more important role in his evaluation of episcopal candidates. For Aquinas, the bishop ought to be driven by love of God and neighbor, unshakeable in his dedication to serve the Lord and the faithful in his preaching and governing ministry.

St. Thomas provides basic criteria that can prove helpful for judging the suitability of persons for episcopal ministry. At certain times in the Church's history, this insight into the qualities of a good episcopal candidate led to the practice of selecting men from religious orders (monastic orders in particular). This makes sense since those in the religious state who have been passively perfected in charity are likely well-suited to serve as bishops in the station of active perfectors, though this is by no means a foregone conclusion. In any event, the criteria for suitable bishops given in the PE and as explained by Aquinas place a premium on unswerving commitment to Christ and the Church, over and above any other skills, admittedly requisite but secondary and frankly more mundane.

Additionally, St. Thomas's understanding of the episcopacy as a "good work" of perfecting others in charity can greatly benefit contemporary theological discourse. His notion of the episcopal *status perfectionis* makes intelligible the bishop's powers of order and jurisdiction and it functions as the principle that organizes the various activities that are executed by one holding these powers. If the acts of those powers are not moved by the intention to perfect others in holiness, these powers are stripped of their proper meaning and purpose, being co-opted for ends ulterior to the episcopacy as it ought to be exercised in the Church. The duties to preach boldly, judge fairly, discipline courageously and charitably, and conduct oneself with humility in order to care for the spiritual and temporal needs of the faithful is understood correctly when seen in light of the Dionysian hierarchical principle that the superior brings his subjects to spiritual perfection, to *theosis*, through acts of fraternal charity. The sacramental, magisterial, and juridical actions of the bishop derive their intelligibility and force from the nature of the episcopal office as an active state of perfection.

The recovery of Aquinas's understanding of the essence of the episcopacy will not only assist contemporary theologians in articulating the presence and purpose of grace in the bishop's office, satisfying O'Meara's aspirations, but it will also direct attention to the fact that the bishop's office itself is constituted by a special communication of grace and the Holy Spirit. Above all, Aquinas shows that the episcopal office *itself* is a precious and singular kind of grace given to the Church for the salvation of souls.

Our cultural context is a climate in which the notion of hierarchy itself is radically challenged. By and large, this has resulted from a toxic notion of authority as tyrannical domination—a notion both anemic and fundamentally flawed. To be sure, the many documented cases of abuses of authority on the private, public, local, national, and global levels warrant opposition and must be resisted. But this in no way nullifies the role of authority as such and its exercise, properly understood and executed. The Christian notion of hierarchical authority is founded on both a natural and supernatural understanding of holy governance. With respect to nature, the very warrant for judging particular instances of authoritative action as unjust or abusive is predicated exclusively upon a proper understanding of due authority as something naturally ordered to the welfare of those subject to it. No one reasonably condemns parents or the state (or even bishops!) when their authority is successfully employed in order to provide fundamental goods for those under their charge, such as food, clothing, shelter, health care, education, and the like. In fact, the successful procurement of many of these benefits is happily ignored as something working as intended. The supernatural understanding of divine authority builds on this natural notion and Christ himself both teaches it and serves as its exemplar. Acknowledging that the rulers of the gentiles lord their authority abusively over their subjects, Christ tells those to whom he entrusts the spiritual authority of the Kingdom: "It shall not be so among you; but whoever will be great among you must be your servant, and whoever would be first among you must be your slave" (Mt 20:25–26). This correct natural and supernatural understanding of authority underlies the instructions given to prelates in the PE. In his commentaries, Aquinas elaborates these directives, providing both their rational basis and the episcopal duties that follow from them.

Though the study undertaken in this book does not provide a

thoroughgoing theological evaluation of Aquinas's theology of the episcopacy in his PE lectures, it lays the foundation for such a study or, rather, set of studies. The full work of critically assessing the theology in St. Thomas's PE lectures would certainly require: (1) a full treatment of how Thomas receives and develops the hierarchical theology of Pseudo-Dionysius, (2) determining what part that reception and development plays in his PE lectures (and this study shows, in part, that it is a small but important part), and (3) evaluating how this theology of the hierarchy is or is not in harmony with the Pauline texts of the PE. And ascertaining the latter further requires a determination of whether Aquinas was a good interpreter of these epistles in particular, and of St. Paul's writings in general.

This study provides the benefit of thoroughness and depth at the cost of the breadth that would be provided by those further critical studies. Specifically, the aim of this work was to discover and accurately summarize St. Thomas's theology of the episcopacy in his PE lectures in order to make an initial contribution that would find its completion in future works that pursue one or more of the elements listed above. With that said, identifying precisely *what* Aquinas claims is the more restricted but nonetheless advantageous purpose of this book. As such, this study could be construed as a work of "positive theology" or, more precisely, of *ressourcement*: recovering the riches that Thomas sets forth in his PE commentaries. In doing so I hope to lay the necessary foundation for those further studies since Aquinas's theology cannot be critically evaluated until what he actually says is known with precision. That, I hope, is the primary value of this book.

By contextualizing Aquinas's theology of the episcopacy in his PE lectures in light of his thirteenth-century contemporaries and in light of his writings on the episcopacy in the rest of his *opera* (chapter 2), this work highlights the unique contribution of Aquinas with his Dionysian-inspired understanding of the episcopacy as a *status perfectionis*. With respect to the writings of Pseudo-Dionysius, my intent in this work was to provide enough background for the reader to understand how Thomas understood Pseudo-Dionysius's *Ecclesiastical Hierarchy* without definitively resolving the technical question of how great a role this hierarchical theology plays in Aquinas's PE commentaries. As such, there is little in this work beyond what is necessary to understand the two instances in the entire set of PE lectures in which Aquinas explicitly cites Dionysius.[4] Despite the lack of such further critical studies, this critical examination of St. Thomas's PE commentaries affords a rich theological deposit that should yield fruit for the renewal of Thomistic studies, for the theology of the episcopacy, and above for all the enlivening of the life and ministry of bishops in loving service to their neighbors and to Christ, our Lord.

4. Namely, *In 1 Tim*, cap. 3, lect. 2, [109], and cap. 6, lect. 3, [270].

Bibliography

PRIMARY SOURCES: THE WORKS OF THOMAS AQUINAS

Aquinas, Thomas. *Commentum in Quatuor Libros Sententiarum*. In *Sancti Thomae Aquinatis Doctoris Angelici Ordinis Praedicatorum Opera Omnia*, vols. 6–7.2. Reprint of the Parma edition. New York: Musurgia, 1948.

———. "*Contra Impugnantes Dei cultum et religionem*." In *Opuscula theologica*, edited by Raymundo Spiazzi, 2:5–110. Turin: Marietti, 1954.

———. "*De commendatione et partitione sacrae scripturae*." In *Opuscula theologica*, edited by R. A. Verardi and R. M. Spiazzi, 1:435–43. Turin: Marietti, 1954.

———. "*De perfectione vitae spiritualis*." In *Opuscula theologica*, ed. Spiazzi, 2:111–53. Turin: Marietti, 1954.

———. *Quaestiones quodlibetales*. Edited by R. Spiazzi. Turin: Marietti, 1956.

———. *Summa Contra Gentiles*. Leonine manual edition. Rome: Apud sedem Commissionis Leoninae, 1934.

———. *Summa Theologiae*. 3rd ed. Torino: Edizioni San Paolo [Leonine edition], 1999.

———. *Super Epistolas S. Pauli Lectura*. Edited by Raphael Cai. 2 vols. Turin: Marietti, 1952.

———. *Super Evangelium S. Ioannis Lectura*. Edited by Raphael Cai. Turin: Marietti, 1952.

———. *Super Evangelium S. Matthaei Lectura*. Edited by Raphael Cai. Turin: Marietti, 1951.

OTHER PRIMARY SOURCES

Albertus Magnus. *Opera Omnia*. Edited by Augustus Borgnet. Paris: Vivès, 1890.

———. *Opera Omnia*. Edited by Maria Burger. Cologne: Monasterii Westfalorum in Aedibus Aschendorff, 1999.

Augustine of Hippo. "Contra adversarium legis et prophetarum." In *PL* 42, cols. 603–66.

———. "De bono conjugali." In *PL* 40, cols. 373–96.
———. "De civitate Dei." In *PL* 41, cols. 13–804.
Bonaventure. *Opera Omnia*. Edited by Luigi da Parma Canali et al. Quaracchi: Collegii S. Bonaventurae, 1882–1902.
Gratian, Johannes. *Decretum magistri Gratiani*. Edited by Aemilius Ludwig Richter and Emil Friedberg. Graz: Akad. Druck- und Verl.-Anst., 1959.
Hugh of St. Victor. *The Didascalicon of Hugh of St. Victor*. Translated by Jerome Taylor. New York: Columbia University Press, 1991.
———. *On the Sacraments of the Christian Faith*. Translated by Roy J. Deferrari. Cambridge, Mass.: The Mediaeval Academy of America, 1951.
———. "Quaestiones et decisiones in Epistolas S. Pauli." In *PL* 175, cols. 593–608A.
Jerome. "Commentariorum in epistolam ad Titum." In *PL* 26, cols. 555–600C.
Peter the Chanter. "Verbum abbreviatum." In *PL* 205, cols. 23–369A.
Peter Lombard. "Collectaneorum in Paulum continuatio." In *PL* 192, cols. 325–94D.
———. *Sententiae in IV Libris Distinctae*. 3rd edition. Rome: Grottaferrata, Editiones Collegii S. Bonaventurae Ad Claras Aquas, 1981.
Pseudo-Dionysius the Areopagite. *Pseudo-Dionysius: The Complete Works*. New York: Paulist Press, 1987.
Tanner, Norman P., ed. *Decrees of the Ecumenical Councils*. 2 vols. London: Sheed & Ward Ltd., 1990.
Walafridus Strabo. "Glossa Ordinaria." In *PL* 114, cols. 623–42B.

SECONDARY SOURCES

Andrée, Alexander. "Anselm of Laon Unveiled: The *Glossa Svper Iohannem* and the Origins of the *Glossa Ordinaria* on the Bible." *Mediaeval Studies* 78 (2011): 217–60.
———. "Laon Revisited: Master Anselm and the Creation of a Theological School in the Twelfth Century." *The Journal of Mediaeval Latin* 22 (2012): 257–81.
Baglow, Christopher T. *"Modus Et Forma": A New Approach to the Exegesis of Saint Thomas Aquinas with an Application to the Lectura super epistolam ad Ephesios*. Rome: Pontificio Instituto Biblico, 2002.
Balthasar, Hans Urs von. *Explorations in Theology*, vol. 1: *Word Made Flesh*. Translated by A. V. Littledale and Alexander Dru. San Francisco, Calif.: Ignatius Press, 1989.
Bataillon, Louis-Jacques, Gilbert Dahan, and Pierre-Marie Gy, eds. *Hughues de Saint-Cher* (+1263): *Bibliste et Théologien*. Turnhout: Brepols, 2004.
Black, C. Clifton. "St. Thomas' Commentary on the Johannine Prologue: Some Reflections on its Character and Implications." *Catholic Biblical Quarterly* 48 (1986): 681–98.

Bouëssé, Humbert. "Épiscopat et sacerdoce, pt 2: l'opinion de Saint Thomas." *Revue des Sciences Religieuses* 28 (1954): 368–91.

Boyle, John F. "Aquinas' Roman Commentary on Peter Lombard." *Annuario Filosófico* 39 (2006): 477–96.

———. "St. Thomas Aquinas and Sacred Scripture." *Pro Ecclesia* 4 (1996): 92–104.

Callan, Charles J. "The Bible in the Summa Theologica of St. Thomas Aquinas." *Catholic Biblical Quarterly* 9 (1947): 33–47.

Chenu, Marie-Dominique. *Aquinas and his Role in Theology*. Translated by Paul Philibert. Collegeville, Minn.: Liturgical Press, 2002.

———. *Nature, Man, and Society in the Twelfth Century: Essays on New Theological Perspectives in the Latin West*. Edited and translated by Jerome Taylor and Lester Little. Toronto: University of Toronto Press, 1997.

———. *Toward Understanding St. Thomas*. Translated by A. M. Landry and D. Hughes. Chicago: Henry Regnery Press, 1964.

Childs, Brevard. *Biblical Theology of the Old and New Testaments*. Minneapolis, Minn.: Fortress Press, 1992.

Cochini, Christian. *Origines Apostoliques du Célibat Sacerdotal*. Paris: P. Lethielleux, 1981.

Congar, Yves. "Apostolicité de ministère et apostolicité de doctrine: Essai d'explication de la Réaction protestante et de la Tradition catholique." In Congar, *Ministères et communion ecclésiale*, 51–94. Paris: Éditions du Cerf, 1971.

———. "Aspects ecclésiologiques de la querelle entre mendiants et séculiers dans la seconde moitié du XIIIe siècle et le début du XIVe." *Archives d'histoire doctrinale et littéraire du Moyen Age* 28 (1961): 35–151.

———. *L'Eglise de saint Augustin à l'époque moderne*. Paris: Éditions du Cerf, 1970.

———. *Église et papauté*. Paris: Éditions du Cerf, 1994.

———. "The Idea of the Church in St. Thomas Aquinas." *The Thomist* 1 (1939): 331–59.

Congar, Yves, and B.-D. Dupuy, eds. *L'Épiscopat et l'église universelle*. Unam Sanctam 39. Paris: Éditions du Cerf, 1962.

d'Alverny, Marie-Thérèse. "Translations and Translators." In *Renaissance and Renewal in the Twelfth Century*, edited by Robert Louis and Giles Constable with Carol Lanham. Toronto: University of Toronto Press (in association with the Medieval Academy of America), 1999.

Darquennes, Achilles. *De Juridische Structuur van de Kerk volgens Sint Thomas van Aquino*. Recueil de Travaux d'Histoire et de Philologie. Leuven: Bibliothèque de l'Université, 1949.

Denifle, Heinrich. "Quel livre servait de base à l'enseignment des Maîtres en Théologie dans l'Université de Paris?" *Revue Thomiste* 2 (1894): 129–61.

Domanyi, Thomas. *Der Römerbriefkommentar des Thomas von Aquin: Ein Beitrag zur Untersuchung seine Auslegungsmethoden*. Basler und Berner Studien zur historischen und systematischen Theologie 39. Bern: Peter Lang, 1979.

Ellis, Robinson. *A Commentary on Catullus*. Oxford: Clarendon Press, 1889.
Fehlner, Peter D. *The Role of Charity in the Ecclesiology of St. Bonaventure*. Rome: Editrice Miscellanea Francescana, 1965.
Gaisser, Julia Haig. *Catullus*. Oxford: Wiley-Blackwell, 2009.
Gillon, Louis Bertrand. "L'Épiscopat, état de perfection." In *L'Evêque dans l'église du Christ*, edited by Humbert Bouëssé and Antré Mandouze, 221–36. Paris: Desclée de Brouwer, 1963.
Gilson, Étienne. *The Christian Philosophy of St. Thomas*. Translated by L. K. Shook. New York: Random House, 1956.
Ginther, James R. "There is a Text in this Classroom: The Bible and Theology in the Medieval University." In *Essays in Medieval Philosophy and Theology in Memory of Walter H. Principe, C.S.B.: Fortresses and Launching Pads*, edited by James R. Ginther and Carl N. Still, 31–51. Aldershot: Ashgate, 2005.
Glorieux, Palemon. "Essai sur les commentaires scripturaires de saint Thomas et leur chronologie." *Recherches de Théologie Ancienne et Médiévale* 17 (1950): 237–66.
Heid, Stefan. *Zölibat in der Frühen Kirche: Die Anfänge einer Enthaltsamkeitspflicht für Kleriker in Ost und West*. Paderborn: F. Schöningh, 1997.
Horst, Ulrich. *Bischöfe und Ordensleute: cura principalis animarum und via perfectionis in der Ekklesiologie des hl. Thomas von Aquin*. Berlin: Akademie Verlag, 1999.
Hütter, Reinhard and Matthew Levering, eds. *Ressourcement Thomism: Sacred Doctrine, the Sacraments, and the Moral Life*. Washington, D.C.: The Catholic University of America Press, 2010.
Johnson, Luke Timothy. *The Anchor Bible: The First and Second Letters to Timothy*. New York: Doubleday, 2001.
Kelly, J. N. D. *The Pastoral Epistles*. Peabody, Mass.: Hendrickson, 1960.
Knight, George. *The Pastoral Epistles, A Commentary on the Greek Text*. Grand Rapids, Mich.: Eerdmans, 1992.
Komonchak, Joseph A. "Authority and Conversion or: The Limits of Authority," *Cristianesimo nella Storia* 21 (2000): 207–29.
Lamb, Matthew. "Introduction." In *Commentary on St. Paul's Epistle to the Ephesians by St. Thomas Aquinas*, 3–36. Albany, N.Y.: Magi Books, 1966.
Lécuyer, J. "Aux origines de la théologie thomiste de l'Épiscopat." *Gregorianum* 35 (1954): 56–89.
———. "Les étapes de l'enseignement thomiste sur l'Épiscopat." *Revue Thomiste* 57 (1957): 29–52.
Loewe, Raphael. "The Medieval History of the Latin Vulgate." In *The Cambridge History of the Bible*, edited by G. W. H. Lampe, 102–54. Cambridge: Cambridge University Press, 1969.
Louth, Andrew. *The Church in History*, vol. 3: *Greek East and Latin West: The Church AD 681–1071*. Crestwood, N.Y.: St. Vladimir's Seminary Press, 2007.
Mahoney, Edward P. "Albert the Great on Christ and Hierarchy." In *Christ Among*

the Medieval Dominicans: Representations of Christ in the Texts and Images of the Order of Preachers, edited by Kent Emery, Jr., and Joseph Wawrykow. Notre Dame, Ind.: University of Notre Dame Press, 1999.

Maltha, A. H. "Heiligheid en macht van de bisschop volgens Thomas van Aquino." In *Episcopale Munus: recueil d'études sur le ministère épiscopal offertes en hommage à Son Excellence Mgr J. Gijsen*, 287–310. Edited by Joannes Matthijs Gijsen, Philippe Delhaye, and Leo Elders. Assen: Van Gorcum, 1982.

Mandonnet, Pierre. "Chronologie des écrits scripturaires de saint Thomas [1–3]." *Revue Thomiste* 33 (1928): 27–45, 116–55, 211–45.

McGovern, Thomas. *Priestly Celibacy Today*. Downers Grove, Ill.: Midwest Theological Forum, 1997.

Minnis, Alastair J. *Medieval Theory of Authorship: Scholastic Literary Attitudes in the Later Middle Ages*. London: Scolar Press, 1984.

Mirsky, Mark, and David Stern, eds. *Rabbinic Fantasies: Imaginitive Narratives from Classical Hebrew Literature*. New Haven, Conn.: Yale University Press, 1998.

Molloy, Noel. "Hierarchy and Holiness: Aquinas on the Holiness of the Episcopal State." *The Thomist* 39 (1975): 198–252.

Morris, Colin. *The Papal Monarchy: The Western Church from 1050 to 1250*. Oxford: Oxford University Press, 1989.

Murphy, Roland. "Patristic and Medieval Exegesis—Help or Hindrance?" *Catholic Biblical Quarterly* 43 (1981): 505–10.

Nederman, Cary, and John Jaursen. *Difference and Dissent: Theories of Toleration in Medieval and Early Modern Europe*. Lanham, Md.: Rowman and Littlefield, 1996.

O'Meara, Thomas F. "Divine Grace and Human Nature as Sources for the Universal Magisterium of Bishops." *Theological Studies* 64 (2003): 683–706.

Orrieux, L. M. "L'Evêque 'perfector' selon le Pseudo-Denys et saint Thomas." In *L'Evêque dans l'Eglise du Christ*, edited by Humbert Bouëssé and Antré Mandouze, 237–42. Paris: Desclée de Brouwer, 1963.

Paretsky, Albert. "The Influence of Thomas the Exegete on Thomas the Theologian: The Tract on Law (Ia-IIae, qq. 98–108) as a Test Case." *Angelicum* 71 (1994): 549–77.

Persson, P. E. *Sacra Doctrina: Reason and Revelation in Aquinas*. Oxford: Blackwell, 1970.

Pesch, Otto Herman. "Paul as Professor of Theology: The Image of the Apostle in St. Thomas' Theology." *The Thomist* 38 (1974): 584–605.

Post, Gaines, Kimon Giocarinis, and Robert Kay. "The Medieval Heritage of a Humanistic Ideal: *Scientia donum Dei est, unde vendi non potest*." *Traditio* 11 (1955): 195–234.

Prügl, Thomas. "Thomas Aquinas as Interpreter of Scripture." In *The Theology of Thomas Aquinas*, edited by Joseph Wawrykow and Rik van Nieuwenhove, 386–415. Notre Dame, Ind.: University of Notre Dame Press, 2005.

Ramírez, Santiago María. *De Episcopatu ut Sacramento deque Episcoporum Collegio*. Salamanca: Instituto Histórico Dominicano de San Esteban, 1996.
Rouse, Mary A., and Richard H. Rouse. *Authentic Witnesses: Approaches to Medieval Texts and Manuscripts*. Notre Dame, Ind.: University of Notre Dame Press, 1991.
Rousseau, O. "La doctrine du ministère épiscopal et ses vicissitudes dans l'église d'Occident." In *L'Épiscopat et l'église universelle*, edited by Y. Congar and D. Dupuy, *Unam Sanctum* 39:279–308. Paris: Éditions du Cerf, 1962.
Ryan, Thomas. *Thomas Aquinas as Reader of the Psalms*. Notre Dame, Ind.: University of Notre Dame Press, 2000.
Saward, John. "The Grace of Christ in His Principal Members: St. Thomas Aquinas on the Pastoral Epistles." In *Aquinas on Scripture*, edited by Thomas G. Weinandy, Daniel A. Keating, and John P. Yocum, 197–221. London: T&T Clark, 2005.
Smalley, Beryl. *The Gospels in the Schools c. 1100–c. 1280*. London: Hambledon Press, 1985.
———. *The Study of the Bible in the Middle Ages*. 2nd rev. ed. Oxford: Basil Blackwell, 1952.
Spicq, Ceslas. *Esquisse d'une Histoire de l'Exégèse Latine au Moyen Age. Bibliothéque Thomiste 26*. Paris: J. Vrin, 1944.
———. *Saint Paul, Les Épitres Pastorales*. Paris: Librairie Lecoffre, 1947.
Stenger, Robert P. "The Development of a Theology of the Episcopacy from the Decretum of Gratian to the Writings of Saint Thomas Aquinas." PhD diss., The Catholic University of America, 1963.
Stickler, Alfons. *Der Klerikerzölibat: Seine Entwicklungsgeschichte und seine theologischen Grundlagen*. Abensberg: Kral Verlag, 1993.
Świerzawski, Wacław. "L'exégèse biblique et la théologie spéculative de s. Thomas d'Aquin." *Divinitas* 18 (1974): 138–53.
Torrell, Jean-Pierre. *Saint Thomas Aquinas. Volume 1, The Person and His Work*. Translated by Robert Royal. 2nd rev. ed. Washington, D.C.: The Catholic University of America Press, 2005.
———. "Saint Thomas et l'histoire." *Revue Thomiste* 105 (2005): 355–409.
Valkenberg, Wilhelmus G. B. M. *Words of the Living God. Place and Function of Holy Scripture in the Theology of St. Thomas Aquinas*. Utrecht: Peeters, 2000.
Valton, E. "Évêques. Questions théologiques et canoniques." In *DTC* 5.2, cols. 1701–25.
Villemin, Laurent. *Pouvoir d'ordre et pouvoir de juridiction: Histoire théologique de leur distinction*. Paris: Éditions du Cerf, 2003.

TEXTS RELATED TO THIS STUDY

Albaric, Michel. "Hugh de Saint-Cher et les concordances bibliques latines (XIIIe–XVIIIe siècles)." In *Hugues de Saint-Cher (+1263): Bibliste et Théologien*, edited by L.-J. Bataillon, 467–79. Turnhout: Brepols, 2004.

Aquinas, Thomas. *Aristotle: On Interpretation*. Translated by Jean T. Oesterle. *Mediaeval Texts in Translation* 11. Milwaukee, Wis.: Marquette University Press, 1962.

———. *Thomae Aquinatis opera omnia cum hypertextibus in CD-ROM*. Edited by Roberto Busa. Milan: Licosa/Editel, 1992.

Baldner, Steven. "The Use of Scripture for the Refutation of Error according to St. Thomas Aquinas." In *Hamartia*, edited by Donald V. Stump, 149–69. New York: Edwin Mellen Press, 1983.

Barr, James. *Holy Scripture: Canon, Authority, Criticism*. Philadelphia: Westminster Press, 1983.

Bataillon, Louis-Jacques. "La diffusione manoscrita e stampata dei commenti biblici di San Tommaso d'Aquino." *Angelicum* 71 (1994): 579–90.

Benson, Robert, and Giles Constable. *Renaissance and Renewal in the Twelfth Century*. Cambridge, Mass.: Harvard University Press, 1982.

Benson, Robert L. *The Bishop-Elect: A Study in Medieval Ecclesiastical Office*. Princeton, N.J.: Princeton University Press, 1968.

Blanche, Albert. "Le sens littéral des Écritures d'après saint Thomas d'Aquin." *Revue Thomiste* 14 (1906): 192–212.

Boadt, Lawrence. "St. Thomas Aquinas and the Biblical Wisdom Tradition." *The Thomist* 49 (1985): 575–611.

Bouëssé, Humbert, and Antré Mandouze, eds. *L'Evêque dans l'église du Christ*. Paris: Desclée De Brouwer, 1963.

Bourke, Vernon J. *Aquinas' Search for Wisdom*. Milwaukee, Wis.: Bruce Publishing, 1965.

———. *Thomistic Bibliography 1920–1940*. *The Modern Schoolman*, supplement to volume 21. St. Louis, Mo., 1945.

Bourke, Vernon J., and T. L. Miethe. *Thomistic Bibliography 1940–1978*. Westport, Conn.: Greenwood Press, 1980.

Boyle, Leonard E. "The Quodlibets of St. Thomas and Pastoral Care." *The Thomist* 38 (1974): 232–56.

Busa, Roberto. *Index Thomisticus S. Thomae Aquinatis Operum Omnium Indices et Concordantiae*. 50 vols. Stuttgart-Bad Cannstatt: Fromman-Holzboog, 1974–80.

Chenu, Marie-Dominique, ed. *La théologie comme Science au XIIIe Siècle*. Vol. 33, *Biblioteque Thomiste*. Paris: J. Vrin, 1957.

———. *St. Thomas d'Aquin et la théologie*. Paris: Éditions du Seuil, 1959.

Colunga, A. "El método histórico en el estudio de la Escritura segundo Tomás." *La Ciencia Tomista* 35 (1927): 30–51.

Congar, Yves. *Etudes d'ecclésiologie médiévale*. In his *Collected Studies* (CS168). London: Variorum Reprints, 1983.

———. "L'Apostolicité de l'Église selon S. Thomas d'Aquin." *Revue des sciences philosophiques et théologiques* 44 (1960): 209–24.

———. *L'ecclésiologie du haut Moyen âge: de saint Grégoire le Grand à la désunion entre Byzance et Rome*. Paris: Éditions de Cerf, 1968.

———. "St. Thomas et les archidiacres." *Revue Thomiste* 57 (1957): 657–71.

———. *Thomas d'Aquin: sa vision de théologie et de l'église*. In his *Collected Studies* (CS190). London: Variorum Reprints, 1984.

———. "Valeur et portée oecuméniques de quelques principes herméneutiques de saint Thomas d'Aquin." *Revue des Sciences Philosophiques et Théologiques* 57 (1973): 611–26.

———. "Vision de l'Eglise chez S. Thomas d'Aquin." *Revue des sciences philosophiques et théologiques* 62 (1978): 523–41.

Congar, Yves, and B.-D. Dupuy, eds. *La collégialité épiscopale: Histoire et théologie*. Unam Sanctam 52. Paris, Éditions du Cerf, 1965.

Cuéllar, Miguel Ponce. *La Naturaleza de la Iglesia sugún Santo Tomas. Estudio del Tema en el Comentario al "Corpus Paulinum."* Pamplona: Ediciones Universidad de Navarra, 1979.

Decker, Bruno. "Schriftprinzip und Ergänzungstradition in der Theologie des hl. Thomas von Aquin." In Decker, *Schrift und Tradition*, 191–221. Essen: Hans Driewer, 1962.

Dondaine, Antoine. "Autour des sécrétaires de saint Thomas." In Dondaine, *Die Metaphysik im Mittelalter: ihr Ursprung und ihre Bedeutung*, 745–54. Berlin: Walter de Gruyter, 1963.

———. *Secrétaires de Saint Thomas*. Rome: Editori di s. Tommaso, 1956.

Dubois, M. "Mystical and Realistic Elements in the Exegesis and Hermeneutics of Thomas Aquinas." In *Creative Biblical Exegesis: Christian and Jewish Hermeneutics through the Centuries*, edited by Benjamin Uffenheimer and H. G. Reventlow, 39–54. Sheffield: JSOT Press, 1988.

Dulles, Avery. "The Church according to St. Thomas Aquinas." In Dulles, *A Church to Believe In*, 149–69. New York: Crossroad, 1982.

Durantel, J. *Saint Thomas d'Aquin et le Pseudo-Denys*. Paris: Librarie F. Alcan, 1919.

Eschmann, Ignatius T. "A Catalogue of St. Thomas's Works." In Étienne Gilson, *The Christian Philosophy of St. Thomas Aquinas*, 381–437. Translated by L. K. Shook. New York: Random House, 1956.

Evans, G. "Exegesis and Authority in the Thirteenth Century." In *Ad litteram: authoritative texts and their medieval readers*, edited by Mark D. Jordan and Kent Emery, 93–111. Notre Dame, Ind.: University of Notre Dame Press, 1992.

———. *The Language and Logic of the Bible. The Earlier Middle Ages*. Cambridge: Cambridge University Press, 1984.

Froehlich, Karl. "Aquinas, Thomas." In *Historical Handbook of Major Biblical Interpreters*, edited by Donald K. McKim, 85–91. Downers Grove, Ill.: InterVarsity Press, 1998.

Gardeil, Ambrose. "Les procédés exégétiques de S. Thomas." *Revue Thomiste* 11 (1903): 428–57.

Gaudemet, Jean. "Recherches sur l'épiscopat médiéval en France." In *Proceedings of the Second International Congress of Medieval Canon Law*, 139–54. Vatican City: S. Congregatio de seminariis et studiorum universitatibus, 1965.

Gibson, M. "The Place of the glossa ordinaria in Medieval Exegesis." In *Ad litteram: Authoritative Texts and Their Medieval Readers*, edited by Mark D. Jordan and Kent Emery, 5–27. Notre Dame, Ind.: University of Notre Dame Press, 1992.
Grant, Robert M. *A Short History of the Interpretation of the Bible*. Rev. ed. New York: Macmillan, 1963.
Haggard, Frank Powell. "An Interpretation of Thomas Aquinas as a Biblical Theologian with Special Reference to his Systematizing of the Economy of Salvation." PhD diss., Drew University, 1972.
Halligan, Nicholas. "Teaching of St. Thomas Aquinas in regard to the Apostles." *American Ecclesiastical Review* 144 (1961): 32–47.
Hankey, Wayne. "Dionysian Hierarchy in Thomas Aquinas: Tradition and Transformation." In *Denys l'Aréopagite et sa postérité en Orient et en Occident*, 405–38. Paris: Institut d'Études Augustiniennes, 1997.
Holzmeister, Urban. "Die Exegetischen Schriften des hl. Thomas v. Aquin." *Zeitschrift für katholische Theologie* (1923): 327–28.
Horst, Ulrich. "Darf man das Bischofsamt erstreben?: Thomas von Aquin und die Sonderstellung des Bischops in der Kirche." In *Für euch Bischof—mit euch Christ: Festschrift für Friedrich Kardinal Wetter zum siebzigsten Geburtstag*, edited by Manfred Weitlauff and Peter Neuner, 179–93. St. Ottilien: EOS Verlag, 1998.
Johnson, John F. "Biblical Authority and Scholastic Theology." In *Inerrancy and the Church*, edited by John D. Hannah, 67–97. Chicago: Moody Press, 1984.
Jordan, Mark D. "Thomas Aquinas." In *Dictionary of Biblical Interpretation: K–Z*, edited by John H. Hayes, 573–75. Nashville, Tenn.: Abingdon Press, 1999.
Kennedy, Robert George. "Thomas Aquinas and the Literal Sense of Sacred Scripture." PhD diss., University of Notre Dame, 1985.
Le Bras, Gabriel. *Institutions ecclésiastiques de la Chrétienté médiévale*, vol. 12.2: *Histoire de l'Eglise*. Edited by Augustin Fliche and Victor Martin. Paris: Bloud and Gay, 1964.
Légendre, A. "La bible dans la Somme théologique." *Revue des Facultés Catholiques de l'Ouest* 21 (1911): 9–33.
Light, Laura. "Versions et révisions du texte biblique." In *Le Moyen Age et la Bible*, edited by P. Riché and G. Lobrichon, 55–93. Paris: Éditions Beauchesne, 1984.
Lonergan, Bernard. *Verbum: Word and Idea in Aquinas*. Edited by David B. Burrell. Notre Dame, Ind.: University of Notre Dame Press, 1967.
Lubac, Henri de. *Exégèse Médiévale: Les Quatre Sens de l'Écriture*. 4 vols. Paris: Aubier, 1964.
Luscombe, David E. "Thomas Aquinas and Conceptions of Hierarchy in the Thirteenth Century." In *Thomas von Aquin: Werk und Wirkung im Licht neuerer Forschungen*, edited by Albert Zimmermann. Berlin: Walter de Gruyter, 1988.

Lyonnet, Stanislas. "L'actualité de saint Thomas exégète." In Lyonnet, *Tommaso d'Aquino nel suo settimo centenario*, 4:9–28. Naples: Edizione Domenicane Italiane, 1974.

Mandonnet, Pierre. "Chronologie des écrits scripturaires de saint Thomas [4–6]." *Revue Thomiste* 34 (1929): 53–69, 132–45, 489–519.

Mandonnet, Pierre, and J. Destrez. *Bibliographie Thomiste*. 2nd edition. Paris, 1960.

Maquart, F. X. "S. Thomas commentateur de la Sainte Ecriture." *Cahiers du Cercle Thomiste* 1 (1926): 153–69.

McGuckin, Terence. "St. Thomas Aquinas and Theological Exegesis of Sacred Scripture." *New Blackfriars* 74 (1993): 197–213.

McNally, R. E. "Medieval Exegesis." *Theological Studies* 22 (1961): 445–54.

Ménard, Etienne. *La Tradition: Révélation, Écriture, Église selon s. Thomas d'Aqin*. Bruges: Desclée de Brouwer, 1964.

Minnis, Alastair J., and A. B. Scott, eds. *Medieval Literary Theory and Criticism: c. 1100–c. 1375: The Commentary Tradition*. Oxford: Clarendon Press, 1991.

O'Connor, Donal J. "The Concept of Mystery in Aquinas' Exegesis, Pt. I-II." *The Irish Theological Quarterly* 36 (1969): 183–210, 261–82.

Pelster, Franz. "Echtheitsfragen bei den exegetischen Schriften des hl. Thomas von Aquin." *Biblica* 4 (1923): 300–311.

Ploeg, J. van der. "The Place of Holy Scripture in the Theology of St. Thomas." *The Thomist* 10 (1947): 398–422.

Pope, Hugh. *St. Thomas as an Interpreter of Holy Scripture*. Oxford: Basil Blackwell, 1924.

Revuelta, Jose M. "Los Comentarios Bíblicos de Santo Tómas." *Scripta Theologica* 3 (1971): 539–79.

Reyero, Maximino Arias. *Thomas von Aquin als Exeget: die Prinzipien seiner Schriftdeutung und seine Lehre von den Schriftsinnen*, vol. 3: *Sammlung Horizonte, neue Reihe*. Einsiedeln: Johannes Verlag, 1971.

Riché, P., and G. Lobrichon, eds. *Le Moyen Age et la Bible*, vol. 4: *Bible de tous les temps*. Paris: Beauchesne, 1984.

Robilliard, J.-A. "Sur la notion de condition (status) en S. Thomas." *Revue des sciences philosophiques et théologiques* 25 (1936): 104–7.

Rossi, Margherita Maria. "La 'divisio textus' nei commenti scritturistici di S. Tommaso d'Aquino: Un procedimento solo esegetico?" *Angelicum* 71 (1994): 537–48.

Saul, P. Damianus. "Die Scriftgelehrsamkeit des hl. Thomas von Aquin." *Theologie und Glaube* (1927): 258–64.

Seidl, S. H. "Thomas von Aquin und die moderne Exegese." *Zeitschrift für katholische Theologie* 93 (1971): 29–44.

Sheets, John. "The Scriptural Dimension of St. Thomas." *American Ecclesiastical Review* 144 (1961): 154–73.

Shooner, H. V., and F. Stegmüller. "*Repertorium biblicum Medii Aevi*, vol. 4–5 (compte rendu)." *Bulletin Thomiste* 10 (1957–59): 99–112.

Smalley, Beryl. "The Bible in the Middle Ages." In *The Church's Use of the Bible: Past and Present*, edited by D. E. Nineham, 57–71. London: SPCK, 1963.

———. "Glossa Ordinaria." In *Theologische Realenzyklopädie*, edited by Gerhard Krause, 452–57. Berlin: de Gruyter, 1984.

Spicq, Ceslas. "Saint Thomas d'Aquin Exégète." In *Dictionnaire de Théologie Catholique*, edited by E. Mangenot, A. Vacant, and E. Amann, 15.1, cols. 694–738. Paris: Libraire Letouzey et Ané, 1946.

Stegmüller, Friedrich. *Repertorium biblicum Medii Aevi*. 11 vols., CSIC. Madrid: Matriti, 1940–80.

Stiegman, Emero. "Charism and Institution in Aquinas." *The Thomist* 38 (1974): 723–33.

Stump, Eleonore. "Biblical Commentary and Philosophy." In *The Cambridge Companion to Aquinas*, edited by Norman Kretzmann and Eleonore Stump, 252–68. Cambridge: Cambridge University Press, 1993.

———. "Revelation and biblical exegesis: Augustine, Aquinas, and Swinburne." In *Reason and the Christian religion: essays in honour of Richard Swinburne*, edited by Alan G. Padgett, 161–97. Oxford: Clarendon Press, 1994.

Świerzawski, Wacław. "God and the Mystery of his Wisdom in the Pauline Commentaries of St. Thomas Aquinas." *Divus Thomas* 74 (1971): 466–500.

Synave, Paul, OP. "La Doctrine de saint Thomas d'Aquin sur la sens littéral des Ecritures." *Revue Biblique* 35 (1926): 40–65.

———. "Le canon scriptuaire de saint Thomas." *Revue Biblique* (1924): 522–33.

———. "Les commentaires scripturaires de saint Thomas d'Aquin." *La Vie Spirituelle* 8 (1923): 455–69.

Synave, Paul, OP, and Pierre Benoit, OP. *Prophecy and Inspiration. A Commentary on the Summa Theologica II-II, Questions 171–178*, Translated by T. L. Sheridan and A. R. Dulles. New York: Desclée, 1961.

Thiel, Detlef. "Necessarius fuit usus Scripturae: Thomas von Aquin uber Schriftlichkeit und Schreiben." *Perspektiven der Philosophie* 26 (2000): 227–62.

Tholuck, Augustinus. *De Thoma Aquinate atque Abaelardo Interpretibus Novi Testamenti*. Halle: E. Anton, 1842.

Torrance, T. F. "Scientific Hermeneutics according to St. Thomas Aquinas." *Journal of Theological Studies* 13 (1962): 259–89.

Valkenberg, Wilhelmus G. B. M. "Readers of Scripture and Hearers of the Word in the Medieaeval Church." *Concilium* 26 (1991): 1, 47–57.

Van Ackeren, Gerald F. *Sacra Doctrina: The Subject of the First Question of the Summa Theologica of St. Thomas Aquinas*. Rome: Catholic Book Agency, 1952.

Vosté, Jacques-Marie. "Exegesis Novi Testamenti et sancti Thomae Summa theologica." *Angelicum* 24 (1947): 3–19.

———. "Medieval Exegesis." *Catholic Biblical Quarterly* 10 (1948): 229–46.

———. "Sanctus Thomas Aquinas Epistularum S. Pauli Interpres." *Angelicum* 19 (1942): 256–76.

Waldstein, Michael. "On Scripture in the Summa Theologiae." *The Aquinas Review* 1 (1994): 73–94.

Weisheipl, James A. *Friar Thomas D'Aquino: His Life, Thought, and Works.* Washington, D.C.: The Catholic University of America Press, 1974.

———. "The Johannine Commentary of Friar Thomas." *Church History* 45 (1976): 185–95.

Zimmermann, Albert, ed. *Thomas von Aquin: Werk und Wirkung im Licht neuerer Forschungen. Miscellanea Mediaevalia* 19. Berlin: Walter de Gruyter, 1988.

Index

acolyte, 21, 35, 51n72, 131
Albert the Great, 20, 22–28, 30–31, 241, 244–45, 247
Alexander of Hales, 22, 27–28
alms, 60, 143
almsgiving, 45, 53n77
ambition, 41, 134, 136
anger, 119, 144–45, 166, 191, 193, 200, 215–16, 229
assiduousness, 173, 181, 203–4, 232
authority, 16, 35, 42, 49, 50n70, 54, 56n86, 62n102, 64–65, 86, 101n106, 103n110, 111–12, 126n80, 127, 130–31, 138, 142, 147–48, 153–54, 167, 170–71, 184, 194, 205, 222–23, 236, 238
avarice, 144–45, 165, 167, 186, 204, 215–16
Avicenna, 24

Baglow, Christopher, 94, 95n88, 242
Balthasar, Hans Urs von, 101–2, 242
biblical exegesis, 70, 78, 81n42, 82, 84–88, 93–94, 98, 242, 245, 248–51; literal sense, 17, 86–88, 90, 93–94, 95n90, 97–98, 126, 173n4, 249
bishop: blameless, 140–41, 212–13, 215, 229; consecration of, ix, 6n11, 7–10, 13, 15–16, 37, 40, 100, 103, 109, 139, 155, 157–58, 167, 170–71, 178, 181, 188, 231, 233; contemplative life of, 12, 14, 30, 33, 36, 38, 41, 45, 60n96, 67–68, 102, 133–34, 136–37, 144, 147, 170, 217, 233–35; continence, 141, 214n31; distinguished, 140, 142–43; duty to correct others, 55, 100, 109n16, 110, 121n57, 127, 160–62, 164, 167, 171, 192, 198–99, 202n133, 205, 211, 215, 219–20, 222n73, 228, 230, 234–35; duty to judge, 64, 101, 106, 145–46, 161–63, 167, 171, 230, 234, 237; duty to rebuke error, 162, 200, 220; duty to study Scripture, 14, 198, 229; governing, x, 4, 10, 26, 31–33, 41–42, 44n59, 46, 48, 57, 59n95, 100, 103, 105–10, 125, 127, 135n108, 138n116, 140, 142, 145–47, 150–51, 153–55, 158, 160, 169, 171, 199, 201, 209, 214–16, 232–34, 237–38; hospitable, 140, 143, 151, 216; husband of one wife, 56, 140–41, 213–14, 229; as image or representative of Christ, 2, 10, 14, 33, 46, 48, 56–57, 62, 64–65, 141, 151, 161, 170; judging accused priests, 106, 161–62; kind, 216; knowledge of difficult matters, 32, 35, 47, 123, 137, 147, 171, 192, 194–95, 203, 210, 220, 231; knowledge of law, 32, 137; as mediator, x, 19, 33, 57, 65, 67–68, 107, 111, 113, 115, 137, 170; reputation, 140, 147, 211; as spiritual father of the faithful, 58n89, 143n134, 146, 169, 171, 183, 203, 208, 215, 229; spiritual life of, ix, 109, 169, 206n4, 207–8; as spiritual perfector, 4, 6n10, 10–12, 20, 22, 24, 27n24, 30n32, 31, 33, 36, 39, 41, 44, 46n64, 65, 66n106, 101, 138, 198, 237, 245; as spouse of his

bishop (cont.)
  church, 28, 29n29, 32, 56, 62, 63n102, 65; as successor of the apostles, 25, 46, 51n73, 52, 56, 64–65, 69, 145; teaching, x–xi, 3–4, 10, 13–15, 17, 31–32, 36, 38, 43, 45–47, 49, 53, 54n80, 55–56, 62n102, 68, 100, 103, 105, 110, 112n23, 115–16, 118, 120, 125, 127, 129, 135, 138, 140, 143–44, 147, 150–55, 158–61, 164, 169–70, 173, 180, 182–83, 185, 190, 194, 198–202, 205, 208, 214–15, 217–18, 220–22, 224–26, 229–30, 232–35
blasphemy, 26, 122, 126, 192
Bonaventure of Bagnoregio, 20, 22–24, 27–29, 61, 242, 244
Boyle, John, 76n20, 83, 85, 96n96, 243
bribes, 145, 167

Callan, Charles, 78n30, 243
care of souls, 46, 122
celibacy, 142n128, 245
charity (*caritas*), ix–x, 1, 4, 12–15, 19–20, 26, 31, 37–40, 42–43, 49, 50n70, 52, 54, 58–59, 60n96, 66, 105, 107, 115, 118–20, 122, 124–26, 127n83, 128, 135–39, 143, 149–50, 152–54, 159, 165–66, 170, 178, 181, 185, 187–88, 191, 193, 202, 204–5, 222, 233–37; fraternal, 4, 13–15, 66–68, 103, 136, 174, 176, 185, 193, 202–4, 236–37
chastity, 11, 19, 39, 43, 68, 140–41, 146, 153–54, 159, 222
Christ, ix–xi, 1, 4, 7, 12, 22, 25–28, 32–33, 39, 42, 46–47, 49, 52–62, 63n102, 64, 92, 94n83, 98–99, 101–2, 109, 111–12, 114, 116, 120, 122–24, 127, 129, 134n103, 135, 137, 141, 144–45, 147, 149n158, 150–51, 154, 157, 163, 165, 167, 170–71, 173n4, 174–76, 179–83, 186–88, 195–96, 199, 202, 204, 210, 213–14, 223–24, 229, 234, 236–38, 240, 244–46; the Good Shepherd, ix, 58–59, 173; the grace of, 10n23, 16, 97, 99, 103, 157, 182, 246; the head of the Church, 25, 46; the kingdom of, 187; mystical body of (*Corpus Christi mysticum*), 7–8, 15–16, 25, 32, 32n41, 53; the Prophet, 14; Spouse of the universal Church, 32, 56, 62, 63n102, 65, 141, 213–14, 229; true body of (*Corpus Christi verum*), 7–8, 25, 35, 158
Cochini, Christian, 141–42, 243
concordance, 79–80, 246
concupiscence, 144
confirmation, 7, 30–31, 48–49
Congar, Yves, 6n10, 62n99, 69, 101, 105n4, 108n15, 243, 246–48
conscience, 31, 42, 118–21, 125, 148n153
continence, 141, 214n31, 216
correctoria, 77–80
courage, x, 167, 177–78, 182, 186, 192, 200–201, 204, 235, 237
covetousness, 41, 68, 136, 140, 145, 186

deacon, 11, 21–22, 25, 27n24, 30, 34–35, 47–48, 51, 54n78, 130–32, 144, 148, 157n186; female, 148n153
Denifle, Heinrich, 85, 89n67, 89n70, 243
devil, 61, 126, 147, 183, 192
divisio textus, 90, 95–97, 104, 110, 130, 174–75, 192, 250
Dominican, 11, 24n11, 52, 60–61, 70–73, 77–79, 82, 92, 245–46
drunkenness, 142, 144, 215–16

ecclesiology, xi, 16–17, 23, 28, 105, 244
envy, 165, 192, 215
episcopacy: established by Christ, 61, 106–8, 122; as exercise of fraternal charity, 14–15; power of jurisdiction (*potestas iurisdictionis*), 3–4, 8, 28, 37, 235, 237; power of order (*potestas ordinis*), 3–4, 8, 15, 25, 28, 48, 158; sacramentality of, x, 4–10, 14, 21–22, 25, 28, 29n29, 31, 37, 51n72, 157–58, 177n16; as a state of perfection, x, 1, 4, 8n15, 10–13, 19–20, 27, 29, 36, 38–41, 45, 49–50, 54, 66–68, 101, 134, 138, 140, 233, 236–37; vow at episcopal consecration, 42, 46, 66–67, 139, 167, 170–71, 185, 188, 202–3, 232
error, 100, 115, 120, 125, 150, 183, 189–90,

192, 198–200, 209, 218–19, 221, 227–28, 230
Eucharist, 6n11, 7, 10, 25, 27, 30–32, 35, 48, 64, 158, 169n235
excommunication, 31, 118n42, 122, 126–28, 164, 171, 174, 194, 202–3, 228
exorcist, 21, 35, 51n72, 131

faith, x, 2, 10, 38, 43, 46–48, 56–58, 63, 83, 86, 98, 105, 108–13, 115–20, 125–26, 128–29, 136–37, 147, 148n153, 149–50, 153–54, 164–71, 174, 176, 177n13, 179–81, 187–91, 193–96, 200, 202–5, 207–11, 214, 215n34, 217, 220, 224–30, 233–34; articles of, 86, 210, 218, 230; deposit of, 108, 169–70; mysteries of, 1, 31, 34n47, 35, 38, 42, 47–48, 57, 102, 144, 148n153, 149, 226, 233, 250–51; rule of, 58, 116, 174n7
false doctrine, 108, 110, 115–18, 120–22, 125–26, 149n158, 165, 170, 180, 190, 192, 194–95, 199, 204, 209, 211, 219–22, 228–30, 235
fasting, 53n77, 152, 232
fear, 119, 162, 167, 173, 174, 177–78, 187, 193
Fehlner, Peter, 28, 244
finances, 145
first principles, 18n46, 28, 86–87, 218, 229–30
forgiveness, 25, 64, 88, 109, 127, 141, 235
Fourth Lateran Council, 112, 126, 127n83, 128
Franciscan order, 27, 60–61, 77

Gerard of Abbeville, 11n25, 61, 65
Glossa ordinaria, 40, 71, 77, 79n36, 80–81, 114n29, 123n65, 133, 156n184, 160n195, 161, 176, 219, 242, 249, 251
gluttony, 215, 219
grace, ix, xi, 2–10, 13, 15–17, 22, 24, 34, 36–38, 40, 42, 56, 59, 66, 69, 88, 97, 99–103, 105, 109, 111, 113–15, 122–23, 129, 139n117, 144, 147, 149, 151, 155, 157–58, 168–171, 175–79, 182–83, 188, 191, 198–99, 201–4, 210, 220, 223–24, 231, 233, 235, 238, 245–46

Gratian, 6n10, 21, 62n102, 88n63, 112, 213n30, 242, 246
greed, 186, 192, 215–16, 229

Halligan, Nicholas, 52, 53n75, 57, 249
hate, 148, 193
hierarchy, xi, 2, 23–28, 30n32, 63n102, 66n106, 69, 105, 107, 113, 138, 238–39, 244–45, 249
heresy, 109, 150
heretic, 15, 53, 100, 109n16, 126, 127n83, 174–75, 183, 190, 201–3, 205–9, 211–12, 218, 220–21, 224, 227–28, 230, 234, 235
hierarchy, xi, 2, 11, 13, 19, 23–28, 30, 40, 61, 63n102, 66n106, 69, 102, 105, 107, 109, 113, 122, 130–31, 137–38, 233, 237–39
holiness, 1, 6n10, 11–13, 30, 32, 40, 42, 49, 69, 101–3, 109, 115, 136, 141, 149, 166, 170, 216, 224, 235–38, 245
Holy Spirit, ix, 3, 17, 38, 45, 55, 100–101, 114, 123, 155, 157, 171, 176–78, 181, 188, 197, 199, 202, 204, 219, 231, 233, 235, 238
honorarium, 161, 186
hope, 111–12, 119, 180, 191, 193, 195
Horst, Ulrich, 6n10, 11–12, 15, 244, 249
Hugh of St. Cher, 77–81, 242, 246
Hugh of St. Victor, 22–24, 82, 89–90, 113n25, 114n29, 117n40, 163n207, 206, 242
humility, 26, 111–12, 127, 136, 192, 220, 237

incontinence, 141n127, 192–93
intemperance, 141
Isidore of Seville, 21

John Paul II (pope), ix
Johnson, Luke Timothy, 76n22, 80, 117n40, 244
jurisdiction, 8n15, 10, 25, 31, 37, 44, 50, 61, 63, 65, 235, 237
justice, 39, 102, 106–7, 110, 120n50, 121–22, 125, 145, 151, 163, 165–66, 195, 197–98, 200–201, 226

Kelly, J. N. D., 125n76, 149n158, 244
knowledge, 24, 32, 34, 45n62, 49, 50n70, 59, 92, 116n37, 119n47, 128–29, 135, 137, 143, 149–50, 155, 168, 195–97, 201n125, 205, 208–10, 217, 220, 224–27, 229, 234
Komonchak, Joseph, 101–2, 244

Lamb, Matthew, 77n25, 78n29, 83n49, 95n93, 96, 244
law, 32, 34n46, 88n63, 94n83, 95n90, 105, 116, 118–19, 121–22, 124, 137, 148n153, 170, 173n4, 213, 225–26, 245, 248
lectio divina, 89, 91
lector, 21, 35, 51n72, 72, 131
Lécuyer, Joseph, 6, 9–10, 13, 15, 37, 40n53, 157, 177n16, 244
lust, 119, 215

Magister in Sacra Pagina, xi, 86, 93n78
magisterium, x, 2, 3, 14, 37, 43, 49, 101, 109, 124, 135, 143–44, 177, 222, 231, 233–34, 237, 245
Mahoney, Edward, 24, 25n16, 26, 27n23, 244
Mandonnet, Pierre, 72–73, 245, 250
married clergy, 141, 214n31
martyrdom, x, 40, 100, 109n16, 171–75, 181–83, 186–88, 201, 203–5, 232, 235
meekness, 26, 119, 145, 165–66, 191, 204, 223
mendicant controversy, 19–20, 29, 44, 52, 60–69
mercy, 88, 98–99, 109, 111, 113–14, 122–23, 127, 141, 151–52, 165–66, 170, 174–76, 184, 196, 205, 224, 235–36
mildness, 144, 191, 205, 220
modesty, 140, 143, 191–92, 205
Molloy, Noel, 6n10, 11–15, 33n45, 46, 47nn67–68, 48n69, 56n86, 61, 62n99, 65–67, 68n114, 245

obedience, 11, 19, 39, 43–44, 59, 124, 128, 136
O'Meara, Thomas, 2–3, 231, 238, 245
order, grades of, 21–22, 25, 32n41, 39, 41, 131–32, 137, 157

papacy, 28
Pastores Gregis, ix–xi
patience, 123, 144, 165–66, 173, 191–92, 195, 200, 205, 220
peace, 88, 111, 113–15, 145, 176, 191–93, 210
persecution, 59, 100, 172–73, 175, 177, 180–81, 183, 192, 195–96, 203–4, 232
Pesch, Otto, 90, 93, 94n83, 95n89, 96, 97n97, 245
Peter Lombard, 7, 20–23, 25, 28–30, 33, 71, 76–77, 81, 114, 174n7, 176n10, 206, 242–43
Peter the Chanter, 90–92, 242
piety, 53n77, 110, 150–53, 158–59, 165, 171, 184–86, 190–92, 195–96, 203, 210, 232, 236
Pius XII: *Sacramentum Ordinis*, 7n11
poor, 54, 108, 145n144
pope, 22, 26–28, 36–37, 42, 44, 46, 63–65
porter, 21, 35, 51n72, 131
poverty, 11, 19, 39, 43, 60
prayer, 126, 128, 150, 173, 232, 235
preaching, 15, 19–20, 33–34, 36, 38, 44–48, 56–57, 60–65, 79n32, 87, 89, 91–92, 98, 100, 105, 109, 112–13, 123, 126, 129, 137–38, 144n137, 149–51, 160–61, 166–67, 169–71, 174–81, 183, 185–88, 190, 198–204, 209–10, 223–24, 229, 232–34, 236–37
pride, 133, 147, 192, 201n125, 215, 229
priest, 8, 10–11, 21–22, 25, 27, 30–36, 40, 44, 47–48, 51, 55n85, 62–65, 130–31, 137, 142n128, 144, 156n186, 160, 164, 245
priesthood, 16, 22, 25, 28, 31, 51, 109–10, 132, 156n186, 158, 160, 163–64, 170, 206, 234
Proclus, 24, 75
prophecy, 56, 123, 155–56, 232
prudence, 42, 140, 142, 160, 189, 192, 214, 222, 234
Prügl, Thomas, 16, 76, 83, 85, 245
Pseudo-Dionysius the Aereopagite, 1, 4, 10, 19–20, 23–25, 30, 33n46, 34n47, 40, 44–46, 48, 51n73, 63,

65–66, 68–69, 75, 101–2, 115n34, 130–31, 138, 239–40, 242
purity, 68, 118–20, 121n53, 148n153, 236

Ramírez, Santiago María, 6n11, 246
Reginald of Piperno, 5n9, 72, 74–75, 82–83, 131
repentance, 127, 141, 191–92, 205
reportatio, 5n9, 72, 74–75, 82–83
righteousness, 39, 43, 191, 195, 207, 216

sacred doctrine (*sacra doctrina*), 1n1, 18, 36, 49, 86n59, 86–87, 210, 225–26, 229, 235, 244–45, 251
salvation, 14n40, 42, 57–58, 63, 92, 115–16, 120, 122–23, 128–29, 150, 159, 167, 171, 173, 180, 187–89, 196, 201–3, 207–8, 217, 234–36, 238, 249
schism, 37, 169n235
science (*scientia*), 32n41, 49, 59, 86–87, 92, 210, 129n92, 143n136, 155n183, 168n232, 208n8, 210, 217–18, 225–26, 229–30, 247
Scripture, x–xi, 14, 27, 30, 32, 34, 70–72, 75–76, 78, 81, 83–87, 89, 91–93, 94n84, 95, 97, 110, 113n25, 137n113, 142, 144n137, 155, 195–99, 205, 218–19, 226, 229, 234, 243, 245–46, 247, 249–52
Second Vatican Council on bishops, x, 2, 231; *Christus Dominus*, 2, *Lumen Gentium*, 7n11, 158n189
shame, 127, 135n108, 177–80, 186, 189–90, 204, 222
sin, 25, 39, 42, 65n105, 68, 88, 98, 113–15, 122, 126–27, 134n106, 138, 140–41, 147, 151, 152n164, 162–66, 176, 183, 189, 192, 200, 203, 212–15, 222, 224, 229, 232, 235
sloth, 177, 215
Smalley, Beryl, 71n3, 77n25, 78n27, 81n43, 83n49, 86, 89, 91n75, 93, 246, 251
sobriety, 140–42, 178, 216
solicitude, 100, 162, 172–74
Spicq, Ceslas, 70, 72n9, 80–82, 87, 98, 117n40, 246, 251

spiritual warfare, 110, 116, 123–26, 165–66, 181, 183–84, 204
state of perfection (*status perfectionis*), x, 1, 4–5, 8n15, 10–16, 19–20, 22, 27–29, 36, 38–41, 45, 49–50, 54, 66–68, 101–3, 134, 138–40, 233, 235–37, 239
Stenger, Robert, 6–8, 10, 13–15, 37, 158, 246
subdeacon, 21, 35, 51n72, 131
suffering, x, 43, 58, 109n16, 144, 172, 177, 179–82, 186–87, 195–96, 203–5, 230
Świerzawski, Wacław, 84, 246, 251

temperance, 119, 178, 204
temporal goods, 41, 136, 145, 168, 182
Thomistic ressourcement, xi, 1–2, 69, 101–2, 231, 235, 237, 239
Torrell, Jean-Pierre, 15, 62n101, 65–66, 71–76, 78–79, 82–83, 89, 92–93, 98, 99n104, 157n187, 227n91, 246
tribulation, 174–75, 181
Trinity, 24

unbelievers, 15, 140, 146–47, 174, 181, 186, 188–92, 200, 202–5
University of Paris, 19, 61, 71, 75, 77, 81, 83, 85–6, 89, 92

vice, 3, 15, 17, 37, 55n83, 91, 102, 140, 144–45, 170, 185, 186n59, 192–93, 201n125, 211, 215, 230, 233
violence, 192, 215–16
virtue: 2–3, 5, 14n35, 15, 17, 31, 44, 53, 57, 69, 102, 107, 109, 118–21, 137, 141–42, 143n134, 145, 147, 151–52, 154, 165–67, 169–70, 174, 178, 180, 185, 191, 195, 211, 214–16, 229, 233; moral, x, 119–20, 137, 141, 231; theological, 119, 195, 204

William of St. Amour, 19–20, 61–62
wisdom, 14, 38, 47, 57, 60, 101, 107–8, 111–12, 139, 179, 191, 218–19, 225, 230, 234, 236
worship, 32, 92, 110, 115–16, 128, 130, 148, 150–52, 184, 190, 196

THOMISTIC RESSOURCEMENT SERIES

Series Editors: Matthew Levering
Thomas Joseph White, OP

Aquinas and the Theology of the Body
The Thomistic Foundations of John Paul II's Anthropology
Thomas Petri, OP

Angels and Demons
A Catholic Introduction
Serge-Thomas Bonino, OP
Translated by Michael J. Miller

The Incarnate Lord
A Thomistic Study in Christology
Thomas Joseph White, OP

The Mystery of Union with God
Dionysian Mysticism in Albert the Great and Thomas Aquinas
Bernhard Blankenhorn, OP

Introduction to the Mystery of the Church
Benoît-Dominique de La Soujeole, OP
Translated by Michael J. Miller

Christ and Spirituality in St. Thomas Aquinas
Jean-Pierre Torrell, OP
Translated by Bernhard Blankenhorn, OP

The Trinity
An Introduction to Catholic Doctrine on the Triune God
Gilles Emery, OP
Translated by Matthew Levering

www.ingramcontent.com/pod-product-compliance
Lightning Source LLC
Chambersburg PA
CBHW022042290426
44109CB00014B/952